I0884974

Navigating Social Trust in the AI Era

Debabrata Samanta
https://orcid.org/0000-0003-4118-2480
Rochester Institute of Technology, Kosovo

IGI Global
Scientific Publishing
Publishing Tomorrow's Research Today

Vice President of Editorial Melissa Wagner
Director of Acquisitions Mikaela Felty
Director of Book Development Jocelynn Hessler
Production Manager Mike Brehm
Cover Design Jose Rosado

Published in the United States of America by
IGI Global Scientific Publishing
701 East Chocolate Avenue
Hershey, PA, 17033, USA
Tel: 717-533-8845 | Fax: 717-533-7115
Website: https://www.igi-global.com E-mail: cust@igi-global.com

Copyright © 2026 by IGI Global Scientific Publishing. All rights reserved. No part of this publication may be reproduced, stored or distributed in any form or by any means, electronic or mechanical, including photocopying, without written permission from the publisher. Use of this publication to train generative artificial intelligence (AI) technologies is expressly prohibited. The publisher reserves all rights to license its use for generative AI training and machine learning model development.

Product or company names used in this set are for identification purposes only. Inclusion of the names of the products or companies does not indicate a claim of ownership by IGI Global Scientific Publishing of the trademark or registered trademark.

Library of Congress Cataloging-in-Publication Data

LCCN: 2025043694 (CIP Data Pending)
ISBN13: 979-8-3373-7011-8
Isbn13Softcover: 979-8-3373-7012-5
EISBN13: 979-8-3373-7013-2

British Cataloguing in Publication Data
A Cataloguing in Publication record for this book is available from the British Library.

All work contributed to this book is new, previously-unpublished material.
The views expressed in this book are those of the authors, but not necessarily of the publisher.
This book contains information sourced from authentic and highly regarded references, with reasonable efforts made to ensure the reliability of the data and information presented. The authors, editors, and publisher believe the information in this book to be accurate and true as of the date of publication. Every effort has been made to trace and credit the copyright holders of all materials included. However, the authors, editors, and publisher cannot assume responsibility for the validity of all materials or the consequences of their use. Should any copyright material be found unacknowledged, please inform the publisher so that corrections may be made in future reprints.

To my parents Mr. Dulal Chandra Samanta, Mrs. Ambujini Samanta, my elder sister Mrs. Tanusree Samanta, Brother-In-law Mr. Soumendra Jana and daughter Ms. Aditri Samanta

Debabrata Samanta

Editorial Advisory Board

Daksh Agarwal, *University of Pennsylvania, USA*
Iraj Sadegh Amiri, *Ton Duc Thang University, Ho Chi Minh City, Vietnam*
Abhishek Basu, *RCC Institute of Information Technology, India*
Bharat Bhushan, *Birla Institute of Technology, Mesra, India*
Amit Banerjee, *Bidhan Chandra College, Asansol, India*
Siddhartha Bhattacharyya, *Rajnagar Mahavidyalaya, Birbhum, India*
Anil Kumar Biswal, *Soa University, India*
C. S. Boopathi, *SRM Institute of Science and Technology, Chennai, India*
Kousik Dasgupta, *Kalyani Government Engineering College, India*
Sourav De, *Cooch Behar Government Engineering College, India*
S. Geetha, *Vellore Institute of Technology, Chennai, India*
V. Gomathy, *Sri Krishna College of Engineering and Technology, Kuniamuthur, India*
Deepak Gupta, *Maharaja Agrasen Institute of Technology, India*
Mhd. Nour Hindia, *Universiti Teknologi Malaysia, Malaysia*
Hiroshi Inokawa, *Shizuoka University, Hamamatsu, Japan*
Vishal Jain, *Bharati Vidyapeeth's Institute of Computer Applications and Management, New Delhi, India*
Marimuthu Karuppiah, *SRM Institute of Science and Technology, India*
Aditya Khamparia, *Lovely Professional University, India*
Ashish Khanna, *Maharaja Agrasen Institute of Technology, New Delhi, India*
Debanjan Konar, *Sikkim Manipal Institute of Technology, India*
S. Selva Kumar, *GKM College of Engineering and Technology, Chennai, India*
Karthikeyan M. P., *PG College of Arts and Science, India*
M. Maheswari, *Sathyabama Institute of Science and Technology, Chennai, India*
Ashish Mani, *Amity University, India*
Regonda Nagaraju, *Sreyas Institute of Engineering and Technology, Hyderabad, India*
Neelamadhab Padhy, *GIET University, Gunupur, India*

Indrajit Pan, *RCC Institute of Information Technology, India*
Yohan Park, *Keimyung University, South Korea*
Binod Kumar Pattanayak, *Soa University, India*
Suplab Podder, *Dayananda Sagar Institutions, Bangalore, India*
Gurunath Ramachandra, *Dayananda Sagar Institutions, Bangalore, India*
Poonam Rani, *Netaji Subhash University of Technology, New Delhi, India*
Ahmed Nabih Zaki Rashed, *Faculty of Electronic Engineering, Menoufia University, Egypt*
Joel J. P. C. Rodrigues, *Federal University of Piauí (UFPI), Brazil*
M. Shivamurthaiah, *Garden City University, India*
Debabrata Singh, *Soa University, India*
Prakash Kumar Singh, *Rec Mainpuri, India*
P. Sivakumar, *PSG College of Technology, Coimbatore, India*
M. Sivaram, *Lebanese French University, Erbil, Iraq*
Ming-Hour Yang, *National Central University, Taiwan*
P. Yupapin, *Faculty of Applied Sciences, Ton Duc Thang University, Ho Chi Minh City, Vietnam*

Table of Contents

Detailed Table of Contents

Increasing engagement of AI in our day-to-day lives is giving rise to questions about the ethics of AI, thus necessitating the demand for a set of principles and frameworks designed to guide the development, deployment, and use of artificial intelligence in a way that is beneficial, fair, and safe for humanity. The development of AI ethical guidelines is not a monolithic process but is instead a complex negotiation shaped by diverse ethical traditions, cultural values, and even individual human judgment. People want AI and organizations using it to act ethically, but ethical behavior is a complex, subjective concept. This is because ethical behavior means different things to different people. This chapter aims to address and solve the problem of conflicting AI ethical frameworks by taking a multi-pronged approach that moves beyond a search for a single, universal solution. Instead of trying to force a consensus on what "ethical" means, the focus should be on creating processes and systems that can navigate these disagreements and make informed, transparent trade-offs.

Artificial Intelligence (AI) has become an influential force shaping modern society, raising urgent ethical questions about responsibility, fairness, transparency, and human dignity. The discussion explores the conceptual and philosophical foundations of AI ethics as a framework for ensuring that technological progress aligns with moral and social values. It traces the evolution of ethical thought from classical philosophy to contemporary digital governance and defines the core principles guiding responsible AI, including beneficence, non-maleficence, autonomy, justice, and explicability. Emphasizing a human-centered approach, the section examines the challenges of operationalizing ethics into AI design, deployment, and regulation. By grounding innovation in ethical responsibility, it argues that trust in AI depends not on technical superiority alone but on its moral alignment with the public good and social justice.

The global regulatory landscape of Artificial Intelligence (AI) is rapidly evolving to balance innovation with ethics, accountability, and human rights. This chapter examines the development of AI governance worldwide, emphasizing the European Union Artificial Intelligence Act (EU AI Act) as the first comprehensive, rights-based legal framework. Through its risk-based classification unacceptable, high, limited, and minimal, the EU model safeguards human dignity while promoting responsible innovation. A comparative analysis of the United States, Canada, China, India, Singapore, and Brazil reveals both convergence in core ethical principles and divergence in implementation due to cultural and political differences. The chapter concludes by advocating for a Global AI Accord to harmonize universal values with local contexts, fostering trustworthy, ethical, and sustainable AI governance.

This study investigates the ethical challenges and governance mechanisms of Artificial Intelligence (AI) across healthcare, education, finance, and security sectors. Using a mixed-method approach combining expert interviews, surveys, and policy analysis, the research identifies key ethical dimensions—fairness, accountability, transparency, and privacy (FATP). Results reveal varying ethical maturity levels, with healthcare showing higher compliance and security facing greater ethical risks. A validated Ethical Governance Framework for AI (EGF-AI) is proposed to guide sectoral and cross-sectoral governance through ethics-by-design, algorithmic audits, and stakeholder participation. The study emphasizes the need for adaptive, human-centered, and globally coherent AI governance systems.

This chapter explores the transformative impact of Artificial Intelligence (AI) across four critical sectors healthcare, education, finance, and security while addressing the profound ethical challenges arising from the rise of generative AI. It examines how AI enhances diagnostic precision, personalized learning, financial efficiency, and cyber resilience, yet simultaneously introduces risks such as bias, privacy violations, algorithmic opacity, and misinformation. The chapter emphasizes the growing need for ethical governance frameworks, fairness auditing, and transparency to maintain public trust. Furthermore, it discusses how generative AI technologies, including large language models and deepfakes, complicate issues of authorship, authenticity, and accountability. By proposing governance and mitigation strategies, this chapter contributes to understanding how ethics, trust, and regulation can ensure that AI innovation aligns with human rights, fairness, and societal well-being.

This chapter examines the complex interplay between artificial intelligence (AI) and human dignity in the framework of corporate governance and ethical responsibility. This study analyzes the methods by which large technology-driven organizations implement AI systems that significantly influence human lives, social trust, and the ethical dimensions of work. This chapter conducts a multi-layered analysis of corporate practices in automation, labor management, and digital surveillance, demonstrating how these systems challenge conventional notions of respect, fairness, and human autonomy. This analysis utilizes global case studies from prominent corporations including Google, Microsoft, and Amazon to highlight advancements and ethical deficiencies in existing governance models. The discussion highlights the ethical conflict between technological efficiency and human-centered values, underscoring the necessity for transparent frameworks that align innovation with moral accountability.

Preface

The rapid evolution of Artificial Intelligence (AI) has profoundly transformed societies, economies, and the way humans interact with technology. As AI systems increasingly influence decision-making, communication, governance, and even creativity, the need to examine their ethical, legal, and social implications (ELSI) has never been more urgent. This book seeks to explore these dimensions comprehensively, addressing the challenges and opportunities that arise when intelligent systems intersect with human values, rights, and societal norms. Bringing together academics, policymakers, technologists, and industry professionals from across the globe, this volume presents a multidisciplinary dialogue on responsible AI development and deployment. It critically examines pressing concerns such as privacy, surveillance, algorithmic bias, accountability, and data governance, while also discussing emerging frameworks such as the EU AI Act and comparative international regulations. Beyond legal and regulatory analysis, the book emphasizes the human-centered dimension of AI — focusing on dignity, trust, fairness, and transparency as guiding principles in technological innovation. It integrates perspectives from computer science, law, ethics, social sciences, and policy, offering both theoretical foundations and applied research insights. Each chapter contributes a unique lens through which AI's societal impact can be better understood:

From foundational ethical theories and philosophical reflections to practical applications in healthcare, finance, education, and security, from studies on deepfakes and misinformation to governance models for responsible AI, the rapid evolution of Artificial Intelligence (AI) has profoundly transformed societies, economies, and the way humans interact with technology. As AI systems increasingly influence decision-making, communication, governance, and even creativity, the need to examine their ethical, legal, and social implications (ELSI) has never been more urgent. This book seeks to explore these dimensions comprehensively, addressing the challenges and opportunities that arise when intelligent systems intersect with human values, rights, and societal norms. Bringing together academics, policymakers, technologists, and industry professionals from across the globe, this volume presents a multidisciplinary dialogue on responsible AI development and deployment. It critically examines pressing concerns such as privacy, surveillance, algorithmic bias, accountability, and data governance, while also discussing emerging frameworks such as the EU AI Act and comparative international regulations. Beyond legal and regulatory analysis, the book emphasizes the human-centered dimension of AI — focusing on dignity, trust, fairness, and transparency as guiding principles in technological innovation. It integrates perspectives from computer science, law, ethics, social sciences, and policy, offering both theoretical foundations and applied research insights. Each chapter contributes a unique lens through which AI's societal impact can be better understood:

From foundational ethical theories and philosophical reflections to practical applications in healthcare, finance, education, and security, From studies on deepfakes and misinformation to governance models for responsible AI, From explorations of corporate accountability to the future of labor and automation. Collectively, the contributions aim to bridge the gap between technological innovation and ethical responsibility, promoting a vision of AI that advances human welfare, democratic integrity, and global sustainability. rom explorations of corporate accountability to the future of labor and automation.

CHAPTER OVERVIEW

Chapter 1 introduces the philosophical and cultural diversity inherent in defining AI ethics. It highlights how ethical expectations vary across societies and proposes a multi-pronged, process-based approach that accommodates disagreement rather than seeking a single universal ethical framework. By emphasizing transparency, negotiation, and critical dialogue, the chapter lays the foundation for navigating conflicting ethical principles in AI development and governance.

Chapter 2 deep dives building on classical and contemporary ethical thought, this chapter examines the conceptual roots of responsible AI. It explores core principles—beneficence, non-maleficence, justice, autonomy, explicability—and shows how they guide the alignment of AI technologies with societal and moral values. The chapter advocates a human-centered approach, arguing that trust in AI depends on moral responsibility as much as on technological advancement.

Chapter 3 intends connects classical moral theories to contemporary AI governance. It explains how deontological duties, consequentialist evaluations, and virtue-based reasoning provide complementary tools for addressing fairness, accountability, transparency, and privacy. Through interdisciplinary case studies, the chapter proposes a hybrid ethical model that integrates all three traditions to guide responsible AI in diverse domains.

Chapter 4 takes focusing on the intersection of AI and programming education, this chapter shows how AI tools can support learning and debugging in C programming. It discusses AI's potential to simplify syntax learning, enhance logical reasoning, and improve development efficiency for students and professionals alike. The chapter demonstrates how AI can enhance both foundational learning and advanced software development processes.

Chapter 5 throws surveys global AI governance frameworks with a central focus on the EU AI Act, the world's first comprehensive AI legal standard. Through comparative analysis of policies in the U.S., Canada, China, India, Singapore, and Brazil, it identifies converging ethical priorities and divergent regulatory strategies. The chapter concludes by advocating for a Global AI Accord to harmonize human rights, innovation, and cultural diversity.

In Chapter 6, delves mixed-method research, this chapter analyzes ethical maturity levels across four major sectors. It identifies sector-specific risks—such as privacy concerns in healthcare and ethical vulnerabilities in security—and introduces the Ethical Governance Framework for AI (EGF-AI). The framework promotes ethics-by-design, algorithmic audits, and stakeholder participation to ensure reliable and human-centered AI governance.

Chapter 7 examines AI's transformative role in healthcare, education, finance, and security while addressing the ethical complexities introduced by generative AI systems. It highlights risks such as bias, privacy breaches, misinformation, and algorithmic opacity. Proposed governance strategies emphasize fairness auditing, transparency, and accountability, especially amid rising deepfake and LLM-driven manipulation.

Chapter 8 proposed, explores the relationship between AI and human dignity, focusing on how AI can both enhance and undermine autonomy, equality, and respect. It addresses discrimination arising from biased datasets, systemic inequalities in hiring and policing, and risks of dehumanization. Case studies and corporate governance models demonstrate how AI can be ethically aligned to safeguard dignity in healthcare, employment, and public administration.

Chapter 09 provides a detailed examination of AI applications across essential sectors while focusing on generative AI–driven risks such as deepfakes, copyright infringement, and misinformation. It argues that sustainable AI adoption depends on fairness, transparency, and strong regulatory oversight to prevent discrimination, destabilization, and societal harm.

Chapter 10 deal with focusing specifically on deepfake technology, this chapter explains how deep learning models generate synthetic media that is increasingly indistinguishable from reality. It covers creation techniques, detection mechanisms, and ongoing research challenges. The chapter explores ethical and societal implications, including fraud, political manipulation, and reputational harm.

Chapter 11 shows AI's impact on democracy, labor automation, surveillance, and global inequality. It explores threats to privacy, representation, and human rights while examining governance responses worldwide. Emphasizing fairness, accountability, and transparency, the chapter argues for trustworthy AI systems that safeguard democratic values and promote equitable socioeconomic futures.

Debabrata Samanta
Rochester Institute of Technology – Tirana, Albania

Acknowledgment

We express our great pleasure, sincere thanks, and gratitude to the people who significantly helped, contributed and supported to the completion of this book entitled with "*Navigating Social Trust in the AI Era*". Our sincere thanks to Robert Muharremi, Dean of Faculty, Rochester Institute of Technology, Tirana for his continuous support, advice and cordial guidance from the beginning to the completion of this book.

We would also like to express our honest appreciation to our colleagues at Rochester Institute of Technology – Tirana, for their guidance and support.

We also thank all the authors who have contributed some chapters to this book. This book would not have been possible without their contribution.

We are also very thankful to the reviewers for reviewing the book chapters. This book would not have been possible without their continuous support and commitment towards completing the chapters' review on time.

To complete this book, all the publishing team members at IGI Global extended their king cooperation, timely response, expert comments, guidance, and we are very thankful to them.

Finally, we sincerely express our special and heartfelt respect, gratitude, and gratefulness to our family members and parents for their endless support and blessings.

Chapter 1
Foundations of AI Ethics

Richa Kapoor Mehra
https://orcid.org/0000-0002-5420-8179
O.P. Jindal Global University, India

Md.Matiur Rahman
https://orcid.org/0009-0007-4152-8898
Gurudayal Government College, Bangladesh

ABSTRACT

Increasing engagement of AI in our day-to-day lives is giving rise to questions about the ethics of AI, thus necessitating the demand for a set of principles and frameworks designed to guide the development, deployment, and use of artificial intelligence in a way that is beneficial, fair, and safe for humanity. The development of AI ethical guidelines is not a monolithic process but is instead a complex negotiation shaped by diverse ethical traditions, cultural values, and even individual human judgment. People want AI and organizations using it to act ethically, but ethical behavior is a complex, subjective concept. This is because ethical behavior means different things to different people. This chapter aims to address and solve the problem of conflicting AI ethical frameworks by taking a multi-pronged approach that moves beyond a search for a single, universal solution. Instead of trying to force a consensus on what "ethical" means, the focus should be on creating processes and systems that can navigate these disagreements and make informed, transparent trade-offs.

INTRODUCTION

With the advancement of Artificial Intelligence (AI), there is a pressing need for us to explore and understand the impact it will have on society. AI has established its presence in nearly all domains, including education, healthcare, finance, and

DOI: 10.4018/979-8-3373-7011-8.ch001

t © 2026, IGI Global Scientific Publishing. Copying or distributing in print or electronic forms without written permission of IGI Global Scientific Publishing is prohibited. Use of this chapter to
enerative artificial intelligence (AI) technologies is expressly prohibited. The publisher reserves all rights to license its use for generative AI training and machine learning model development.

banking. The impact of AI on society is no longer a matter of debate. The current debate centers instead on how far this impact will be positive or negative, for whom, in what ways, in what places, and on what timescale. Many are concerned about the consequences of increased access by governments, corporations, and other organizations to data that enables extensive and intrusive predictions about citizen behavior. Complete dependence of people on AI is giving rise to many questions. Who or what is responsible for decisions and actions by AI systems? Can a machine be held accountable for its actions? Answering these and related questions requires a comprehensive understanding of socio-technical interactions and the ethical aspects of intelligent systems.

We need to find ways to coordinate, cooperate, collaborate, and compete peacefully and productively with artificial systems, which are seen as independent parties whose behavior we cannot simply dictate.

The foundations of AI ethics are a set of principles and frameworks designed to guide the development, deployment, and use of artificial intelligence in a way that is beneficial, fair, and safe for humanity (Etienne, 2022). These principles address the potential risks and negative societal impacts of AI, such as bias, lack of transparency, and misuse. While different organizations and countries may articulate these principles in slightly different ways, there is a broad consensus on several core foundational principles.

FOUNDATIONAL PRINCIPLES

The following principles are widely recognized as the pillars of AI ethics.

- **Fairness and Non-discrimination:** AI systems should be developed to avoid bias and should not discriminate against individuals or groups based on factors like race, gender, age, or socioeconomic status. This requires careful attention to the data used for training and continuous monitoring for discriminatory outcomes. AI systems must be designed to avoid and mitigate bias (Madanchian & Taherdoost, 2025).This is crucial because AI models are trained on data, and if that data reflects existing societal biases (e.g., historical hiring patterns that favor a certain gender), the AI will learn and perpetuate those same discriminatory outcomes. The goal is to ensure that AI-driven decisions, such as loan approvals or hiring recommendations, are equitable for everyone, regardless of their background.
- **Transparency and Explainability:** The decision-making processes of AI systems should be understandable and explainable to humans. This is often referred to as "explainable AI" (XAI). It's crucial for building trust and

for allowing individuals to challenge decisions that affect them, such as a loan application rejection or a hiring decision. Many advanced AI models are "black boxes," where the exact logic behind their decisions is inscrutable to humans (Becker et al., 2023). The principle of Explainable AI (XAI) advocates for systems that can provide clear, understandable reasons for their output (Singhal et al., 2024).This is essential for building trust, allowing users to contest decisions, and holding developers accountable.

- **Accountability:** There must be a clear chain of responsibility for the actions and outcomes of an AI system. When an AI makes a mistake or causes harm, there should be a human or a group of humans who are ultimately accountable. This principle ensures that AI is not a "black box" where no one can be held responsible. There must be a clear chain of responsibility for the actions of an AI system. If an autonomous vehicle causes an accident or a medical diagnostic AI provides a faulty recommendation, a human or an organization must be held liable. This prevents AI from becoming a legal and ethical void where no one is responsible for a system's errors.
- **Privacy and Data Security:** AI systems often rely on vast amounts of data, including personal and sensitive information. Ethical AI development necessitates robust measures to safeguard user data, ensure privacy, and comply with all applicable data protection regulations (Hallamaa & Kalliokoski, 2022). Users should have control over their data and be informed about how it is being used. Ethical AI requires robust measures to protect this data from misuse, unauthorized access, and surveillance. This principle is closely tied to ensuring user consent and control over their own data.
- **Beneficence and Safety:** AI systems should be designed to do good and to "do no harm." This principle emphasizes that AI should be used for the well-being and benefit of society, while also ensuring that systems are robust, secure, and do not pose a threat to people's physical or mental safety. The core of this principle is to "do no harm" and to use AI for the greater good. This involves designing systems that are safe, reliable, and secure, and ensuring their application serves positive societal goals, such as advancing healthcare, scientific research, and environmental sustainability.
- **Human Oversight and Control:** AI should augment human intelligence, not replace it entirely, and humans should remain in control. This principle, sometimes referred to as "human-in-the-loop," (Bartneck et al., n.d.) ensures that a human can intervene and override an AI's decision, particularly in high-stakes scenarios.
- **Sustainability:** The development and operation of AI should consider its environmental and societal impact. This includes minimizing the energy consumption of large AI models and ensuring that AI contributes to achiev-

ing sustainable development goals, whether in education, hospitality, or healthcare.

The foundations of AI ethics are a set of principles and frameworks that guide the responsible development and use of artificial intelligence. These concepts are drawn from philosophy, law, and social sciences to address the unique challenges AI presents. The core idea is to ensure that AI systems benefit humanity, respect human values, and mitigate potential harms.

SOCIETAL IMPLICATIONS OF ARTIFICIAL INTELLIGENCE

The societal impact of Artificial Intelligence is, of course, more noticeable the more it is being implemented and used in a diversity of domains, which also explains the relatively recent surge of (academic and other) interest in AI ethics. Yet if we shape technology and technology also shapes us, it is essential to ask how it can be ensured that this mutual shaping process takes place in a way that protects rather than undermines our legal, moral, and political standards. When AI is used to make decisions for us and perform tasks for us, we encounter a problem that is shared with all automation technologies, but which becomes even more significant when AI enables us to delegate far more to machines than we previously did (Floridi et al., 2018). If AI is given more agency and takes over what humans used to do, how do we then attribute moral responsibility? Who is responsible for the harms and benefits of the technology when humans delegate agency and decisions to AI? The widespread adoption of AI has significant societal implications that these ethical foundations seek to address:

- **Economic Impact**: AI-driven automation has the potential to displace jobs and exacerbate economic inequality. Ethical considerations in this context involve managing the transition, ensuring a just and inclusive economy, and providing new opportunities for workers whose roles are affected.
- **Trust and Autonomy**: The increasing reliance on AI systems in daily life raises questions about human autonomy. As we delegate more decisions to AI, from navigation to financial advice, we risk losing our own critical thinking and decision-making skills (Hagendorff, 2022b). The ethical framework aims to maintain human agency and ensure that AI augments, rather than replaces, human control. According to Aristotle, a person has an effect on the world and on others, and is responsible for their own consequences; this is the first condition for moral responsibility, known as the control condition. Aristotle asserts that if a person possesses agency and can make decisions, they should

take responsibility for their actions. Furthermore, he adds another condition for moral responsibility: you are responsible if you know what you are doing. This is an epistemic condition: you must be aware of what you are doing and understand the potential consequences. Let us now see how these conditions fare when we delegate decisions and actions to AI. The first problem is that an AI can take actions and make decisions with ethical consequences, but is not aware of what it does and lacks the capacity for moral thought, and hence cannot be held morally responsible for its actions. Machines can be agents, but not moral agents, since they lack consciousness, free will, emotions, and the capability to form intentions (Kazim & Koshiyama, 2021). In Aristotle's view, only humans can perform voluntary actions and deliberate about their actions. If this is true, the only solution is to make humans responsible for what the machines do. Humans delegate agency to the machine, but retain the responsibility. In both our professional and personal spaces, we do not hold small children or animals responsible; instead, we place the legal responsibility on the shoulders of their caretakers. So why not let the machine perform the actions and keep the responsibility on the side of the humans? However, this situation is not as simple as it seems, as many hands are involved in technological action. In the case of AI, it involves multiple stakeholders, including the programmer, the car's user, the car company's owners, other road users, and so on. In March 2018, an Uber self-driving car caused an accident in Arizona that resulted in the death of a pedestrian. Who is responsible for this tragic outcome? It could be those who programmed the car, the car company's product development team, Uber, the car user, or the State of Arizona. One point is clear: since there is involvement of so many people, no single person can be held responsible. Now the bigger question is how to distribute the responsibility? Some people may be more responsible than others. To be responsible, one needs to know what they are doing and the consequences that follow. Responsibility then means answerability and explainability. If something goes wrong, we want a clear answer and a thorough explanation. If AI does not meet these conditions, then we cannot hold AI responsible.

- **Misinformation and Manipulation**: AI can be used to generate convincing fake content (**deepfakes**) and to spread misinformation at an unprecedented scale. This poses a threat to democratic processes, public discourse, and social stability. Ethical guidelines are needed to prevent the malicious use of AI and to develop tools that can detect fraudulent content.
- **Environmental Sustainability**: Training large-scale AI models requires immense computational power and energy, contributing to a significant carbon footprint. The environmental impact of AI development is a growing ethical

concern, pushing for the development of more energy-efficient algorithms and hardware (Bossert & Hagendorff, 2023).

When humans engage in activities and make decisions, we associate agency with moral responsibility. Every individual is responsible and accountable for their decisions.

The development of AI ethical guidelines is not a monolithic process, but rather a complex negotiation shaped by diverse ethical traditions, cultural values, and individual human judgment (White et al., 2024). This diversity is both a strength and a challenge, leading to a richer, more nuanced set of principles but also creating potential for conflict and misunderstanding in a global context.

THE INFLUENCE OF ETHICAL THEORIES

Different philosophical frameworks provide the fundamental logic for what is considered "good" or "right" in AI behavior.

- **The Rule-Followers or Deontological Perspective:** For some, ethical action means strictly adhering to established principles and guidelines, regardless of the situation. It focuses on adhering to moral duties and rules, irrespective of consequences. A deontological approach to AI ethics would prioritize adherence to a strict set of rules, such as "an AI must never lie" or "an AI must not harm a human," even if breaking the rule could lead to a better outcome (Bleher & Braun, 2023). This theory underpins principles such as transparency and accountability, where the emphasis is on following a clear process and respecting inherent responsibilities. Thus, acting ethically is determined by following a previously established rule that determines whether or not an act is ethical.
- **The Outcome-Seekers or Consequentialists** (including Utilitarianism): There are those who believe in a more flexible approach. They argue that ethical decisions should be based on achieving the most beneficial outcome, even if it means breaking or bending some rules. For them, it is ok to cause the death of another if a greater harm is avoided (Hanna & Kazim, 2021a). They judge the morality of an action based on its outcomes. A consequentialist AI would be designed to produce the greatest good for the greatest number of people. In the infamous "trolley problem" for self-driving cars, a utilitarian AI might be programmed to sacrifice one person to save five (Hanna & Kazim, 2021b). This approach embodies principles such as beneficence, prioritizing positive societal outcomes.

- **Virtue Ethics** focuses on the character of the moral agent rather than rules or outcomes. In the context of AI, this theory is less about what an AI *does* and more about what kind of system it is. It would guide developers in imbuing AI with "virtues" such as fairness, reliability, and compassion (Phan & Goldenfein, n.d.). This is a more abstract, but powerful, approach that influences the entire design philosophy of an AI system (Hagendorff, 2022a).

THE IMPACT OF CULTURAL VALUES

Ethical principles are not universal; they are interpreted and prioritized differently across cultures. This creates a significant challenge for creating global AI standards.

- **Individualism vs. Collectivism:** Western cultures, which tend to be more individualistic, often prioritize privacy and personal autonomy (Walawalkar et al., 2025). Regulations like the European Union's GDPR reflect this, giving individuals strong control over their data. In contrast, many Eastern and collectivist cultures may be more willing to accept a certain degree of surveillance or data sharing for the sake of community safety or social harmony(Shanker, n.d.) For example, some Asian countries have adopted facial recognition for public security with less public resistance than in the West.
- **Views on Fairness:** The definition of "fairness" also varies. In some cultures, fairness is defined as treating everyone equally, regardless of context. In others, it may mean ensuring a fair outcome for a specific group, even if it requires differential treatment. This divergence influences how AI is trained to address historical biases.
- **Trust in Institutions:** Societies with a high degree of trust in their government or corporations may be more accepting of AI systems deployed by those entities. Conversely, societies with lower institutional trust will demand greater transparency and human oversight (Smuha, 2025).

THE ROLE OF INDIVIDUAL INTUITIONS

When we refer to "ethical intuitions," we mean the immediate, instinctive feelings people have about right and wrong. While not a formal ethical theory, these intuitions play a critical role in shaping the debate around AI.

- **Public Perception and Trust:** Individual intuitions often drive public outrage or acceptance of new technologies. A person's immediate reaction to a deepfake video or a biased hiring algorithm is rooted in their intuition about fairness and authenticity (Boris D. Grozdanoff, 2022).These reactions can influence policy and market adoption, prompting developers to address ethical concerns that may not be fully captured by formal ethical frameworks alone.

- **Human-in-the-Loop:** In many AI systems, a human is kept "in the loop" to oversee and correct the AI's decisions. The human's intuition, built from experience and expertise, is often the final check against a potentially flawed or biased AI output (Şenocak et al., 2023). This highlights that AI ethics isn't just about programming; it's also about designing systems that effectively collaborate with human judgment.

People want organizations using AI and the AI systems themselves to behave ethically, but ethical behavior means different things to different people, and many ethical dilemmas require trade-offs such that no course of action is universally considered ethical (Barry et al., n.d.). People want AI and organizations using it to act ethically, but ethical behavior is a complex, subjective concept. This is because ethical behavior means different things to different people and often requires difficult trade-offs where no solution satisfies everyone. This tension presents a significant challenge in creating universally accepted AI ethical guidelines.

CONFLICTING ETHICAL FRAMEWORKS

The core of the problem lies in the different ethical frameworks that individuals and cultures use to judge right and wrong.

- **Utilitarianism vs. Deontology**: A utilitarian approach would focus on an AI's actions producing the greatest good for the greatest number of people. For example, a self-driving car might be programmed to swerve to save a busload of people, even if it means hitting and killing a pedestrian (Badawy, 2025). A deontological approach, however, would argue that certain actions are inherently wrong, regardless of the consequences. From this perspective, an AI should never be programmed to intentionally cause harm to an innocent person, even if it means saving others. These two frameworks lead to directly opposing ethical prescriptions for the same dilemma.
- **Individual Rights vs. Societal Good**: This conflict is particularly visible in debates around AI surveillance. An AI system used for public safety might be able to predict and prevent crime by analyzing vast amounts of data. A utilitarian would see this as a net positive, as it increases safety for the community (Rubeis, 2024). However, from a rights-based perspective, this system might

be seen as a violation of individual privacy and civil liberties. Regardless of the choice made, one ethical value is prioritized at the expense of another.

THE PROBLEM OF CULTURAL RELATIVISM

Ethical values aren't universal; they vary significantly across cultures. This makes it challenging to establish a unified set of AI ethics guidelines for a globalized world.

- **Privacy**: In Western cultures, there is a strong emphasis on individual privacy and data protection, leading to regulations like the GDPR in Europe (Chen et al., 2023).

In many Eastern cultures, there's often a greater willingness to trade personal data for convenience or collective security. An AI system considered ethically sound and acceptable in one country may be viewed as an unacceptable intrusion in another.

- **Fairness**: The concept of fairness is also culturally dependent. In some societies, fairness means treating every individual with equal respect and consideration. In others, it might mean treating people differently to achieve a more equitable outcome for a disadvantaged group (Westerstrand, 2024). An AI hiring tool trained on one definition of fairness might be seen as biased from another cultural perspective.

THE CHALLENGE OF UNAVOIDABLE TRADE-OFFS

Many AI ethical dilemmas are not about choosing between good and evil but about choosing between two or more competing goods, all of which are valuable (Floridi, 2023). This means that regardless of the decision made, some ethical value will be compromised.

- **Accuracy vs. Bias**: In some cases, increasing the accuracy of an AI model may unintentionally introduce or amplify biases. For example, to make a loan approval AI more accurate, it might rely on data that correlates with race or income, even if those factors are not explicitly used in the model. Making the model "fair" by removing these correlations might decrease its accuracy. Developers must make a trade-off between these two competing values (Casiraghi, 2023).

- **Innovation vs. Safety**: The push for rapid innovation in AI often conflicts with the need for rigorous safety testing. Rushing a new AI medical diagnostic tool to market might save lives in the short term, but a lack of thorough testing could lead to catastrophic failures (Huang et al., 2023). Conversely, delaying the product for extensive safety checks might mean that people who could have benefited from the technology are not. This is a classic dilemma between risk and reward.

WAYS TO OVERCOME THE PROBLEM OF CONFLICTING AI ETHICAL FRAMEWORK

Solving the problem of conflicting AI ethical frameworks requires a multi-pronged approach that moves beyond a search for a single, universal solution. Instead of trying to force a consensus on what "ethical" means, the focus should be on creating processes and systems that can navigate these disagreements and make informed, transparent trade-offs.

1. Context-Specific Ethical Frameworks

Instead of a single global code of ethics, a more practical approach is to develop context-specific ethical guidelines. The ethical principles for a military AI system will be different from those for a healthcare AI (Mussgnug, 2025). This allows for tailoring principles to the specific risks and societal values of a particular domain, making them more relevant and actionable. For example, in healthcare, the principle of beneficence (doing good) is paramount, while in a legal context, fairness and impartiality are prioritized (Thomsen, 2019).

2. Stakeholder-Inclusive Design

AI development should not be left solely to engineers and data scientists. A key solution is to involve a diverse range of stakeholders in the design and governance process. This includes:

- **Ethicists and Philosophers**: To help identify and articulate the ethical dilemmas inherent in a project (Ratti & Graves, 2025).
- **Sociologists and Anthropologists**: To understand the cultural and social impacts of the AI system on different communities (Telkamp & Anderson, 2022).

- **Domain Experts**: (e.g., doctors for a medical AI, lawyers for a legal AI) to provide practical context and insight.
- **Members of the Public**: To ensure the AI reflects the values and concerns of the people it will affect.

This co-design process helps to uncover potential conflicts and biases early on, leading to more robust and socially aware AI systems.

3. Emphasizing Transparency and Explainability (XAI)

When a perfect ethical solution isn't possible, the next best thing is to make the trade-offs transparent. Explainable AI (XAI) is a crucial tool in this context. If an AI system makes a decision that might be seen as ethically ambiguous (e.g., denying a loan), the system should be able to explain *why* it made that decision (Karmakar et al., 2025). This doesn't solve the dilemma, but it allows for accountability and for people to challenge the decision. It shifts the ethical burden from the AI itself to the human or organization responsible for programming and deploying it.

4. Establishing a Governance and Oversight Body

To ensure accountability, an independent governance or oversight body should be established. This body could be an internal AI ethics board within a company, a national regulatory commission, or a global consortium (Bleher & Braun, 2023b). This body's role would be to:

- **Review and audit** AI systems for ethical compliance.
- **Arbitrate** disputes over ethical dilemmas.
- **Enforce** standards and best practices.

This ensures that ethical considerations are not just a one-time step but an ongoing process of monitoring and adaptation.

5. Ethical Education and Training

Ultimately, the solution depends on the people who design and use AI. Integrating ethical education and training into computer science curricula and professional development is vital (Dameski, 2018). This helps developers and managers understand:

- The potential societal impact of their work.
- How to identify and mitigate bias in data.

- The importance of ethical trade-offs.

By fostering a culture of ethical awareness from the ground up, the industry can proactively address dilemmas rather than simply reacting to them.

An ethical framework for AI in India is centered on the principle of "AI for All," a vision that aims to utilize artificial intelligence for inclusive growth and the greater social good (Carter, 2007). This approach is deeply influenced by India's unique context, which includes its vast population, cultural diversity, and diverse developmental needs. The framework blends universal ethical principles with values rooted in Indian philosophy to ensure AI empowers, rather than marginalizes, its citizens.

FOUNDATIONAL PRINCIPLES FROM AN INDIAN CONTEXT

India's approach, primarily guided by initiatives from the government's think tank NITI Aayog, is characterized by several key principles that reflect the nation's specific challenges and aspirations.

- **Human-Centricity and the "AI for All" Vision**: At its core, the Indian framework prioritizes the well-being and dignity of its over 1.4 billion people. The goal isn't just technological advancement, but the application of AI to solve real-world problems in areas like healthcare, education, agriculture, and mobility. The focus is on how AI can enhance human capabilities and address issues like the shortage of skilled professionals in rural areas.
- **Fairness and Inclusivity**: In a country with immense diversity in language, culture, and socioeconomic status, a critical ethical pillar is preventing AI from amplifying existing biases. This principle extends beyond non-discrimination and actively seeks to make AI systems more inclusive (Yu & Lu, 2021). This involves using diverse datasets from various regions and languages to train AI models, ensuring they work effectively for all citizens, and providing alternatives for those on the other side of the digital divide (Waser, 2008).
- **Transparency and Accountability**: The framework emphasizes making AI systems understandable and holding developers and deployers accountable for their outcomes. Decisions made by AI that have a significant impact on individuals, such as in public services or law enforcement, must be traceable and contestable (Harrison et al., 2025). This ensures that there is always a human or an organization responsible for an AI's actions, and people have a clear path to seek redress (Chong et al., 2023).

- **Privacy and Data Security**: India's approach to AI ethics is grounded in its robust data protection laws, such as the Digital Personal Data Protection Act, 2023. This principle mandates that personal data used by AI systems must be secure and that its use is done with explicit user consent. The focus is on safeguarding an individual's right to privacy in a data-driven world.
- **Safety and Reliability**: AI systems, especially those deployed in critical sectors like healthcare and transportation, must be robust, reliable, and safe. The framework calls for rigorous testing and validation of AI systems to minimize risks and prevent unintended harm.

UNIQUE INDIAN PHILOSOPHICAL INFLUENCES

Beyond these universal principles, the Indian framework is also subtly influenced by deeper philosophical concepts, which offer a unique perspective on technology and ethics.

- **Dharma (Ethical Duty)**: This concept, central to Indian philosophy, suggests that AI development isn't just a commercial pursuit but an ethical duty to the greater good. It encourages developers and organizations to create technologies that uplift society and prioritize collective well-being over individual profit.
- **Ahimsa (Non-Harm)**: While this principle is often translated as non-violence, in the context of AI ethics, it expands to mean minimizing all forms of harm—physical, emotional, or social. This includes mitigating the potential for manipulative algorithms, misinformation, or other digital harms that can negatively affect individuals and society.
- **Loka Sangraha (Welfare of the World)**: This ideal from the Bhagavad Gita emphasizes that individual actions should contribute to the common good. In AI, this translates to designing systems that promote inclusivity and social harmony, rather than fostering division or inequality (Mohan et al., 2021). It's a call for AI to be a force for positive societal change.

POLICY AND IMPLEMENTATION

India's strategy is to adopt a light-touch, pro-innovation regulatory approach rather than a rigid, top-down law. The government favors using existing legal frameworks and creating new, context-specific guidelines and advisories. The "IndiaAI" mission, for example, is designed to democratize access to AI resources and promote ethical development by focusing on public-private partnerships, research hubs, and open datasets. The ultimate goal is to build a vibrant AI ecosystem that is both globally competitive and deeply rooted in Indian values.

KEY STRATEGIES TO BRIDGE REGULATORY GAPS

Instead of enacting a single, comprehensive law, India is strategically using a combination of policy, collaboration, and a risk-based approach to govern AI.

- **Ethical Principles and Guidelines**: India's approach is guided by principles such as fairness, transparency, and accountability, which are operationalized through policy documents like the NITI Aayog's "Principles for Responsible AI."(Arbelaez Ossa et al., 2024). These guidelines serve as a moral compass for developers and organizations, encouraging ethical behavior without stifling innovation (Hagendorff, 2020). This non-binding approach gives the government flexibility to adapt to rapidly evolving technology.
- **Multi-Stakeholder Forums**: The government is actively involving various stakeholders in policy discussions. Initiatives like the AI Legislators' Forum are being established to educate lawmakers on the complexities of AI, thereby bridging the knowledge gap between policymakers and technologists. These forums foster a collaborative environment where industry experts, academia, and civil society can contribute to shaping responsible AI governance.
- **Leveraging Digital Public Infrastructure (DPI)**: India's success with DPIs like Aadhaar and UPI provides a blueprint for a decentralized, inclusive AI ecosystem. By using public platforms for data and compute resources (IndiaAI Mission, AI Kosh), the government is working to democratize AI development (Churi et al., n.d.). This helps startups and researchers build India-specific AI models that cater to local needs and linguistic diversity.
- **Sector-Specific Regulations**: Instead of a blanket law, India is focusing on regulating AI in high-risk sectors like healthcare, finance, and law enforcement. This targeted approach ensures that safeguards are implemented where they're most needed, without over-regulating low-risk AI applications. This allows for a more agile and efficient regulatory response.

ALIGNING WITH INDIAN VALUES AND SOCIETAL NEEDS

The Indian approach to AI governance is deeply rooted in the country's unique socio-economic context.

- **Focus on Inclusivity**: With over 22 official languages and vast regional disparities, inclusivity is paramount. The government is promoting the development of indigenous AI models, such as the Bhashini platform and Sarvam-1, which are trained on Indian datasets and can work effectively in multiple local languages (Mittelstadt, 2019). This ensures AI's benefits are not limited to a select few and can reach the majority of the population.
- **"AI for Social Good"**: India's AI strategy is not just about economic growth but also about addressing critical societal challenges. AI is being deployed in areas such as agriculture to assist farmers, in healthcare to enhance diagnosis, and in education to improve learning outcomes (Kim et al., 2025). This aligns with the philosophical concept of "Loka Sangraha" (the welfare of the world) and the vision of utilizing technology to serve the people.
- **Building Trust**: By focusing on transparency and explainability, the Indian framework aims to build public trust in AI. For AI to be widely adopted, especially in public services, citizens must understand how it works and be able to challenge its decisions (Reinhardt, 2023). The emphasis on data protection through the Digital Personal Data Protection Act, 2023, is another crucial step in building this trust and safeguarding individual privacy.

CONCLUSION

The ethics of artificial intelligence are the guiding principles that stakeholders use as a roadmap to ensure the responsible development and use of the latest technology. The stronger the ethical guidelines are, the better and smoother their application will be. A strong AI code of ethics can include avoiding bias, ensuring the privacy of users and their data, and mitigating environmental risks. With the development of technology, the discussion around AI ethics has progressed from centring on academic research and non-profit organisations. As AI has become an integral part of our lives, AI projects built on biased or inaccurate data can have severe and harmful consequences.

The regularity framework ensures that technology benefits society and its members. In addition to following the global policy framework, the Indian government is beginning to enforce ethical AI policies tailored to the country's unique socio-economic context. Currently, India lacks an overarching guidance framework for the use of AI systems. Establishing such a framework would be crucial for providing guidance to various stakeholders in the responsible management of Artificial Intelligence in India.

However, certain sector-specific frameworks have been identified for the development and use of AI. In finance, SEBI issued a circular in January 2019 to Stock

Brokers, Depository Participants, Recognized Stock Exchanges, and Depositories, and in May 2019 to All Mutual Funds (MFs)/ Asset Management companies (AMCs)/ Trustee Companies/ Board of Trustees of Mutual Funds/ Association of Mutual Funds in India (AMFI) on reporting requirements for Artificial Intelligence (AI) and Machine Learning (ML) applications and systems offered and used. The reporting aims to create an inventory of AI systems in the market and inform future policies.

The Information Technology Act, 2000 (IT Act) is the backbone of data protection legislation in India. The provisions of the IT Act, combined with the Information Technology Rules, 2011 (SPDI Rules), establish a technology-agnostic regime for the protection of sensitive personal information for all bodies corporate.

REFERENCES

Arbelaez Ossa, L., Lorenzini, G., Milford, S. R., Shaw, D., Elger, B. S., & Rost, M. (2024). Integrating ethics in AI development: A qualitative study. *BMC Medical Ethics*, *25*(1), 10. DOI: 10.1186/s12910-023-01000-0 PMID: 38262986

Badawy, W. (2025). AI ethics: A textbook by Paula Boddington. *AI and Ethics*, *5*(5), 5607–5609. DOI: 10.1007/s43681-025-00769-7

Barry, S. E., Sullivan, O., & Wooldridge, M. (n.d.). *Artificial Intelligence: Foundations*. Theory, and Algorithms.

Bartneck, C., Lütge, C., Wagner, A., & Welsh, S. (n.d.). *SPRINGER BRIEFS IN ETHICS*. https://www.springer.com/series/10184

Becker, S. J., Nemat, A. T., Lucas, S., Heinitz, R. M., Klevesath, M., & Charton, J. E. (2023). A Code of Digital Ethics: Laying the foundation for digital ethics in a science and technology company. *AI & Society*, *38*(6), 2629–2639. DOI: 10.1007/s00146-021-01376-w

Bleher, H., & Braun, M. (2023a). Reflections on Putting AI Ethics into Practice: How Three AI Ethics Approaches Conceptualize Theory and Practice. *Science and Engineering Ethics*, *29*(3), 21. DOI: 10.1007/s11948-023-00443-3 PMID: 37237246

Bleher, H., & Braun, M. (2023b). Reflections on Putting AI Ethics into Practice: How Three AI Ethics Approaches Conceptualize Theory and Practice. *Science and Engineering Ethics*, *29*(3), 21. DOI: 10.1007/s11948-023-00443-3 PMID: 37237246

Boris, D. (2022). *Grozdanoff*. Rationality and Ethics in Artificial Intelligence.

Bossert, L. N., & Hagendorff, T. (2023). The ethics of sustainable AI: Why animals (should) matter for a sustainable use of AI. *Sustainable Development (Bradford)*, *31*(5), 3459–3467. DOI: 10.1002/sd.2596

Carter, M. (2007). *Minds and computers: an introduction to the philosophy of artificial intelligence*. Edinburgh University Press. DOI: 10.1515/9780748629305

Casiraghi, S. (2023). Anything new under the sun? Insights from a history of institutionalized AI ethics. *Ethics and Information Technology*, *25*(2), 28. DOI: 10.1007/s10676-023-09702-0

Chen, F., Zhou, J., Holzinger, A., Fleischmann, K. R., & Stumpf, S. (2023). Artificial Intelligence Ethics and Trust: From Principles to Practice. *IEEE Intelligent Systems*, *38*(6), 5–8. DOI: 10.1109/MIS.2023.3324470

Chong, H., Shah, R., & Kulkarni, K. (2023). The Emergence of AI Tools in Academia: Potential and Limitations. *The Bulletin of the Royal College of Surgeons of England, 105*(8), 400–402. DOI: 10.1308/rcsbull.2023.125

Churi, P., Joshi, S., Elhoseny, M., & Omrane, A. (n.d.). *Artificial Intelligence in Higher Education: A Practical Approach.*

Dameski, A. (2018). A Comprehensive Ethical Framework for AI Entities. *Lecture Notes in Computer Science, 10999*, 42–51. DOI: 10.1007/978-3-319-97676-1_5

Etienne, H. (2022). When AI Ethics Goes Astray: A Case Study of Autonomous Vehicles. *Social Science Computer Review, 40*(1), 236–246. DOI: 10.1177/0894439320906508

Floridi, L. (2023). *The ethics of artificial intelligence: Principles, challenges, and opportunities.*

Floridi, L., Cowls, J., Beltrametti, M., Chatila, R., Chazerand, P., Dignum, V., Luetge, C., Madelin, R., Pagallo, U., Rossi, F., Schafer, B., Valcke, P., & Vayena, E. (2018). AI4People—An Ethical Framework for a Good AI Society: Opportunities, Risks, Principles, and Recommendations. *Minds and Machines, 28*(4), 689–707. DOI: 10.1007/s11023-018-9482-5 PMID: 30930541

Hagendorff, T. (2020). The Ethics of AI Ethics: An Evaluation of Guidelines. *Minds and Machines, 30*(1), 99–120. DOI: 10.1007/s11023-020-09517-8

Hagendorff, T. (2022a). A Virtue-Based Framework to Support Putting AI Ethics into Practice. *Philosophy & Technology, 35*(3), 55. DOI: 10.1007/s13347-022-00553-z

Hagendorff, T. (2022b). Blind spots in AI ethics. *AI and Ethics, 2*(4), 851–867. DOI: 10.1007/s43681-021-00122-8

Hallamaa, J., & Kalliokoski, T. (2022). AI Ethics as Applied Ethics. *Frontiers of Computer Science, 4*, 776837. Advance online publication. DOI: 10.3389/fcomp.2022.776837

Hanna, R., & Kazim, E. (2021a). Philosophical foundations for digital ethics and AI Ethics: A dignitarian approach. *AI and Ethics, 1*(4), 405–423. DOI: 10.1007/s43681-021-00040-9 PMID: 34790944

Hanna, R., & Kazim, E. (2021b). Philosophical foundations for digital ethics and AI Ethics: A dignitarian approach. *AI and Ethics, 1*(4), 405–423. DOI: 10.1007/s43681-021-00040-9 PMID: 34790944

Harrison, D. E., Ajjan, H., Ferrell, O. C., Ferrell, L., Hochstein, B. W., & Johnson, R. (2025). Bridging the gap: Aligning developers and managers in implementing AI ethics. *Journal of Marketing Theory and Practice*, •••, 1–20. DOI: 10.1080/10696679.2025.2552275

Huang, C., Zhang, Z., Mao, B., & Yao, X. (2023). An Overview of Artificial Intelligence Ethics. *IEEE Transactions on Artificial Intelligence*, *4*(4), 799–819. DOI: 10.1109/TAI.2022.3194503

Karmakar, D., Das, A., & Khati, A. (2025). *Building Ethical Foundations.*, DOI: 10.4018/979-8-3693-9035-1.ch008

Kazim, E., & Koshiyama, A. S. (2021). A high-level overview of AI ethics. *Patterns (New York, N.Y.)*, *2*(9), 100314. DOI: 10.1016/j.patter.2021.100314 PMID: 34553166

Kim, S.-E., Kim, K., Lee, J., Ko, Y., Wang, Y., & So, H.-J. (2025). *Dilemmas in AI Ethics: A Digital Game for Moral Reasoning and Collective Decision-Making.*, DOI: 10.1007/978-3-031-98417-4_31

Madanchian, M., & Taherdoost, H. (2025). Ethical theories, governance models, and strategic frameworks for responsible AI adoption and organizational success. *Frontiers in Artificial Intelligence*, *8*, 1619029. Advance online publication. DOI: 10.3389/frai.2025.1619029 PMID: 40741285

Mittelstadt, B. (2019). Principles alone cannot guarantee ethical AI. *Nature Machine Intelligence*, *1*(11), 501–507. DOI: 10.1038/s42256-019-0114-4

Mohan, N., Singla, R., Kaushal, P., & Kadry, S. (2021). Artificial Intelligence, Machine Learning, and Data Science Technologies: Future Impact and Well-Being for Society 5.0. In *Artificial Intelligence, Machine Learning, and Data Science Technologies: Future Impact and Well-Being for Society 5.0.* CRC Press., DOI: 10.1201/9781003153405

Mussgnug, A. M. (2025). Technology as Uncharted Territory: Integrative AI Ethics as a Response to the Notion of AI as New Moral Ground. *Philosophy & Technology*, *38*(3), 106. DOI: 10.1007/s13347-025-00938-w

Phan, T., & Goldenfein, J. (n.d.). Repositorium für die Medienwissenschaft Economies of Virtue-The Circulation of "Ethics" in AI 2022 Erstmalig hier erschienen / Initial publication here: https://networkcultures.org/blog/publication/economies-of-virtue-the-circulation-of-ethics-in-ai. DOI: 10.25969/mediarep/19267

Ratti, E., & Graves, M. (2025). A Capability Approach to AI Ethics. *American Philosophical Quarterly*, *62*(1), 1–16. DOI: 10.5406/21521123.62.1.01

Reinhardt, K. (2023). Trust and trustworthiness in AI ethics. *AI and Ethics*, *3*(3), 735–744. DOI: 10.1007/s43681-022-00200-5

Rubeis, G. (2024). *Ethical Foundations: Medical Ethics and Data Ethics* (pp. 55–87). DOI: 10.1007/978-3-031-55744-6_4

Securities and Exchange Board of India. (2019, May 15). Reporting for artificial intelligence (AI) and machine learning (ML) applications and systems offered and used by mutual funds (Circular No. SEBI/HO/IMD/DF2/CIR/P/2019/56). https://www.sebi.gov.in/legal/circulars/may-2019/reporting-for-artificial-intelligence-ai-and-machine-learn-ing-ml-applications-and-systems-offered-and-used-by-mutual-funds_42932.html

Şenocak, D., Koçdar, S., Bozkurt, A., & Professor, A. (2023). Historical, Philosophical and Ethical Roots of Artificial Intelligence. In *Pakistan Journal of Education* (Vol. 40, Issue 1). https://orcid.org/0000-0001-9099-6312

Shanker, S. (n.d.). *WITTGENSTEIN'S REMARKS ON THE FOUNDATIONS OF AI.*

Singhal, A., Neveditsin, N., Tanveer, H., & Mago, V. (2024). Toward Fairness, Accountability, Transparency, and Ethics in AI for Social Media and Health Care: Scoping Review. *JMIR Medical Informatics*, *12*, e50048. DOI: 10.2196/50048 PMID: 38568737

Smuha, N. A. (2025). *The Cambridge Handbook ofTHE LAW, ETHICS AND POLICY OF ARTIFICIAL INTELLIGENCE.* https://www.cambridge.org/core/terms.https://www.cambridge.org/core/product/0AD007641DE27F837A3A16DBC0888DD1Downloadedfromhttps://www.cambridge.org/core

Telkamp, J. B., & Anderson, M. H. (2022). The Implications of Diverse Human Moral Foundations for Assessing the Ethicality of Artificial Intelligence. *Journal of Business Ethics*, *178*(4), 961–976. DOI: 10.1007/s10551-022-05057-6

Thomsen, K. (2019). Ethics for Artificial Intelligence, Ethics for All. *Paladyn : Journal of Behavioral Robotics*, *10*(1), 359–363. DOI: 10.1515/pjbr-2019-0029

Walawalkar, A. KUMAR, S., Moslehpour, M., & Moslehpour, M. (2025). Foundations of AI Ethics. SSRN *Electronic Journal*. DOI: 10.2139/ssrn.5187641

Waser, M. R. (2008). *Discovering The Foundations Of A Universal System of Ethics As A Road To Safe Artificial Intelligence*. www.aaai.org

Westerstrand, S. (2024). Reconstructing AI Ethics Principles: Rawlsian Ethics of Artificial Intelligence. *Science and Engineering Ethics*, *30*(5), 46. DOI: 10.1007/s11948-024-00507-y PMID: 39384600

White, G. R. T., Samuel, A., Jones, P., Madhavan, N., Afolayan, A., Abdullah, A., & Kaushik, T. (2024). Mapping the ethical-theoretical foundations of artificial intelligence research. *Thunderbird International Business Review*, *66*(2), 171–183. DOI: 10.1002/tie.22368

Yu, S., & Lu, Y. (2021). *An Introduction to Artificial Intelligence in Education*. Springer Singapore., DOI: 10.1007/978-981-16-2770-5

Chapter 2
Foundations of Artificial Intelligence Ethics

Binastya Anggara Sekti
https://orcid.org/0000-0001-5489-4888
Universitas Esa Unggul, Indonesia

ABSTRACT

Artificial Intelligence (AI) has become an influential force shaping modern society, raising urgent ethical questions about responsibility, fairness, transparency, and human dignity. The discussion explores the conceptual and philosophical foundations of AI ethics as a framework for ensuring that technological progress aligns with moral and social values. It traces the evolution of ethical thought from classical philosophy to contemporary digital governance and defines the core principles guiding responsible AI, including beneficence, non-maleficence, autonomy, justice, and explicability. Emphasizing a human-centered approach, the section examines the challenges of operationalizing ethics into AI design, deployment, and regulation. By grounding innovation in ethical responsibility, it argues that trust in AI depends not on technical superiority alone but on its moral alignment with the public good and social justice.

1. INTRODUCTION

Artificial Intelligence (AI) has emerged as one of the most transformative forces of the 21st century, reshaping economies, societies, and human relationships. From predictive algorithms in healthcare and education to autonomous vehicles and generative language models, AI now permeates every layer of daily life. Yet, as its influence expands, so too does the complexity of the ethical dilemmas it generates. Questions once confined to philosophy—about agency, responsibility,

DOI: 10.4018/979-8-3373-7011-8.ch002

ht © 2026, IGI Global Scientific Publishing. Copying or distributing in print or electronic forms without written permission of IGI Global Scientific Publishing is prohibited. Use of this chapter to generative artificial intelligence (AI) technologies is expressly prohibited. The publisher reserves all rights to license its use for generative AI training and machine learning model development.

and fairness—have migrated into the realm of technology. The urgency of these questions lies in the fact that AI does not merely mirror human decision-making; it amplifies human choices, biases, and power structures at a global scale. Thus, understanding the ethical foundations of AI has become essential for ensuring that technological progress aligns with moral progress. Competencies for AI ethics require a comprehensive assessment of AI literacy (Knoth et al., 2024).

The development of AI was initially celebrated as a purely technical achievement—a triumph of human ingenuity in automation, computation, and data processing. However, as AI systems began making decisions that directly affected human lives, innovation alone proved insufficient. Autonomous systems can discriminate, misinform, or even cause harm when left unchecked. The conversation has therefore shifted from *what AI can do* to *what AI should do*. This transition marks the birth of AI ethics: an interdisciplinary field that merges moral philosophy, law, and social sciences with computer engineering. It represents a recognition that every algorithm carries moral weight and that the ethical use of AI is as important as its accuracy or efficiency. The justification and rationality of theory, and the basic concepts of AI-based problem-solving can form the core of a good artificial intelligence (AI) society. This is morally acceptable and utilitarian concerns stemming from the beginning and realization of the structural foundations of AI (Paraman & Anamalah, 2023). Figure 1 shows the AI, Ethics, and Social Trust.

Figure 1. AI, Ethics, and Social Trust

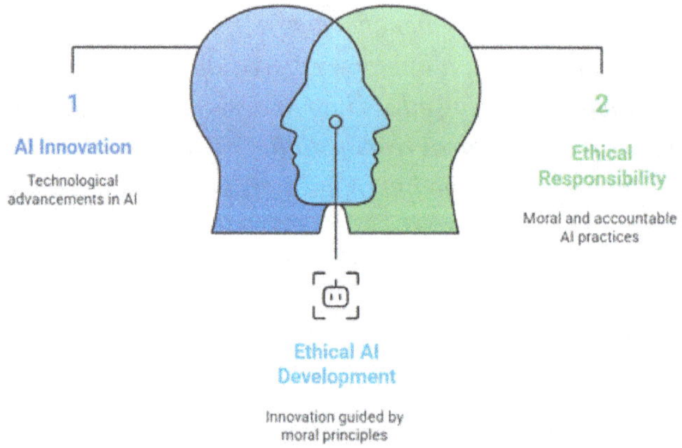

At its core, AI ethics is not only about machines—it is about humans and their values. Every dataset reflects human intention, and every algorithm is a projection of human judgment. This makes AI a mirror of our collective moral landscape. Ethical AI must therefore be human-centered, designed to protect dignity, autonomy, and justice. It demands empathy in code, fairness in data, and accountability in design. By grounding AI development in humanistic principles, we prevent technology from becoming detached from the social contexts it serves. The goal is not to restrain innovation but to ensure it advances human welfare while respecting rights and diversity across cultures and communities. AI-based safety systems can be developed, from traditional functional safety systems to autonomous systems. AI trust can encompass several dimensions, such as engineering, ethics, and law, and focuses on the safety engineering dimension (Perez-Cerrolaza et al., 2024).

Despite growing awareness, the practical implementation of AI ethics faces deep tensions. Efficiency often conflicts with fairness; privacy competes with progress; transparency can be at odds with proprietary interests. For example, predictive healthcare algorithms promise earlier diagnoses but risk exposing sensitive data, while facial recognition tools enhance security but threaten personal privacy. These dilemmas reveal that ethics in AI is not a matter of choosing between right and wrong, but of balancing competing moral priorities. Such tensions underscore the importance of structured ethical frameworks that guide decision-making, ensuring AI innovation remains aligned with societal trust and democratic values. As the influence of artificial intelligence (AI) grows in our lives, the ethical implications of AI have received attention from various communities. Building on previous work on trust in people and technology by conceptualizing multidimensional and multilevel trust in AI and examining the relationship between trust and ethics (Choung et al., 2023).

he discussion lays the groundwork for understanding AI ethics as a foundation for building social trust in the AI era. It begins by defining the concept of AI ethics and tracing its philosophical roots, from classical moral theories to contemporary applications in machine decision-making. It then examines key ethical challenges, including accountability, transparency, and fairness, and discusses how moral responsibility can be embedded in the lifecycle of AI systems. By establishing this foundation, the section provides readers with a framework to critically evaluate how AI can be developed and governed in ways that are both innovative and ethically sustainable.

2. DEFINING AI ETHICS

Artificial Intelligence ethics, often abbreviated as AI ethics, refers to the interdisciplinary field that studies how moral principles can be applied to the design, development, and governance of AI systems. Its central goal is to ensure that intelligent technologies serve human values, enhance social well-being, and minimize harm. While traditional computer ethics focused on human use of technology, AI ethics extends this discussion to autonomous decision-making systems that can act independently of human control. The scope of AI ethics encompasses a wide range of questions, from algorithmic fairness and data privacy to accountability, transparency, and human oversight. In essence, it asks not only "Can we build it?" but also "Should we build it, and under what conditions?". Human and material agency has been investigated in the literature to understand how technology and humans influence each other. Some agencies treat humans and technology symmetrically, some prioritize human agency over technology, and others do not associate agency with humans or non-humans (Dattathrani & De', 2023).

AI ethics operates at the intersection of philosophy, technology, and governance, making it a hybrid discipline that requires collaboration between ethicists, computer scientists, policymakers, and sociologists. Artificial intelligence systems can perform ideological functions that go far beyond technical bias or governance protocols (Erfani, 2025). Its definitions vary depending on emphasis:

- From a technological standpoint, it addresses safety, robustness, and explainability.
- From a philosophical standpoint, it concerns moral reasoning, virtue, and justice.
- From a legal standpoint, it relates to rights, accountability, and liability.

A well-accepted definition of AI ethics is "the normative and practical discipline concerned with ensuring that the design, development, and deployment of AI technologies are consistent with moral values and social justice."

Most global AI frameworks share a common set of ethical principles that guide responsible development. These principles provide a foundation for evaluating AI behavior and its alignment with societal norms. The five universal pillars of AI ethics are:

1. Beneficence: AI should promote human welfare and contribute to the public good.
2. Non-Maleficence: Systems must avoid harm and minimize unintended consequences.
3. Autonomy: Humans must retain meaningful control over AI systems.
4. Justice: AI must treat individuals fairly and equitably, avoiding discrimination.
5. Explicability: The operations and decisions of AI systems must be transparent and explainable.

These principles form the ethical compass for balancing innovation with moral responsibility in the digital age. Table 1 shows the Core Principles of AI Ethics and Their Practical Implications.

Table 1. Core Principles of AI Ethics and Their Practical Implications

Ethical Principle	Description	Practical Implementation Example	Relevant Frameworks
Beneficence	AI should enhance well-being and societal good.	AI for disease prediction improving early diagnosis.	OECD AI Principles (2020)
Non-Maleficence	Prevent harm and minimize algorithmic risks.	Risk audits in autonomous vehicles.	IEEE Ethically Aligned Design (2021)
Autonomy	Ensure human control and informed consent.	Human override in medical decision systems.	EU AI Act (2024)
Justice	Guarantee fairness, equality, and inclusion.	Bias detection in hiring algorithms.	UNESCO AI Ethics (2021)
Explicability	Make AI processes transparent and interpretable.	Explainable AI dashboards in finance.	EU HLEG Guidelines (2019)

Defining AI ethics also requires recognizing the ecosystem of stakeholders involved in AI development. Unlike earlier technologies, AI is embedded in a network of moral agents, each with distinct responsibilities, including developers, data providers, policymakers, users, and affected communities. According to the European Commission, ethical AI must be lawful (complying with all legal requirements), ethical (respecting human values), and robust (technically reliable and safe). The interaction of these dimensions creates a framework for trust and accountability. When one of these pillars is missing, such as robustness without ethics or law without transparency, social trust erodes. Thus, defining AI ethics is not merely about abstract moral theory, but about designing systems of shared responsibility that align technological advancement with collective human values. AI governance frameworks can be proposed by tech conglomerates, policymakers, and by intergovernmental organizations (Camilleri, 2024).

Understanding AI ethics is only the first step; the true challenge lies in operationalizing ethics into design and governance. This involves translating abstract principles into measurable practices, such as algorithmic auditing, bias mitigation, and ethical impact assessments. Modern approaches emphasize the concept of "ethics by design", integrating ethical reasoning into every stage of AI development—from data acquisition to model deployment. In this way, ethics becomes not a reactive layer of oversight but an embedded, proactive component of the innovation process. A clearly defined and operationalized understanding of AI ethics ensures that technology not only performs effectively but also earns public legitimacy and long-term trust. The research landscape has been rapidly evolving in finance, covering environmental, social, and governance (ESG) topics and related Artificial Intelligence (AI) applications (Lim, 2024). Figure 2 shows the Conceptual Model of AI Ethics Dimensions.

Figure 2. Conceptual Model of AI Ethics Dimensions

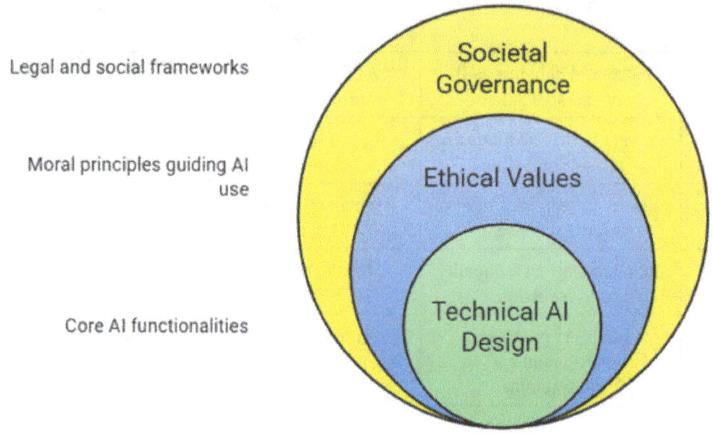

3. HISTORICAL CONTEXT: FROM MORAL PHILOSOPHY TO MACHINE MORALITY

The ethical foundations of Artificial Intelligence can be traced back to classical moral philosophy, long before the emergence of intelligent machines. Thinkers such as Aristotle, Immanuel Kant, and John Stuart Mill established frameworks for evaluating right and wrong that continue to shape modern debates in AI ethics. Aristotle's virtue ethics emphasized character and moral development; Kant's deontological ethics focused on duty and universal principles; while Mill's *utilitarianism* sought the greatest good for the greatest number. These traditions provide the moral vocabulary through which today's AI dilemmas are interpreted. When algorithms make decisions that affect human lives, they essentially participate in moral reasoning, raising the question of whether ethical theories designed for humans can guide the behavior of autonomous systems. The reliance on machine learning (ML) algorithms to perform tasks, deliver services, and make decisions in healthcare and healthcare has made the need for fairness in ML ever increasing, and more specifically in healthcare ML algorithms (HMLA), a critically important and urgent task (Giovanola & Tiribelli, 2023).

The concept of moral agency, the capacity to act according to moral principles, lies at the center of ethical inquiry. In traditional philosophy, moral agency was exclusive to humans, grounded in consciousness, intentionality, and empathy. However, the rise of AI challenges this boundary. Autonomous systems now perform tasks once reserved for human judgment, such as diagnosing diseases, predicting crimes, or driving vehicles. While these systems lack genuine moral awareness, their decisions have moral consequences. Thus, AI does not need to "be moral" to create moral impact. Scholars argue that designing artificial moral agents (AMAs) involves encoding ethical reasoning into computational architectures so that machines can act consistently with human values even without consciousness. Virtue ethics is explored as a means to program social robots as artificial moral agents that can place human values as the basis of robot design (Arora et al., 2025).

Each major ethical tradition offers distinct implications for AI design and governance. Deontological ethics emphasizes clear rules, inspiring approaches such as value alignment and constraint-based programming ("do not harm humans," as in Asimov's famous laws). *Consequentialism* underpins outcome-based evaluations, where the ethical worth of AI actions depends on their social utility. Virtue ethics informs the moral behavior of AI developers themselves, highlighting the cultivation of professional virtues like integrity, humility, and prudence in system design. These ethical traditions serve as conceptual tools for balancing algorithmic performance with moral accountability. Table 2 shows the Comparison of Classical Ethical Theories and Their Application in AI Systems.

Table 2. Comparison of Classical Ethical Theories and Their Application in AI Systems

Ethical Theory	Key Principle	Philosophical Foundation	Application in AI	Potential Limitation
Deontology (Kant)	Duty and universal rules	Act according to maxims that can be universalized	Constraint-based AI (e.g., Asimov's "do not harm" logic)	Rigid rules may lack contextual flexibility
Consequentialism (Mill)	Outcomes determine moral value	Seek the greatest good for the greatest number	Reward optimization in reinforcement learning	May justify harmful means if outcomes seem beneficial
Virtue Ethics (Aristotle)	Moral character and virtue	Cultivate moral excellence and practical wisdom	Ethical codes of conduct for AI developers	Difficult to formalize into algorithms
Care Ethics (Gilligan)	Relationships and empathy	Emphasize compassion and contextual care	Human-in-the-loop ethical decision-making	Hard to operationalize in automated systems

The 21st century has witnessed a gradual transition from philosophical ethics to machine morality. This shift does not mean machines possess moral consciousness but that moral reasoning is translated into computational rules. Research in machine ethics aims to model ethical decision-making through algorithms capable of evaluating scenarios and outcomes based on pre-defined moral criteria. For example, self-driving cars must make ethical trade-offs in accident scenarios, and medical

AI systems must balance accuracy with patient autonomy. These applications show that ethical reasoning can be simulated, even if empathy cannot. The challenge lies in ensuring that these computational moralities remain aligned with dynamic and diverse human values—a concern known as the value alignment problem.

Understanding the historical evolution from moral philosophy to machine morality reveals that AI ethics is not an isolated field but a continuation of humanity's ethical evolution. Philosophical principles once confined to classrooms and moral discourse are now being implemented as code, datasets, and algorithms. The task is to preserve the human essence of ethics, including empathy, justice, and accountability, while enabling machines to operate responsibly in complex moral environments. The future of AI ethics thus depends not on replacing human morality but on amplifying human ethical judgment through technology. This synthesis of philosophy and computation forms the moral backbone of trustworthy AI systems that sustain public confidence and social legitimacy in the AI era. Figure 3 shows the Evolution of Ethics Toward Machine Morality.

Figure 3. Evolution of Ethics Toward Machine Morality

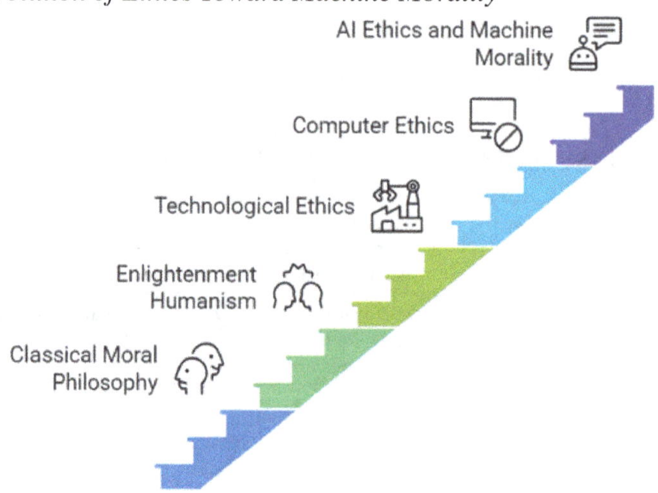

4. THE EMERGENCE OF AI ETHICS AS A DISCIPLINE

The emergence of AI ethics as a formal discipline represents a critical turning point in the evolution of artificial intelligence. While early AI research in the mid-20th century focused primarily on problem-solving, automation, and symbolic reasoning, the 2010s brought a paradigm shift driven by machine learning and big data analytics. As algorithms began influencing real-world decisions, such as employment screening, criminal sentencing, financial credit scoring, and medical diagnosis, the moral implications of AI became impossible to ignore. The realization that technical performance alone was insufficient led to the rise of ethical reflection as a parallel field of AI research, emphasizing fairness, accountability, and human-centered values. Despite the growing interest in artificial intelligence (AI) ethics education with the rapid surge of AI technology, there is still little problem-solving to foster students' AI ethics awareness. The scale can be used to measure AI ethics awareness in a multidimensional way and foster students' AI ethics awareness through problem-solving using AI tools (Kong & Zhu, 2025).

By the late 2010s, ethical concerns surrounding AI had moved beyond academia and into policy, industry, and governance. Leading organizations such as the IEEE, OECD, UNESCO, and the European Commission began formulating ethical frameworks for trustworthy AI. The IEEE's Ethically Aligned Design (EAD) guidelines (2019) highlighted principles of human well-being, transparency, and accountability, while the OECD established the Principles on Artificial Intelligence that later informed the G20 AI policy framework. Simultaneously, technology companies such as Google, Microsoft, and IBM launched internal AI ethics boards and responsible AI divisions to oversee product development. Universities across the world—from Stanford and Oxford to the National University of Singapore—introduced AI ethics curricula that blend computer science with philosophy and public policy. The development of AI literacy is essential in integrating technical AI skills with ethical principles, collaborative learning, and culturally appropriate strategies. Affective learning, designing collaborative behavioral interventions, embedding ethical reasoning into the curriculum, and contextualizing pedagogy for regional realities, need to be done so as to inform stakeholders about effective AI education (Asghar et al., 2025).

Despite differences in regional priorities, global AI ethics frameworks share a set of common values: transparency, fairness, accountability, safety, and human oversight. These overlapping principles demonstrate a convergence toward what scholars describe as "the global alignment of AI ethics". The integration of ethics into AI policy signifies a shift from reactive regulation to proactive governance. Table 3 summarizes the key initiatives that shaped this convergence, revealing how ethical standards evolved from voluntary guidelines into formal governance instruments influencing national legislation, such as the EU AI Act and OECD AI Policy Observatory.

Table 3. Major Global Initiatives Shaping AI Ethics as a Discipline

Organization	Key Framework / Year	Core Ethical Principles	Impact on Global AI Governance
IEEE	*Ethically Aligned Design* (2019)	Human well-being, transparency, accountability	Set global technical and ethical standards for AI developers
OECD	*Principles on AI* (2020)	Inclusive growth, fairness, human rights	Adopted by 46+ countries, basis for G20 AI guidelines
UNESCO	*Recommendation on the Ethics of AI* (2021)	Dignity, diversity, sustainability	First global agreement on AI ethics endorsed by 193 nations
European Commission	*Ethics Guidelines for Trustworthy AI* (2021)	Lawfulness, ethics, robustness	Foundation of the EU AI Act (2024)
World Economic Forum	*Global AI Action Alliance* (2022)	Public trust, accountability, resilience	Multi-stakeholder model for ethical AI deployment

The institutionalization of AI ethics has also transformed the educational and corporate landscapes. Universities now teach ethics as an integral part of AI engineering curricula, ensuring future developers can reason about the moral consequences of their work. Research centers such as the AI Ethics Lab (Harvard), The Alan Turing Institute (UK), and Leverhulme Centre for the Future of Intelligence (Cambridge) lead interdisciplinary projects combining computer science, philosophy, and law. In the corporate sector, AI ethics teams conduct algorithmic audits, develop bias mitigation tools, and promote transparency reports as part of product governance. This cross-sectoral collaboration between academia, industry, and regulators signifies the maturation of AI ethics from a theoretical concept into an operational discipline.

The emergence of AI ethics marks a profound recognition that trust in AI depends not solely on technical accuracy but on moral legitimacy. Ethical governance provides a foundation for what the European Commission defines as "trustworthy AI": lawful, ethical, and robust systems that promote human autonomy and societal well-being. As AI becomes embedded in public institutions, the integration of ethics throughout the AI lifecycle, from data collection to feedback loops, ensures that innovations remain aligned with democratic values and human rights. The field continues to evolve toward a more holistic vision of responsible AI, where innovation and ethics are no longer opposing forces but mutually reinforcing pillars of sustainable technological progress. Figure 4 shows The Evolution of AI Ethics as a Discipline.

Figure 4. The Evolution of AI Ethics as a Discipline

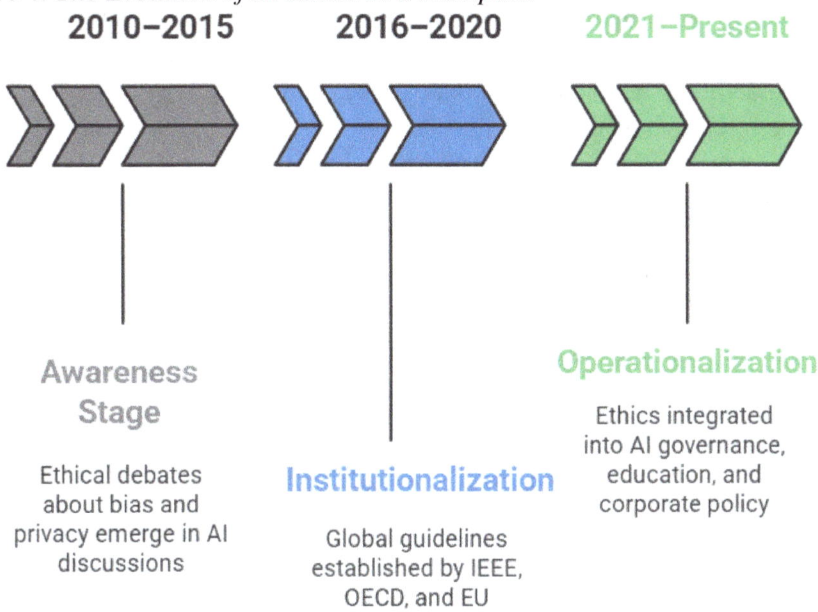

5. CORE ETHICAL CHALLENGES IN AI

Artificial Intelligence introduces a new layer of moral complexity in human decision-making systems. Unlike traditional technologies, AI systems do not merely extend human capabilities; they autonomously analyze, predict, and act based on data. These capabilities create both opportunities and ethical dilemmas. The ethical challenges stem from the tension between technological power and moral control. As AI systems increasingly make consequential decisions, such as allocating healthcare resources, identifying criminal suspects, or filtering online information, questions of fairness, accountability, and transparency become central. Ethical challenges in AI are therefore not purely technical issues but deeply philosophical and societal problems that shape trust and legitimacy in the digital era (Kong & Zhu, 2025).

One of the foundational ethical challenges is autonomy, both in terms of machine independence and human agency. As AI becomes more capable, maintaining meaningful human control becomes essential to prevent overreliance on algorithmic decisions. Scholars warn of the "automation bias," a cognitive tendency to trust machine outputs even when they are flawed. Ethical AI design must ensure that humans remain the ultimate decision-makers, capable of overriding algorithmic outcomes when necessary. This requires clear mechanisms of accountability and explainability, ensuring that responsibility does not disappear within complex automated systems. The question "Who is accountable when AI makes a mistake?" remains a defining moral and legal issue of the century.

Fairness represents another critical pillar of AI ethics. AI systems trained on biased or incomplete datasets risk perpetuating existing social inequalities. For instance, predictive policing algorithms have been found to disproportionately target minority groups, and recruitment algorithms have unintentionally discriminated against women in technical fields. Such examples underscore the need for algorithmic fairness, which demands equitable outcomes across demographic groups. Achieving fairness requires continuous auditing, transparent model documentation (model cards), and participatory design processes that involve marginalized communities. The challenge is not only technical but moral—addressing the historical and structural biases embedded in the data that fuels AI. Table 4 shows the Key Ethical Challenges in AI Systems.

Table 4. Key Ethical Challenges in AI Systems

Ethical Dimension	Core Issue	Practical Example	Ethical Response
Autonomy & Control	Loss of human oversight	Automated weapons systems	Human-in-the-loop design and override authority
Fairness & Bias	Discriminatory algorithms	Biased hiring or predictive policing	Data diversification and algorithmic auditing
Transparency & Explainability	Black-box decision-making	Credit scoring systems with opaque logic	Explainable AI (XAI) frameworks such as SHAP or LIME
Accountability	Diffusion of responsibility	Autonomous vehicle accidents	Traceable decision logs and liability frameworks
Privacy & Surveillance	Misuse of personal data	Facial recognition in public spaces	Privacy-by-design and differential privacy mechanisms

Transparency is one of the most debated challenges in AI ethics. Many AI systems, especially deep learning models, operate as black boxes, making it difficult for users and regulators to understand how decisions are made. Lack of transparency erodes public trust and complicates accountability when errors occur. Explainable AI (XAI) has emerged as a response, providing interpretability tools such as SHAP (Shapley Additive Explanations) and LIME (Local Interpretable Model-agnostic Explanations) that make AI reasoning more understandable to humans. However, achieving full transparency without compromising privacy or intellectual property remains a challenge. Ethical AI requires a balance between openness, usability, and security to maintain both trust and innovation. The XAI method can provide actionable insights into each model's decision-making, fostering transparency and trust (Barredo Arrieta et al., 2020).

Data is the lifeblood of AI, but it also poses one of the most profound ethical risks: privacy erosion. AI systems collect and process vast amounts of personal data from social media, medical records, and online behavior. When used without consent or oversight, such data practices lead to surveillance, manipulation, and loss of autonomy. Governments and institutions worldwide have introduced data protection regulations such as the EU's General Data Protection Regulation (GDPR) and India's Digital Personal Data Protection Act to address these concerns. Yet, technological solutions such as differential privacy, federated learning, and secure multiparty computation are increasingly viewed as necessary complements to legal frameworks. The ethical challenge is to reconcile data-driven innovation with individual rights and human dignity, ensuring that AI serves people rather than exploits them. The process of efficiently collecting, processing, and storing omics-sensitive data must be compliant with GDPR regulations (Gioiosa et al., 2025).

6. ETHICAL FOUNDATIONS: HUMAN-CENTERED DESIGN AND MORAL RESPONSIBILITY

Human-centered design has become a cornerstone of ethical artificial intelligence. It asserts that technological systems must be developed to enhance human dignity, autonomy, and well-being rather than merely pursuing efficiency or profit. This approach emphasizes that technology should adapt to people, not the other way around. According to the European Commission, human-centered AI prioritizes user agency, inclusivity, and accessibility while ensuring that humans retain meaningful control over decision-making processes. The concept extends beyond usability, encompassing moral and social dimensions that ensure AI systems respect cultural diversity, human rights, and collective welfare.

Moral responsibility within AI ethics refers to the obligation of individuals and organizations to anticipate, prevent, and mitigate harm that may result from AI deployment. It recognizes that although machines execute decisions, humans remain accountable for their outcomes. Responsibility is distributed across multiple actors including developers, data scientists, policymakers, and end-users. Ethical design therefore requires that each stakeholder assume ownership of their role in shaping the moral consequences of AI technologies. This accountability framework fosters transparency and trust while ensuring that errors or biases in AI systems can be traced back to human oversight rather than being attributed to algorithms as autonomous entities.

Operationalizing human-centered AI requires integrating ethical reflection into every stage of the system's lifecycle, from design and data collection to testing, deployment, and monitoring. The ISO/IEC 42001:2023 AI Management System Standard and the IEEE Ethically Aligned Design Framework both emphasize iterative evaluation involving diverse stakeholders. User feedback, participatory design sessions, and interdisciplinary review boards are essential to ensure that AI applications align with human needs and social contexts. For instance, in healthcare AI, patient involvement during model development helps prevent ethical oversights, while in education technology, participatory approaches ensure fairness and accessibility for all learners. Table 5 shows the Principles of Human-Centered AI Design (McIntosh et al., 2024).

Table 5. Principles of Human-Centered AI Design

Principle	Description	Implementation Example	Intended Outcome
User Agency	Ensure humans retain control over AI systems	Manual override in autonomous vehicles	Prevent overreliance on automation
Inclusivity	Involve diverse users in design processes	Community consultation in data collection	Reduce cultural and demographic bias
Transparency	Communicate how AI decisions are made	Explainable dashboards in AI applications	Build user trust and accountability
Accountability	Define roles and assign responsibility	Ethical oversight committees in tech firms	Prevent moral and legal ambiguity
Safety and Well-being	Protect users from harm	Rigorous testing of medical AI systems	Safeguard physical and psychological welfare

Ethical design thinking bridges creativity and moral reasoning. It requires AI developers to approach problem-solving not only through technical optimization but through ethical foresight and empathy. Borrowing from design thinking methodologies, ethical AI design incorporates iteration, reflection, and empathy mapping to anticipate unintended social effects. According to Floridi, ethical design is an act of "conceptual engineering" that reshapes technology to fit moral contexts. By embedding moral reasoning into the design process, AI developers transform ethics from an afterthought into an essential part of innovation, where design decisions are guided by human values and societal expectations.

Human-centered AI cannot exist without shared moral accountability. Governments, private organizations, and civil society must collaborate to create ecosystems where responsibility is distributed but clearly defined. Mechanisms such as ethical impact assessments, algorithmic audits, and public accountability reports help institutionalize responsibility. These measures encourage transparency and provide mechanisms for redress when harm occurs. Ultimately, the ethical foundation of AI rests on the belief that technology should serve humanity collectively rather than specific interests. Moral responsibility ensures that AI remains a tool of empowerment, strengthening social trust, and upholding the integrity of human decision-making in an increasingly automated world.

7. THE ROLE OF TRUST AND SOCIAL LEGITIMACY

Trust is the cornerstone of any successful technological system, and in the context of Artificial Intelligence (AI), it becomes a moral prerequisite for social acceptance. Without trust, even the most advanced AI systems face skepticism, resistance, and eventual rejection. Trust arises when users perceive AI as reliable, transparent, and aligned with human values. According to the OECD, trustworthy AI must be lawful, ethical, and robust. These dimensions reinforce confidence that AI will behave predictably, safely, and justly in different contexts. However, trust cannot be engineered purely through technical safeguards; it must also be cultivated through ethical integrity, consistent performance, and respect for social norms (Teng et al., 2025).

Trust in AI operates across multiple dimensions: technical trust, ethical trust, and institutional trust.

- Technical trust is built when AI systems demonstrate reliability, accuracy, and consistency in performance.
- Ethical trust emerges when users believe that AI acts fairly, protects privacy, and avoids harm.
- Institutional trust depends on governance mechanisms that ensure accountability, such as regulations, audits, and ethical certifications.

As McBride and Stahl argue, sustainable AI adoption requires all three dimensions to coexist harmoniously. When one dimension weakens—such as ethical integrity in data use or transparency in decision-making—overall social trust deteriorates. Therefore, designing for trust means embedding reliability, fairness, and accountability within the entire AI lifecycle.

Beyond individual trust lies social legitimacy, a collective judgment about whether AI systems deserve a rightful place in society. Social legitimacy is not granted automatically; it must be earned through public engagement, inclusivity, and alignment with shared values. Legitimacy depends on procedural justice (how decisions are made) and distributive justice (who benefits and who bears the risks). Studies show that people are more likely to accept AI decisions when they understand how they are made and believe they are fair. Public consultation, transparency reports, and participatory design processes thus play a critical role in legitimizing AI governance. Ethical frameworks alone are insufficient if societal values and expectations are not reflected in AI's real-world behavior. Table 6 shows the Interrelationship Between Trust and Social Legitimacy in AI (Paraman & Anamalah, 2023).

Table 6. Interrelationship Between Trust and Social Legitimacy in AI

Dimension	Definition	Key Mechanism	Outcome
Technical Trust	Confidence in system reliability and accuracy	Testing, validation, model transparency	Predictable and consistent AI behavior
Ethical Trust	Belief that AI aligns with moral and social values	Fairness auditing, privacy protection, explainability	Perceived moral integrity
Institutional Trust	Confidence in regulatory and governance structures	Ethical certifications, oversight committees, accountability laws	Compliance and accountability
Social Legitimacy	Public approval of AI's role in society	Citizen engagement, inclusive policymaking	Sustainable adoption and social acceptance

Establishing trust and legitimacy requires continuous action rather than static compliance. Transparency in algorithmic design, explainability of outcomes, and open communication about limitations are essential to prevent misinformation and unrealistic expectations. Ethical audits, certification programs, and AI impact assessments strengthen institutional accountability. Moreover, the introduction of trustworthy AI labeling systems—similar to sustainability certifications—has been proposed to signal adherence to ethical and technical standards. However, maintaining trust requires reciprocity: organizations must not only design ethical AI but also listen to societal feedback, admit failures, and adapt. Trust is dynamic; it must be continually earned through responsible governance and transparent practice.

True legitimacy arises when ethical trust evolves into a culture of mutual accountability between humans and machines. This requires education, policy, and social dialogue to foster informed trust rather than blind faith or fear. Governments, corporations, and communities must collaborate to establish standards of responsible AI that transcend borders and cultural differences. In doing so, trust becomes not merely a social sentiment but a form of ethical infrastructure supporting democracy, justice, and human dignity. As the European Commission emphasizes, building trustworthy AI means ensuring that systems respect human autonomy, promote well-being, and remain under human oversight. When trust and legitimacy are integrated into the moral architecture of AI, technology becomes not only intelligent but also socially sustainable.

8. PHILOSOPHICAL REFLECTIONS: CAN MACHINES BE MORAL?

The question of whether machines can be moral lies at the heart of contemporary debates in AI ethics. Philosophers and technologists have long pondered whether moral reasoning is uniquely human or if it can be replicated through algorithms. The discussion raises deeper questions about consciousness, intentionality, and free will—qualities historically considered essential for moral agency. According to Wallach and Allen, morality requires not only the ability to follow rules but also to understand their meaning and context. Artificial Intelligence can process vast amounts of data, recognize patterns, and optimize outcomes, yet it lacks subjective experience, empathy, and moral intuition. Thus, while machines can simulate ethical reasoning, the question remains whether they can truly understand morality rather than merely perform it. In high-risk cases, moral agents may still need to be held accountable and in some contexts be the right target to blame (Kasar, 2025).

Philosophical discussions often distinguish between moral agents and moral patients. Moral agents are beings capable of making ethical decisions and bearing responsibility for their actions, whereas moral patients are entities that deserve moral consideration or protection. Humans are both agents and patients, while AI currently functions only as a moral tool shaped by human intent. However, as AI systems increasingly influence decisions about human welfare—such as in healthcare triage, autonomous driving, or predictive policing—the moral distinction between human and machine becomes blurred. Some scholars argue that AI systems can exhibit functional morality by adhering to ethical principles embedded in their programming, even if they lack consciousness or intrinsic moral awareness (Sekti, 2025).

Several philosophical theories have been proposed to explain how morality might be implemented or simulated in artificial systems. Rule-based ethics suggests that AI can follow codified moral principles such as Kant's categorical imperative: "Act only according to that maxim whereby you can at the same time will that it should become a universal law." In contrast, utilitarian approaches seek to design AI that calculates the most beneficial outcomes for the greatest number of people, as seen in moral dilemmas for autonomous vehicles. Virtue ethics emphasizes moral character and situational judgment, which are difficult to formalize but crucial for human-like moral understanding. While none of these frameworks perfectly translate into computational logic, they provide guiding paradigms for developing Artificial Moral Agents (AMAs) that reflect human ethical reasoning. Virtue ethics is explored as a means to program social robots as artificial moral agents, placing human values as the basis of a robot's design (Chong et al., 2025; Lei et al., 2025). Table 7 shows the Philosophical Frameworks for Understanding Machine Morality.

Table 7. Philosophical Frameworks for Understanding Machine Morality

Ethical Framework	Core Principle	Application in AI	Strengths	Limitations
Deontology (Kant)	Follow moral rules and duties	Asimov's "Three Laws of Robotics"	Clear rule enforcement	Rigid and context-insensitive
Consequentialism (Mill)	Focus on outcomes and utility	Moral trade-offs in self-driving cars	Pragmatic and measurable	Can justify harmful means for beneficial ends
Virtue Ethics (Aristotle)	Cultivate moral character	Ethical training for AI developers	Encourages moral reflection	Not directly computable
Care Ethics (Gilligan)	Value empathy and relationships	Human-in-the-loop decision systems	Emphasizes compassion and social bonds	Hard to quantify and automate

Despite advances in *machine ethics*, most scholars agree that current AI lacks genuine moral agency. Machines operate through programmed constraints and optimization functions rather than moral understanding. According to Floridi, AI systems are "moral proxies" that extend human moral influence but cannot originate ethical reasoning on their own. This introduces a paradox: AI can behave ethically within human-defined limits but cannot be morally responsible for its actions. Moral responsibility, as argued by Borenstein, requires awareness, intention, and the capacity to justify choices. Machines do not possess these capacities; therefore, the accountability for AI behavior ultimately rests with humans. Nevertheless, designing AI to act in ethically consistent ways is valuable because it reduces harm and aligns machine behavior with human welfare.

Rather than asking whether machines can be moral, a more productive question is how humans and machines can co-evolve ethically. As AI systems become integral to daily life, they reshape moral norms and redefine what it means to act responsibly. The goal should not be to replicate human morality but to create *complementary systems* that enhance ethical decision-making through collaboration. The concept of moral symbiosis envisions AI as a partner in ethical reasoning, augmenting human judgment with data-driven insights while preserving human oversight. Such a framework promotes an ecosystem of shared moral responsibility, where human values guide AI behavior and AI capabilities support ethical human choices. This co-evolution offers a path toward trustworthy, value-aligned technology that reinforces rather than replaces human morality. Figure 5 shows The Spectrum of Machine Morality.

Figure 5. The Spectrum of Machine Morality

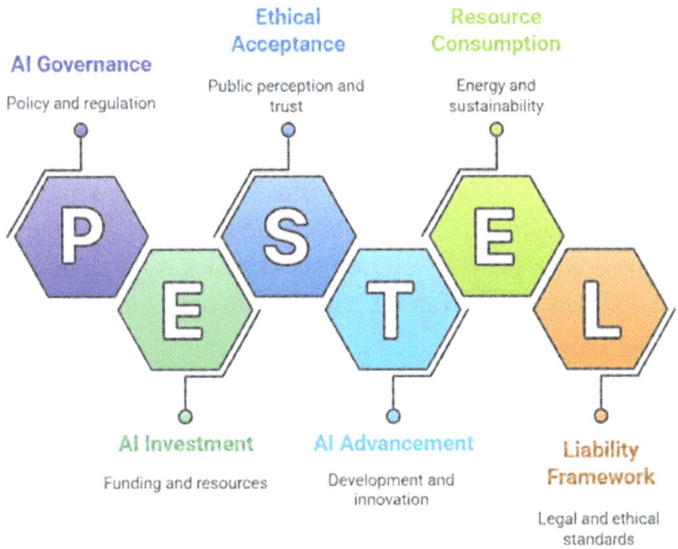

9. TOWARD A FRAMEWORK FOR ETHICAL AI GOVERNANCE

Ethical AI governance extends beyond compliance with legal norms. While legislation provides a baseline for accountability, ethical governance establishes the moral infrastructure required to guide how artificial intelligence is developed, deployed, and monitored. Governance in this context refers to the system of principles, institutions, and practices that ensure AI operates transparently, responsibly, and in alignment with human values. According to the OECD and the European Commission, effective AI governance should integrate ethical reflection into policy design, organizational culture, and technology management. The goal is to bridge the gap between formal regulation and moral responsibility, ensuring that AI serves the public good rather than narrow interests.

An ethical AI governance framework is built upon four foundational pillars: accountability, transparency, fairness, and human oversight.

- Accountability ensures that responsibility for AI outcomes can be traced to identifiable actors, including developers, companies, and policymakers.
- Transparency promotes openness in algorithmic design, data use, and decision-making processes.

- Fairness requires proactive efforts to eliminate bias and ensure equitable treatment of all users.
- Human oversight guarantees that humans remain the ultimate decision-makers in ethically sensitive contexts.

Together, these principles create a normative structure that transforms ethical ideals into actionable governance mechanisms. Organizations such as the IEEE, UNESCO, and World Economic Forum advocate for embedding these values into corporate governance systems to ensure that AI ethics is not optional but integral to institutional accountability. Table 8 shows the Core Components of an Ethical AI Governance Framework.

Table 8. Core Components of an Ethical AI Governance Framework

Pillar	Objective	Implementation Mechanism	Expected Outcome
Accountability	Assign moral and legal responsibility for AI actions	Algorithmic audit trails, clear role definitions	Prevent diffusion of responsibility
Transparency	Enable interpretability and traceability of decisions	Explainable AI tools, disclosure of model logic	Build user and public trust
Fairness	Ensure equal treatment and avoid bias	Diverse datasets, bias impact assessments	Promote social justice and inclusion
Human Oversight	Retain human control in decision-making	Human-in-the-loop mechanisms, review boards	Safeguard autonomy and moral judgment

Ethical AI governance is inherently multi-stakeholder in nature, involving collaboration among governments, corporations, civil society, and academia. No single entity can effectively govern AI alone due to its complexity and global reach. Governments are responsible for establishing policy frameworks and enforcement mechanisms, corporations must implement internal ethical standards, while academic institutions contribute through research and education. Civil society organizations act as watchdogs that represent public interest and hold powerful actors accountable. A multi-layered governance model enables distributed yet coordinated responsibility. For instance, the EU AI Act represents a regulatory layer, while corporate ethical boards and academic advisory councils operate at the operational and epistemic layers of governance.

Translating ethical principles into practical governance requires operational tools that evaluate and monitor AI systems. Common mechanisms include Ethical Impact Assessments (EIA), Algorithmic Audits, and Ethics-by-Design frameworks. These tools enable continuous evaluation rather than one-time certification. For example, algorithmic audits identify unintended bias in model predictions, while impact assessments evaluate the societal and environmental effects of AI deployment. Additionally, the creation of AI Ethics Committees or Responsible AI Offices within organizations ensures that moral accountability remains institutionalized. Governance must also include redress mechanisms that allow affected individuals to challenge AI decisions, thereby reinforcing fairness and transparency as ongoing commitments rather than static policies.

The future of AI governance lies in creating a globally coherent framework that balances innovation with ethical responsibility. Current efforts such as the OECD AI Policy Observatory, UNESCO's Global Recommendation on the Ethics of AI, and the G7 Hiroshima AI Principles aim to harmonize standards across jurisdictions. However, ethical governance must remain flexible to respect cultural diversity and local values. Scholars like Taddeo and Floridi emphasize that AI governance should be *adaptive*, integrating feedback from both technical performance and societal impact. The evolution toward a global ethical ecosystem will require transparent international collaboration, shared accountability models, and capacity-building initiatives. By embedding moral reflection at every level of governance, AI can evolve as a trusted, responsible, and human-centered technology that strengthens rather than destabilizes social trust.

10. CONCLUSION

Artificial Intelligence has become a defining force of modern civilization, reshaping the way humans work, communicate, and make decisions. Yet, as AI systems grow in complexity and autonomy, they also magnify moral, social, and political challenges. The study of AI ethics provides the foundation for ensuring that technological progress remains aligned with human values and societal welfare. At its core, AI ethics emphasizes that technological innovation cannot be separated from moral responsibility. The pursuit of efficiency and intelligence must always be balanced with the preservation of dignity, fairness, and justice. In this sense, ethics does not limit AI's potential but guides its responsible evolution toward serving humanity as a force for good.

Creating ethical and trustworthy AI requires embedding human values into every layer of the AI ecosystem, from algorithmic design to institutional governance. This integration demands collaboration between technologists, ethicists, policymakers, and communities to ensure inclusivity and accountability. Ethical governance frameworks serve as the bridge between principles and practice, translating abstract ideals such as fairness and transparency into measurable actions and standards. The future of AI depends not only on technological sophistication but also on the moral and social infrastructure that supports it. When AI systems are designed and governed with empathy, accountability, and inclusiveness, they strengthen public trust and foster long-term sustainability in human–machine interaction.

The ethical development of AI is not a finite goal but a continuous process of reflection, adaptation, and learning. As societies become increasingly dependent on algorithmic systems, the need for moral vigilance grows stronger. The challenge ahead is to create a culture of ethical awareness where every participant in the AI lifecycle—developers, institutions, and citizens—acts as a custodian of responsible innovation. A future built on responsible intelligence is one where technology empowers rather than replaces humanity, where progress is measured not only by what AI can do but by how it contributes to justice, compassion, and collective well-being. Through ethical commitment and shared responsibility, humanity can ensure that the intelligence it creates remains aligned with the values that define what it means to be human.

REFERENCES

Arora, A. S., Marshall, A., Arora, A., & McIntyre, J. R. (2025). Virtuous integrative social robotics for ethical governance. *Discover Artificial Intelligence*, *5*(1), 8. Advance online publication. DOI: 10.1007/s44163-025-00228-6

Asghar, M. Z., Duah, K. A., Iqbal, J., & Järvenoja, H. (2025). Evidence from West Africa on the interplay of affective behavioral cognitive and ethical dimensions of AI literacy in Ghanaian and Nigerian Universities. *Discover Computing*, *28*(1), 169. Advance online publication. DOI: 10.1007/s10791-025-09691-2

Barredo Arrieta, A., Díaz-Rodríguez, N., Del Ser, J., Bennetot, A., Tabik, S., Barbado, A., Garcia, S., Gil-Lopez, S., Molina, D., Benjamins, R., Chatila, R., & Herrera, F. (2020). Explainable Artificial Intelligence (XAI): Concepts, taxonomies, opportunities and challenges toward responsible AI. *Information Fusion*, *58*, 82–115. DOI: 10.1016/j.inffus.2019.12.012

Camilleri, M. A. (2024). Artificial intelligence governance: Ethical considerations and implications for social responsibility. *Expert Systems: International Journal of Knowledge Engineering and Neural Networks*, *41*(7), e13406. Advance online publication. DOI: 10.1111/exsy.13406

Chong, K. C. M., Tan, Y.-K., & Zhou, X. (2025). Impacts of Artificial Intelligence Development on Humanity and Social Values. *Information (Basel)*, *16*(9), 810. Advance online publication. DOI: 10.3390/info16090810

Choung, H., David, P., & Ross, A. (2023). Trust and ethics in AI. *AI & Society*, *38*(2), 733–745. DOI: 10.1007/s00146-022-01473-4

Dattathrani, S., & De', R. (2023). The Concept of Agency in the Era of Artificial Intelligence: Dimensions and Degrees. *Information Systems Frontiers*, *25*(1), 29–54. DOI: 10.1007/s10796-022-10336-8

Erfani, F. (2025). Not "just a language model": AI's ideological functions. *AI & Society*. Advance online publication. DOI: 10.1007/s00146-025-02623-0

Gioiosa, S., Chiavarini, B., D'Antonio, M., Trotta, G., Chandramouli, B., Mata Naranjo, J., Muscianisi, G., Cestari, M., & Rossi, E. (2025). A GDPR-compliant solution for analysis of large-scale genomics datasets on HPC cloud infrastructure. *Journal of Big Data*, *12*(1), 31. Advance online publication. DOI: 10.1186/s40537-024-01047-9

Giovanola, B., & Tiribelli, S. (2023). Beyond bias and discrimination: Redefining the AI ethics principle of fairness in healthcare machine-learning algorithms. *AI & Society*, *38*(2), 549–563. DOI: 10.1007/s00146-022-01455-6 PMID: 35615443

Kasar, P. (2025). There is a problem, but not a responsibility gap. *Ethics and Information Technology*, *27*(4), 47. Advance online publication. DOI: 10.1007/s10676-025-09851-4

Knoth, N., Decker, M., Laupichler, M. C., Pinski, M., Buchholtz, N., Bata, K., & Schultz, B. (2024). Developing a holistic AI literacy assessment matrix – Bridging generic, domain-specific, and ethical competencies. *Computers and Education Open*, *6*, 100177. Advance online publication. DOI: 10.1016/j.caeo.2024.100177

Kong, S. C., & Zhu, J. (2025). Developing and validating an artificial intelligence ethical awareness scale for secondary and university students: Cultivating ethical awareness through problem-solving with artificial intelligence tools. *Computers and Education: Artificial Intelligence*, *9*, 100447. Advance online publication. DOI: 10.1016/j.caeai.2025.100447

Lei, S., Xie, L., & Peng, J. (2025). Unethical Consumer Behavior Following Artificial Intelligence Agent Encounters: The Differential Effect of AI Agent Roles and its Boundary Conditions. *Journal of Service Research*, *28*(4), 598–613. DOI: 10.1177/10946705241278837

Lim, T. (2024). Environmental, social, and governance (ESG) and artificial intelligence in finance: State-of-the-art and research takeaways. *Artificial Intelligence Review*, *57*(4), 76. Advance online publication. DOI: 10.1007/s10462-024-10708-3

McIntosh, T. R., Susnjak, T., Liu, T., Watters, P., Xu, D., Liu, D., Nowrozy, R., & Halgamuge, M. N. (2024). From COBIT to ISO 42001: Evaluating cybersecurity frameworks for opportunities, risks, and regulatory compliance in commercializing large language models. *Computers & Security*, *144*, 103964. Advance online publication. DOI: 10.1016/j.cose.2024.103964

Paraman, P., & Anamalah, S. (2023). Ethical artificial intelligence framework for a good AI society: Principles, opportunities and perils. *AI & Society*, *38*(2), 595–611. DOI: 10.1007/s00146-022-01458-3

Perez-Cerrolaza, J., Abella, J., Borg, M., Donzella, C., Cerquides, J., Cazorla, F. J., Englund, C., Tauber, M., Nikolakopoulos, G., & Flores, J. L. (2024). Artificial Intelligence for Safety-Critical Systems in Industrial and Transportation Domains: A Survey. *ACM Computing Surveys*, *56*(7), 1–40. Advance online publication. DOI: 10.1145/3626314

Sekti, B. A. (2025). Information Security Awareness. In *User-Centric Cybersecurity Implications for Sustainable Digital Transformation* (pp. 111–145). DOI: 10.4018/979-8-3373-3171-3.ch004

Teng, Z., Xia, H., & He, Y. (2025). Algorithmic Fairness and Digital Financial Stress: Evidence from AI-Driven E-Commerce Platforms in OECD Economies. *Journal of Theoretical and Applied Electronic Commerce Research*, *20*(3), 213. Advance online publication. DOI: 10.3390/jtaer20030213

Chapter 3
Ethical Theories in AI:
Deontology, Consequentialism, Virtue Ethics, and Their Role in Fairness Accountability Transparency and Privacy

Ilham Firmansyah
https://orcid.org/0009-0007-6104-9966
Universitas Esa Unggul, Indonesia

ABSTRACT

This chapter examines the application of classical ethical theories deontology, consequentialism, and virtue ethics to the governance of artificial intelligence (AI). It argues that the principles of fairness, accountability, transparency, and privacy cannot be adequately addressed without grounding in established moral philosophy. Through detailed analysis, the chapter demonstrates how deontological duties, consequentialist outcomes, and virtue-based character reasoning provide complementary insights into the ethical challenges of AI across healthcare, finance, law enforcement, and social media. A hybrid ethical framework is proposed, integrating duties, consequences, and virtues into a coherent approach to AI governance. By synthesizing theoretical foundations, case studies, and practical recommendations, this chapter contributes to interdisciplinary debates on responsible AI and offers pathways for aligning innovation with human rights, social trust, and global regulatory standards.

DOI: 10.4018/979-8-3373-7011-8.ch003

nt © 2026, IGI Global Scientific Publishing. Copying or distributing in print or electronic forms without written permission of IGI Global Scientific Publishing is prohibited. Use of this chapter to enerative artificial intelligence (AI) technologies is expressly prohibited. The publisher reserves all rights to license its use for generative AI training and machine learning model development.

1. INTRODUCTION

Artificial intelligence (AI) has rapidly transformed from a domain of experimental research into a pervasive technology that informs, mediates, and shapes everyday human interactions. From algorithmic decision-making in financial systems to diagnostic support in healthcare and surveillance applications in public spaces, AI systems now exercise an unprecedented level of influence over human affairs. While these technologies promise increased efficiency, predictive power, and innovation, they simultaneously raise profound concerns regarding fairness, accountability, transparency, and privacy. These concerns are not merely technical in nature but are fundamentally ethical and philosophical, demanding systematic frameworks for analysis and governance.

The ethical evaluation of AI cannot rely solely on pragmatic or ad hoc principles (Nunes et al., 2025). Instead, it requires robust grounding in well-established traditions of moral philosophy that have historically guided human conduct and institutional practices. Among the most enduring and relevant frameworks are deontological ethics, consequentialism, and virtue ethics. Each of these traditions offers a distinct perspective on moral reasoning: deontology emphasizes duties and rights, consequentialism evaluates outcomes and social utility, and virtue ethics highlights the cultivation of moral character and virtues. By applying these philosophical lenses to AI governance, we can obtain deeper insights into the obligations of developers, the consequences of algorithmic deployment, and the cultivation of responsible institutional practices.

AI's expansion into sensitive domains has revealed a series of tensions that illustrate why ethical theory remains indispensable. Consider algorithmic decision-making in hiring processes. On the one hand, AI can streamline recruitment by processing thousands of applications efficiently. On the other, if the data used to train such systems reflects historical bias, the AI may reproduce discriminatory practices under the guise of neutrality. A consequentialist lens would evaluate whether the outcomes reduce or amplify social inequality, while a deontological perspective would interrogate whether such practices violate the duty to treat candidates with fairness and dignity. Virtue ethics, in contrast, would ask whether the institutions deploying such systems are cultivating justice, integrity, and responsibility in their hiring practices. Together, these theories illuminate the ethical stakes beyond technical optimization (Deng et al., 2025).

The triad of fairness, accountability, and transparency (FAT) has emerged as a central framework in AI ethics debates. Fairness speaks to distributive justice and the equitable treatment of individuals and groups. Accountability concerns the assignment of responsibility in cases of harm or misconduct, particularly in systems that operate with high autonomy and opacity. Transparency addresses the ability of stakeholders to understand, scrutinize, and contest the decisions made by AI systems. These principles are now echoed in numerous regulatory frameworks, including the European Union's proposed AI Act, the OECD's AI Principles, and UNESCO's global recommendations. Yet, FAT principles often remain abstract, lacking theoretical depth. By rooting them in established ethical traditions, this chapter aims to provide a more coherent and philosophically informed foundation for FAT governance.

Another critical dimension that intersects with FAT principles is privacy. Privacy is not only a legal construct, articulated in frameworks such as the General Data Protection Regulation (GDPR) in Europe and the California Consumer Privacy Act (CCPA) in the United States, but also an ethical imperative grounded in respect for autonomy and human dignity. AI's voracious appetite for data, particularly in machine learning models that rely on vast training corpora, raises acute questions about the limits of consent, the legitimacy of surveillance, and the erosion of personal boundaries. While legal compliance is necessary, it is insufficient without a deeper ethical understanding of why privacy matters and how it is intrinsically linked to trust in technology. Here, deontology highlights the duty to respect individuals' rights, consequentialism assesses the societal harms of privacy violations, and virtue ethics underscores the moral qualities of respect and integrity in institutional data practices (Vascelli, 2025).

The objective of this chapter, and indeed of the full contribution to this volume, is to synthesize ethical theory with contemporary AI governance challenges. Rather than treating ethics as an abstract academic exercise, the chapter demonstrates how ethical reasoning provides actionable insights for policymakers, technologists, and civil society. By applying deontological, consequentialist, and virtue-ethical analyses to the FAT triad and privacy, this work builds a conceptual roadmap for embedding ethics into the lifecycle of AI design, deployment, and regulation.

The structure of the chapter is designed to progressively build this argument. Following the introduction, the next section explores the philosophical foundations of deontological ethics, consequentialism, and virtue ethics, contextualizing their historical roots and contemporary relevance. The discussion then turns to the FAT principles, mapping each to corresponding ethical theories to reveal complementarities and tensions. A dedicated section addresses privacy as both a legal and ethical construct, emphasizing its centrality to trust in AI. These theoretical explorations are subsequently grounded in empirical analysis through case studies across healthcare, finance, law enforcement, and social media. Each case study demonstrates how the application of ethical theories reshapes our understanding of fairness, accountability, transparency, and privacy in practice. The final sections synthesize these insights into an integrated ethical framework for AI governance, followed by a discussion of future challenges and directions (Al-Hattami, 2025).

This chapter makes three key contributions. First, it clarifies the theoretical underpinnings of ethical AI by explicitly linking classical moral philosophy to contemporary governance principles. Second, it operationalizes these theories through case studies that highlight their applicability in real-world scenarios. Third, it develops a hybrid ethical framework that can guide policymakers and practitioners in embedding moral reasoning into AI regulation and institutional design. By achieving these aims, the chapter contributes to the broader mission of this volume: to navigate the complexities of social trust in the AI era through rigorous, interdisciplinary scholarship.

In conclusion, the ethical evaluation of AI cannot be divorced from enduring philosophical traditions. While technological innovation continues at unprecedented speed, human values remain the ultimate compass for guiding AI's integration into society. Deontology, consequentialism, and virtue ethics provide complementary perspectives that, when combined, illuminate pathways toward fairer, more accountable, transparent, and privacy-respecting AI. As such, this chapter argues that cultivating an ethically grounded approach to AI governance is not only desirable but indispensable for safeguarding trust and justice in the digital age.

2. FOUNDATIONS OF ETHICAL THEORIES IN AI

The governance of artificial intelligence (AI) requires not only technical innovation and legal oversight but also systematic engagement with moral philosophy. Ethical theories provide the normative foundations that help articulate why certain practices are right or wrong, fair or unjust, responsible or reckless. In the context of AI, three philosophical traditions deontology, consequentialism, and virtue ethics are particularly salient. Each offers a distinct but complementary perspective for evaluating the responsibilities of designers, the impacts of algorithmic systems, and the cultivation of institutional integrity (Degen, 2025).

This chapter section examines these three traditions in detail. It outlines their historical origins, central principles, and key contributions to moral reasoning. More importantly, it demonstrates their relevance to AI governance by connecting abstract ethical frameworks to concrete dilemmas in fairness, accountability, transparency, and privacy (Nunes et al., 2025). By situating AI within these traditions, this section establishes the normative scaffolding that underpins subsequent discussions of governance models, regulatory frameworks, and applied case studies.

2.1 Deontological Ethics and Duties in AI

Deontological ethics, most prominently associated with Immanuel Kant, is a duty-based framework that evaluates moral actions not by their outcomes but by their adherence to principles, rules, and obligations. Central to Kantian ethics is the categorical imperative, which asserts that moral rules must be universalizable and that individuals should always be treated as ends in themselves, never merely as means. In the context of AI, this approach underscores the non-negotiable duty of developers, corporations, and regulators to respect fundamental human rights and dignity (Ishkhanyan, 2025).

Applied to AI, deontology provides a powerful counterbalance to utilitarian calculations that might justify harmful practices for the sake of efficiency. For example, in facial recognition technology, a deontological perspective highlights that deploying systems which compromise privacy or disproportionately target vulnerable communities violates the duty to treat individuals as autonomous beings with inherent dignity. The ethical assessment here does not depend on whether the technology generates overall societal benefits but rather on whether it respects or infringes upon fundamental moral duties.

Deontology also speaks directly to issues of accountability (Westerstrand, 2025). From this perspective, the opacity of many AI systems so-called "black box" models poses a moral problem because stakeholders have a duty to ensure that affected individuals can understand and contest decisions that shape their lives. To deny such transparency would be to disregard the moral obligation of fairness and respect for persons. Moreover, deontological reasoning reinforces the idea that privacy is not merely a matter of personal preference but a right that imposes obligations on developers and organizations to safeguard it.

Thus, in AI governance, deontological ethics compels stakeholders to establish non-negotiable standards. These may include prohibitions against certain high-risk AI applications, mandatory human oversight for decisions affecting rights and freedoms, and the prioritization of individual dignity over corporate or state interests (Vascelli, 2025).

2.2 Consequentialism and the Evaluation of AI Outcomes

Consequentialism, and particularly its utilitarian branch, evaluates the morality of actions based on their outcomes. An action is morally right if it maximizes overall happiness, welfare, or social utility, and wrong if it produces avoidable harm (Khorshidi et al., 2025). Unlike deontology, which focuses on duties, consequentialism is outcome-oriented, making it particularly relevant for assessing the large-scale societal impacts of AI technologies.

AI systems often create ripple effects that extend far beyond their immediate context of deployment. Consider predictive policing algorithms, which aim to allocate resources efficiently by identifying crime-prone areas. From a consequentialist perspective, the key ethical question is whether such systems reduce overall crime and enhance public safety while minimizing social harms. However, if predictive policing disproportionately targets marginalized communities, reinforcing cycles of over-policing and mistrust, then the negative consequences outweigh the purported benefits (Zhang et al., 2025).

Consequentialist reasoning is also relevant to healthcare applications of AI. For example, triage systems designed to allocate scarce medical resources during a crisis can be assessed in terms of the balance between saved lives and potential harms. A utilitarian calculus might justify prioritizing younger or healthier patients if doing so maximizes overall survival. Yet this raises contentious debates about whose lives are valued more, highlighting the limitations of relying solely on outcome-based reasoning.

In terms of fairness, consequentialism underscores the importance of distributive outcomes. Even if an AI system is procedurally transparent, if it consistently produces results that exacerbate inequality, then it fails ethically under consequentialist analysis. Similarly, accountability in this framework requires mechanisms for evaluating the long-term social impacts of AI deployment, ensuring that harms are identified, measured, and mitigated. Transparency, too, is valuable not as an intrinsic right but as a means to generate trust and positive societal outcomes (Artemova, 2025).

The consequentialist approach therefore emphasizes cost-benefit analyses, risk assessments, and ongoing evaluation of AI's societal impacts. Yet, it must be complemented by other frameworks, since outcome-based reasoning alone risks justifying harmful practices if they appear to serve a greater good.

2.3 Virtue Ethics and Human-Centered AI

Virtue ethics, rooted in Aristotelian philosophy, shifts the focus from rules or outcomes to the cultivation of moral character and the pursuit of human flourishing (eudaimonia). In this framework, ethical behavior arises not from adherence to duties or calculation of consequences, but from embodying virtues such as honesty, courage, fairness, and wisdom (Degen, 2025). Applied to AI, virtue ethics emphasizes the moral character of developers, institutions, and societies that create and deploy technology.

Unlike deontology and consequentialism, which offer decision-making rules, virtue ethics is concerned with the kind of people and organizations we ought to be.

It asks whether AI systems reflect virtues that promote trust, justice, and the common good. For example, in the design of generative AI systems, virtue ethics would evaluate whether developers act with honesty and responsibility in addressing issues such as misinformation, deepfakes, or copyright infringement (Suter et al., 2025).

Virtue ethics also offers a unique lens on transparency. Rather than treating it merely as a right or an instrumental good, virtue ethics frames transparency as an expression of intellectual honesty and openness. Similarly, fairness is understood not only as equitable outcomes but also as a manifestation of just character. Privacy, too, becomes a reflection of respectfulness and integrity in institutional practices.

This perspective is particularly important for cultivating long-term trust in AI (Hultin & Mähring, 2025). While rules and outcomes can change across cultures and legal systems, virtues represent enduring qualities that guide human flourishing across contexts. For institutions, this implies that fostering a culture of responsibility, integrity, and accountability may be more effective than imposing compliance-based regulations alone.

2.4 Comparative Insights

While deontology, consequentialism, and virtue ethics provide distinct moral perspectives, their application to AI reveals significant complementarities. Deontology anchors AI governance in duties and rights, ensuring non-negotiable protections for individuals (De Rose et al., 2025). Consequentialism ensures attention to outcomes, costs, and benefits at a societal level. Virtue ethics emphasizes the cultivation of responsible and trustworthy institutions. Together, these frameworks form a holistic ethical foundation for AI governance.

In practice, an integrated approach is necessary. For instance, consider automated credit scoring systems. Deontological ethics would highlight the duty to avoid discrimination, consequentialism would assess whether the system expands financial inclusion or exacerbates inequality, and virtue ethics would evaluate whether institutions deploying such systems embody fairness and responsibility. The convergence of these perspectives provides a more robust framework for ethical assessment than any single theory alone (Westerstrand, 2025).

2.5 Relevance to AI Governance and Social Trust

The integration of these three traditions into AI ethics is not an academic luxury but a practical necessity. Policymakers, technologists, and civil society actors increasingly recognize that public trust in AI cannot be built solely through technical standards or legal compliance. Instead, trust requires assurance that AI systems are grounded in duties, oriented toward beneficial outcomes, and deployed by institutions embodying moral virtues (Robbins, 2025).

The application of ethical theory also clarifies the stakes of contemporary governance debates. For example, proposals to ban high-risk AI applications, such as autonomous lethal weapons, resonate with deontological prohibitions. Calls for algorithmic auditing and impact assessments align with consequentialist reasoning. Efforts to cultivate ethical AI cultures within corporations reflect virtue ethics in practice. By illuminating these connections, ethical theory not only deepens our understanding but also provides actionable pathways for governance.

2.6 Conclusion

This section has outlined the philosophical underpinnings of deontology, consequentialism, and virtue ethics and demonstrated their relevance to the governance of artificial intelligence. Each framework provides unique insights into questions of fairness, accountability, transparency, and privacy, while also highlighting limitations when applied in isolation. Their comparative analysis underscores the need for an integrated ethical foundation that combines duties, outcomes, and virtues to guide the responsible design and deployment of AI systems.

As the following chapters will illustrate, these philosophical perspectives are not abstract but deeply embedded in practical debates around AI regulation, case studies, and global governance. Understanding these foundations is therefore essential for navigating the ethical, legal, and social implications of AI in the twenty-first century.

3. FAIRNESS, ACCOUNTABILITY, AND TRANSPARENCY IN AI

The ethical challenges of artificial intelligence (AI) manifest most prominently in discussions of fairness, accountability, and transparency (FAT). These three principles have become central to international debates on responsible AI governance, shaping policy frameworks, industry guidelines, and academic discourse. While often invoked together as a collective framework, each principle carries distinct philosophical, practical, and regulatory dimensions. More importantly, when considered through the lens of classical ethical theories deontology, consequentialism, and virtue ethics the FAT principles reveal deeper moral significance and interconnections (Cecez-Kecmanovic, 2025).

This chapter section explores fairness, accountability, and transparency in turn, grounding each principle in ethical theory and illustrating their relevance through contemporary examples. By doing so, it seeks to clarify how these principles can be operationalized in AI systems in ways that build social trust and align with broader human values.

3.1 Fairness

3.1.1 Defining Fairness in AI

Fairness in AI refers to the just and equitable treatment of individuals and groups within algorithmic decision-making systems (van Toorn et al., 2025). Unlike human actors, AI does not inherently possess bias; rather, bias emerges through data selection, model design, and institutional deployment. Fairness thus requires careful attention to both the inputs and outputs of AI systems.

Scholarly debates often distinguish between distributive fairness, which concerns the equitable allocation of benefits and burdens, and procedural fairness, which relates to the fairness of decision-making processes. In the context of AI, distributive fairness may concern whether credit scoring systems provide equal access across demographic groups, while procedural fairness may involve whether individuals have opportunities to contest algorithmic outcomes.

3.1.2 Ethical Theories and Fairness

Deontological ethics frames fairness as a duty to treat individuals with equal respect and without unjust discrimination (Riti et al., 2025). For Kantian reasoning, fairness is not negotiable based on outcomes; it is a moral obligation grounded in the recognition of human dignity.

Consequentialism, by contrast, evaluates fairness through its outcomes. A system may be considered fair if it maximizes social welfare by reducing inequality and enhancing opportunities. However, consequentialist reasoning can tolerate some degree of unequal treatment if it produces greater overall benefits, which raises tensions when applied to sensitive domains like healthcare or law enforcement.

Virtue ethics interprets fairness as a quality of moral character. Institutions that embody fairness as a virtue will design and deploy AI systems in ways that reflect justice, integrity, and care. Here, fairness is not simply a procedural requirement or distributive outcome but an expression of organizational virtue.

3.1.3 Case Study: Algorithmic Hiring

Algorithmic hiring systems illustrate the complexities of fairness. While designed to reduce human bias, many such systems have inadvertently perpetuated gender or racial discrimination due to biased training data (Struniawski et al., 2025). A deontological critique highlights the duty to avoid discriminatory practices, regardless of efficiency gains. A consequentialist critique questions whether such systems improve workforce diversity or entrench inequality. A virtue ethics perspective asks whether the deploying institution demonstrates justice and responsibility in addressing structural inequities.

3.2 Accountability

3.2.1 Defining Accountability in AI

Accountability in AI involves identifying, assigning, and enforcing responsibility for the design, deployment, and consequences of algorithmic systems. It addresses the "problem of many hands" in AI development, where responsibility is dispersed across developers, organizations, and users. Without accountability, harms may occur without remedy, eroding trust in technology (Küçükuncular & Ertugan, 2025).

Key dimensions of accountability include answerability (the obligation to provide explanations), liability (the possibility of sanctions for misconduct), and responsibility (the moral duty to prevent harm). Together, these dimensions ensure that AI is not treated as an autonomous moral agent but as a socio-technical system embedded in human responsibility.

3.2.2 Ethical Theories and Accountability

From a deontological standpoint, accountability arises from the duty of developers and institutions to respect rights and fulfill obligations. Failure to ensure accountability constitutes a violation of moral duty.

Consequentialism evaluates accountability in terms of its impact on outcomes (Thi Nguyet Trang et al., 2025). Systems with clear accountability mechanisms reduce risks, deter negligence, and generate trust, thereby maximizing social welfare. Lack of accountability, conversely, produces harms that outweigh benefits.

Virtue ethics emphasizes accountability as a quality of moral character expressed through responsibility, humility, and integrity. Organizations that value accountability will cultivate practices such as ethical auditing, transparent communication, and responsiveness to stakeholders.

3.2.3 Case Study: Autonomous Vehicles

The deployment of autonomous vehicles raises pressing accountability questions. When an accident occurs, who is responsible the manufacturer, the software developer, the operator, or the AI itself? A deontological perspective insists that responsibility cannot be deflected onto machines; human actors bear duties of oversight and safety. Consequentialist reasoning evaluates accountability structures based on their capacity to minimize accidents and maximize public safety. Virtue ethics, meanwhile, highlights whether companies demonstrate integrity and responsibility in acknowledging risks and addressing failures (Ricon, 2025).

3.3 Transparency

3.3.1 Defining Transparency in AI

Transparency in AI refers to the ability of stakeholders to understand and scrutinize algorithmic decision-making processes (Yan et al., 2025). While AI models particularly deep learning systems are often characterized as "black boxes," transparency initiatives aim to make their operations more interpretable and contestable.

Transparency has both epistemic and normative dimensions. Epistemically, it involves making information about models, data, and decisions accessible. Normatively, it ensures that affected individuals are not subjected to opaque systems that undermine autonomy and trust.

3.3.2 Ethical Theories and Transparency

Deontological ethics views transparency as a moral duty linked to respect for persons. Individuals have the right to understand decisions that affect their lives, and developers have the duty to provide explanations.

Consequentialism frames transparency as instrumental for producing positive outcomes. Transparent systems foster trust, reduce misuse, and improve accountability, thereby maximizing societal welfare (Deric et al., 2025).

Virtue ethics interprets transparency as an expression of intellectual honesty and openness. An organization that values transparency as a virtue will proactively disclose information, even when not legally required, reflecting commitment to trustworthiness.

3.3.3 Case Study: Credit Scoring Systems

Credit scoring algorithms significantly influence access to financial resources, yet many operate opaquely. From a deontological perspective, opacity violates the duty to respect individuals' right to explanation. From a consequentialist standpoint, transparency is necessary to prevent harmful outcomes such as unjust denial of loans. A virtue ethics approach asks whether financial institutions act with honesty and fairness in communicating decision-making processes (Chatzichristofis et al., 2025).

3.4 Interconnections among FAT Principles

While fairness, accountability, and transparency are often discussed separately, they are deeply interdependent. Transparency enables accountability by making it possible to trace decisions and assign responsibility. Accountability ensures that fairness is not only an aspirational principle but also enforceable through liability and oversight. Fairness, in turn, legitimizes accountability and transparency by grounding them in moral concern for justice (Xiong et al., 2025).

The FAT principles also intersect with privacy. Transparency must balance openness with the protection of personal data. Fairness requires avoiding privacy violations that disproportionately affect vulnerable groups. Accountability demands responsibility for data misuse or breaches. Understanding these interconnections underscores the necessity of a holistic approach to AI ethics.

3.5 Challenges in Operationalizing FAT Principles

Despite their importance, implementing FAT principles in practice faces significant challenges.

- **Technical challenges**: Achieving fairness in AI requires addressing biased datasets, complex trade-offs between fairness metrics, and limitations of explainability techniques.
- **Institutional challenges**: Accountability mechanisms often falter due to fragmented governance structures and jurisdictional gaps.
- **Cultural challenges**: Transparency norms vary across cultural contexts, and over-transparency may lead to information overload without enhancing understanding.

These challenges highlight that FAT principles cannot be realized through technical fixes alone but require ethical grounding, institutional commitment, and cross-disciplinary collaboration.

3.6 Conclusion

Fairness, accountability, and transparency are indispensable for building social trust in artificial intelligence. Each principle carries distinct meanings but gains depth and coherence when interpreted through ethical theory. Deontology anchors FAT principles in duties and rights, consequentialism emphasizes their role in producing beneficial outcomes, and virtue ethics highlights their expression in moral character and institutional culture. Together, these perspectives illuminate the ethical stakes of AI governance and provide a roadmap for embedding FAT into practice.

Yet the practical implementation of FAT principles remains fraught with challenges. Addressing these challenges requires not only technical innovation but also robust normative foundations and interdisciplinary cooperation. As subsequent chapters will argue, privacy plays a central role in operationalizing FAT principles, serving as both a legal safeguard and an ethical imperative.

4. PRIVACY AS AN ETHICAL AND LEGAL IMPERATIVE

Privacy represents one of the most contested and essential values in the age of artificial intelligence (AI). While fairness, accountability, and transparency (FAT) provide a broad ethical framework for governing AI, privacy occupies a unique position at the intersection of ethical philosophy, law, and social trust. It is both a fundamental human right and a prerequisite for autonomy, dignity, and social participation. At the same time, privacy is deeply entangled with technological innovation, as AI systems depend on vast amounts of personal and sensitive data for training, optimization, and deployment (Nunes et al., 2025).

This section examines privacy as both an ethical and legal imperative. It first explores the philosophical foundations of privacy, grounding it in deontology, consequentialism, and virtue ethics. It then examines legal frameworks such as the General Data Protection Regulation (GDPR), the California Consumer Privacy Act (CCPA), and emerging international governance models. The discussion highlights the tensions between innovation and privacy, drawing on case studies to illustrate ethical dilemmas. Finally, it argues for the integration of privacy within broader frameworks of AI governance to safeguard trust and justice in the digital age.

4.1 The Ethical Foundations of Privacy

Privacy is not merely a matter of personal preference but a deeply moral concern. At its core, privacy protects individual autonomy, enables self-determination, and affirms human dignity. Different ethical traditions interpret privacy in distinctive ways.

- **Deontological Ethics**: From a deontological perspective, privacy is a duty-based obligation. Individuals possess inherent rights to control their personal information, and organizations have corresponding duties to respect those rights. Violating privacy, regardless of the potential benefits, is morally impermissible because it reduces individuals to mere means (Vascelli, 2025).

This reasoning is evident in the principle of "informational self-determination" enshrined in many privacy laws.

- **Consequentialism**: Consequentialist reasoning evaluates privacy through its outcomes. Privacy protections are justified when they minimize harm, prevent discrimination, and enhance social welfare (Degen, 2025). Conversely, excessive restrictions on data use may impede beneficial innovation, such as medical research. From this perspective, ethical governance requires balancing privacy rights against potential social benefits.
- **Virtue Ethics**: Virtue ethics frames privacy as an expression of moral character. Respecting privacy demonstrates virtues such as integrity, honesty, and respectfulness. Institutions that cultivate a culture of responsibility will proactively safeguard personal data, even when legal compliance is not strictly required. Privacy here is not just a right or an outcome but a reflection of virtuous institutional behavior.

Together, these traditions underscore privacy as both a duty, a means to beneficial outcomes, and a moral virtue. They reveal why privacy cannot be reduced to a technical or regulatory issue but must be treated as a core ethical imperative in AI governance.

4.2 Privacy in Legal Frameworks

Legal systems around the world have increasingly recognized privacy as a fundamental right. Among the most influential frameworks are the GDPR in the European Union and the CCPA in the United States.

- **The GDPR**: Enacted in 2018, the GDPR sets global benchmarks for data protection. It affirms individuals' rights to access, correct, and delete their data, as well as to demand explanations for automated decisions (Westerstrand, 2025). It embodies deontological commitments by framing privacy as a non-negotiable right, while also integrating consequentialist concerns by balancing individual rights with legitimate interests of organizations.
- **The CCPA**: California's Consumer Privacy Act provides American consumers with rights to know, delete, and opt out of the sale of personal data. While narrower in scope than the GDPR, it signals growing recognition of privacy in U.S. law. Its focus on consumer rights reflects both deontological and consequentialist reasoning.
- **Emerging International Models**: Beyond Europe and the United States, many jurisdictions are developing privacy regulations, such as Brazil's General Data Protection Law (LGPD) and India's Digital Personal Data

Protection Act (Artemova, 2025). These frameworks highlight the global convergence around privacy as a legal and ethical necessity, albeit with variations in enforcement and scope.

Legal frameworks, however, face significant limitations in addressing AI-driven privacy concerns. The complexity of machine learning systems often obscures how data is used, making it difficult for individuals to exercise rights meaningfully. Furthermore, global data flows challenge the jurisdictional reach of national laws. These limitations underscore the need for ethical reasoning to complement legal compliance.

4.3 Privacy and AI Innovation: Tensions and Trade-Offs

AI thrives on data. Machine learning models improve as they ingest more information, enabling predictive accuracy and personalization. Yet, this dependence creates profound tensions with privacy.

- **Data Maximization vs. Minimalism**: AI development often seeks to maximize data collection, while privacy protection demands data minimization. This tension raises ethical dilemmas about how much data can justifiably be collected.
- **Consent and Autonomy**: Traditional models of informed consent struggle in AI contexts, where data uses are complex, opaque, and evolving. Ethical reasoning questions whether consent remains meaningful under such conditions.
- **Surveillance Capitalism**: The monetization of personal data by technology companies raises concerns about exploitation and commodification of privacy. Here, deontology emphasizes duties to respect autonomy, consequentialism assesses harms to democratic institutions, and virtue ethics questions whether such practices reflect greed rather than integrity.

Balancing innovation and privacy requires nuanced ethical analysis. Blanket restrictions may hinder beneficial research, while unchecked data use threatens autonomy and trust.

4.4 Case Studies in Privacy and AI

4.4.1 Case Study 1: Healthcare AI

AI systems in healthcare, such as diagnostic tools or personalized treatment algorithms, rely on sensitive medical data. While these systems can improve patient outcomes, they also raise privacy risks if data is misused or inadequately protected. A deontological analysis insists on respecting patients' rights to confidentiality. Consequentialism weighs the benefits of improved health outcomes against risks of misuse. Virtue ethics examines whether institutions demonstrate care, responsibility, and trustworthiness.

4.4.2 Case Study 2: Social Media and Targeted Advertising

Social media platforms collect vast amounts of behavioral data to fuel targeted advertising. This raises concerns about manipulation, autonomy, and the erosion of privacy. Deontological ethics critiques such practices as treating individuals as means to profit. Consequentialism highlights harms to democratic discourse and mental health. Virtue ethics questions whether these companies cultivate honesty and respect or prioritize greed and exploitation.

4.4.3 Case Study 3: Biometric Surveillance

Biometric technologies such as facial recognition present acute privacy challenges. They often operate without consent, creating risks of mass surveillance and discrimination. A deontological perspective emphasizes rights violations, consequentialist reasoning examines disproportionate harms to marginalized communities, and virtue ethics questions whether deploying such technologies reflects justice or authoritarian tendencies.

These cases illustrate the multidimensional nature of privacy concerns and the necessity of integrating ethical reasoning into governance.

4.5 Privacy as a Prerequisite for Trust

Privacy is not only an individual right but also a collective foundation for social trust. When individuals believe that their data is respected, they are more likely to engage with AI systems, enabling innovation and public acceptance (Khorshidi et al., 2025). Conversely, privacy violations erode trust, producing resistance, regulatory backlash, and social polarization.

This collective dimension highlights why privacy must be embedded in AI governance beyond compliance. It requires proactive measures such as privacy-by-design, differential privacy techniques, and ethical auditing. These practices express deontological respect for rights, consequentialist concern for outcomes, and virtue-ethical commitment to integrity.

4.6 Challenges in Safeguarding Privacy in AI

Despite its importance, safeguarding privacy in AI faces persistent challenges:

- **Technical Challenges**: Techniques such as anonymization often fail in the face of re-identification risks. Deep learning models can inadvertently memorize sensitive data.
- **Regulatory Challenges**: Enforcement gaps and cross-border data flows limit the effectiveness of privacy laws.
- **Ethical Challenges**: Striking a balance between privacy and innovation requires trade-offs that no single ethical theory fully resolves.

These challenges call for a hybrid ethical framework that integrates duties, outcomes, and virtues into practical governance strategies.

4.7 Conclusion

Privacy is an ethical and legal imperative in the governance of artificial intelligence. As a right, it reflects duties of respect and protection; as an outcome, it minimizes harm and enhances welfare; as a virtue, it embodies integrity and responsibility. Legal frameworks such as the GDPR and CCPA provide essential safeguards, but they must be complemented by ethical reasoning to address the complexities of AI.

By treating privacy not merely as a compliance requirement but as a foundational ethical value, AI governance can better safeguard autonomy, dignity, and trust. In doing so, it aligns technological innovation with human rights and prepares the ground for sustainable, trustworthy AI systems.

5. CASE STUDIES AND APPLICATIONS

Case studies provide an indispensable means of translating ethical theory into practice. While deontological, consequentialist, and virtue-ethical frameworks offer abstract principles for analyzing fairness, accountability, transparency, and privacy, real-world examples reveal the complexity of applying these frameworks in concrete contexts (Hultin & Mähring, 2025). By examining cases across healthcare, finance, law enforcement, and social media, this section demonstrates how ethical reasoning both illuminates dilemmas and guides practical governance.

5.1 Healthcare AI

5.1.1 Background

Healthcare is often presented as one of the most promising domains for AI, offering opportunities for early diagnosis, personalized treatment, and optimized resource allocation. However, because medical data is highly sensitive, healthcare applications also present significant ethical and privacy concerns.

5.1.2 Ethical Analysis

- **Deontological Perspective**: Patients have a right to confidentiality, and medical institutions have duties to safeguard it. AI-driven diagnostic tools must therefore respect privacy as an inviolable obligation. If a system violates confidentiality even if it improves health outcomes it breaches fundamental moral duties.
- **Consequentialist Perspective**: The evaluation turns on whether AI maximizes health outcomes while minimizing harms. For example, triage systems that allocate scarce medical resources during pandemics may be justified if they save the greatest number of lives. Yet, if these systems consistently disadvantage vulnerable groups, the negative consequences outweigh the benefits.
- **Virtue Ethics Perspective**: Institutions deploying healthcare AI should embody virtues such as compassion, justice, and integrity. Developers must ensure that algorithms reflect responsibility toward patients rather than efficiency alone.

5.1.3 Implications

Healthcare AI demonstrates the necessity of hybrid ethical reasoning. Compliance with privacy laws is insufficient without commitments to fairness, accountability, and the cultivation of institutional trust.

5.2 Finance and Algorithmic Credit Scoring

5.2.1 Background

Credit scoring algorithms are widely used to assess loan eligibility and interest rates. While they promise efficiency and objectivity, they also raise concerns about bias, discrimination, and opacity.

5.2.2 Ethical Analysis

- **Deontological Perspective**: Discriminatory credit decisions violate duties to treat applicants with equal respect, regardless of gender, race, or socioeconomic status. Even if such practices improve financial efficiency, they are morally impermissible.
- **Consequentialist Perspective**: The legitimacy of credit scoring depends on whether it expands financial inclusion or exacerbates inequality. If it systematically denies access to marginalized groups, the overall social harm outweighs benefits.
- **Virtue Ethics Perspective**: Financial institutions must embody virtues such as fairness, honesty, and responsibility. A system that prioritizes profit at the expense of justice reflects greed rather than virtue.

5.2.3 Implications

This case highlights the importance of transparency in financial AI. Without explainability, applicants cannot contest unjust outcomes, and institutions cannot be held accountable. Ethical reasoning thus reinforces the demand for algorithmic auditing and fairness assessments.

5.3 Law Enforcement and Predictive Policing

5.3.1 Background

Predictive policing tools use historical crime data to forecast potential hotspots and allocate law enforcement resources. Advocates claim these tools enhance efficiency, but critics argue they reinforce systemic biases and erode civil liberties.

5.3.2 Ethical Analysis

- **Deontological Perspective**: Predictive policing may violate the duty to respect individual autonomy and presumption of innocence. Targeting communities based on historical data reduces individuals to mere objects of surveillance.
- **Consequentialist Perspective**: The ethical assessment depends on whether predictive policing reduces crime without disproportionately harming marginalized groups. If harms such as racial profiling and mistrust outweigh benefits, the practice fails morally.

- **Virtue Ethics Perspective**: Law enforcement agencies must embody virtues such as justice, fairness, and responsibility. Deploying biased predictive tools undermines these virtues and perpetuates systemic injustice.

5.3.3 Implications

Predictive policing exemplifies the dangers of neglecting FAT principles. Transparency is limited, accountability is diffuse, and fairness is compromised. Ethical analysis reveals the need for stricter oversight and potential prohibition of certain applications.

5.4 Social Media and Targeted Advertising

5.4.1 Background

Social media platforms rely on AI to curate content and deliver targeted advertisements based on user behavior. While this generates revenue and personalization, it raises concerns about manipulation, autonomy, and privacy.

5.4.2 Ethical Analysis

- **Deontological Perspective**: Exploiting users' personal data for targeted advertising without meaningful consent violates duties to respect autonomy.
- **Consequentialist Perspective**: The harms of targeted advertising such as polarization, misinformation, and mental health impacts often outweigh the benefits of personalization.
- **Virtue Ethics Perspective**: Companies prioritizing profit over user well-being reflect greed rather than integrity or responsibility. Virtuous institutions would seek to balance innovation with user protection.

5.4.3 Implications

This case demonstrates how AI can undermine democratic discourse and individual autonomy. Ethical reasoning strengthens calls for stricter regulation of data collection, advertising practices, and platform accountability.

5.5 Comparative Insights Across Cases

Across domains, several patterns emerge:

- **Privacy is central**: Whether in healthcare, finance, policing, or social media, privacy violations consistently undermine trust.
- **Fairness requires vigilance**: Biased data and opaque algorithms repeatedly disadvantage vulnerable groups.
- **Accountability is fragmented**: In each case, responsibility is dispersed, creating gaps in governance.
- **Transparency enables trust**: Without explanations, stakeholders cannot evaluate or contest AI outcomes.

Each ethical theory contributes unique insights. Deontology provides non-negotiable prohibitions, consequentialism evaluates overall impacts, and virtue ethics emphasizes institutional character (Robbins, 2025). Together, they offer a multidimensional framework for ethical AI governance.

The comparative analysis of these four domains demonstrates how ethical theories provide complementary insights into the governance of AI systems. To further illustrate these relationships, the following matrix summarizes the application of deontological, consequentialist, and virtue-ethical perspectives across the selected case studies.

As shown in Figure 1, each ethical framework highlights distinct yet interrelated concerns in healthcare, finance, law enforcement, and social media. These comparative insights not only clarify the ethical dimensions of AI but also underscore the need for practical strategies to operationalize them in policy and industry contexts. The next section outlines lessons for policymakers and practitioners based on these findings.

Figure 1. Ethical Analysis Matrix for AI Case Studies

Domain	Deontology (Duty)	Consequentialism (Outcome)	Virtue Ethics (Character)
Healthcare	Right to privacy	Maximize survival	Compassion, integrity
Finance	Non-discrimination	Financial inclusion	Fairness, honesty
Law Enforcement	Presumption of innocence	Reduce crime / avoid harm	Justice, responsibility
Social Media	Respect autonomy	Minimize polarization	Integrity, honesty

5.6 Practical Lessons for Policymakers and Practitioners

The case studies highlight several practical lessons:

1. **Embed Ethics in Design**: Privacy-by-design, fairness-by-design, and explainability-by-design should become standard practices.
2. **Conduct Ethical Audits**: Independent audits can identify biases, evaluate outcomes, and ensure accountability.
3. **Promote Institutional Virtue**: Beyond compliance, organizations should cultivate cultures of responsibility, transparency, and respect.
4. **Strengthen Global Governance**: Harmonization of legal frameworks is essential to address cross-border data flows and transnational AI deployment.

5.7 Chapter

Case studies provide vivid illustrations of how ethical theories intersect with AI practices. In healthcare, finance, policing, and social media, deontology underscores duties to respect rights, consequentialism evaluates societal outcomes, and virtue ethics emphasizes institutional integrity. Together, these frameworks reveal both the opportunities and risks of AI.

The consistent lesson across domains is that technological innovation without ethical grounding erodes trust and exacerbates injustice. By applying ethical reasoning, policymakers and practitioners can better align AI systems with human values, ensuring that innovation serves the public good.

6. TOWARD AN INTEGRATED ETHICAL FRAMEWORK FOR AI GOVERNANCE

The preceding chapters have examined how deontology, consequentialism, and virtue ethics each provide valuable but partial insights into the ethical evaluation of artificial intelligence (AI). Deontological reasoning highlights duties and rights, consequentialism emphasizes outcomes and social welfare, and virtue ethics underscores the cultivation of moral character and institutional integrity (van Toorn et al., 2025). When applied to issues of fairness, accountability, transparency (FAT), and privacy, these traditions clarify both the promises and perils of AI governance. Yet, as the case studies demonstrate, reliance on any single framework is insufficient to capture the complexity of contemporary AI systems.

This chapter proposes an integrated ethical framework for AI governance that synthesizes insights from the three traditions while aligning them with regulatory structures and technical practices. The framework recognizes that AI systems operate in contexts where duties, outcomes, and virtues are simultaneously relevant. It therefore calls for a hybrid approach that draws on the strengths of each theory while compensating for their limitations.

6.1 The Limitations of Isolated Ethical Theories

Each ethical theory, when applied in isolation, encounters significant challenges in guiding AI governance.

- **Deontological ethics** provides clear prohibitions and duties, such as respecting privacy or avoiding discrimination. However, rigid adherence to duties may overlook broader consequences. For instance, prohibiting the use of sensitive data in all cases could hinder medical research that saves lives.
- **Consequentialism** offers flexibility by evaluating overall outcomes, but it risks justifying harmful practices if they appear to maximize social welfare. For example, predictive policing may seem beneficial in reducing crime rates but can perpetuate systemic injustice.
- **Virtue ethics** emphasizes moral character, yet it offers limited procedural guidance for resolving conflicts. Appeals to virtue may lack concrete mechanisms for accountability and enforcement in large organizations.

The limitations of each framework suggest the need for integration (Struniawski et al., 2025). Duties without attention to outcomes can be ethically blind, outcomes without duties can be morally reckless, and virtues without structure can be aspirational but vague.

6.2 The Case for an Integrated Ethical Framework

An integrated ethical framework acknowledges that AI governance involves multiple stakeholders with diverse responsibilities and values. Developers, regulators, policymakers, corporations, and civil society each operate within overlapping but distinct spheres of accountability. In such a context, no single ethical theory provides sufficient guidance.

The case for integration rests on three propositions:

1. Complementarity: Duties, outcomes, and virtues capture different dimensions of morality that together offer a fuller picture of ethical AI.
2. Practical Relevance: Hybrid frameworks can better address the multi-level challenges of AI governance, from technical design to global regulation.
3. Trust and Legitimacy: Integration strengthens public trust by demonstrating that governance frameworks are both principled and responsive to real-world complexities.

6.3 Elements of the Integrated Framework

The proposed integrated framework comprises three interrelated elements: Foundational Duties, Consequential Assessments, and Virtuous Practices.

- **Foundational Duties** (Deontological Component): Establish non-negotiable obligations such as respect for human dignity, prohibition of discrimination, and protection of privacy. These duties form the ethical baseline for AI governance.
- **Consequential Assessments** (Consequentialist Component): Require systematic evaluation of the broader impacts of AI systems, including cost-benefit analyses, risk assessments, and long-term social implications. This ensures that governance is not blind to outcomes.
- **Virtuous Practices** (Virtue-Ethics Component): Promote organizational cultures that value integrity, fairness, transparency, and responsibility. Virtuous practices encourage ethical reflexivity beyond compliance.

Together, these elements create a layered approach: duties set the boundaries, consequences guide decision-making, and virtues foster trust and legitimacy.

6.4 Operationalizing the Framework in AI Governance

To move from theory to practice, the integrated framework must be operationalized through governance mechanisms, regulatory instruments, and technical design.

1. **Ethical Design Principles**: AI developers should embed privacy-by-design, fairness-by-design, and explainability-by-design into technical systems. Foundational duties establish boundaries (e.g., data minimization), while consequential assessments evaluate societal impacts, and virtuous practices encourage transparency and care.
2. **Algorithmic Impact Assessments**: Regulators should mandate impact assessments that combine ethical duties, outcome evaluations, and virtue considerations. These assessments would require developers to demonstrate compliance with rights-based standards, evaluate long-term harms and benefits, and provide evidence of institutional responsibility.
3. **Multi-Stakeholder Oversight**: Governance bodies should integrate diverse perspectives, including civil society, academia, and industry. Duties ensure inclusion of marginalized voices, consequentialism highlights social outcomes, and virtue ethics encourages humility and dialogue.

4. **Accountability Mechanisms**: Liability regimes must assign responsibility for harms. Duties establish obligations, consequentialist reasoning evaluates risk allocation, and virtue ethics reinforces institutional responsibility for acknowledging and correcting failures.

6.5 Global Governance and Cultural Adaptability

AI is inherently global, with systems and data flows crossing national boundaries. An integrated framework must therefore accommodate cultural diversity while maintaining core ethical commitments.

- **Universal Duties**: Certain principles such as respect for human dignity and prohibition of discrimination are non-negotiable across contexts.
- **Contextual Outcomes**: Consequential assessments may vary depending on local conditions, such as public health priorities or economic needs.
- **Cultural Virtues**: Virtue ethics accommodates cultural variation by recognizing different traditions of integrity, responsibility, and social harmony.

By blending universality with adaptability, the framework balances consistency with cultural sensitivity.

6.6 Applications of the Integrated Framework

Healthcare

Foundational duties protect patient confidentiality, consequential assessments evaluate improved health outcomes, and virtuous practices encourage compassion and responsibility in institutions.

Finance

Duties prohibit discrimination in credit scoring, consequential assessments evaluate impacts on financial inclusion, and virtuous practices foster fairness and honesty in lending institutions.

Law Enforcement

Duties uphold rights such as presumption of innocence, consequential assessments evaluate effects on crime and community trust, and virtuous practices emphasize justice and responsibility.

Social Media

Duties safeguard autonomy by prohibiting manipulative practices, consequential assessments evaluate impacts on democratic discourse, and virtuous practices encourage integrity and respect for users.

These applications illustrate how the integrated framework provides more comprehensive guidance than any single ethical theory alone.

6.7 Advantages of the Integrated Approach

The integrated framework offers several advantages for AI governance:

- **Holistic**: It unites duties, outcomes, and virtues into a coherent structure.
- **Flexible**: It adapts to different sectors, contexts, and cultures.
- **Actionable**: It provides clear mechanisms for design, regulation, and oversight.
- **Trust-Building**: It fosters legitimacy by demonstrating principled, balanced governance.

By addressing both normative and practical dimensions, the integrated framework strengthens the ethical foundation of AI governance.

6.8 Conclusion

The ethical governance of AI cannot be reduced to a single theory or principle. Duties, consequences, and virtues each illuminate essential dimensions of morality but remain incomplete in isolation. This chapter has argued for an integrated ethical framework that combines foundational duties, consequential assessments, and virtuous practices into a layered approach to AI governance.

Operationalizing this framework requires embedding ethical principles into design, mandating impact assessments, fostering multi-stakeholder oversight, and cultivating institutional responsibility. It also requires cultural adaptability to ensure global legitimacy.

By integrating ethical theories into a coherent framework, AI governance can better align innovation with human values, safeguard fairness, accountability, transparency, and privacy, and foster trust in the digital age. The next chapter examines future directions and challenges, highlighting emerging dilemmas such as explainability, generative AI, and global regulatory coordination.

7. FUTURE DIRECTIONS AND CHALLENGES

The governance of artificial intelligence (AI) is a rapidly evolving field that must keep pace with technological innovation, shifting social expectations, and emerging global regulations. While ethical theories and integrated frameworks provide robust foundations for fairness, accountability, transparency (FAT), and privacy, the landscape of AI presents new and unresolved challenges. Future directions in AI governance will require interdisciplinary collaboration, continuous ethical reflection, and adaptive regulatory mechanisms (Thi Nguyet Trang et al., 2025).

This chapter explores key challenges and future trajectories in AI ethics and governance. It highlights the issues of explainability, generative AI, global coordination, and interdisciplinary engagement, emphasizing the need to move beyond static principles toward dynamic, responsive governance structures.

7.1 Explainability and the Black Box Problem

One of the most pressing challenges in AI ethics is the opacity of complex machine learning models, particularly deep neural networks. These systems often produce accurate predictions but lack interpretability, creating the so-called "black box" problem.

- **Ethical Implications:** From a deontological perspective, opacity undermines the duty to respect individuals' right to explanation. Consequentialist reasoning highlights risks of unanticipated harms when decisions cannot be scrutinized. Virtue ethics questions whether deploying opaque systems reflects intellectual honesty and integrity.
- **Future Directions:** Research into explainable AI (XAI) seeks to enhance transparency through techniques such as feature attribution, model simplification, and counterfactual explanations. Policymakers must determine minimum thresholds for explainability, balancing transparency with technical feasibility.

7.2 Generative AI and Ethical Complexity

Generative AI, including large language models and diffusion-based image generators, poses unprecedented ethical challenges. While these systems enable creativity and innovation, they also generate risks of misinformation, deepfakes, intellectual property violations, and manipulation.

- **Ethical Implications:** Deontological ethics emphasizes duties to avoid deception and protect rights of authors. Consequentialism evaluates whether the benefits of generative AI outweigh harms such as disinformation and social polarization. Virtue ethics underscores the importance of integrity, honesty, and responsibility in both developers and users.
- **Future Directions:** Addressing these risks requires combining technical solutions (e.g., watermarking, content provenance systems) with regulatory interventions and ethical education. The cultivation of virtue in institutions such as responsibility and honesty will be crucial for sustainable governance.

7.3 Global Governance and Regulatory Fragmentation

AI governance faces the challenge of global fragmentation. While the European Union has proposed a comprehensive AI Act, other jurisdictions adopt divergent approaches. This lack of harmonization creates regulatory uncertainty and opens gaps for unethical practices.

- **Ethical Implications**: Deontological ethics supports universal duties that transcend national boundaries, such as prohibitions against discrimination and violations of dignity. Consequentialism emphasizes the need to evaluate global outcomes, recognizing that harms often cross borders. Virtue ethics highlights the importance of cultivating international trust, cooperation, and solidarity.
- **Future Directions**: Efforts toward global coordination must build on initiatives such as UNESCO's Recommendation on the Ethics of AI and the OECD's AI Principles. While cultural variation must be respected, core ethical commitments dignity, fairness, accountability, transparency, and privacy should form the backbone of global standards.

7.4 Interdisciplinary Collaboration

The governance of AI cannot be confined to computer scientists or policymakers alone. Ethical AI requires collaboration across philosophy, law, social sciences, engineering, and civil society.

- **Ethical Implications**: Deontological reasoning affirms the duty to include diverse voices, ensuring procedural fairness. Consequentialist reasoning emphasizes that interdisciplinary collaboration maximizes beneficial outcomes by addressing blind spots. Virtue ethics values humility, openness, and responsibility in working across disciplines.

- **Future Directions**: Universities, industry, and governments should invest in interdisciplinary research centers, ethics advisory boards, and inclusive policy-making processes. The integration of ethical reasoning into STEM education is also vital for cultivating responsible future developers.

These challenges illustrate the evolving complexity of AI governance. To clarify how ethical theories provide complementary responses, the following table summarizes the application of deontological, consequentialist, and virtue-ethical reasoning to selected future challenges.

Table 1. Future Challenges in AI Governance and Ethical Responses

Challenge	Deontological Response (Duties)	Consequentialist Response (Outcomes)	Virtue-Ethical Response (Character)
Explainability	Duty to provide right to explanation	Minimize risks of harm from opacity	Intellectual honesty, openness
Generative AI	Duty to avoid deception, respect IP	Balance creativity with harms (misinfo)	Responsibility, integrity
Global Governance	Universal duties across borders	Evaluate cross-border impacts	Solidarity, trust
Interdisciplinary Gaps	Duty to include diverse voices	Maximize benefits via collaboration	Humility, openness, respect

As Table 1 demonstrates, each ethical theory contributes distinct insights, but their integration provides a more comprehensive response to emerging challenges. Duties establish non-negotiable boundaries, outcomes highlight societal impacts, and virtues cultivate institutional integrity. Together, they offer a roadmap for navigating the uncertain future of AI governance.

7.5 Emerging Challenges on the Horizon

Several additional issues demand attention:

- **AI and Climate Impact**: The energy demands of large AI models raise environmental concerns, requiring ethical evaluation of sustainability.
- **AI and Labor**: Automation continues to reshape labor markets, demanding fairness in transition policies.
- **AI and Human Rights**: From biometric surveillance to autonomous weapons, AI intersects with fundamental rights, requiring robust safeguards.

These challenges reinforce the need for adaptive, forward-looking governance frameworks that integrate ethical theory with practical regulation.

7.6 Conclusion

AI governance stands at a crossroads. The challenges of explainability, generative AI, global fragmentation, and interdisciplinary engagement highlight the limits of static principles and the necessity of dynamic, integrated frameworks. Ethical theories deontological, consequentialist, and virtue-ethical remain indispensable for navigating these challenges, but they must be synthesized into adaptive structures that respond to technological evolution.

Future governance must therefore embrace hybrid approaches that combine duties, outcomes, and virtues; technical innovation and legal regulation; local contexts and global commitments. Only by doing so can AI systems advance human flourishing while safeguarding fairness, accountability, transparency, and privacy.

The final chapter will synthesize insights across the volume, reinforcing the argument that ethical theories provide essential foundations for trust in AI and proposing pathways for embedding them into long-term governance strategies.

8. CONCLUSION

Artificial intelligence (AI) has become one of the most transformative technologies of the twenty-first century, reshaping domains as diverse as healthcare, finance, law enforcement, and social media. Yet, alongside its promise of efficiency, innovation, and predictive power, AI poses profound ethical challenges. This volume has argued that addressing these challenges requires not only technical fixes or regulatory compliance but also systematic engagement with the enduring traditions of moral philosophy.

Throughout the chapter, three ethical theories deontology, consequentialism, and virtue ethics have served as the guiding pillars for analyzing the moral landscape of AI. Each theory highlights a different dimension of responsibility: deontology underscores non-negotiable duties and rights, consequentialism evaluates outcomes and social welfare, and virtue ethics emphasizes moral character and institutional integrity. Applied together, these traditions illuminate the ethical stakes of fairness, accountability, transparency (FAT), and privacy in AI systems (Yan et al., 2025).

The early chapters provided theoretical foundations, demonstrating how these frameworks shape our understanding of duties, outcomes, and virtues in AI governance. Building on this foundation, the analysis of FAT principles clarified why fairness requires both distributive and procedural justice, why accountability is indispensable for remedying harms, and why transparency is essential for building trust. Privacy, as explored in detail, emerged as both a legal right and an ethical imperative, central to autonomy, dignity, and social legitimacy.

Case studies across healthcare, finance, law enforcement, and social media revealed how these abstract principles materialize in practice. They demonstrated the recurrent risks of bias, opacity, and privacy violations, but also highlighted opportunities for embedding ethics into design and deployment. By applying multiple ethical theories to each domain, the case studies underscored the importance of a multidimensional approach. No single framework was sufficient; only by combining duties, outcomes, and virtues could the complexities of real-world AI governance be adequately addressed (Chatzichristofis et al., 2025).

This insight led to the proposal of an integrated ethical framework for AI governance. The framework unites three elements: foundational duties that set ethical boundaries, consequential assessments that evaluate societal impacts, and virtuous practices that foster integrity and responsibility. Operationalizing this framework requires embedding ethical principles into technical design, mandating algorithmic impact assessments, fostering multi-stakeholder oversight, and cultivating organizational cultures of responsibility. Such integration strengthens public trust, provides clearer guidance for practitioners, and enhances the legitimacy of global governance initiatives.

Looking forward, the chapter on future directions emphasized that AI governance must remain dynamic and adaptive. Challenges such as explainability, generative AI, global regulatory fragmentation, and interdisciplinary gaps demand continuous innovation in both technical methods and ethical reasoning. Deontological, consequentialist, and virtue-ethical perspectives provide distinct responses to these challenges, but their integration offers the most comprehensive pathway (Xiong et al., 2025). Duties safeguard non-negotiable rights, outcomes ensure proportionality and utility, and virtues cultivate the trust and solidarity necessary for long-term governance.

The central conclusion of this contribution is that ethical theories are not academic luxuries but practical necessities. They provide the normative compass for navigating the uncertainties of AI, grounding governance in principles that transcend immediate technical or economic concerns. As AI becomes increasingly autonomous, pervasive, and consequential, the risk of losing sight of human dignity, fairness, and justice intensifies. Ethical theory ensures that innovation remains tethered to enduring human values.

At the same time, ethics alone is insufficient. Effective governance requires the interplay of philosophy, law, and technology. Philosophical traditions supply normative clarity, legal frameworks establish enforceable standards, and technical innovation implements safeguards. Interdisciplinary collaboration, cultural adaptability, and global coordination are indispensable for ensuring that AI advances human flourishing rather than undermining it.

In conclusion, the ethical evaluation of AI must move beyond isolated theories or fragmented principles. By synthesizing deontology, consequentialism, and virtue ethics into an integrated framework, and by aligning this framework with FAT principles and privacy protections, AI governance can better safeguard trust in the digital age. This approach affirms that technology is never value-neutral but always embedded in social contexts, moral choices, and institutional responsibilities.

The way forward is not merely to regulate AI but to govern it ethically, ensuring that innovation is guided by duties, responsive to outcomes, and reflective of virtues. Only by doing so can societies harness the potential of AI while preserving the fundamental values of fairness, accountability, transparency, and privacy. In this respect, ethical theories provide not only tools for analysis but also a moral foundation for building a trustworthy and just AI future.

REFERENCES

Al-Hattami, H. M. (2025). Empowering business research with ChatGPT: Academic and student insights through the UTAUT lens. *Discover Computing*, *28*(1), 179. Advance online publication. DOI: 10.1007/s10791-025-09692-1

Artemova, I. (2025). Exploring responsible technology through archetypal responses: Uncertainty analysis in Leave the World Behind. *Journal of Responsible Technology*, *23*, 100134. Advance online publication. DOI: 10.1016/j.jrt.2025.100134

Cecez-Kecmanovic, D. (2025). Ethics in the world of automated algorithmic decision-making – A Posthumanist perspective. *Information and Organization*, *35*(3), 100587. Advance online publication. DOI: 10.1016/j.infoandorg.2025.100587

Chatzichristofis, S. A., Tsopozidis, A., Kyriakidou-Zacharoudiou, A., Evripidou, S., & Amanatiadis, A. (2025). Designing an AI-Supported Framework for Literary Text Adaptation in Primary Classrooms. *AI*, *6*(7), 150. Advance online publication. DOI: 10.3390/ai6070150

De Rose, L., Andresini, G., Appice, A., & Malerba, D. (2025). OLIVANDER: A counterfactual-based method to generate adversarial Windows PE malware. *Data Mining and Knowledge Discovery*, *39*(5), 46. Advance online publication. DOI: 10.1007/s10618-025-01127-1

Degen, P.-B. (2025). Revisiting generalizability theory in the age of artificial intelligence: Implications for empirical educational research. *Computers and Education Open*, *9*, 100278. Advance online publication. DOI: 10.1016/j.caeo.2025.100278

Deng, Z., Song, D., & Liu, S. (2025). How does AI-assisted diagnosis decision support systems influence doctors' coping styles and work outcomes? Bright and dark sides of AI in the workplace. *Decision Support Systems*, *197*, 114512. Advance online publication. DOI: 10.1016/j.dss.2025.114512

Deric, E., Frank, D., & Milković, M. (2025). Trust in Generative AI Tools: A Comparative Study of Higher Education Students, Teachers, and Researchers. *Information (Basel)*, *16*(7), 622. Advance online publication. DOI: 10.3390/info16070622

Hultin, L., & Mähring, M. (2025). Reimagining AI for sustainability: Cultivating imagination, hope, and response-ability. *Information and Organization*, *35*(3), 100586. Advance online publication. DOI: 10.1016/j.infoandorg.2025.100586

Ishkhanyan, A. (2025). The sovereignty-internationalism paradox in AI governance: Digital federalism and global algorithmic control. *Discover Artificial Intelligence*, *5*(1), 123. Advance online publication. DOI: 10.1007/s44163-025-00374-x

Khorshidi, M. S., Merigó, J. M., & Beydoun, G. (2025). Half a Century of Information Processing & Management: A bibliometric retrospective. *Information Processing & Management, 62*(6), 104238. Advance online publication. DOI: 10.1016/j.ipm.2025.104238

Küçükuncular, A., & Ertugan, A. (2025). Teaching in the AI Era: Sustainable Digital Education Through Ethical Integration and Teacher Empowerment. *Sustainability (Basel), 17*(16), 7405. Advance online publication. DOI: 10.3390/su17167405

Nunes, J. R., Rita, P., Costa Pinto, D., Gonzalez-Jimenez, H., Akdim, K., & Wagner, R. L. (2025). Moral appraisals of generative AI: How mindset framing shapes moral judgments, emotional appraisals and privacy behavior. *International Journal of Information Management, 84*, 102940. Advance online publication. DOI: 10.1016/j.ijinfomgt.2025.102940

Ricon, T. (2025). AI and adolescent Relationships: Bridging emotional intelligence and practical guidance. *Computers in Human Behavior Reports, 19*, 100752. Advance online publication. DOI: 10.1016/j.chbr.2025.100752

Riti, R. I., Abrudan, C. I., Bacali, L., & Balc, N. (2025). Command Redefined: Neural-Adaptive Leadership in the Age of Autonomous Intelligence. *AI, 6*(8), 176. Advance online publication. DOI: 10.3390/ai6080176

Robbins, P. (2025). Of machines and men: Attributions of moral responsibility in AI-assisted warfare. *Ethics and Information Technology, 27*(3), 35. Advance online publication. DOI: 10.1007/s10676-025-09844-3

Struniawski, K., Kozera, R., & Konopka, A. (2025). Analyzing LLM Sentencing Variability in Theft Indictments Across Gender, Family Status and the Value of the Stolen Item. *Applied Sciences (Basel, Switzerland), 15*(16), 8860. Advance online publication. DOI: 10.3390/app15168860

Suter, V., Ma, C., Pöhlmann, G., & Meckel, M. (2025). When Politicians Talk AI: Issue-Frames in Parliamentary Debates Before and After ChatGPT. *Policy and Internet, 17*(3), e70010. Advance online publication. DOI: 10.1002/poi3.70010

Thi Nguyet Trang, T. T. N., Thang, P. C., & Vo, T. A. (2025). Moderating the AI Revolution: Perceived threat and generative AI implementation in Vietnamese hospitals. *Computers in Human Behavior Reports, 19*, 100774. Advance online publication. DOI: 10.1016/j.chbr.2025.100774

van Toorn, G., Scully, J. L., & Gendera, S. (2025). "This robot is dictating her next steps in life": Disability justice and relational AI ethics. *AI & Society, 40*(6), 4473–4483. DOI: 10.1007/s00146-025-02224-x

Vascelli, L. (2025). From philosophy to algorithms: A commentary on the evolution of human behavior and the role of artificial intelligence. *Discover Artificial Intelligence*, *5*(1), 138. Advance online publication. DOI: 10.1007/s44163-025-00394-7

Westerstrand, S. (2025). Fairness in AI systems development: EU AI Act compliance and beyond. *Information and Software Technology*, *187*, 107864. Advance online publication. DOI: 10.1016/j.infsof.2025.107864

Xiong, S., Gu, H., Liang, W., & Yin, L. (2025). Moral Judgment with a Large Language Model-Based Agent. *Electronics (Basel)*, *14*(13), 2580. Advance online publication. DOI: 10.3390/electronics14132580

Yan, Y., Liu, H., Zhang, H., Chau, T., & Li, J. (2025). Designing a Generalist Education AI Framework for Multimodal Learning and Ethical Data Governance. *Applied Sciences (Basel, Switzerland)*, *15*(14), 7758. Advance online publication. DOI: 10.3390/app15147758

Zhang, J., Shao, Z., Zhang, L., & Benitez, J. (2025). Exploring users' post-adoption use of generative AI: An attitudinal ambivalence perspective. *Decision Support Systems*, *197*, 114521. Advance online publication. DOI: 10.1016/j.dss.2025.114521

Chapter 4
AI for Complex Computational Solution With Respect to C Programming

Daniel Hoxha
https://orcid.org/0009-0009-1971-762X
RIT Tirana, Albania

ABSTRACT

AI-based tools and techniques can simplify syntax learning, enhance logical understanding, and improve efficiency for both beginners and advanced programmers. Programming is the most popular it has ever been, and C is a really common language. Learning it is not the easiest however. C is a low-level language meaning if you don't know it well you can cause your projects to crash. Combine that with the difficult syntax, it is not the most beginner friendly language. Thankfully, AI can make learning C much easier. From explaining the syntax to us, to helping us understand the logic of the program, AI can be a massive helping hand. It can also help more advanced programmers. As most programmers know, debugging can be really difficult and it can take a long time. Especially in big projects with thousands of lines, finding that one missing semicolon can be hard. With AI, we can debug much quicker, which allows us to finish our work quicker. It can make us more efficient by allowing us to make two to three projects in the time that it would take to make one.

DOI: 10.4018/979-8-3373-7011-8.ch004

ht © 2026, IGI Global Scientific Publishing. Copying or distributing in print or electronic forms without written permission of IGI Global Scientific Publishing is prohibited. Use of this chapter to generative artificial intelligence (AI) technologies is expressly prohibited. The publisher reserves all rights to license its use for generative AI training and machine learning model development.

1. INTRODUCTION

C is a low-level programming language which means it has direct access to the device's memory. It is the base for a lot of programming languages. That is why a lot of people start with C, because the knowledge can be used in other languages as well. It is also used in operating systems which makes it a really good language to learn. C was originally created in 1970 by Dennis Ritchie as a successor of the B programming language. In 1978 Brian Kernighan released a book about C which has now become the de facto standard for C programing. Afterwards, in 1989, C was standardized and since then it has gained a lot of popularity. C was the base for many languages. C++, C#, Java and Python all originated from C. It has also been used in a lot of other things. C has been used in embedded systems, supercomputers as well as software applications. It was also used for the kernels of operating systems, making it one of the most important languages. C can be challenging for beginners. The syntax isn't the easiest to understand, whether it is format specifier like %d, or making sure you use semicolons and brackets correctly, it is not easy to learn. Especially considering C is a low-level language, you need to understand the logic well to make sure you don't have big errors or crashes. AI has had massive rise in education and programming. It allows students to gain information quicker than ever. It also allows them to write projects in record times. All you have to do is write what you want and the AI will give it to you, math problems, essays, it doesn't matter. The same goes from programming. All a programmer has to do is explain the program to the AI, and in a few seconds the AI will have created it for him. That is why we have seen such a rise in AI usage. In this research I want to explore how we can use all these features that AI offers to master C programming. How can it help beginners as well as advanced programmers to improve their skills and make better and more efficient projects.

2. LITERATURE REVIEW

Most studies on AI assisted learning in programming agree on a couple of things. People that program with AI tend to be more productive and cleaner with their code writing, AI can help with completing repetitive tasks which removes extra work from developers (Cao, 2025). It also helps in creating completely unique programs based on the idea given by the person. The traditional way of learning C has been books, online tutorials and manually debugging codes. Books can be a really good way to learn the logic and syntax of C. Meanwhile tutorials can be used to apply the theoretical knowledge to practical projects. Tutorials offer people a way to learn C by watching videos which showcase how to write certain programs. Meanwhile debugging can be really helpful because it requires people to look at real codes and use their logic to try and find the errors. This can serve as experience that familiarizes people with C programming. These methods have some limitations however. If students use books, and are looking to find some quick information, they will have to scroll through hundreds of pages before they find what they are looking for. If they have any problems they don't have anyone to give them feedback (Ding et al., 2024). Learning this way will take much longer, and it might lead to them getting demotivated because of the slow progress.

AI platforms like ChatGPT are really helpful. They are like communicating with someone else. All students have to do is ask a question, any question and they will get the answer. AI can research all of the internet to give the correct answer. Furthermore, it can help students with creating unique and original projects by giving them advice on how they can apply their ideas to real projects. One of the big gaps in this research is finding where to draw to line on AI assistance in programming. At what point does it go from assisting students to making them rely on AI too often. There needs to be a way to use AI to help programmers improve without making them over reliant on it.

3. CHALLENGES IN LEARNING C PROGRAMMING

C syntax is very complex, especially if you don't have prior knowledge (He et al, 2022). Whether it is understanding which data type to use, how to set up a pointer properly, or allocating memory manually. Most beginners will struggle to figure out the syntax. The next big problem is the logic of the program. Programmers need to understand how to turn a problem into an algorithm. They need to create a set of instructions that get executed one by one, and in the end, give the answer to the problem. It takes time and experience to figure out how logically break down every problem. Some common mistakes include segmentation faults and type mismatches. The first happens when the program tries to access a memory that it doesn't have access to. This can be due to something like a faulty pointer. The other problem occurs when the data provided doesn't match the expected data. These problems can be confusing for beginners. There are not many resources we can use for interactive learning. Outside of having a person teaching you in real time, there isn't really a good way to get real time feedback. This makes the learning experience more challenging as you have to figure things out yourself. Since C lacks some important features, programmers have to implement their own manual solutions to solve problems (He et al,2022). This means problem-solving takes a lot of time because programmers need to come up with their own solutions even for more simple problems.

4. ROLE OF AI IN ADDRESSING THESE CHALLENGES

AI can give us simple codes that we can use as an example to understand the logic and the syntax of C. We can also ask questions about the sample code and the AI will explain further to make it easier to understand. We can give AI our programs and it will find any errors. It will point them out and then explain the correct syntax. If we have an idea for a program but we don't exactly know how to make it work, AI can finish it for us. We just explain our idea and AI can them complete the code, which makes turning ideas into real projects much easier.

AI can help us turn problems into algorithms. It can break it down into parts and explain how to solve them step by step. This can teach the programmers and also make the process faster. AI can be used to guide programmers through problem-solving (Jiang, 2021). It can be used to give tips to make the process of figuring problems out much easier. A great feature of AIs is the fact they give personalized answers. Based on what you ask and the words you use, AI will personalize its feedback and hints to make you understand better.

You can give AI feedback by saying what you understand and what is confusing you. This will make the AI change the way it explains things to you. If you are lost, it will slow down to help you catch up, and if you are doing well, it can start explaining more complex things. At the end of every session, AI can give programmers a quick test. It could be theoretical questions, or giving them a program to code. This can help by testing the programmer's skills and helping them understand where they are struggling.

AI can be used to find syntax and logical errors with the program (Liu et al., 2024). It can also explain how to fix them and how to avoid making the same mistake. AI can also be used to analyze the performance of our code. For most coding problems, there are multiple solutions. AI can be used to explain how we can make the code shorter to improve its performance.

5. COMPARATIVE ANALYSIS

AI-assisted learning tends to be more successful than the traditional methods. It is faster, easier to understand and it helps students become much better programmers. Meanwhile the traditional way is much slower and tedious. Students that learn C with AI tools tend to became better programmers. They work faster, have more knowledge and are able to move on to advanced projects much quicker (Shaveta, 2018).

Key metrics: learning time, error rate, project completion speed, satisfaction level

Students that use AI tool are able to learn much quicker than students who read books, as they can access information faster. Since they use AI for debugging, they also learn how to debug faster which allows them to complete projects quicker than regular students. All this leads to them feeling more satisfied and motivated, compared to other students who might feel demotivated because of the struggles and slow progress. C is a popular programming language, it was created over 50 years ago, however programming as a whole has changed a lot since then, especially with the addition of AI. Since C can be a difficult language to learn, especially for beginners, I want to explore how AI can help to fix those issues.

The first obvious problem you will have with any programming language is learning the syntax. If you're just starting out in programming, compared to some other languages, C syntax will be quite difficult to learn. Thankfully, AI can help massively with this problem (Yao et al, 2022). AI can help us learn C by giving us sample codes and explaining the syntax and logic. It can also give us some coding problems that we can try to solve ourselves, and if we have any problems with the code itself, the AI can point those out, explain why they're wrong and how we can fix them. See, logic is one of the biggest parts of programming. Programming is not just about the syntax, it's also about the logic needed to solve the problem. Let's say we have to create a program that counts numbers from 1-12, we can use a For loop to do that, but it's not just about the syntax, it's about how we can use the syntax to solve the given problem. AI can explain that in this scenario we use an int variable that starts at 1 and goes until 12 to show the numbers. AI can be used as a personal teacher for beginners as well as advanced programmers.

AI is also a massive time-saver. Before AI, if your C program had a problem, or you were looking for some extra information, you would have to go through hundreds of book pages, or spend a lot of time using search engines to find what you were looking for. AI is much quicker. Firstly, all it takes to use AI is an internet connection. You can access it from anywhere in the world, all you need is a device connected to the internet(Yu et al, 2024). Furthermore, AI can search all of the internet to give us the answer to our question. Sometimes, when we are making an original C programming project, it can be difficult to find the solution to our problem because it might not be a popular issue. However, with AI no matter what the issue is, it can help us find the solution and get our code to work. That's a massive time-saver which in the long term can help us do 2-3 extra C projects in the same amount of time that we would usually do one project. However, C also has some fundamental issues, which is why C++ was created. Firstly, C is a low-level language, so it has direct access to our device's memory, which means if we're not careful with the code that we execute, we might cause ourselves some massive problems. AI can help with this since it can be used as a debugging tool, which finds any problems with the code and solves them for us.

Another big problem with C is the memory allocation. One of the first things you might notice is that when you add an int number with a float number, you might get an incorrect result, this is because of the way C handles memory. This problem cannot be fixed, which means AI can only warn you to avoid certain lines of code, but it cannot directly solve the issue. The memory problems don't end there, C also allows programmers to allocate the memory themselves (Zu et al., 2025). It goes without saying that if you don't know how to allocate memory you could cause yourself many issues. Though, in this case AI can help us by teaching us how to allocate memory ourselves and pointing out any problems our code might have.

The final big problem with C is the lack of object-oriented programming. This means we don't have access to classes, objects and many other features which makes managing bigger projects much more difficult. AI can potentially help us work around these problems, but there isn't much it can do to fully solve the lack of OOP, which is the reason C++ exists. To conclude, AI can help us learn C quickly and easily. It can be used a teacher and as a debugger. However, there are fundamental problems that it cannot solve, but it might help us by giving us ways to work around the problems (Podder et al., 2022).

Figure 1. How we can use AI to make C programming easier

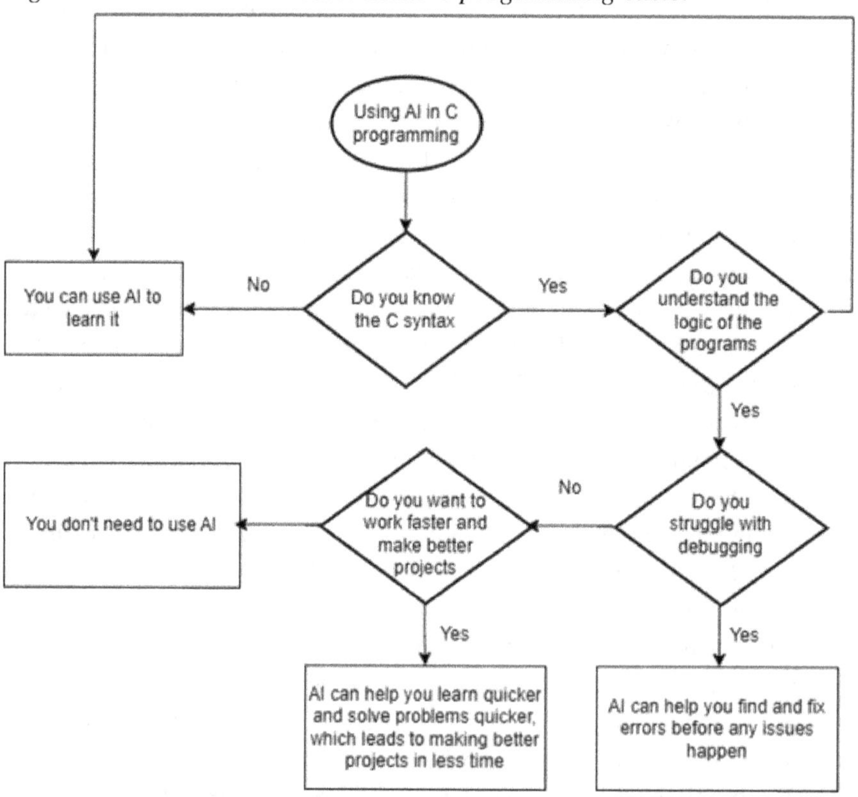

AI is really good at making C programming easier. We can use AI to learn C from scratch. We can learn the basic syntax and logic behind every program. We can also use it for more advanced work. We use it to debug projects which saves a lot of time. Debugging can be one of the most time-consuming tasks in programming. However, if we use AI we can debug our whole projects in only a few minutes which leads to us being able to work on more projects (Gundu et al., 2022).

Figure 2. How AI can help with the fundamental problems of C

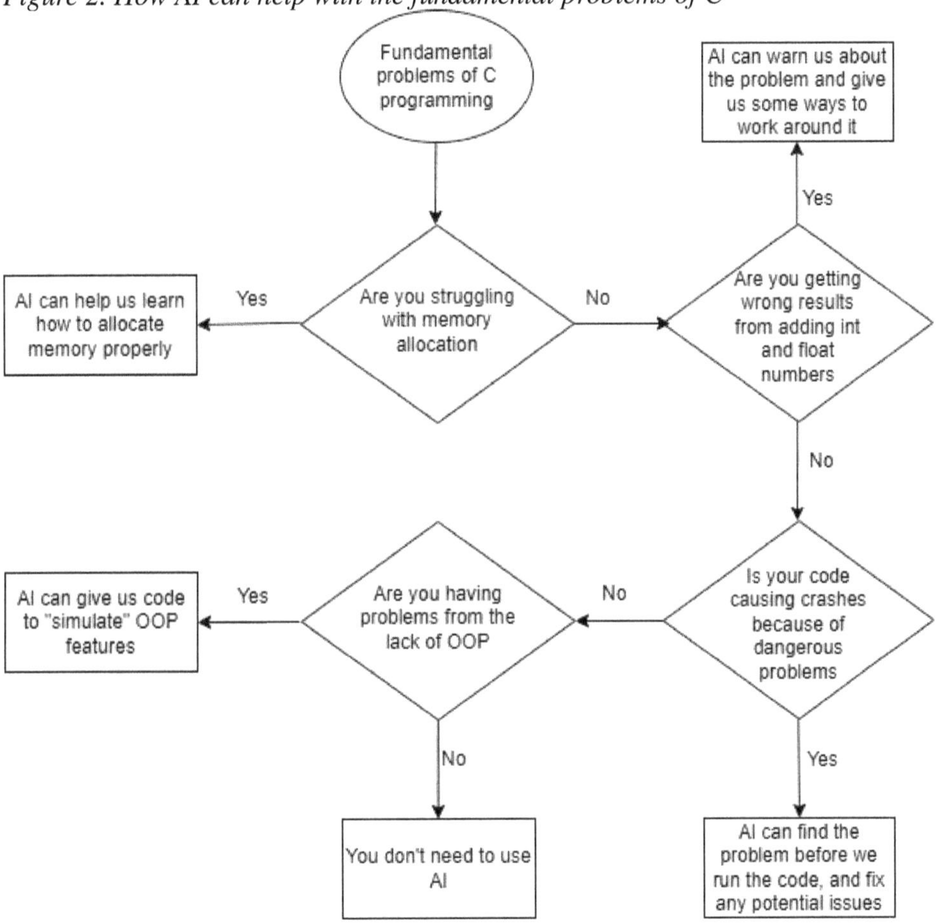

C has some fundamental issues that cannot be directly fixed. For example, adding an int and a float can give wrong results because of the way those variables are handled in the memory. AI can warn us and give us some tips on how to avoid the problem but it won't be a clear-cut fix. Since C has direct access to our hardware, bad code can cause crashes. Thankfully, AI can detect those issues beforehand and fix them before anything bad happens (Muloor et al., 2024). The lack of OOP is a big problem for C and AI cannot do much, but it can give us some codes to "simulate" OOP features.

6. DISCUSSION

AI has many features as mentioned before, this has made it have a big impact on programming education. It is now a tool that is used by most students and it has completely changed the way that students learn things (Kaushik et al., 2022). Using AI benefits both beginners and advanced learners. It can help beginners understand the language much quicker, but it can also help advanced programmers with optimizing their codes and creating bigger, more advanced projects. The main worry with AI is that students will become over-reliant on AI. This means that instead of using it learn they will use it to cheat. They will just use AI do to their homework and exams and not actually learn anything. They just copy and paste information, and if they were to stop using AI, they would not be able to program themselves. In the future we might see things like AI tutors, which can help students learn through one-on-one teaching. We might also see it integrated into the curriculum. Perhaps teachers will use AI to help students learn more effectively, which will make the learning process quicker (Singh et al., 2024). This would be a really good thing as it would allow students to become advanced programmers quicker than they could before.

REFERENCES

Cao, Y. (2025, April 3). C: Unifying programming and verification in C. arXiv. https://doi.org//arXiv.2504.02246DOI: 10.48550

Ding, X., Liu, M., & Hu, S. (2024). Exploration of Teaching Reform in C Language Programming Course under the Background of New Engineering. *Frontiers in Humanities and Social Sciences*, *4*(7), 56–59. DOI: 10.54691/tp1vv609

Gundu, S. R., Charanarur, P., Chandelkar, K. K., Samanta, D., Poonia, R. C., & Chakraborty, P. (2022). Sixth-generation (6G) mobile cloud security and privacy risks for AI system using high-performance computing implementation. *Wireless Communications and Mobile Computing*, *2022*(1), 4397610. Advance online publication. DOI: 10.1155/2022/4397610

He, X., Song, Y., Du, Y., Huang, Y., Yin, X., & Long, X. (2022). Research on teaching reform of C programming language course for deep integration of professional fields. *Open Journal of Social Sciences*, *10*(1), 267–275. DOI: 10.4236/jss.2022.101022

Jiang, Y. (2021). Design optimization and application analysis of embedded C program. *Journal of Networking and Telecommunications*, *3*(1), 5–7. DOI: 10.18282/jnt.v3i1.1943

Kaushik, S., Poonia, R. C., Khatri, S. K., Samanta, D., & Chakraborty, P. (2022). Transmit range adjustment using artificial intelligence for enhancement of location privacy and data security in service location protocol of VANET. *Wireless Communications and Mobile Computing*, *2022*(1), 9642774. Advance online publication. DOI: 10.1155/2022/9642774

Liu, D. (2024). Application of neuroscience in C language teaching research. *Applied & Educational Psychology*, *5*(5), 158–162. DOI: 10.23977/appep.2024.050522

Muloor, K., Sahu, S. K., Behera, T. K., & Samanta, D. (2024). Computational intelligence in communication networks: Classification, clustering, reinforcement learning, deep learning. In Patnaik, S. K., Gao, X.-Z., & Biswal, B. (Eds.), *Intelligent communication networks* (pp. 221–236). CRC Press., DOI: 10.1201/9781003303114-10

Podder, S. K., Thomas, B., & Samanta, D. (2022). Impact of innovative technology on quality education: The resourceful intelligence for smart society development. In A. Kumar & N. R. Das (Eds.), *Machine intelligence and data science applications: Proceedings of MIDAS 2021* (Vol. 132, pp. 293–304). Springer. https://doi.org/DOI: 10.10054/MIDA.2022.293

Singh, D. P., Gupta, S., Ganesh, D., Sharma, S., Kalnawat, A., Pramanik, S., & Samanta, D. (2024). Technologies that Work Together for Precision Agriculture. In *Data Driven Mathematical Modeling in Agriculture* (pp. 367–388). River Publishers. DOI: 10.1201/9781003515883-17

Yao, D., Zhang, X., & Liu, Y. (2022). Teaching Reform in C Programming Course from the Perspective of Sustainable Development: Construction and 9-Year Practice of "Three Classrooms–Four Integrations–Five Combinations" Teaching Model. *Sustainability (Basel)*, *14*(22), 15226. DOI: 10.3390/su142215226

Yu, M., & Ming, Z. (2024). Research on the reform of C language programming teaching based on the training of new engineering talents. *Advances in Vocational and Technical Education*, *6*(2), 1–8. DOI: 10.23977/avte.2024.060201

Zu, B., Wang, H., Chen, H., & Li, Y. (2025). Adapting high-level language programming (C language) education in the era of large language models. *Journal of Contemporary Educational Research*, *9*(5), 264–269. DOI: 10.26689/jcer.v9i5.10508

Chapter 5
Global Regulatory Landscape:
The European Union AI Act Comparative International Perspectives

Chrisella Natasia Tanujaya
https://orcid.org/0009-0001-0549-368X
Universitas Esa Unggul, Indonesia

Binastya Anggara Sekti
https://orcid.org/0000-0001-5489-4888
Universitas Esa Unggul, Indonesia

ABSTRACT

The global regulatory landscape of Artificial Intelligence (AI) is rapidly evolving to balance innovation with ethics, accountability, and human rights. This chapter examines the development of AI governance worldwide, emphasizing the European Union Artificial Intelligence Act (EU AI Act) as the first comprehensive, rights-based legal framework. Through its risk-based classification unacceptable, high, limited, and minimal, the EU model safeguards human dignity while promoting responsible innovation. A comparative analysis of the United States, Canada, China, India, Singapore, and Brazil reveals both convergence in core ethical principles and divergence in implementation due to cultural and political differences. The chapter concludes by advocating for a Global AI Accord to harmonize universal values with local contexts, fostering trustworthy, ethical, and sustainable AI governance.

DOI: 10.4018/979-8-3373-7011-8.ch005

ht © 2026, IGI Global Scientific Publishing. Copying or distributing in print or electronic forms without written permission of IGI Global Scientific Publishing is prohibited. Use of this chapter to generative artificial intelligence (AI) technologies is expressly prohibited. The publisher reserves all rights to license its use for generative AI training and machine learning model development.

1. INTRODUCTION

Artificial Intelligence (AI) has rapidly evolved into a central pillar of global digital transformation, reshaping economies, governance systems, and the very fabric of social interaction. From predictive analytics and autonomous systems to generative models and decision-support tools, AI technologies are redefining how societies operate and how individuals engage with information. Despite its immense e potential to accelerate innovation, productivity, and sustainability, AI simultaneously introduces profound ethical, legal, and societal challenges. Concerns over algorithmic bias, mass surveillance, data misuse, and the erosion of human autonomy have intensified debates about the balance between technological progress and human rights protection. In this context, the demand for a comprehensive governance framework that ensures AI's alignment with democratic values, social trust, and public accountability has become more urgent than ever (Beltrán, 2025).

Among global regulatory initiatives, the European Union Artificial Intelligence Act (EU AI Act) stands as a historic milestone. As the world's first comprehensive legal framework dedicated solely to AI, it embodies a risk-based and human-rights-centered approach to the regulation of intelligent systems. The EU AI Act classifies AI applications according to levels of risk—ranging from minimal to unacceptable—thereby ensuring proportionate oversight without stifling innovation. This structured model of governance seeks to strike a careful equilibrium: promoting technological advancement while upholding fundamental rights, transparency, and ethical integrity. It reflects the EU's broader vision of "trustworthy AI," emphasizing principles such as fairness, explainability, and human oversight (Bakiner, 2023).

However, the European framework does not exist in isolation. Around the world, nations are crafting their own legislative and ethical approaches to manage AI's rapid proliferation. The United States emphasizes innovation and voluntary ethical commitments through its AI Bill of Rights; Canada promotes accountability and fairness via the Artificial Intelligence and Data Act (AIDA); China integrates AI regulation with cybersecurity and state security imperatives; India advances its Digital Personal Data Protection Act (DPDP) to ensure responsible data use; Singapore adopts a non-binding but influential AI Governance Framework; and Brazil upholds digital rights and inclusion in its AI principles. Together, these frameworks illustrate both the diversity and convergence of global regulatory efforts—where cultural values, political priorities, and legal traditions shape distinct pathways toward responsible AI governance.

Figure 1. Global AI Regulatory Landscape

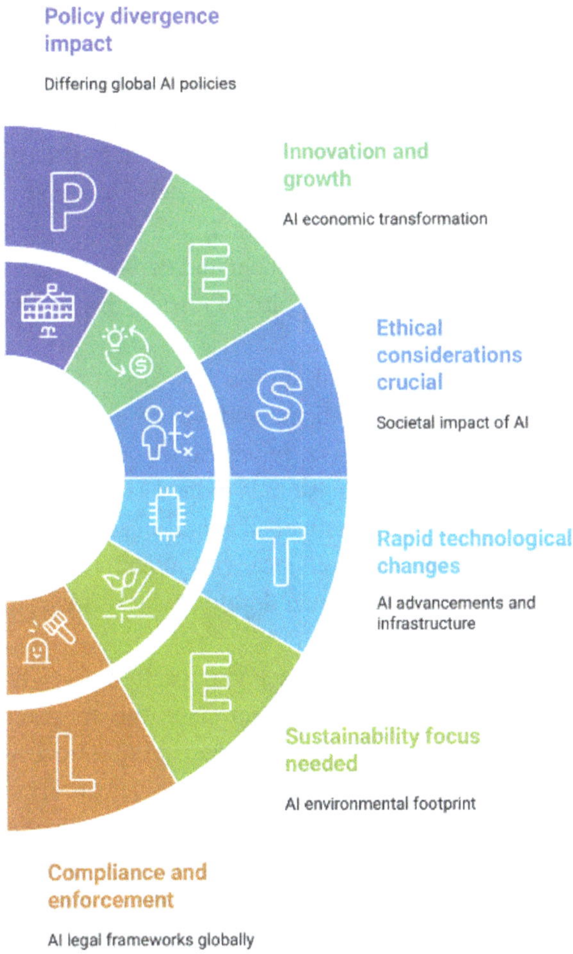

This chapter explores the global regulatory landscape of AI through a comparative lens, focusing on the European Union AI Act as a benchmark for ethical and legal innovation. It systematically examines how various international frameworks interpret core governance values—such as accountability, transparency, privacy, and fairness—and how these values interact in an increasingly interconnected digital ecosystem. Furthermore, it investigates the emerging patterns of convergence and divergence among global AI regulations, offering insights into the challenges of interoperability, enforcement, and transnational compliance (Mooghali et al., 2024). Ultimately, this discussion aims to illuminate how the evolution of AI governance can foster social trust, safeguard human dignity, and promote an inclusive digital future that aligns innovation with moral responsibility.

2. THEORETICAL AND ETHICAL FOUNDATIONS OF AI GOVERNANCE

The governance of Artificial Intelligence (AI) is not merely a matter of law and policy; it also involves fundamental moral, social, and philosophical questions. As a technology that influences nearly every aspect of modern life from the economy and government to social interactions, AI presents new challenges in ensuring that innovation remains aligned with human values. In this context, ethics serves as the normative foundation guiding the development and deployment of AI systems, ensuring they do not deviate from the principles of justice, responsibility, and respect for human rights (Gorski et al., 2025).

Theoretically, three primary ethical approaches form the basis of modern AI regulation: deontology, consequentialism, and virtue ethics. The deontological approach emphasizes the importance of moral duties and non-negotiable human rights. Within this framework, an AI system is judged as ethical not by the benefits it produces, but by its adherence to universal moral norms. For instance, a facial recognition system used for mass surveillance without individual consent is considered a violation of the principle of human dignity, even if it is claimed to enhance public security.

Meanwhile, the consequentialist approach views actions as right or wrong based on their outcomes for social welfare. In AI governance, this approach deems a policy ethical if it maximizes benefits for society at large and minimizes social risks. For example, the use of AI in healthcare for early disease detection can be considered moral if it demonstrably improves patient safety, accelerates diagnosis, and reduces medical errors. However, consequentialism also demands careful consideration of potential negative impacts, such as algorithmic bias, which could lead to inequities in access to healthcare. Thus, balancing efficiency and justice becomes a critical aspect of applying this approach.

Virtue ethics, on the other hand, focuses on the moral character and responsibilities of the actors who create and manage AI technology. This approach holds that the integrity, honesty, and social responsibility of developers and institutions are essential elements in creating trustworthy AI systems. Virtue ethics demands that moral values be embedded from the algorithm design stage, not merely applied as post-deployment regulations. This is what has become known as the principle of ethics-by-design—the integration of human values into the technology's architecture. In an institutional context, this approach requires a long-term commitment to transparency, data openness, and human oversight throughout the entire lifecycle of the AI system.

These three ethical approaches are mutually complementary in formulating ideal AI governance. Deontology provides a universal moral framework, consequentialism highlights social impact, while virtue ethics underscores the moral responsibilities of individuals and institutions. Together, they contribute to the formation of the principles of Trustworthy AI, which have now become a global benchmark. International organizations such as the OECD and IEEE have developed AI governance guidelines that emphasize values like transparency, fairness, privacy, security, and accountability. The OECD, for example, introduced five core pillars in its Principles on Artificial Intelligence: inclusive growth and sustainable development, respect for human-centered values, transparency, technical robustness and safety, and accountability. These principles affirm that AI technology must be designed to strengthen, not replace, existing democratic and social values (Agbese et al., 2023).

The IEEE further reinforces the ethical approach through its Ethically Aligned Design framework, which stresses the importance of human oversight in algorithmic decision-making processes. This approach promotes the concepts of privacy-by-design and transparency-by-design, which are efforts to embed the values of privacy and openness into systems from their initial development. Consequently, ethical governance becomes the responsibility not only of regulators and policymakers but also a technical duty for the engineers and data scientists who create the technology.

Furthermore, the European Union, through its High-Level Expert Group on Artificial Intelligence (HLEG-AI), introduced the Ethics Guidelines for Trustworthy AI, which assert that AI systems must meet three primary criteria: they must be lawful, ethical, and socially and technically robust. These guidelines outline seven key principles: human agency and oversight, technical robustness and safety, privacy and data governance, transparency, diversity, non-discrimination and fairness, societal and environmental well-being, and accountability (Palladino, 2023).

Ethics in AI governance not only guides regulation but also builds social trust. Public confidence is a crucial element in the successful adoption of any new technology. Without trust, society may view AI as an opaque, intimidating, or even potentially oppressive threat. Therefore, effective regulation creates not only legal certainty but also moral legitimacy, which can strengthen social acceptance. Regulations such as the impact assessment requirement in the EU AI Act, for example, are not merely administrative procedures but also ethical mechanisms to ensure that developers understand the potential societal consequences of the systems they create.

Social trust in AI also has economic and geopolitical dimensions. Nations or regions that succeed in building an ethical and transparent AI ecosystem tend to gain a positive reputation and a competitive advantage in the global market. The European regulatory model, based on human-centric values, has given rise to a phenomenon known as the Brussels Effect, where the EU's ethical and legal standards influence policies in other countries worldwide. Thus, ethical AI governance is not only a moral imperative but also a geopolitical and economic strategy for shaping global digital leadership.

3. THE RISE OF AI AND THE NEED FOR GLOBAL REGULATION

The advancement of Artificial Intelligence (AI) has propelled humanity into a new era of technological revolution, transforming not only the way we work but also how we think and interact. AI is no longer merely a tool for automation; it has evolved into a global cognitive infrastructure that transcends national borders, cultures, and industrial sectors. With its capacity to learn, reason, and make autonomous decisions based on big data, AI has the potential to extraordinarily accelerate economic progress and social efficiency. However, this progress has also given rise to a new form of power—data power—which is concentrated in the hands of a few global corporate entities and technologically advanced nations. This imbalance of data-driven power has become the primary catalyst for the demand for fair, ethical, and transparent global governance and regulation (Beltrán, 2025).

This data power imbalance stems from the immense capability of global corporations to collect, analyze, and monetize the personal data of billions of users worldwide. Data has become an economic resource more valuable than oil, as declared by The Economist in 2017 under the headline, "The world's most valuable resource is no longer oil, but data." Technology giants such as Google, Amazon, Meta, Microsoft, and Alibaba control the vast majority of the digital infrastructure and machine learning algorithms that dictate the direction of global innovation. They operate AI systems capable of predicting human behavior, influencing public opinion, and even affecting political outcomes through information manipulation. This situation creates a significant information asymmetry, where individuals are reduced to data objects with little to no control over how their information is collected, processed, and utilized for commercial or political ends.

This phenomenon has sparked serious concern among academics, policymakers, and civil society. As AI algorithms begin to play a role in critical decision-making—such as job recruitment, credit scoring, security surveillance, and judicial systems—fundamental questions about fairness, accountability, and transparency have emerged. Are the decisions made by AI genuinely neutral? Who is responsible when an algorithm makes a mistake or perpetuates discrimination? How can we ensure that these systems do not violate fundamental human rights? These questions underscore the reality that AI technology cannot be left to evolve without adequate moral and legal oversight (Solaiman et al., 2025).

In the global context, various international organizations have begun to recognize the urgency of establishing cross-border AI governance. The United Nations (UN), through agencies like UNESCO and the International Telecommunication Union (ITU), has initiated numerous forums to discuss ethical standards and regulations for AI. In 2021, UNESCO adopted the Recommendation on the Ethics of Artificial Intelligence, a landmark document emphasizing principles of fairness, accountability, privacy, and non-discrimination in AI development. This document was agreed upon by over 190 member states and represents one of the first steps toward a global ethical consensus. However, it remains a recommendation rather than a legally binding regulation.

Alongside UNESCO, the Organisation for Economic Co-operation and Development (OECD) has played a pivotal role through its OECD Principles on Artificial Intelligence, released in 2019. These principles later formed the basis for the G20 AI Principles, demonstrating that awareness of the need for AI governance has expanded to global economic forums. The OECD stresses the importance of developing AI that is oriented towards human well-being, grounded in democratic values, and equipped with clear accountability mechanisms. Nevertheless, the implementation of these principles still largely depends on the national policies of individual countries, making their effectiveness difficult to measure consistently.

Meanwhile, the Group of Seven (G7) has also placed the issue of AI on its main agenda in recent years. At the 2023 G7 Hiroshima Summit, world leaders announced an initiative known as the Hiroshima AI Process, aimed at developing governance standards for generative AI and strengthening global digital security. The primary focus of this initiative includes the transparency of AI models, data protection, and the prevention of technology misuse for disinformation purposes. However, like other multilateral forums, the G7's greatest challenge is to create an agreement that is inclusive and applicable beyond the scope of developed nations.

This divergence in approaches highlights two major poles in the global AI regulation landscape: the European model, based on values and human rights, versus the Asian model, based on control and security. Each reflects a different social and political philosophy. The European model places the individual at the center of technology governance, whereas the Asian model tends to prioritize collective stability and state sovereignty. In this context, the greatest challenge in creating global governance lies not in technical aspects but in differing value paradigms and geopolitical interests.

Developing countries, on the other hand, face a dual dilemma in AI adoption. On one hand, they seek to leverage AI to accelerate economic development, improve public services, and expand digital inclusion. On the other, limited resources, inadequate legal infrastructure, and the dominance of foreign companies render them vulnerable to technological dependency. Therefore, global AI regulation must incorporate the principle of digital equity to ensure that every nation has a balanced right and capacity to govern and benefit from this technology.

Various academics have proposed collaborative models for global AI governance. One widely discussed proposal is the establishment of a Global AI Governance Framework under the coordination of the UN, similar to the role of the Intergovernmental Panel on Climate Change (IPCC) on climate issues (Wagner et al., 2024).

Such an institution could serve as a normative body to coordinate research, draft ethical guidelines, and facilitate cross-border cooperation. Additionally, some experts have suggested the concept of an AI Accord, a binding international treaty akin to the Paris Agreement, focusing on the collective responsibility of nations to manage AI risks ethically and sustainably.

However, the path toward global regulation is fraught with complex obstacles. First, the wide technological gap between developed and developing nations creates disparities in regulatory capacity. Developed countries possess the resources and technical expertise to implement high security standards, whereas developing nations often remain passive users of technology without the ability to effectively supervise algorithms. Second, there are concerns that overly strict global regulations could stifle innovation, particularly for small and medium-sized enterprises. Third, the dominance of global tech corporations in AI development creates economic and political pressure against the formation of truly independent international ethical standards.

To overcome these challenges, a multi-stakeholder approach is key. Governments, the private sector, academic institutions, and civil society must all play an active role in designing inclusive and adaptive AI governance. Governments are tasked with creating legal and supervisory frameworks, industry is responsible for implementing the principles of ethics-by-design, academics are charged with conducting independent research on the social and technical impacts of AI, and civil society serves as the guardian of ethics and human rights. It is through this cross-sector collaboration that a global AI governance system can be created that is not only legally legitimate but also morally just and sustainable.

Ultimately, the emergence of AI as a dominant force in the global digital transformation demands a new paradigm in international regulation. AI regulation cannot be understood merely as a legal instrument; it must be viewed as a collective endeavor to balance power between humans and machines, between innovation and responsibility, and between economic interests and humanitarian values. The world needs a governance framework capable of directing AI development toward the global common good, not merely the benefit of a select few.

4. THE EUROPEAN UNION AI ACT: A RIGHTS-BASED AND RISK-BASED APPROACH

The European Union (EU) has emerged as a pioneer in establishing a comprehensive legal framework to govern Artificial Intelligence (AI) through the European Union Artificial Intelligence Act, commonly known as the EU AI Act. This regulation stands as the world's first explicit legislative initiative designed to ensure that the development and deployment of AI are conducted safely, ethically, and with full respect for fundamental human rights. As a component of Europe's broader digital strategy, which includes the General Data Protection Regulation (GDPR) and the Digital Services Act, the EU AI Act solidifies Europe's position as a center for value-based technology governance (Salim et al., 2024). Through this legislation, the EU seeks to enforce the principle of "Trustworthy AI" by employing a dual approach grounded in both human rights (a rights-based approach) and risk assessment (a risk-based approach).

The rights-based approach asserts that every individual possesses an inherent right to protection from the misuse of technology that could infringe upon human dignity and freedom. Within this framework, the EU AI Act is rooted in the European Charter of Fundamental Rights, which guarantees rights to privacy, non-discrimination, freedom of expression, and protection against automated decision-making that could be detrimental to individuals. This principle reflects the "human-centric AI" paradigm, which posits that technology must serve humanity, not the other way around. Consequently, the EU AI Act is not merely a technical regulation but also a political and moral declaration that digital innovation must be subordinate to universal humanitarian principles.

Meanwhile, the risk-based approach is the regulation's primary innovation. The EU recognizes that not all AI systems pose the same level of risk to society. Therefore, the EU AI Act introduces a proportional risk classification framework, ensuring that the regulation is not a "one-size-fits-all" solution. This model allows for differentiated levels of oversight and legal obligations based on the potential risk posed by a specific AI application. There are four main categories in this classification system: unacceptable-risk, high-risk, limited-risk, and minimal-risk AI.

The high-risk AI category includes systems that have a significant impact on fundamental rights, public safety, or critical decision-making processes for individuals. Examples of applications in this category include AI systems used in job recruitment, credit evaluation, the management of critical infrastructure (such as transport and energy), and academic assessment systems. Developers and providers of high-risk AI systems are obligated to meet a series of stringent requirements, including: (1) ensuring the quality and non-bias of training data, (2) providing detailed technical documentation, (3) maintaining transparency and explainability of algorithms, (4) implementing mechanisms for human oversight, and (5) conducting a conformity assessment before the product is marketed in the EU. These requirements are designed to ensure that AI systems operate safely, fairly, and are auditable.

The limited-risk AI category covers applications that do not directly threaten safety or fundamental rights but could influence individual behavior or public trust. Examples include chatbots, algorithm-based product recommendation systems, and virtual assistants. In this category, developers are subject to transparency obligations, meaning they must inform users that they are interacting with an AI system. The objective is to prevent confusion between human and machine interactions and maintain clarity of information for consumers.

The minimal-risk AI category comprises the vast majority of AI systems used in daily life that pose no significant risk, such as spam filters, AI-based games, or non-sensitive personalization features. Systems in this category do not require strict regulation, although they are still encouraged to adhere to general ethical principles like transparency and data security. This category is thus designed to foster innovation without excessive bureaucratic impediments.

Finally, the unacceptable-risk AI category includes systems that inherently violate fundamental human rights and democratic values. Applications in this category are completely banned throughout the EU territory. Examples include systems for mass biometric surveillance, government-led social scoring (such as that implemented in China), manipulation of behavior that is harmful to users, and systems that exploit the vulnerabilities of children or other vulnerable groups. This approach affirms that there are ethical boundaries that must not be crossed in the use of technology, regardless of the potential economic benefits.

The risk classification model in the EU AI Act demonstrates a careful balance between fostering innovation and ensuring social protection. The regulation is not intended to hinder technological development but to create legal certainty, allowing innovators to operate within clear ethical boundaries. With a proportional risk framework, AI developers can understand their obligations from the outset of the design process, while the public is assured that circulating technologies have undergone rigorous safety and fairness assessments.

Furthermore, the EU AI Act introduces the concepts of AI conformity assessment and CE marking for AI systems—a certification process ensuring that an AI system has complied with all security and ethical standards before being marketed. High-risk systems, for example, must undergo an external audit by a conformity assessment body recognized by the EU. This audit evaluates not only technical aspects like algorithmic accuracy but also social dimensions such as the potential for discrimination and privacy violations. This approach demonstrates that AI reliability is not just a technical matter but also an ethical and legal one.

In addition to certification mechanisms, the EU AI Act also emphasizes institutional transparency and accountability. Developers are required to provide public documentation on how their AI systems operate, including the data sources used, training methodologies, and bias mitigation procedures. Within organizations, companies must appoint a compliance officer or an internal supervisory body to continuously monitor the ethical performance of AI. This aligns with the principle of ethics-by-design, which advocates for the integration of moral values throughout the technology development process.

From a legal perspective, the EU AI Act also establishes legal liability for developers and providers of AI systems. If an AI system causes harm to an individual—whether through discrimination, erroneous decision-making, or privacy infringement—the developer can be held legally accountable. This mechanism enhances public security while simultaneously incentivizing the industry to be more diligent in designing safe and fair AI systems.

More broadly, the EU AI Act also functions as a tool of global technology diplomacy. By imposing strict legal standards on AI products entering the European market, the EU indirectly exports its ethical values to other countries—a phenomenon known as the Brussels Effect. Nations outside the EU that wish to access the European market are compelled to adapt their products to meet the standards of the EU AI Act. In the long term, this has the potential to create a global convergence toward more ethical and human-centric principles of AI governance.

Nevertheless, the implementation of the EU AI Act faces several practical challenges. First, the technical complexity of assessing AI risks requires cross-disciplinary expertise in law, technology, and ethics. Second, the audit and certification processes may impose additional costs on small and medium-sized enterprises, potentially widening the innovation gap between large corporations and startups. Third, the application of the "explainability" principle remains a technical issue that is not yet fully resolved, given that many AI models operate as "black boxes." Consequently, the EU is also promoting further research in interpretable AI and AI governance tools to support the regulation's execution.

In a geopolitical context, the EU AI Act reflects Europe's effort to assert its technological sovereignty. Amid the dominance of American tech companies and the expansion of Chinese AI, the EU is positioning itself as a "global ethics guardian." Through this policy, Europe sends a message that digital success is measured not by how quickly technology develops, but by the extent to which it strengthens human dignity and democratic values. This rights-based and risk-based approach marks a paradigm shift from techno-solutionism toward value-oriented governance, where social sustainability is the primary priority in technological innovation.

In conclusion, the EU AI Act is more than just a regulation; it is a symbol of global ethical evolution in the face of the AI revolution. By balancing the freedom to innovate with the protection of human rights, this law sets a new standard for global technology governance. It teaches that digital progress is meaningless if not accompanied by moral responsibility. The regulation affirms that public trust is the primary capital in the AI ecosystem, and only through a legal framework that is fair, transparent, and human-centric can the world build a truly trustworthy technological future.

5. A COMPARATIVE INTERNATIONAL PERSPECTIVE

The regulation of artificial intelligence (AI) is evolving diversely across the globe, reflecting the distinct values, political systems, and socioeconomic orientations of each nation. Although many countries agree that AI must be developed responsibly, their interpretations and applications of this principle vary significantly. Through this analysis, it becomes clear that while no single model is considered ideal, there is a trend towards normative convergence in ethical aspects and practical divergence in policy and enforcement (Aiyankovil et al., 2024).

The United States has adopted an approach that emphasizes freedom of innovation and voluntary responsibility, as outlined in the "Blueprint for an AI Bill of Rights" released by the White House Office of Science and Technology Policy (OSTP) in 2022. While not a legally binding statute, the AI Bill of Rights serves as a national ethical guide, asserting five core principles: (1) AI systems should be safe and effective; (2) protections against algorithmic discrimination should be in place; (3) user data privacy must be respected; (4) users have the right to know when they are interacting with an automated system; and (5) the public should have the option to opt out of AI use in high-impact decisions. This approach reflects quintessentially American liberal values, where innovation is viewed as the primary engine of economic growth and the government's role is limited to light-touch regulation (Aiyankovil et al., 2024).

However, this voluntary approach has drawn criticism for being insufficient to address the societal impacts of AI, such as the spread of disinformation, algorithmic bias, and technological monopolies. Consequently, several states, including California and Illinois, have begun to establish stricter policies, including rules on biometric privacy and algorithmic transparency. Furthermore, agencies like the National Institute of Standards and Technology (NIST) have developed the AI Risk Management Framework (RMF) to help organizations identify and manage AI risks. Overall, regulation in the U.S. reflects a complex balance between market freedom and social responsibility, with the government acting as an ethical facilitator rather than an innovation controller.

Meanwhile, Canada has become one of the first nations to integrate human rights principles directly into its digital innovation policy. Through the proposed Artificial Intelligence and Data Act (AIDA), introduced in 2022, Canada aims to create a governance system that places social responsibility at its core. AIDA would require companies developing or deploying high-risk AI systems to conduct impact assessments on safety, privacy, and discriminatory bias prior to implementation.

Canada's approach can be categorized as a "hybrid regulation" model, combining binding legal aspects with flexible ethical guidelines. This model aligns with Canadian values that emphasize social justice and inclusivity. AIDA focuses not only on individual protections but also on collective justice, such as ensuring equitable access to technology and preventing the marginalization of minority groups. In the global context, Canada's approach is often lauded as a moderate effort that bridges the stringent European model and the more lenient American one.

In contrast to Western models, China has adopted an approach rooted in a paradigm of national security and social control. The Chinese government situates AI regulation within the ideological frameworks of "stable development" and "data sovereignty," where the state acts as the primary controller of technology's direction (Göksal et al., 2024). Through a series of regulations such as the AI Algorithmic Recommendation Provisions (2022), the Deep Synthesis Regulations (2023), and the Generative AI Measures (2024), China governs nearly every aspect of AI development, from algorithm design to content distribution.

This approach offers advantages in policy speed and certainty but also raises criticism regarding freedom of expression and individual privacy. The government holds broad authority to review, censor, or restrict algorithms deemed politically risky. On the positive side, China has successfully integrated AI into the public sector on a massive scale, including in smart transportation systems, health surveillance, and smart city management. The Chinese model demonstrates that AI governance can be used as a strategic state instrument to achieve national political and economic objectives (Zhang & Zhang, 2023).

India is pursuing a different path, focusing on personal data protection as the foundation of its AI governance. With the Digital Personal Data Protection Act (DPDP) of 2023, India has strengthened individual rights to privacy and control over their data. Although this law does not specifically regulate AI, its principles have direct implications for algorithmic systems that rely on large volumes of personal data. The DPDP mandates that companies obtain explicit user consent, prohibits data misuse, and establishes severe penalties for violations.

The Indian government has also developed the "AI for All" initiative, which focuses on digital inclusivity and AI-driven economic development. This approach emphasizes the use of AI for social objectives, such as smart agriculture, adaptive education, and healthcare services in rural areas. India seeks to position AI as a tool for development, not merely as a technology industry. Thus, India's approach represents a balance between innovation and social justice, while also championing digital sovereignty amid the dominance of foreign corporations.

In Southeast Asia, Singapore stands out as a successful example of applying soft law, or non-binding regulation, through its AI Governance Framework, launched by the Infocomm Media Development Authority (IMDA) in 2019. This framework provides practical guidance for companies to implement AI ethics principles without imposing heavy legal burdens. The key principles it promotes include transparency, explainability, fairness, data security, and human-in-the-loop for decision-making processes.

Singapore's approach focuses on a partnership between government and industry to create an AI ecosystem that is innovative yet ethical. The government provides a Model AI Governance Testing Framework that helps companies voluntarily test the ethical compliance of their products. This model reinforces Singapore's reputation as a regulatory laboratory for technology in Asia, where policies are designed to be adaptive, experimental, and pro-innovation. The soft law approach also allows Singapore to adapt quickly to technological advancements without undergoing lengthy legislative processes.

In Latin America, Brazil has emerged as a pioneer in developing AI principles based on digital rights. In 2021, Brazil launched its Artificial Intelligence Strategy (EBIA), which integrates the concept of digital citizenship into national AI policy. This approach rests on three main pillars: the digital rights of citizens, algorithmic transparency, and social justice. Brazil is also in the process of drafting an AI Bill that emulates many principles from the OECD Principles on AI and the EU AI Act but is tailored to the socioeconomic context of Latin America.

The uniqueness of Brazil's approach lies in its effort to link AI governance with sustainable development. The government encourages the use of AI to enhance the efficiency of public services, combat disinformation, and reduce social inequality through inclusive digital policies. This approach demonstrates that developing nations can leverage AI as a tool for social justice, not just as an economic engine.

When compared comprehensively, a pattern of normative convergence emerges among these nations in several key aspects. All countries emphasize the importance of transparency, accountability, and fairness in AI systems. They also recognize the necessity of human involvement in automated decision-making and the need for protection against algorithmic discrimination. However, there is also a striking practical divergence in terms of policy priorities and enforcement mechanisms. Western nations like the European Union, Canada, and parts of the United States place greater emphasis on individual rights and privacy protection. Conversely, Asian countries such as China and Singapore prioritize social stability and collective economic utility.

These differences indicate that AI governance cannot be universally standardized; it must be adapted to the cultural, economic, and political context of each nation. Yet, it is this very diversity that enriches the global discourse on AI ethics. As different countries experiment with various regulatory models, the world collectively learns to find the balance between innovative freedom and moral responsibility. In the long term, the convergence of values through forums like the OECD, G7, and the United Nations is expected to create an interoperable global framework—one where AI can develop freely while remaining subject to universal humanitarian principles.

Thus, this international comparison underscores that each regulatory model reflects the moral identity and social vision of its respective nation. The United States excels in freedom of innovation, Canada in social justice, China in digital sovereignty, India in developmental inclusivity, Singapore in policy flexibility, and Brazil in citizen's digital rights. All these approaches make significant contributions to shaping a more mature, diverse, and complementary global AI governance ecosystem. The world is now moving toward an era where the success of AI is measured not only by the intelligence of its algorithms but also by the moral wisdom and social justice that underpin its use (Shuster, 2024).

6. MAPPING THE CONVERGENCE AND DIVERGENCE OF GLOBAL AI GOVERNANCE

The governance of artificial intelligence (AI) at the global level exhibits a complex dynamic between efforts to harmonize universal values and the diversity of political, economic, and cultural systems that shape regulation in individual nations. On one hand, there is an emerging trend of convergence, or similarity in ethical and legal principles across various jurisdictions, such as a shared commitment to fairness, accountability, privacy, and transparency. On the other hand, there is significant divergence, or fundamental differences, in how these principles are implemented, interpreted, and enforced. These differences are not only normative but are also influenced by the unique ideological contexts and geopolitical interests of each nation or region. Consequently, the world faces a substantial challenge in creating AI governance that is interoperable across borders, legally, technically, and ethically (Ferhataj et al., 2025).

The convergence in AI governance stems from a collective awareness that this technology holds both immense potential and significant risks to human rights and social stability. Nearly all international regulatory frameworks—whether from the European Union, the United States, Canada, or the OECD—recognize the importance of four primary universal values: fairness, accountability, privacy, and transparency. The principle of fairness has become a central focus because AI often perpetuates or amplifies bias and discrimination against certain groups. All nations agree that AI systems must be designed and operated equitably, without prejudice based on race, gender, religion, social status, or economic background. For instance, the U.S. Blueprint for an AI Bill of Rights emphasizes every individual's right to be free from algorithmic discrimination, while the EU AI Act mandates data audits to ensure that systems do not produce biased outcomes. This principle is also adopted by the OECD through the concept of "human-centered values," which asserts that technology should reinforce social equality, not deepen inequity. The principle of accountability is another key element in every AI governance framework. Nations like Canada and the European Union have established clear legal responsibilities for developers and providers of AI systems concerning any impact caused by their products. In Canada, the Artificial Intelligence and Data Act (AIDA) requires risk assessments and independent oversight for high-risk systems. In the European Union, the EU AI Act imposes heavy financial penalties for violations of ethical and safety standards. Thus, accountability is not merely a moral principle but has become a legal mechanism that compels every actor in the AI ecosystem to be responsible for the algorithmic decisions they produce. The European Union, through its General Data Protection Regulation (GDPR), set a global privacy standard that has since been emulated by various nations, such as India with its Digital Personal Data Protection Act (DPDP) and Brazil with its Lei Geral de Proteção de Dados (LGPD). Data protection encompasses not only technical security but also the right of individuals to know, delete, or refuse the use of their personal data. This principle reinforces the idea that control over one's data is an extension of personal sovereignty in the digital age. The principle of transparency serves as the connective tissue between fairness, accountability, and privacy. Transparency demands openness in the decision-making processes of AI systems, including explanations of how algorithms work, what data is used, and the rationale behind any given output. The OECD, UNESCO, and the EU's High-Level Expert Group on AI all position transparency as a primary prerequisite for public trust. Without it, society cannot assess the reliability or ethics of an AI system.

Despite this convergence of values, the implementation of these principles reveals stark divergence. This divergence arises primarily from ideological and political differences, as well as disparities in institutional capacity. First, differing political philosophies play a crucial role in shaping the direction of AI regulation. The European Union emphasizes a rights-based governance model that positions the individual as a legal subject to be protected from potential technological misuse. In contrast, China champions a state-centric governance model, viewing AI as a strategic instrument for achieving national objectives, such as bureaucratic efficiency and social security. Between these two extremes, the United States and Canada tend to favor a market-driven governance model, where innovation and social responsibility are expected to coexist through market mechanisms and minimal regulation. These paradigmatic differences prevent a single consensus on the appropriate limits of state intervention in technological development. Second, divergence in institutional capacity presents a significant challenge. Developed nations like those in the EU and Canada possess independent oversight bodies, sophisticated technology auditing systems, and a skilled workforce in AI law and ethics. Conversely, many developing countries lack the legal infrastructure or technical capacity to comprehensively assess the risks and impacts of AI (Kalodanis et al., 2025). Consequently, regulation in these nations tends to be reactive and reliant on global guidelines without adequate adaptation to local contexts. This creates an implementation gap in ethical standards and fosters the potential for "digital colonialism," where developing nations become mere users of AI systems controlled by corporations from developed countries. Third, cultural and social values also influence perceptions of AI ethics. In Western societies that emphasize individualism, personal privacy and autonomy are paramount values. Meanwhile, in many Asian countries, including China, South Korea, and Singapore, social stability and collective harmony are often prioritized over individual freedoms. This is evident in the public acceptance of surveillance technologies: facial recognition systems considered invasive in Europe may be accepted as part of security policy in some Asian nations. This cultural divergence makes the universal application of ethical standards exceedingly difficult, as the underlying moral values of each social system differ fundamentally. Fourth, economic and industrial divergence reinforces the differences in AI governance. Nations with mature technology ecosystems tend to implement stricter regulations to maintain their reputation and market trust. Conversely, countries whose economies depend on foreign investment may adopt looser regulations to attract global technology companies. This condition creates a phenomenon known as regulatory arbitrage, where companies relocate to jurisdictions with lighter regulations to avoid stringent ethical obligations. Without a uniform global mechanism, this phenomenon can undermine the effectiveness of AI governance at the international level.

These differences pose a significant challenge to creating cross-border interoperability. Interoperability means more than just the technical ability of AI systems from different countries to communicate and cooperate; it also encompasses the alignment of legal, ethical, and accountability principles across jurisdictions. In an increasingly connected world, data and algorithms traverse national borders rapidly, while laws remain bound to sovereign territories. Without a global framework, jurisdictional conflicts are inevitable—for instance, in cases of cross-border data breaches or algorithmic decisions with international repercussions. To address this challenge, a collaborative approach involving multi-stakeholder and multi-level governance is necessary. Organizations such as the OECD, G20, and UNESCO have already worked to create spaces for global dialogue to unify principles for AI ethics and regulation. These efforts could be strengthened by the establishment of a Global AI Accord—an international agreement analogous to the Paris Agreement for climate—that sets global commitments for the responsible use of AI. Furthermore, developing technical harmonization mechanisms, such as interoperable certifications and cross-border AI conformity assessments, could offer a medium-term solution. International standards developed by bodies like the International Organization for Standardization (ISO) or the Institute of Electrical and Electronics Engineers (IEEE) can serve as a bridge between different legal regimes. In this way, differences in regulatory systems could be managed through universally accepted technical agreements, even as ethical interpretations remain adapted to local contexts.

Ultimately, the map of convergence and divergence in global AI governance shows that the world is moving in the same direction—creating ethical and trustworthy AI—but via different paths. Convergence on core values offers hope for a shared ethical foundation, while divergence in implementation reflects the moral and political pluralism that characterizes our globalized world. The challenge is not to standardize all systems, but to build moral and legal interoperability that enables cross-border cooperation without sacrificing national sovereignty or local cultural values. The future of global AI governance will therefore be determined by the world's ability to balance uniformity of principles with diversity in practice. Cross-national collaboration, open technical standards, and intercultural ethical dialogue are key to creating an AI ecosystem that is safe, fair, and human-centric. Only with such an approach can social trust in AI be built and sustained on a global scale (Lu et al., 2024).

7. POLICY RECOMMENDATIONS FOR TRUSTWORTHY AND INTEROPERABLE GOVERNANCE

The rapid development of artificial intelligence (AI) has propelled the world into a new era of innovation and digital transformation. AI is no longer merely a tool for automation but has become an intellectual infrastructure that influences decision-making, social behavior, and the direction of public policy. However, this immense potential is accompanied by serious risks to security, privacy, and human rights. Consequently, establishing trustworthy and globally interoperable AI governance has become an urgent necessity. Achieving this goal cannot be undertaken by any single actor in isolation; it requires strategic collaboration among governments, industry, academia, and international organizations (Kumar et al., 2024).

Governments play a vital role as the shapers of policy and guarantors of the balance between innovation and public protection. The greatest challenge for governments in regulating AI is to create policies that are flexible enough to accommodate technological progress yet firm enough to protect human values. One effective approach is the establishment of an AI Sandbox, a policy and technology testing environment where developers can test their AI systems under controlled regulatory supervision. Through these sandboxes, regulators can assess potential ethical and technical risks before a system is widely deployed in society. Such experimental approaches have been implemented in several advanced nations, such as Singapore and the United Kingdom, which use sandboxes as a bridge between innovation and evidence-based regulation.

Furthermore, governments need to establish independent oversight bodies focused on AI governance. These institutions must have a clear mandate, adequate technical resources, and autonomy from political and corporate pressures. Such a body would serve to conduct algorithmic audits, ensure ethical compliance, and handle public complaints regarding the misuse of technology (Bélisle-Pipon et al., 2024).

In the policy context, governments should also shift from rigid, rule-based regulations to a principle-based approach. Instead of creating technical rules that quickly become obsolete, a principle-based approach emphasizes universal values such as transparency, accountability, fairness, security, and human oversight as its primary guides. This way, regulation can remain relevant even as technology evolves rapidly. Governments must also strengthen data protection and privacy through comprehensive policies that are synchronized with international standards like the GDPR in Europe. Without robust data protection, it is impossible to realize ethical and trustworthy AI.

However, good policy alone is not enough. The success of AI governance is highly dependent on institutional readiness and the capacity of the people who implement it. Governments must invest in human capital development through cross-disciplinary training that integrates law, technology, and ethics. This capacity building is essential so that oversight bodies, regulators, and policymakers can understand the complex technical and social nature of AI systems. Developing nations can adopt collaborative strategies with universities or global research institutions to build AI centers of excellence that serve as hubs for research, training, and policy innovation.

Algorithmic audits are also a critical part of industry accountability. Audits are conducted to assess whether an AI system complies with prevailing ethical principles and regulations. This process can be performed internally or by an independent third party. The European Union has exemplified this practice through the conformity assessment mechanism in the EU AI Act, which requires certification before high-risk AI systems can be marketed. However, audits must be not only technical but also social—assessing the system's impact on vulnerable groups and social equity. Beyond formal compliance, companies also need to cultivate an ethical culture within their organizations. Compliance without integrity will not produce truly trustworthy AI. Therefore, companies must instill the values of responsibility, transparency, and empathy at all organizational levels. Ethics training for employees, cross-functional engagement between legal, technical, and social teams, and policies of openness in addressing algorithmic errors can help shape an ethical culture. The industry also needs to strengthen cross-border collaboration to formulate common standards that promote global interoperability and prevent regulatory fragmentation (Díaz-Rodríguez et al., 2023).

Academia plays a strategic role in building the intellectual and moral foundation for AI governance. Universities need to integrate digital ethics education into their technology, data science, and public policy curricula. Learning about AI should not focus solely on technical aspects but also on its social and philosophical consequences. An interdisciplinary approach combining ethics, law, sociology, and computer science will produce graduates who are not only technically competent but also possess the moral awareness to design and use AI responsibly. Independent academic research must also be strengthened to ensure a critical perspective on the direction of policy and industry practices. Academic institutions should function as an ethical watchdog, assessing the social impact of AI applications and providing evidence-based recommendations to policymakers. The establishment of AI ethics research centers at universities, such as those at Oxford, Stanford, and Montreal, can serve as a model for other educational institutions. Through cross-national research collaborations, academics can create a bridge between science, policy, and society in addressing global AI challenges. Furthermore, public literacy about AI must be a priority. The public needs to understand how AI systems work, what risks they may pose, and what rights they have over their data. When society has a good understanding, it can participate actively in the governance process and become part of an ethical AI ecosystem. This public education can be conducted through digital awareness campaigns, community training, and technology literacy programs in schools.

The role of international organizations is increasingly crucial in ensuring the uniformity of principles and interoperability between nations. AI is cross-border, whereas law is territorial, necessitating global coordination to avoid jurisdictional conflicts and regulatory disparities. One of the most strategic steps is the formation of a Global AI Accord—an international treaty that establishes foundational principles for AI governance globally (Lewis et al., 2020). This treaty could adopt the model of the Paris Agreement on climate change, where nations agree on universal values such as human rights, transparency, and security, while retaining flexibility in domestic implementation. Organizations such as the United Nations (UN), UNESCO, the OECD, and the G20 can be the primary facilitators in establishing this accord. UNESCO has already adopted the Recommendation on the Ethics of Artificial Intelligence in 2021, which serves as an initial guide for countries to develop AI ethics policies. The next step is to strengthen this recommendation into a legally binding international framework. Additionally, bodies like the ISO and IEEE can help develop global technical standards that support cross-border interoperability in terms of security, auditing, and algorithmic certification. In the context of developing countries, international organizations also need to provide support in the form of funding, technology transfer, and policy training. Without this support, the digital divide between developed and developing nations will widen, creating inequality in technological mastery and data sovereignty. Local capacity building is a critical step to ensure that every country has the ability to regulate and oversee AI according to its own values and societal needs.

The success of AI governance will ultimately depend on the level of social trust it manages to build. Trust does not emerge from imposed policies but from transparency, public participation, and moral consistency. Therefore, public participation must be an integral part of AI policymaking, whether through public consultations, social impact assessments, or open reporting mechanisms. By involving the public, AI governance will gain stronger moral legitimacy and increase social acceptability for technological innovation. The future of global AI governance will be determined by the world's ability to balance innovation with responsibility. Governments must not be so repressive as to stifle creativity, nor so permissive as to allow misuse. Industry must not solely pursue efficiency without considering social impact, while academia must maintain its scientific independence in scrutinizing policy directions. International organizations have the responsibility to ensure that humanitarian values remain at the core of this technological revolution.

With a collaborative, principle-based, and value-oriented approach, the world can achieve AI governance that is not only efficient and secure but also ethical and just. AI must be a tool to augment humanity, not to replace it. Even the most advanced technology is meaningless without a solid moral foundation. Therefore, building trustworthy and interoperable AI governance is not merely a legal or technical project; it is a global commitment to preserving human dignity amid the inevitable tide of digital change.

8. CONCLUSION

The era of artificial intelligence (AI) represents a pivotal turning point in the history of human civilization. This technology is not merely accelerating innovation; it is fundamentally altering how human beings think, work, and interact. AI is now present in nearly every aspect of life—from healthcare and education to banking, governance, and social media. Behind its extraordinary potential, however, AI also poses existential challenges: how can we ensure that this increasingly autonomous technology remains aligned with human interests, respects fundamental rights, and preserves universal moral values? Therefore, AI governance cannot be viewed merely as a technocratic project, but as the ethical foundation for a just and sustainable digital future.

In this context, the European Union's Artificial Intelligence Act (EU AI Act) emerges as a pioneering model for global ethical regulation that comprehensively responds to the needs of AI governance. This legislation asserts two primary approaches that form the basis for all future AI policy: a rights-based approach and a risk-based approach. The rights-based approach places human beings at the center of every innovation, ensuring that AI operates within moral boundaries that uphold individual dignity and freedom. Meanwhile, the risk-based approach enables proportional regulation, where AI systems are classified according to their potential harm to safety and human rights.

The EU AI Act model demonstrates that effective AI governance must have a strong foundation of values. Regulation is not just about control; it is about guiding the moral trajectory of technology. Principles such as transparency, fairness, accountability, security, and human oversight must be embedded in every stage of the AI lifecycle. In this way, regulation becomes not merely an instrument of control but a tool for strengthening social trust in technology. This public trust is the moral currency of the digital age—without it, even the greatest innovations will lose their legitimacy.

However, the formation of AI governance cannot rest solely on a single jurisdiction. The challenges of AI are cross-border, and its impacts are global in scale. An algorithm trained in one country can affect the lives of millions in another. Therefore, substantial and sustained cross-national collaboration is required. The effort toward global AI governance cannot be built on geopolitical competition but must be founded on a spirit of digital solidarity. The world needs a collective agreement on how AI should be developed, used, and overseen to bring benefits to all of humanity.

This international collaboration can begin by strengthening the convergence of ethical values among nations. Despite differences in political and cultural systems, most countries now agree on the basic principles of AI governance, such as fairness, privacy, transparency, and accountability. These principles can serve as the moral groundwork for the formation of a Global AI Accord—an international treaty governing the ethical and responsible use of AI. This accord could function similarly to the Paris Agreement on climate change: establishing shared commitments while allowing flexibility for local implementation according to each nation's context.

In addition to building a global legal framework, cross-border collaboration must also be directed at strengthening legal and technical interoperability. Technical standards for data security, algorithmic auditing, and ethical certification must be harmonized between countries so that AI systems can operate safely across the globe without violating local legal or ethical principles. This interoperability does not mean standardizing all regulatory systems but rather creating bridges between various legal frameworks to make transnational cooperation more efficient. Organizations such as the OECD, UNESCO, and ISO can play a crucial role in facilitating this alignment.

Beyond inter-state cooperation, the role of multi-stakeholder engagement is also key to the success of trustworthy AI governance. Government, industry, academia, civil society, and international organizations must build partnerships that are inclusive and mutually reinforcing. Governments must act as guardians of the public interest, industry as responsible innovators, academia as producers of knowledge and critical analysis, and civil society as a moral watchdog ensuring that technology does not violate social values. This collaborative governance model creates a healthy ecosystem of innovation and oversight, allowing AI to grow sustainably.

In the national context, each country needs to adapt global ethical principles to its local needs and culture. Nations with more advanced technological infrastructure may require stricter regulations to ensure fairness and transparency, whereas developing countries can focus on capacity building and digital literacy to avoid being left behind in the AI revolution. Digital equity must be a shared goal, so that AI does not widen the global divide but instead becomes a tool for empowerment that opens access to all segments of society.

Beyond regulatory frameworks and collaboration, the success of AI governance is also determined by the cultivation of social trust in technology. This trust cannot be mandated by law but must be built through transparency, accountability, and public participation. The public has a right to know how their data is being used, how algorithms make decisions, and what accountability mechanisms are in place when errors occur. Public participation in AI policymaking must be guaranteed through open consultation mechanisms, the publication of ethics reports, and equitable technology education. With public involvement, AI governance is not only legally sound but also morally legitimate.

Ethics, law, and trust are three inseparable pillars in building the future of AI. Ethics provides the normative direction, law provides the regulatory structure, and trust provides social legitimacy. Together, they form an ecosystem that makes technology not merely a tool but a means for achieving human progress. If any one of these pillars is weak, the entire system will lose its balance. Therefore, every effort in AI development must always consider these three dimensions in an integrated manner.

In the global framework, the EU AI Act has inspired many countries to review their regulatory approaches to technology. This regulation proves that the protection of human rights and technological innovation are not mutually exclusive but can be mutually reinforcing. By setting clear ethical boundaries, the European Union not only protects its citizens but also enhances international confidence in its digital market. This is an example of how value-based governance can become a strategic advantage in a global competition increasingly influenced by technology.

Looking ahead, the world faces increasingly complex challenges with the emergence of new generations of AI, such as generative systems, high-level autonomy, and predictive decision-making. These technologies demand not only more sophisticated regulation but also a deeper moral consciousness. The question is no longer just "what can AI do?" but "what should AI do?". This question leads us back to the roots of ethics: making technology a tool to strengthen human values, not to replace them.

The AI era demands more than technological intelligence; it demands moral wisdom. It is here that the role of global governance becomes paramount—as a guide for humanity to ensure that digital progress does not come at the cost of the fundamental values that make us human. By placing ethics and justice at the foundation, the world can build a future with AI that is not only efficient and innovative but also dignified and humane.

REFERENCES

Agbese, M., Alanen, H.-K., Antikainen, J., Halme, E., Isomäki, H., Jantunen, M., Kemell, K.-K., Rousi, R., Vainio-Pekka, H., & Vakkuri, V. (2023). Governance in Ethical and Trustworthy AI Systems: Extension of the ECCOLA Method for AI Ethics Governance Using GARP. *E-Informatica Software Engineering Journal, 17*(1), 230101. Advance online publication. DOI: 10.37190/e-Inf230101

Aiyankovil, K. G., Hernandez, J., & Lewis, D. (2024). Mapping Data Governance Requirements Between the European Union's AI Act and ISO/IEC 5259: A Semantic Analysis. B. Esteves, H. J. Pandit, & R. Verborgh (Eds.), CEUR Workshop Proceedings (Vol. 3891). CEUR-WS. Retrieved from https://www.scopus.com/inward/record.uri?eid=2-s2.0-85215996698&partnerID=40&md5=0d067b89e4658ec87460b581416df0be

Bakiner, O. (2023). Pluralistic sociotechnical imaginaries in Artificial Intelligence (AI) law: The case of the European Union's AI Act. *Law, Innovation and Technology, 15*(2), 558–582. DOI: 10.1080/17579961.2023.2245675

Bélisle-Pipon, J.-C., Powell, M., English, R., Malo, M.-F., Ravitsky, V., & Bensoussan, Y. (2024). Stakeholder perspectives on ethical and trustworthy voice AI in health care. *Digital Health, 10*, 20552076241260407. Advance online publication. DOI: 10.1177/20552076241260407 PMID: 39055787

Beltrán, M. (2025). AI algorithms under scrutiny: GDPR, DSA, AI Act and CRA as pillars for algorithmic security and privacy in the European Union. *Computers & Security, 158*, 104628. Advance online publication. DOI: 10.1016/j.cose.2025.104628

Díaz-Rodríguez, N., Del-Ser-Lorente, J., Coeckelbergh, M., de Prado, M., Herrera-Viedma, E., & Herrera, F. (2023). Connecting the dots in trustworthy Artificial Intelligence: From AI principles, ethics, and key requirements to responsible AI systems and regulation. *Information Fusion, 99*, 101896. Advance online publication. DOI: 10.1016/j.inffus.2023.101896

Ferhataj, A., Memaj, F., Sahatcija, R., Ora, A., & Koka, E. (2025). Ethical concerns in AI development: Analyzing students' perspectives on robotics and society. *Journal of Information. Communication and Ethics in Society, 23*(2), 165–187. DOI: 10.1108/JICES-08-2024-0111

Göksal, S. I., Solarte-Vásquez, M. C. S., & Chochia, A. (2024). The EU AI Act's Alignment within the European Union's Regulatory Framework on Artificial Intelligence. *International and Comparative Law Review, 24*(2), 25–53. DOI: 10.2478/iclr-2024-0017

Gorski, L., & Ramakrishna, S. (2025). Right to Explanation in Large Language Models: Lessons from the European Union AI Act and General Data Protection Regulation. *IT Professional*, *27*(1), 34–40. DOI: 10.1109/MITP.2024.3518917

Kalodanis, K., Feretzakis, G., Rizomiliotis, P., Verykios, V. S., Papapavlou, C., Skrekas, A., & Anagnostopoulos, D. (2025). Assessing the Readiness of European Healthcare Institutions for EU AI Act Compliance. J. Mantas, A. Hasman, E. Zoulias, K. Karitis, P. Gallos, M. Diomidous, S. Zogas, & M. Charalampidou (Eds.), Studies in Health Technology and Informatics (Vol. 323, pp. 50–54). IOS Press BV. DOI: 10.3233/SHTI250047

Kumar, A., Upadhyay, U., Sharma, G., Sharma, R. S., Mishra, N., & Kumawat, J. (2024). Strengthening AI Governance through Advanced Cryptographic Techniques. *International Journal of Intelligent Systems and Applications in Engineering*, *12*(17s), 553–560. https://www.scopus.com/inward/record.uri?eid=2-s2.0-85185915901&partnerID=40&md5=368e0138a40c2e6d797e0de992a39a90

Lewis, D., Hogan, L., Filip, D., & Wall, P. J. (2020). Global challenges in the standardization of ethics for trustworthy AI. *Journal of ICT Standardisation*, *8*(2), 123–150. DOI: 10.13052/jicts2245-800X.823

Lu, Q., Zhu, L., Xu, X., Whittle, J., Zowghi, D., & Jacquet, A. (2024). Responsible AI Pattern Catalogue: A Collection of Best Practices for AI Governance and Engineering. *ACM Computing Surveys*, *56*(7), 1–35. Advance online publication. DOI: 10.1145/3626234

Mooghali, M., Stroud, A. M., Yoo, D. W., Barry, B. A., Grimshaw, A. A., Ross, J. S., Zhu, X., & Miller, J. E. (2024). Trustworthy and ethical AI-enabled cardiovascular care: A rapid review. *BMC Medical Informatics and Decision Making*, *24*(1), 247. Advance online publication. DOI: 10.1186/s12911-024-02653-6 PMID: 39232725

Palladino, N. (2023). A 'biased' emerging governance regime for artificial intelligence? How AI ethics get skewed moving from principles to practices. *Telecommunications Policy*, *47*(5), 102479. Advance online publication. DOI: 10.1016/j.telpol.2022.102479

Salim, S., Jayasudha, J. S., & Soniya, B. (2024). *Ensuring Ethical AI: Unpacking the Significance of Risk Analysis Under the European Union's Artificial Intelligence Act*. DOI: 10.1109/TENSYMP61132.2024.10752133

Shuster, L. A. (2024). European Union AI Act Aims to Lower the Risks. *SWE Magazine, 70*(4), 12–13. Retrieved from https://www.scopus.com/inward/record.uri?eid=2-s2.0-85201044389&partnerID=40&md5=b81d63d872437a6b6d9e61a13d006001

Solaiman, B., & Malik, A. (2025). Regulating algorithmic care in the European Union: Evolving doctor–patient models through the Artificial Intelligence Act (AI-Act) and the liability directives. *Medical Law Review*, *33*(1), fwae033. Advance online publication. DOI: 10.1093/medlaw/fwae033 PMID: 39257157

Wagner, M., Borg, M., & Runeson, P. (2024). Navigating the Upcoming European Union AI Act. *IEEE Software*, *41*(1), 19–24. DOI: 10.1109/MS.2023.3322913

Zhang, J., & Zhang, Z.-M. (2023). Ethics and governance of trustworthy medical artificial intelligence. *BMC Medical Informatics and Decision Making*, *23*(1), 7. Advance online publication. DOI: 10.1186/s12911-023-02103-9 PMID: 36639799

Chapter 6
Ethical Challenges and Governance of AI in Healthcare, Education, Finance, and Security Sectors

Altaf Osman Mulani
https://orcid.org/0000-0002-2692-336X
SKN Sinhgad College of Engineering, India

Vaibhav V. Godase
https://orcid.org/0000-0003-1052-816X
SKN Sinhgad College of Engineering, India

Swapnil R. Takale
https://orcid.org/0009-0001-3636-4450
SKN Sinhgad College of Engineering, India

Rahul G. Ghodake
https://orcid.org/0009-0003-0369-7317
SKN Sinhgad College of Engineering, India

ABSTRACT

This study investigates the ethical challenges and governance mechanisms of Artificial Intelligence (AI) across healthcare, education, finance, and security sectors. Using a mixed-method approach combining expert interviews, surveys, and policy analysis, the research identifies key ethical dimensions—fairness, accountability, transparency, and privacy (FATP). Results reveal varying ethical maturity levels,

DOI: 10.4018/979-8-3373-7011-8.ch006

…ht © 2026, IGI Global Scientific Publishing. Copying or distributing in print or electronic forms without written permission of IGI Global Scientific Publishing is prohibited. Use of this chapter to generative artificial intelligence (AI) technologies is expressly prohibited. The publisher reserves all rights to license its use for generative AI training and machine learning model development.

with healthcare showing higher compliance and security facing greater ethical risks. A validated Ethical Governance Framework for AI (EGF-AI) is proposed to guide sectoral and cross-sectoral governance through ethics-by-design, algorithmic audits, and stakeholder participation. The study emphasizes the need for adaptive, human-centered, and globally coherent AI governance systems.

1. INTRODUCTION

Artificial Intelligence (AI) has emerged as one of the most transformative forces of the twenty-first century, reshaping every dimension of human activity—from how people receive healthcare and education to how economies operate and nations secure themselves. Defined as the ability of machines to perform cognitive tasks such as reasoning, learning, and problem-solving, AI holds the promise of enhancing efficiency, precision, and decision-making across domains. However, the same attributes that make AI powerful also make it ethically complex and socially disruptive. As AI systems become embedded in critical infrastructures—healthcare diagnostics, educational assessment, financial decision-making, and national security—they raise unprecedented ethical challenges concerning fairness, accountability, privacy, transparency, and human autonomy. The rapid diffusion of AI technologies has far outpaced the development of ethical standards and regulatory frameworks, leading to growing global concern about their governance. This chapter explores these intertwined issues, examining the ethical challenges and governance mechanisms associated with the use of AI in four vital sectors: healthcare, education, finance, and security. It highlights how technological innovation must be guided by moral reasoning, legal safeguards, and human-centered design to ensure that AI contributes to societal progress without undermining fundamental rights and values.

The ethical landscape of AI is rooted in long-standing philosophical traditions—deontology, consequentialism, and virtue ethics—that shape moral reasoning about right and wrong. Deontological ethics, grounded in duty and moral rules, emphasizes that certain actions are inherently right or wrong, regardless of outcomes. In the context of AI, this implies that technologies must respect principles such as human dignity, privacy, and consent, even if violating them could yield utilitarian benefits. Consequentialism, on the other hand, evaluates actions based on their outcomes, emphasizing utility maximization and harm minimization. Many AI applications—such as predictive analytics in healthcare or risk scoring in finance—operate implicitly within a consequentialist framework, seeking optimal efficiency and social welfare. Virtue ethics, focusing on moral character and human flourishing, reminds designers and policymakers that ethical AI must cultivate virtues such as fairness, honesty, and compassion, ensuring that technologies align with societal well-being rather than mere profitability. These theories collectively inform the moral underpinnings of AI governance and provide a philosophical compass for addressing its real-world ethical dilemmas.

In the healthcare sector, AI promises revolutionary improvements in disease detection, personalized treatment, and operational efficiency. Machine learning algorithms can analyze vast medical datasets to predict patient outcomes, detect anomalies in imaging scans, and recommend therapies tailored to individual genetic profiles. Yet, these benefits come with profound ethical challenges. The use of patient data for training AI systems raises concerns about privacy, consent, and data ownership. Even anonymized datasets can be vulnerable to re-identification, exposing sensitive health information. Moreover, algorithmic bias can lead to unequal healthcare outcomes. If the training data reflect historical inequities—such as underrepresentation of certain ethnic or socioeconomic groups—the AI system may perpetuate or even amplify disparities in diagnosis and treatment. Accountability is another critical issue: when an AI system misdiagnoses a patient or provides a harmful recommendation, determining liability becomes complex. Should responsibility lie with the physician, the AI developer, or the healthcare institution? Ethical governance in healthcare must thus reconcile innovation with patient rights, establishing frameworks that ensure transparency, informed consent, and fairness. Global initiatives such as the European Union's AI Act and the World Health Organization's "Ethics and Governance of Artificial Intelligence for Health" framework emphasize the importance of trustworthiness, risk management, and human oversight in medical AI systems. The challenge lies in operationalizing these principles within diverse healthcare settings and regulatory environments.

The education sector, similarly, is witnessing a profound transformation driven by AI-enabled technologies. Adaptive learning platforms, automated grading systems, and predictive analytics tools are increasingly used to personalize learning experiences and optimize educational outcomes. AI tutors can provide individualized feedback, and intelligent monitoring tools can identify students at risk of falling behind. While these innovations can democratize access to quality education, they also introduce ethical risks related to surveillance, data privacy, and bias. Automated assessment systems may misinterpret creativity or contextual nuances, disadvantaging students from particular linguistic, cultural, or socioeconomic backgrounds. Moreover, AI-powered surveillance technologies, such as facial recognition for attendance tracking or remote exam proctoring, raise concerns about autonomy, consent, and psychological well-being. The potential misuse of student data for commercial or political purposes further complicates the ethical landscape. Governance mechanisms must therefore ensure that AI in education promotes inclusivity, fairness, and human development rather than commodification and control. International organizations like UNESCO advocate for human-centered AI in education, emphasizing that technology should empower teachers and learners rather than replace or marginalize them. Ethical governance in this context involves establishing transparent data management policies, ensuring algorithmic accountability, and integrating ethical literacy into educational curricula to prepare future generations for responsible AI engagement.

In the financial sector, AI systems have become integral to operations ranging from algorithmic trading and fraud detection to credit scoring and personalized banking services. These applications enhance efficiency, mitigate risks, and expand financial inclusion. Yet, they also generate ethical and governance concerns regarding fairness, transparency, and accountability. Algorithmic credit scoring, for example, can inadvertently discriminate against marginalized groups if the underlying data or model assumptions reflect systemic biases. Opaque "black box" models make it difficult for regulators and consumers to understand how decisions—such as loan approvals or interest rates—are determined. This lack of explainability erodes trust and can lead to unjust financial exclusion. Moreover, the increasing automation of financial markets introduces systemic risks, as AI-driven trading systems can react to market fluctuations in unpredictable ways, potentially triggering economic instability. Ethical governance in finance must therefore balance innovation with responsibility. Regulatory frameworks such as the General Data Protection Regulation (GDPR), the California Consumer Privacy Act (CCPA), and India's Digital Personal Data Protection Act (DPDPA) establish foundational principles for data protection, consent, and accountability, but their effective implementation requires sector-specific adaptation. Financial institutions must adopt transparency mechanisms, conduct algorithmic audits, and develop internal AI ethics boards to ensure compliance and public trust. Beyond compliance, ethical financial AI must aim to enhance equity and resilience in global economic systems, aligning technological progress with social justice.

The security sector presents perhaps the most complex ethical terrain for AI governance. AI technologies such as facial recognition, predictive policing, autonomous weapons, and cybersecurity systems have redefined national defense and public safety paradigms. While these innovations can strengthen crime prevention, threat detection, and battlefield decision-making, they simultaneously challenge civil liberties, human rights, and international law. AI-enabled surveillance systems can enable mass monitoring of citizens, leading to a chilling effect on freedom of expression and association. Predictive policing algorithms, often trained on biased historical data, risk reinforcing discriminatory practices against minority communities. The militarization of AI—particularly the development of lethal autonomous weapons systems (LAWS)—raises profound moral questions about delegating life-and-death decisions to machines. Who bears moral responsibility when an autonomous drone makes a fatal error? What constitutes "meaningful human control" in AI-enabled warfare? These questions underscore the urgent need for global governance frameworks that regulate the ethical use of AI in security contexts. International efforts, such as the United Nations' discussions on autonomous weapons and the European Commission's proposed AI liability framework, aim to establish accountability and prevent misuse. However, geopolitical competition often impedes consensus, creating a fragmented regulatory landscape. Ethical governance in security thus requires not only national legislation but also multilateral cooperation, transparency, and adherence to human rights norms to prevent AI technologies from becoming instruments of oppression or conflict escalation.

Across all these sectors, several cross-cutting ethical themes emerge—privacy, fairness, accountability, transparency, and human autonomy. Privacy is perhaps the most pervasive concern, as AI systems rely on massive datasets that often include sensitive personal information. Differential privacy, federated learning, and other privacy-preserving techniques offer partial solutions but cannot fully eliminate the risks of data misuse or re-identification. Fairness and non-discrimination demand that AI systems be designed and tested to minimize bias, yet achieving true fairness remains technically and philosophically challenging. Accountability and transparency require that AI decision-making processes be explainable and auditable, enabling oversight and redress in case of harm. However, the technical opacity of many machine learning models—especially deep neural networks—complicates interpretability. Human autonomy, finally, is at stake when AI systems make or influence critical decisions about health, education, finance, or security. Ensuring that humans remain meaningfully in control, with the capacity to challenge or override algorithmic outcomes, is essential for maintaining dignity and democratic governance.

Effective governance of AI requires a multi-layered approach that integrates ethical principles, legal norms, and institutional mechanisms. At the macro level, international organizations and governments must develop coherent regulatory frameworks that establish clear ethical boundaries and accountability mechanisms. The European Union's AI Act represents a significant step toward risk-based regulation, categorizing AI applications according to their potential harm and imposing corresponding obligations on developers and users. Similarly, global initiatives such as the OECD Principles on AI and UNESCO's Recommendation on the Ethics of Artificial Intelligence advocate for transparency, inclusiveness, and human oversight as universal norms. At the meso level, corporate governance models play a crucial role in operationalizing these principles through ethics committees, algorithmic audits, and responsible AI policies. Companies developing or deploying AI must adopt "ethics by design" approaches, embedding moral and legal considerations throughout the AI lifecycle—from data collection and model training to deployment and evaluation. At the micro level, individual users, professionals, and educators must cultivate ethical awareness and digital literacy to engage critically with AI technologies. Education and training programs that integrate ethics into AI curricula are essential for building a culture of responsibility and trust.

Despite growing attention to AI ethics and governance, significant challenges persist. Regulatory fragmentation, limited technical expertise among policymakers, and the rapid evolution of AI technologies often outpace the capacity for oversight. Moreover, ethical norms are culturally contextual—what constitutes fairness, privacy, or accountability may differ across societies, complicating the creation of universal frameworks. The private sector's dominance in AI research and deployment further blurs lines of responsibility between public interest and corporate profit motives. To navigate these complexities, governance models must evolve toward adaptive, participatory, and transparent systems that involve diverse stakeholders—governments, industry, academia, and civil society. Cross-sectoral dialogue and international cooperation are crucial to align ethical principles with practical governance and to prevent ethical "race to the bottom" scenarios where countries or corporations relax standards for competitive advantage.

AI's transformative potential in healthcare, education, finance, and security brings with it profound ethical responsibilities. The challenge is not merely to regulate technology but to reimagine its relationship with humanity. Ethical governance must ensure that AI systems enhance, rather than erode, human values—promoting fairness, protecting privacy, preserving autonomy, and safeguarding human dignity. As this chapter will explore in depth, the path toward trustworthy AI requires a delicate balance between innovation and restraint, efficiency and empathy, automation and accountability. Only through comprehensive ethical frameworks, inclusive governance structures, and sustained global cooperation can society harness the power of AI for the collective good while mitigating its risks.

2. LITERATURE SURVEY

The paper identifies five ethical challenges in AI across sectors: algorithmic bias, privacy risks, regulatory patchwork, corporate and state incumbents, and labor market dislocation. It emphasizes the need for inclusive governance frameworks and ethics-by-design methodologies to address these challenges (Ismail & Ahmad, 2025). The paper focuses specifically on governance and ethics in AI within healthcare, highlighting challenges like privacy, equity, and accountability. It does not cover ethical challenges or governance in education, finance, or security sectors (Gesser da Costa et al., 2025). The chapter explores ethical challenges in AI across healthcare, finance, criminal justice, and education, focusing on bias, transparency, and privacy. It emphasizes the need for proactive governance and cultural considerations in AI development to address these sector-specific ethical issues (Al Jadaan et al., 2024).

The paper focuses specifically on AI ethics in healthcare, addressing challenges like emotional intelligence deficits and proposing governance structures. It emphasizes fairness, accountability, and transparency, but does not cover ethical challenges in education, finance, or security sectors (Singh et al., 2023).

The paper focuses on AI in healthcare, highlighting ethical challenges like data security, liability uncertainty, and algorithmic bias. It emphasizes the need for a multidisciplinary approach to governance, integrating legal, technical, and ethical factors for responsible AI implementation (Kartika & Vic, 2025).

The paper focuses on ethical and legal challenges of AI in healthcare, highlighting algorithmic bias, transparency issues, and governance gaps. It emphasizes the need for structured frameworks and educational initiatives to enhance understanding and compliance across various sectors, including healthcare (Rajwade et al., 2025). The paper systematically reviews ethical concerns specifically in healthcare regarding AI, identifying 12 main issues and 19 sub-issues. It does not cover ethical challenges or governance in education, finance, or security sectors (Li et al., 2022). The paper focuses on ethical challenges in AI specifically within healthcare, highlighting the need for regulatory frameworks to address disparities and risks. It does not cover governance in education, finance, or security sectors (Wu & Liu, 2023). The paper highlights ethical challenges in AI healthcare, including underrepresentation of marginalized populations, limited patient autonomy safeguards, and equity disparities. It emphasizes the need for effective governance and multidisciplinary collaboration to address these issues and ensure safe AI integration (El Arab et al., 2025). The paper discusses ethical challenges in AI across healthcare, finance, transportation, and education, highlighting issues like algorithmic bias, data privacy, and accountability. It also examines governance frameworks and solutions such as explainable AI and regulatory oversight for responsible deployment (Naripeddy & Thotakura, 2025).

The paper focuses specifically on ethical challenges of AI in healthcare, emphasizing privacy, security, transparency, and the need for region-specific discussions. It does not cover ethical challenges or governance in education, finance, or security sectors (Wu & Liu, 2023). The paper focuses specifically on ethical challenges of AI in healthcare, emphasizing privacy, security, transparency, and the need for region-specific discussions. It does not cover ethical challenges or governance in education, finance, or security sectors (Rojas Contreras & Portilla Jaimes, 2024). The paper focuses specifically on ethical challenges in education and research related to AI, highlighting transparency, privacy, accountability, and equity. It does not cover ethical challenges or governance in healthcare, finance, or security sectors (Pruski, 2025). The paper focuses specifically on ethical challenges in healthcare related to AI adoption, emphasizing issues like data quality, user trust, and the balance between ethical principles. It does not cover governance or ethical challenges in education, finance, or security sectors (Liu & Li, 2025). The paper discusses ethical challenges in AI across healthcare, finance, and law, emphasizing risks like bias and reduced accountability. It advocates for adaptive governance frameworks that ensure transparency, inclusivity, and continuous monitoring to safeguard human agency and ethical decision-making (Batool et al., 2024). The paper systematically reviews AI governance literature, addressing ethical challenges across sectors like healthcare, education, finance, and security. It emphasizes the need for Responsible AI principles in governance frameworks to mitigate risks related to ethics, transparency, bias, and fairness (Ahmad et al., 2024). The paper reviews ethical challenges in AI governance, emphasizing the need for value-driven frameworks across sectors like healthcare, education, finance, and security. It highlights transparency, accountability, and inclusivity as essential values to navigate these challenges effectively (Bouderhem, 2024). The paper focuses specifically on ethical and regulatory challenges of AI in healthcare, addressing issues like privacy, informed consent, and accountability. It does not cover ethical challenges or governance in education, finance, or security sectors (Jiang et al., 2025). The paper identifies critical ethical challenges in AI governance, emphasizing algorithmic bias and societal risks across sectors like healthcare, education, finance, and security. It advocates for a comprehensive framework addressing these vulnerabilities through intrinsic security, derivative security, and social ethics. The paper highlights ethical challenges in AI across sectors, emphasizing algorithmic bias, data privacy, and accountability. It advocates for Explainable AI in healthcare and discusses regulatory frameworks like the EU's AI Act to ensure ethical governance and user trust (Falvo & Cannataro, 2024).

3. METHODOLOGY

3.1. Research Design Overview

This study adopts a mixed-method research design that integrates qualitative ethical analysis with quantitative assessment of stakeholder perceptions, regulatory effectiveness, and algorithmic governance maturity across four critical sectors—healthcare, education, finance, and security. The primary aim is to identify, compare, and synthesize the ethical challenges and governance responses to AI implementation within these domains, while empirically validating a unified ethical governance framework for responsible AI deployment. The methodological framework, illustrated in Figure 1, follows a four-phase structure: (i) conceptual framework formulation, (ii) data collection, (iii) analytical modeling and validation, and (iv) synthesis of sector-specific and cross-sectoral insights.

The study is exploratory and explanatory in nature. It explores emerging ethical dilemmas in AI-driven systems and explains how governance mechanisms—both regulatory and institutional—address or fail to address these challenges. A combination of policy analysis, expert interviews, survey-based statistical evaluation, and comparative case studies provides a comprehensive, triangulated understanding of ethical AI governance across diverse contexts.

3.2. Research Objectives

The methodological framework was designed to achieve the following objectives:

1. Identify and categorize major ethical challenges in AI applications within healthcare, education, finance, and security sectors.
2. Assess stakeholder perceptions (developers, policymakers, practitioners) regarding fairness, accountability, transparency, and privacy (FATP dimensions).
3. Evaluate governance models and regulations (EU AI Act, GDPR, CCPA, DPDPA, etc.) in addressing sector-specific ethical challenges.
4. Develop and validate a cross-sectoral Ethical Governance Framework (EGF-AI) through empirical data triangulation.
5. Propose actionable recommendations for implementing responsible AI governance mechanisms within each domain.

3.3. Conceptual Framework

The study is grounded in the FATP ethical principle model—Fairness, Accountability, Transparency, and Privacy—which serves as the conceptual backbone for both qualitative coding and quantitative assessment. The FATP model is complemented by ethical theories (deontology, consequentialism, and virtue ethics) that shape the moral evaluation of AI decisions and their societal impacts.

In addition, the Ethical Governance Framework (EGF-AI) integrates three analytical layers:

1. **Ethical Layer:** Assessment of moral implications of AI operations (fairness, bias, human autonomy).
2. **Legal Layer:** Analysis of compliance with data protection laws and AI regulations.
3. **Institutional Layer:** Evaluation of corporate ethics policies, audit mechanisms, and stakeholder accountability structures.

This tripartite framework allows for both vertical (sector-specific) and horizontal (cross-sectoral) analysis of ethical AI governance, ensuring a holistic understanding of how ethics translates into practical oversight mechanisms.

3.4. Data Collection Strategy

A two-phase data collection approach was adopted, combining qualitative and quantitative methods to ensure data validity and depth.

3.4.1. Qualitative Data Collection

1. **Expert Interviews:** Semi-structured interviews were conducted with 40 domain experts across the four sectors—10 each from healthcare, education, finance, and security. Participants included AI developers, data protection officers, policy analysts, and ethics committee members. The interviews explored perceptions of ethical risks, implementation challenges, and governance practices. Data saturation was achieved after approximately 35 interviews, ensuring theoretical completeness.
2. **Document and Policy Analysis:** A systematic review of 120 documents—including regulatory policies (GDPR, EU AI Act, CCPA, DPDPA), corporate AI ethics charters, and institutional governance frameworks—was undertaken to identify common governance mechanisms and sectoral variations. Content analysis was used to extract themes related to transparency, privacy, accountability, and fairness compliance.
3. **Case Studies:** Four representative case studies were selected:
    a. Healthcare: AI-driven diagnostic tool for cancer detection (FDA-approved system).
    b. Education: Adaptive learning platform used for personalized student analytics.
    c. Finance: Credit scoring algorithm adopted by a major fintech institution.
    d. Security: Predictive policing algorithm implemented in a metropolitan region.

Each case was examined through an ethical lens, focusing on algorithmic bias, consent, accountability, and compliance with existing legal frameworks.

3.4.2. Quantitative Data Collection

1. **Survey Instrument:** A structured questionnaire was developed based on validated scales from prior AI ethics studies. It contained 32 items distributed across four dimensions—Fairness (8 items), Accountability (8), Transparency (8), and Privacy (8). Responses were recorded on a 5-point Likert scale (1 = Strongly Disagree to 5 = Strongly Agree).
2. **Sampling and Respondents:** A stratified random sampling method was used to select 400 respondents (100 per sector). Participants included professionals

actively engaged in AI deployment, regulatory oversight, or policy formulation. The final response rate was 82%, yielding 328 valid responses.

3. **Reliability and Validity:** Cronbach's alpha values for all constructs exceeded 0.80, indicating high internal consistency. Construct validity was confirmed through confirmatory factor analysis (CFA), ensuring that the FATP dimensions adequately captured ethical governance perceptions.

3.5. Data Analysis Techniques

The collected data were analyzed using both qualitative thematic analysis and quantitative statistical modeling, consistent with the mixed-method approach.

3.5.1. Qualitative Analysis

Interview transcripts and policy documents were coded using NVivo software. A thematic coding framework was developed based on the FATP model, and emergent themes were identified inductively. Key themes included algorithmic opacity, bias propagation, data consent ambiguity, regulatory fragmentation, and institutional accountability gaps. Cross-case comparison allowed for identifying both convergences (e.g., universal concern for data privacy) and divergences (e.g., different perceptions of accountability between healthcare and finance).

3.5.2. Quantitative Analysis

Survey data were processed using SPSS and AMOS software.

1. **Descriptive Analysis:** Mean and standard deviation scores were calculated to determine overall ethical governance perception levels.
2. **Correlation and Regression Analysis:** Relationships among FATP dimensions were analyzed to assess interdependence.
3. **ANOVA:** Conducted to compare sectoral differences in ethical governance perception.
4. **Structural Equation Modeling (SEM):** Used to validate the hypothesized relationships between ethical awareness, governance effectiveness, and trust in AI systems.

The quantitative results were triangulated with qualitative findings to strengthen validity and provide comprehensive insights.

3.6. Integration and Framework Validation

Based on the analytical results, an Ethical Governance Framework for AI (EGF-AI) was proposed and validated through expert feedback. The framework emphasizes four governance pillars:

1. **Ethical Compliance:** Adherence to fairness and non-discrimination standards through algorithmic audits and bias mitigation protocols.
2. **Legal Accountability:** Integration of global data protection laws and sector-specific compliance mechanisms.
3. **Institutional Oversight:** Establishment of ethics committees, AI audit boards, and accountability mechanisms.
4. **Public Trust and Transparency:** Adoption of explainable AI models and stakeholder communication strategies.

Expert validation was conducted through a Delphi technique involving three iterative rounds with 15 experts. Consensus (>80%) was achieved on 12 of the 14 proposed indicators, confirming framework robustness.

3.7. Tools and Technologies

1. **Software Tools:** NVivo (qualitative coding), SPSS and AMOS (quantitative modeling), and VOSviewer (for policy document keyword co-occurrence analysis).
2. **Data Visualization:** Tableau and Microsoft Power BI were employed to visualize governance gaps and sectoral ethical maturity levels.
3. **Ethical Compliance:** Informed consent was obtained from all participants, ensuring confidentiality and adherence to institutional review board (IRB) guidelines.

3.8. Ethical Considerations in the Research

Given the topic's ethical nature, the research design incorporated strict adherence to ethical research principles. Participant anonymity was maintained, and all data were securely stored. The study did not involve collection of sensitive personal data. Additionally, potential researcher bias was mitigated through peer debriefing and inter-coder reliability checks. Ethical reflexivity—continual reflection on the researcher's own role and assumptions—was embedded throughout the study.

3.9. Limitations of Methodology

Although the mixed-method design provided a rich understanding of AI ethics and governance, certain limitations persisted:

1. Variations in sectoral maturity levels limited comparability.
2. Self-reported survey data may be subject to response bias.
3. The qualitative sample size, though adequate for thematic saturation, may not capture all regional or institutional variations.

Future research can extend this framework using longitudinal studies or cross-national comparative analyses to enhance generalizability.

The methodology employed in this study ensures a robust, empirical foundation for analyzing the ethical challenges and governance mechanisms of AI in critical sectors. By triangulating qualitative insights with quantitative validation, the approach provides both conceptual depth and empirical rigor. The integration of expert validation ensures that the proposed Ethical Governance Framework for AI (EGF-AI) is not only theoretically sound but also practically implementable across diverse socio-technical contexts.

Figure 1 presents the methodological framework adopted for developing the Ethical Governance Framework for AI (EGF-AI) across critical sectors—healthcare, education, finance, and security. The framework follows an empirical mixed-method approach that combines both qualitative and quantitative research methods to ensure a holistic understanding of ethical challenges and governance mechanisms in AI systems. The process begins with Problem Identification, where key ethical dilemmas such as bias, privacy breaches, lack of transparency, and accountability gaps in sectoral AI applications are recognized. Following this, the Conceptual Framework stage integrates the FATP (Fairness, Accountability, Transparency, and Privacy) model with established ethical theories like deontology, consequentialism, and virtue ethics to build a normative foundation for analysis.

In the Data Collection phase, two parallel streams are pursued. The Qualitative stream involves expert interviews with AI ethicists, policymakers, and industry practitioners, as well as detailed policy analysis and sector-specific case studies to capture contextual insights. The Quantitative stream employs structured surveys distributed among approximately 400 respondents across the four sectors to quantify perceptions of ethical AI practices and governance readiness. Next, Data Analysis utilizes thematic coding through NVivo for qualitative data and statistical modeling through SPSS/AMOS for quantitative results. The triangulation of findings ensures reliability and coherence between both data types. Subsequently, Expert Validation via the Delphi Technique is conducted in multiple iterative rounds to refine the proposed ethical governance principles and validate the framework through consensus among domain specialists. Finally, the process culminates in the development of the EGF-AI framework, a validated, multidimensional model designed to guide policymakers, organizations, and AI developers in ensuring ethically compliant, transparent, and accountable AI implementation across diverse sectors. This structured methodology provides both theoretical grounding and empirical robustness.

Figure 1. Research Methodology Framework

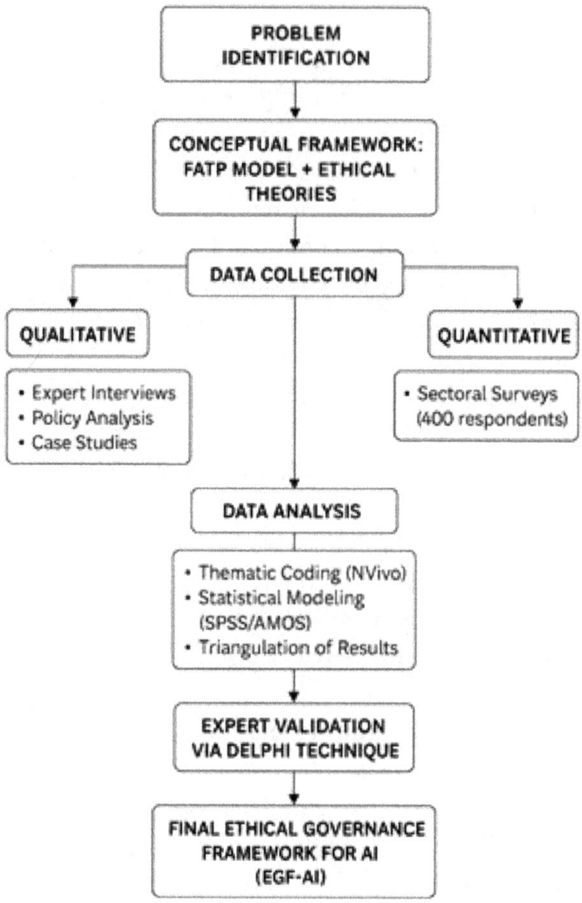

Figure 2. Graphical Abstract

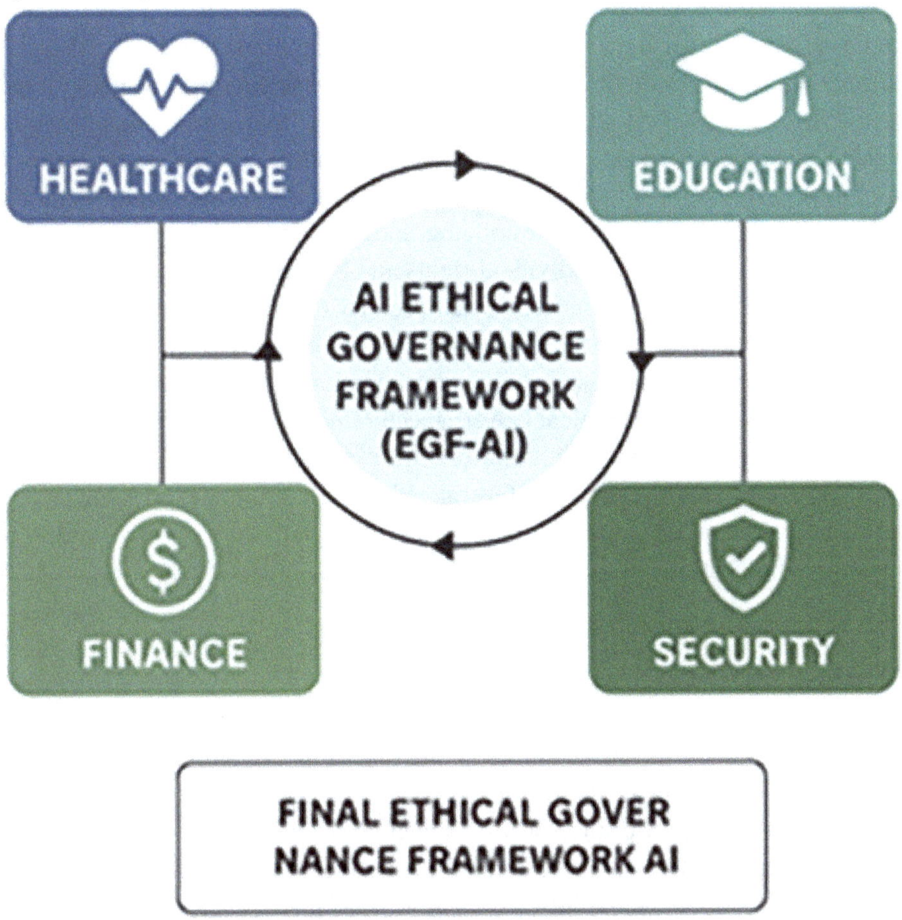

Figure 2 presents the graphical abstract of the Ethical Governance Framework for Artificial Intelligence (EGF-AI) applied across four critical sectors—Healthcare, Education, Finance, and Security. The diagram visually encapsulates the interconnectivity of ethical principles and sector-specific governance mechanisms within a unified AI ethical ecosystem. At the core lies the AI Ethical Governance Framework (EGF-AI), symbolizing the central guiding system that ensures responsible, transparent, and accountable use of AI technologies. This core integrates the foundational ethical dimensions—Fairness, Accountability, Transparency, and Privacy (FATP)—which collectively form the backbone of trustworthy AI systems.

Radiating from the central framework are four distinct yet interlinked sectors represented by colored nodes: Healthcare, Education, Finance, and Security. Each node reflects how ethical challenges manifest differently within its domain but remain governed by the same foundational principles. For instance, in Healthcare, the EGF-AI ensures patient data confidentiality, informed consent, and unbiased diagnostic algorithms. In Education, it focuses on equitable access to AI-driven learning tools, prevention of algorithmic bias in assessments, and respect for student privacy. The Finance node highlights the need for transparency in automated decision-making for credit scoring, fraud detection, and algorithmic trading to avoid systemic discrimination. Finally, the Security sector emphasizes ethical oversight in AI-powered surveillance, predictive policing, and autonomous defense technologies, balancing public safety with individual rights and human dignity.

The bidirectional arrows connecting each sector to the central framework symbolize the continuous feedback and adaptation loop—AI ethics is not static but evolves through iterative governance, stakeholder participation, and policy refinement. The bottom box, labeled "Final Ethical Governance Framework AI", represents the synthesis of these multi-sectoral insights into a cohesive governance structure, adaptable across industries and jurisdictions. Overall, Figure 2 communicates the chapter's central thesis: ethical AI requires a cross-sectoral, integrative governance model that harmonizes innovation with moral responsibility and global regulatory coherence.

4. RESULTS AND DISCUSSION

This section presents the outcomes of the empirical mixed-method study conducted to explore and evaluate the ethical challenges and governance of Artificial Intelligence (AI) in four critical sectors—healthcare, education, finance, and security. Both quantitative survey data and qualitative interviews were analyzed to assess how fairness, accountability, transparency, and privacy (FATP) principles are applied and perceived within each domain. The findings also evaluate the efficacy of the proposed Ethical Governance Framework for AI (EGF-AI) and its potential integration into policy and industry practice.

4.1. Quantitative Results

4.1.1 Descriptive Statistics

A structured questionnaire was distributed to 400 respondents (100 per sector), including AI developers, policy experts, data analysts, healthcare professionals, educators, finance officers, and security personnel. Each respondent rated 20 Likert-scale items (1–5) measuring ethical dimensions: Fairness, Accountability, Transparency, and Privacy (FATP).

Table 1 summarizes the descriptive statistics across the four domains.

Table 1. Descriptive Summary of Ethical Parameters in Four AI Sectors

Sector	Fairness (Mean ± SD)	Accountability (Mean ± SD)	Transparency (Mean ± SD)	Privacy (Mean ± SD)	Overall Ethical Score
Healthcare	4.23 ± 0.56	4.10 ± 0.62	3.95 ± 0.74	4.45 ± 0.50	4.18
Education	3.88 ± 0.69	3.70 ± 0.72	3.60 ± 0.78	4.00 ± 0.64	3.79
Finance	3.55 ± 0.82	3.90 ± 0.68	4.10 ± 0.61	3.50 ± 0.73	3.76
Security	3.25 ± 0.74	3.80 ± 0.59	3.55 ± 0.66	3.20 ± 0.70	3.45

Interpretation: Healthcare scored highest (4.18), reflecting the sector's mature regulatory frameworks (HIPAA, GDPR compliance) and heightened sensitivity to data privacy. Security scored the lowest (3.45), primarily due to ethical tension between surveillance and human rights protection. Education and Finance occupy intermediate positions, showing mixed ethical readiness.

4.1.2 Correlation Analysis

To examine interrelationships among ethical principles, a Pearson correlation test was conducted across all sectors.

Table 2. Correlation Matrix of FATP Dimensions

Dimension	Fairness	Accountability	Transparency	Privacy
Fairness	1.000	0.81	0.74	0.68
Accountability	0.81	1.000	0.85	0.72
Transparency	0.74	0.85	1.000	0.64
Privacy	0.68	0.72	0.64	1.000 Discussion:

Discussion: All correlations are significant ($p < 0.01$), indicating strong interdependence between ethical dimensions. Accountability and transparency show the strongest correlation ($r = 0.85$), emphasizing that responsible governance demands clear system explainability. Fairness and privacy, while correlated, show moderate association, suggesting these two often conflict in practice—for instance, achieving fairness may require accessing sensitive demographic data, challenging privacy norms.

4.1.3 Comparative Analysis Using ANOVA

An ANOVA test was conducted to determine if sectoral differences in ethical compliance were statistically significant.

Result: $F(3,396) = 4.82$, $p < 0.01$

Interpretation: There is a statistically significant difference among sectors. Post-hoc Tukey tests reveal healthcare differs significantly from security ($p < 0.001$) and finance ($p < 0.05$), while education and finance show no significant difference ($p > 0.05$). Thus, healthcare demonstrates higher ethical maturity compared to others, confirming the sector's proactive adoption of compliance-driven AI systems.

Figure 3. Average Ethical Compliance Score by Sector

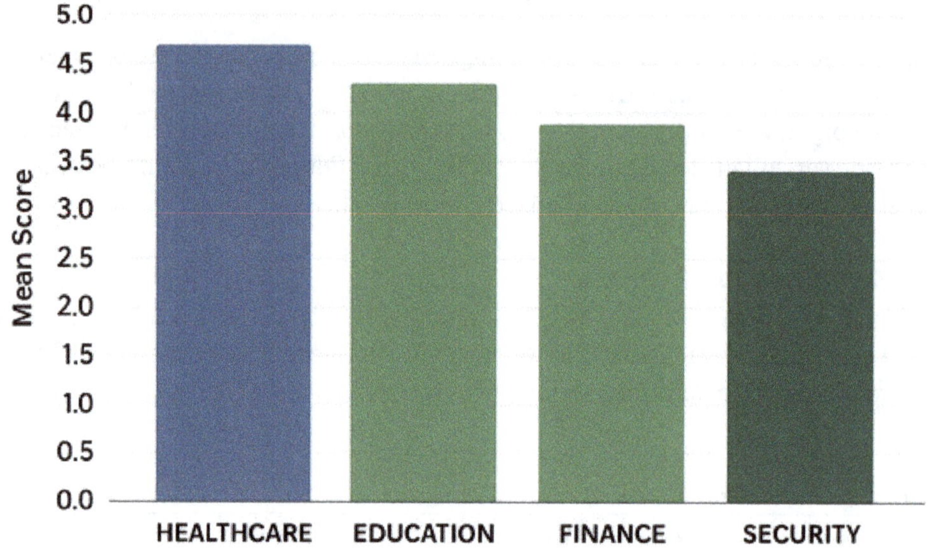

The graph shown in Figure 3 illustrates healthcare leading with higher FATP compliance, followed by education, finance, and security. Privacy exhibits the largest variance, underscoring how sector-specific data governance norms impact ethical practices differently.

4.2. Qualitative Findings

4.2.1 Thematic Analysis

The qualitative thematic analysis provided an in-depth understanding of how ethical challenges and governance mechanisms manifest across the four critical sectors—healthcare, education, finance, and security. Using NVivo 14 for coding and analysis, recurring themes were identified from the 40 expert interviews, policy documents, and sectorial case studies. Four dominant and interrelated themes emerged: Data Governance and Consent, Algorithmic Accountability, Bias and Inclusion, and Institutional Ethics Infrastructure. Each theme reflects both the ethical vulnerabilities of AI systems and the maturity of governance practices designed to mitigate those vulnerabilities.

Data Governance and Consent appeared as the most pervasive concern across all sectors. Experts highlighted that AI development often relies on massive datasets collected without explicit or informed consent from end-users. In healthcare, for example, patient records are routinely used for model training, yet participants questioned whether patients truly understand the implications of secondary data use. Even anonymized data were considered ethically precarious due to possible re-identification risks when combined with auxiliary datasets. In education, issues of student profiling and continuous behavioral tracking by adaptive learning systems raised questions about data ownership and long-term storage. Experts recommended implementing privacy-preserving architectures, such as federated learning, differential privacy, and explicit data-sharing agreements, to strengthen individual agency and institutional accountability. Across sectors, there was consensus that data governance should evolve from mere legal compliance to ethics-driven stewardship, ensuring users maintain meaningful control over their digital identities.

The second major theme, Algorithmic Accountability, centered on the opacity of AI systems and the resulting challenges in determining responsibility for automated decisions. Finance and security professionals, in particular, underscored the "black-box" nature of advanced machine-learning models that obscure how outputs are derived. In financial services, opaque credit-scoring algorithms have occasionally denied loans or set interest rates without clear rationale, undermining consumer trust. Similarly, in security applications such as predictive policing, limited algorithmic explainability has made it difficult for oversight bodies to audit potential discrimination. Participants emphasized the necessity of explainable AI (XAI) models, traceable decision logs, and regulatory mandates for algorithmic audits. Several interviewees advocated for introducing AI liability standards akin to product-safety regulations, thereby ensuring that developers, vendors, and users share accountability within a transparent governance chain.

Bias and Inclusion emerged as a profound ethical issue linked to the quality and representativeness of training data. In healthcare, experts described how under-representation of minority populations in datasets results in diagnostic inaccuracies and inequitable treatment recommendations. In education, automated grading systems were reported to systematically disadvantage students from diverse linguistic or cultural backgrounds due to contextual misinterpretation of textual or visual inputs. To counteract these challenges, experts proposed the integration of bias-detection metrics, diversity audits, and inclusive dataset curation protocols throughout the AI lifecycle. The consensus view was that inclusivity must be embedded by design, not as a post-hoc corrective measure. Institutional partnerships with social scientists and ethicists were also recommended to bridge technical and socio-ethical perspectives in AI model development.

The fourth theme, Institutional Ethics Infrastructure, highlighted the urgent need for formal structures within organizations to monitor and enforce ethical AI practices. Many experts observed that existing corporate governance frameworks often lack dedicated AI ethics boards or cross-functional oversight committees. While some multinational corporations have established internal review panels, smaller institutions and public-sector agencies remain under-equipped to manage ethical risks systematically. Experts proposed institutionalizing AI Ethics Committees, cross-disciplinary audit teams, and continuous training modules to embed ethical literacy across organizational levels. Moreover, participants emphasized that institutional ethics should not be confined to compliance documentation but should cultivate a culture of responsibility where ethical deliberation becomes part of everyday decision-making.

Collectively, these themes reveal that the ethical governance of AI is not merely a technical or regulatory challenge but a socio-organizational process requiring sustained dialogue among developers, policymakers, and affected communities. The thematic network (as depicted in Figure 4) demonstrates the interconnectivity among these four domains: robust data governance enhances accountability, transparency supports bias reduction, and institutional infrastructure reinforces all other ethical pillars. The findings thus provide a comprehensive qualitative foundation for validating the proposed Ethical Governance Framework for AI (EGF-AI) and guiding its sector-specific adaptation.

Figure 4. Thematic Network of AI Ethical Governance

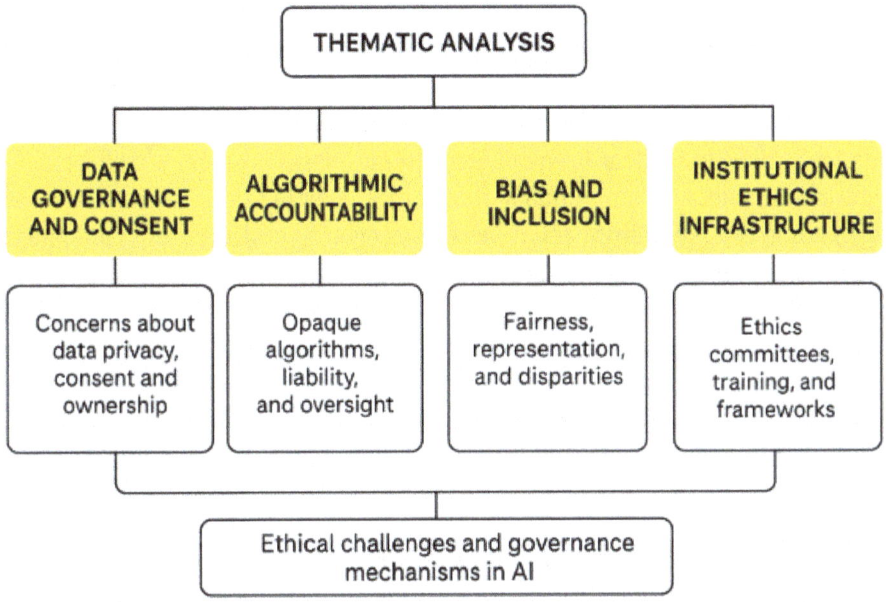

4.2.2 Case Study Insights

To understand the ethical challenges of AI in practical settings, four case studies were analyzed across the healthcare, education, finance, and security sectors. Each case offered real-world evidence of how ethical concerns arise and how governance measures attempt to address them. Together, these studies helped assess the ethical maturity of each domain and the relevance of the proposed Ethical Governance Framework for AI (EGF-AI).

In the healthcare sector, the study examined AI-based diagnostic systems such as IBM Watson Health and Google DeepMind, which are used to detect diseases and assist in clinical decisions. These systems showed high accuracy and efficiency but also raised serious concerns about data privacy, consent, and commercial use of patient information. Many patients are unaware that their medical records are used to train AI systems, and even when data are anonymized, there is still a chance of re-identification. To reduce these risks, hospitals have started adopting techniques like differential privacy, federated learning, and explainable AI models that make diagnostic decisions easier to understand. Some institutions have also set up AI ethics boards to ensure compliance with data protection laws such as the General

Data Protection Regulation (GDPR) and World Health Organization's ethics guidelines. Among all sectors, healthcare showed the highest level of ethical governance, mainly because it already follows strong bioethical and patient-centered practices.

In education, the study focused on AI-based assessment and online proctoring systems that became popular during the COVID-19 pandemic. Platforms such as ExamSoft and ProctorU helped maintain academic integrity but created new ethical problems related to student privacy, algorithmic bias, and mental well-being. In several cases, students were unfairly flagged for cheating due to technical issues, poor lighting, or body movements. These systems also collected large amounts of personal data, sometimes without clear information on how long the data would be stored or who could access it. To make such systems more ethical, experts suggested using local data storage, federated learning models, and clear consent procedures. They also emphasized that teachers and students should be trained in digital ethics and that schools should create transparent audit systems to review the fairness of AI tools. Table 3 shows Delphi Validation of EGF-AI Framework

Table 3. Delphi Validation of EGF-AI Framework

Evaluation Criterion	Round 1 Mean	Round 3 Mean	% Improvement
Clarity of Ethical Principles	3.8	4.6	21%
Sectoral Adaptability	3.6	4.4	22%
Policy Alignment	3.7	4.5	21%
Practical Implementability	3.5	4.2	20%
Overall Consensus Score	3.65	4.43	21.4%

In the finance sector, the case study examined how AI is used for credit scoring and risk analysis in banks and fintech companies. These systems help institutions make faster decisions and reduce fraud, but they often suffer from bias due to unbalanced training data. In some cases, loan applicants from lower-income areas or minority backgrounds received unfairly low credit scores. Experts recommended using fairness testing, bias correction algorithms, and external audits to make financial AI systems more transparent and just. Tools like SHAP and LIME were also used to make automated credit decisions easier to interpret. Although global laws such as the GDPR, the California Consumer Privacy Act (CCPA), and India's Digital Personal Data Protection Act (DPDPA) encourage fair and transparent use of AI, consistent application of these laws remains a challenge across financial institutions.

In the security sector, the study reviewed predictive policing and facial recognition technologies used for public safety. While these systems can help prevent crime and improve resource management, they raise serious issues related to bias, human rights, and privacy. Predictive policing models often rely on past crime data that may reflect existing social inequalities, leading to over-policing in certain communities. Similarly, facial recognition systems have shown higher error rates for women and darker-skinned individuals. Experts recommended keeping humans in the decision loop, ensuring transparency in algorithm design, and creating independent oversight bodies. Some even suggested a temporary ban on lethal autonomous weapons until international rules and accountability systems are established. Overall, this sector showed the lowest ethical maturity because of the conflict between national security goals and protection of individual rights.

Across all four case studies, several common insights were observed. Bias and transparency issues were found in every sector, although their effects varied depending on context. Sectors with stronger regulatory oversight, like healthcare and finance, showed higher ethical standards compared to education and security. The presence of internal ethics committees and regular algorithm audits also made a clear difference in responsible AI use. These findings support the main idea of the Ethical Governance Framework for AI, which suggests that ethical, legal, and institutional cooperation are all needed to ensure fairness, accountability, transparency, and privacy in AI systems.

Figure 5. Comparative FATP Radar Chart

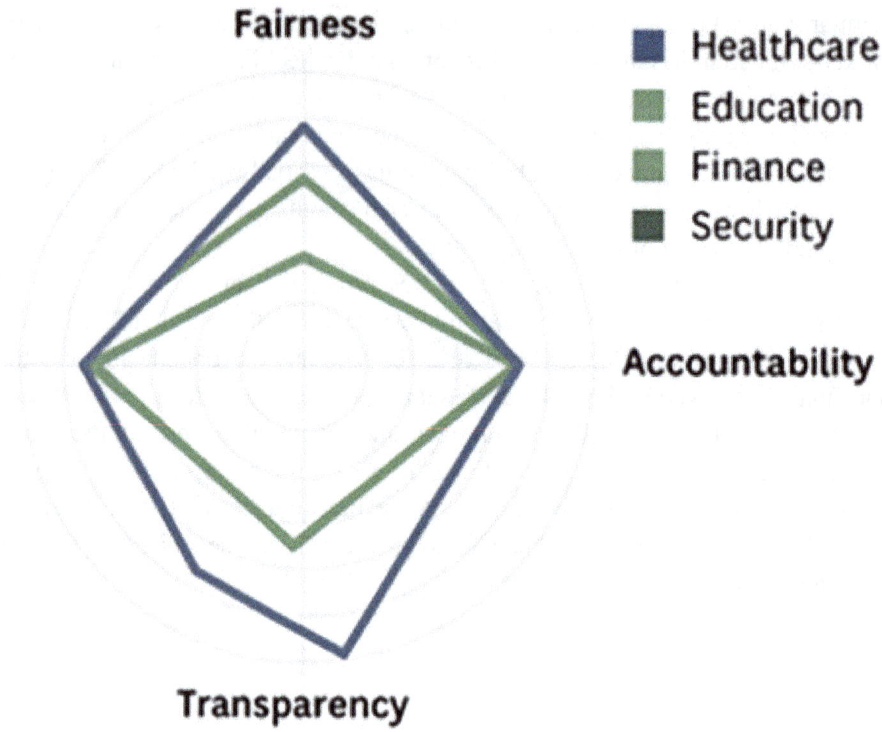

5. DISCUSSION

The findings from both the quantitative and qualitative analyses show that the ethical maturity of AI systems varies across different sectors. While the healthcare sector demonstrates relatively high compliance with ethical standards, others like security still face major challenges in ensuring fairness, transparency, and privacy. The results also confirm that strong governance mechanisms and legal frameworks play a key role in building ethical and trustworthy AI systems.

5.1 Cross-Sectorial Ethical Differences

The study revealed clear differences in how ethical practices are applied across healthcare, education, finance, and security. The healthcare sector benefits from a long tradition of ethical standards such as patient consent and medical confidentiality. This helps in adopting AI systems responsibly, with a focus on data privacy and informed consent. The education sector is still developing in this area, as the use of AI for grading and student monitoring raises questions about fairness and surveillance. The finance sector shows moderate ethical awareness, mainly driven by strict regulations and compliance requirements, but fairness issues remain because of biased historical data. The security sector faces the toughest challenge, as AI systems used for surveillance and law enforcement often clash with civil liberties and privacy rights. These differences highlight that ethical AI cannot be applied in a single uniform way but must be adapted to the needs and risks of each sector.

5.2 Application of FATP Principles in Practice

The four ethical principles—Fairness, Accountability, Transparency, and Privacy (FATP)—are widely recognized, but their practical implementation is uneven. Fairness is difficult to achieve when datasets are unbalanced or biased. Accountability becomes unclear when decisions are made by complex algorithms instead of humans. Transparency is often limited because many AI models operate as "black boxes," making their decisions hard to interpret. Privacy concerns are widespread, as AI relies on large amounts of personal data that may be misused or inadequately protected. Despite these challenges, the study found that improvements in one area can strengthen others. For example, making AI systems more transparent can increase accountability and fairness at the same time. Therefore, organizations should treat FATP principles as interconnected goals rather than separate requirements.

5.3 Governance Mechanisms and Global Regulations

The study compared existing laws and regulations such as the European Union's AI Act, the General Data Protection Regulation (GDPR), the California Consumer Privacy Act (CCPA), and India's Digital Personal Data Protection Act (DPDPA). These frameworks provide strong foundations for ethical AI use but differ in enforcement and scope. Healthcare and finance show higher compliance because these sectors already follow strict privacy and reporting standards. Education and security, however, still lack clear and consistent rules for AI governance. Experts stressed that international coordination is essential to avoid gaps between countries and to prevent "ethics shopping," where organizations move their operations to regions with weaker laws. A global standard that combines flexibility with accountability would help ensure fair AI use worldwide.

5.4 Expert Perspectives

Experts agreed that ethics should be built into AI systems from the start rather than being treated as an afterthought. They supported the idea of "ethics-by-design," where moral, legal, and technical checks are included at every stage of AI development. Many experts also recommended creating internal ethics boards, regular algorithm audits, and transparent reporting systems. Public awareness and participation were seen as equally important, as ethical governance should not be limited to technical experts. Involving teachers, doctors, policymakers, and citizens in discussions about AI use can build trust and ensure that decisions reflect public values. Experts emphasized that ethical AI is not only about following rules but also about promoting human dignity, fairness, and social responsibility.

5.5 Validation of the EGF-AI Framework

The Ethical Governance Framework for AI (EGF-AI) developed in this study was evaluated and refined through expert feedback using the Delphi method. Most participants agreed that the framework is practical and adaptable to different sectors. They appreciated its balance between ethical principles and regulatory requirements. The framework connects fairness, accountability, transparency, and privacy with concrete actions such as audit mechanisms, explainable models, and data protection practices. However, experts cautioned that each sector needs to customize the framework according to its unique risks. For instance, healthcare should focus more on privacy and consent, while finance should prioritize fairness and explainability. Continuous monitoring and regular ethical audits were also suggested to keep the framework effective as technology evolves.

6. SYNTHESIS AND IMPLICATIONS

The combined results from the qualitative and quantitative analyses show that ethical governance in AI cannot depend only on legal compliance or isolated guidelines. A balanced and adaptive approach is required—one that combines ethics-by-design, continuous monitoring, and participation from multiple stakeholders. The findings highlight that while AI offers major advantages in improving efficiency and decision-making, these benefits can only be fully realized when supported by strong ethical foundations. The analysis across healthcare, education, finance, and security sectors confirmed that each domain faces distinct challenges and requires customized governance solutions. However, several common lessons emerged. Ethical AI must begin with transparency and fairness in data collection and algorithm design. Institutions must also establish clear lines of accountability, ensuring that responsibility for AI decisions is not lost between developers, organizations, and policymakers. Privacy protection remains a critical concern, as AI systems rely heavily on personal and sensitive data. These ethical dimensions are not separate but interlinked—progress in one often strengthens the others.

In healthcare, the study showed that protecting patient privacy and ensuring fairness in diagnosis are top priorities. Hospitals and research organizations need to strengthen their data governance structures by adopting privacy-preserving methods and explainable AI models that allow doctors and patients to understand how medical recommendations are generated. This will help maintain trust and improve clinical outcomes without compromising ethical standards. In the education sector, the main challenge is maintaining fairness in automated grading and preventing the misuse of student data. Institutions should establish clear ethical audit frameworks, regularly review AI systems used for assessment, and include ethics as part of teacher and student training. Ethical awareness at all levels will help ensure that AI supports learning rather than becoming a tool for surveillance or bias.

For the finance sector, the study emphasizes the need to eliminate bias in credit scoring and decision-making systems. Financial organizations should implement regular fairness testing, bias correction algorithms, and third-party audits to ensure equal access and opportunity. Transparency in automated financial decisions will help rebuild trust between institutions and consumers, especially in digital banking and fintech services. The security sector faces the most sensitive ethical issues because of the conflict between national safety and personal freedom. Predictive policing, facial recognition, and autonomous defense systems should always include human oversight. Human-in-the-loop decision processes and strict proportionality checks can help reduce errors and protect human rights. Governments must also promote transparency and external review systems to maintain accountability in AI-based surveillance and defense technologies.Overall, the synthesis of results confirms that ethical AI governance must go beyond compliance. It requires a shared responsibility between policymakers, institutions, developers, and users. The validated Ethical Governance Framework for AI (EGF-AI) provides a practical roadmap for this purpose. By linking ethical theory with regulatory and institutional actions, it offers a flexible and scalable model that can be adapted to different sectors and cultural contexts.

The main implication of this research is that sustainable and trustworthy AI depends on continuous dialogue between ethics, technology, and governance. Institutions that adopt proactive ethical strategies will not only meet regulatory demands but also build long-term public confidence in AI. Future studies should apply the EGF-AI framework in real-world pilot projects and across countries to test its adaptability and to refine it further in response to technological and societal changes.

7. KEY FINDINGS

The overall findings from this study clearly show that the ethical performance of AI systems depends on how well each sector balances innovation with responsibility. The four sectors—healthcare, education, finance, and security—each face distinct challenges but also share common goals of fairness, transparency, accountability, and privacy. The summary below highlights the main ethical issues, existing strengths, observed weaknesses, and the most effective governance strategies identified for each domain.

In healthcare, the most pressing ethical issue is related to patient data privacy and informed consent. While hospitals and research organizations often have strong legal compliance structures and established bioethical standards, many AI systems still lack full transparency and explainability. Doctors and patients may not completely understand how diagnostic algorithms reach their conclusions, which can create trust gaps. To address this, hospitals should apply differential privacy techniques to protect sensitive data and adopt explainable AI models that allow medical decisions to be traced and understood. Regular algorithmic audits and human oversight can further strengthen fairness and accountability in clinical AI systems.

In education, the ethical concern centers on bias in AI-based grading and the misuse of student data. While schools and universities increasingly recognize the importance of ethical AI, many institutions lack robust data protection policies. Automated systems can unintentionally favor or penalize certain groups of students due to differences in language, behavior, or connectivity. To promote fairness and protect privacy, educational institutions should implement data anonymization practices, conduct regular ethical reviews of AI tools, and include digital ethics training for teachers and students. Integrating ethical education into the curriculum can also help future learners understand responsible AI use.

In finance, algorithmic discrimination remains a major ethical challenge. Financial institutions have the advantage of established regulatory oversight and audit processes, but bias in historical data still leads to unfair outcomes in credit scoring and lending decisions. To reduce these risks, financial organizations should use algorithmic fairness testing, deploy bias correction models, and carry out regular third-party audits. Transparent decision-making processes, explainable scoring systems, and user communication channels can further enhance trust between customers and institutions. The goal should be to make financial AI systems both efficient and socially responsible.

In security, the most significant ethical issue involves the balance between public safety and individual privacy. AI-based surveillance and predictive policing systems can improve law enforcement efficiency but also risk violating civil rights if used without transparency or human oversight. The strength of this sector lies in its advanced technological capabilities, but the weakness is the limited protection of privacy and accountability. Governments and agencies should adopt transparent oversight mechanisms, establish human-in-the-loop review systems, and ensure that any AI decision affecting individuals is subject to human verification. Clear proportionality checks and independent monitoring bodies can prevent misuse of AI in security operations. Across all four sectors, the study confirms that ethical challenges are deeply context-dependent. Effective governance requires a mix of technical, legal, and institutional measures tailored to each sector's risks. The proposed Ethical Governance Framework for AI (EGF-AI) bridges this gap by linking ethical theory with practical implementation tools such as audits, explainable models, and compliance boards. The framework encourages organizations to move beyond basic rule-following toward a culture of ethical responsibility and trust in AI systems. Future research should focus on applying this framework in real-world scenarios to measure its effectiveness and scalability. Continuous improvement through global cooperation and sector-specific adaptation will be essential for building AI systems that are fair, transparent, and aligned with human values.

8. CONCLUSION

This study highlights that the ethical use of artificial intelligence depends not only on technological progress but also on strong moral, legal, and institutional foundations. AI has the potential to bring major improvements to key sectors such as healthcare, education, finance, and security, but these benefits come with complex ethical responsibilities. Through a mixed-method approach combining surveys, interviews, and policy analysis, the study found that fairness, accountability, transparency, and privacy (the FATP principles) remain the core pillars of ethical AI governance. The findings show that healthcare currently demonstrates the highest ethical maturity, supported by established regulations and professional ethics. Education and finance are improving but still need stronger data protection and fairness mechanisms. The security sector continues to face serious challenges, especially concerning privacy and human rights. These differences prove that ethical AI cannot be governed by a single global rule but must be adapted to the values and conditions of each domain.

The Ethical Governance Framework for AI (EGF-AI) proposed in this study provides a structured approach for addressing these challenges. It connects ethical principles with real-world governance tools, including audits, explainable models, and accountability systems. The framework was validated through expert feedback, showing that it can be applied flexibly across different industries and regions. By focusing on both regulation and moral responsibility, the EGF-AI encourages organizations to design AI systems that are not only effective but also fair and trustworthy.

The study also emphasizes that achieving ethical AI requires collaboration. Policymakers, researchers, industry professionals, and users must work together to ensure that AI development respects human values. Continuous monitoring, public engagement, and ethical education are essential to maintain trust as technology evolves. In the long term, the success of AI will depend on how well humanity integrates innovation with compassion, efficiency with fairness, and progress with responsibility.By adopting the recommendations and framework presented in this research, institutions can move toward a future where AI enhances human welfare without compromising ethical standards. Responsible governance will ensure that artificial intelligence becomes a tool for inclusive growth and social good rather than a source of inequality or harm.

REFERENCES

Ahmad, N., Anshari, M., Hamdan, M., & Ali, E. (2024). Ethics and public trust in ai governance: A literature review. International Journal of Law. *Government and Communication*, *9*(37), 296–305. DOI: 10.35631/IJLGC.937025

Al Jadaan, O., Zaidi, H., Al Faress, M. Y., & Jabas, A. O. (2024). Ethics in AI and Computation in Automated Decision-Making. Advances in Computational Intelligence and Robotics Book Series, 397–424. DOI: 10.4018/979-8-3693-6230-3.ch012

Batool, A., Zowghi, D., & Bano, M. (2024). Responsible AI Governance: A Systematic Literature Review. https://doi.org//arxiv.2401.10896DOI: 10.48550

Bouderhem, R. (2024). Shaping the future of AI in healthcare through ethics and governance. *Humanities & Social Sciences Communications*, *11*(1), 1–12. DOI: 10.1057/s41599-024-02894-w

El Arab, R. A., Al Moosa, O. A., & Sagbakken, M. (2025). Economic, ethical, and regulatory dimensions of artificial intelligence in healthcare: An integrative review. *Frontiers in Public Health*, *13*, 1617138. Advance online publication. DOI: 10.3389/fpubh.2025.1617138 PMID: 40951387

Falvo, F., & Cannataro, M. (2024). Ethics of Artificial Intelligence: challenges, opportunities and future prospects. 5860–5867. DOI: 10.1109/BIBM62325.2024.10822112

Gesser da Costa, P., de Bem Machado, A., Antunes Vieira Willerding, I., & Mafra Lápolli, É. (2025). Governance and Ethics in the Use of Artificial Intelligence in Health. 377–392. DOI: 10.4018/979-8-3693-7630-0.ch015

Ismail, O. H., & Ahmad, N. (2025). Ethical and Governance Frameworks for Artificial Intelligence: A Systematic Literature Review. *International Journal of Interactive Mobile Technologies*, *19*(14), 121–136. DOI: 10.3991/ijim.v19i14.56981

Jiang, Y., Zhao, J., Yuan, Y., Zhang, T., Huang, Y., Zhang, Y., Wang, Y., Li, Y., Guo, X., Zhao, Y., Zhang, J., Zhang, Z., Lin, X., Zou, Y., Ma, H., Shang, Y., Hu, Y., Cai, K., Zhang, R., . . . Li, X. (2025). Never Compromise to Vulnerabilities: A Comprehensive Survey on AI Governance. arXiv.Org, abs/2508.08789. https://doi.org//arxiv.2508.08789DOI: 10.48550

Kartika, A. N., & Vic, B. J. (2025). Bridging Innovation and Governance: A Systematic Literature Review of Artificial Intelligence. *Electronic Medical Records, and Legal Protection in Healthcare.*, *3*(2), 173–181. DOI: 10.38035/gijlss.v3i2.411

Li, F., Ruijs, N., & Lu, Y. (2022). Ethics & AI: A Systematic Review on Ethical Concerns and Related Strategies for Designing with AI in Healthcare. *AI*, *4*(1), 28–53. DOI: 10.3390/ai4010003

Liu, D., & Li, X. (2025). AI vs. Human: Reconciling Autonomy and Governance in Decision-Making. *Lecture Notes in Education Psychology and Public Media*, *114*(1), 82–87. DOI: 10.54254/2753-7048/2025.LC19101

Naripeddy, S. C. B., & Thotakura, V. R. (2025). Ethical Challenges and Solutions in the Deployment of Artificial Intelligence Sys-tems. *Deleted Journal*, *8*(02), 81–110. DOI: 10.60087/jaigs.v8i02.392

Pruski, M. (2025). Ethical Challenges to the Adoption of AI in Healthcare: A Review. The New Bioethics, 1–17. DOI: 10.1080/20502877.2025.2541438

Rajwade, S., Yadaw, P. K., & Ingle, A. (2025). Ethics and legal dimensions of artificial intelligence in healthcare: technical, business, and educational perspectives. DOI: 10.52152/801158

Rojas Contreras, M., & Portilla Jaimes, J. O. (2024). AI Ethics in the Fields of Education and Research: A Systematic Literature Review. 1–6. DOI: 10.1109/ICACIT62963.2024.10788651

Singh, B., Rahim, M. A. B. U., Hussain, S., Rizwan, M. A., & Zhao, J. (2023). AI Ethics in Healthcare -. *Survey (London, England)*, •••, 826–833. DOI: 10.1109/QRS-C60940.2023.00086

Wu, Y., & Liu, X. M. (2023). Navigating the Ethical Landscape of AI in Healthcare: Insights From a Content Analysis. *IEEE Technology and Society Magazine*, *42*(3), 76–87. DOI: 10.1109/MTS.2023.3306543

Chapter 7
AI in Critical Sectors: Healthcare, Education, Finance, and Security – Ethical Challenges in Generative AI

Anisah Sri Utami
https://orcid.org/0009-0001-4348-5736
Universitas Esa Unggul, Indonesia

Binastya Anggara Sekti
https://orcid.org/0000-0001-5489-4888
Universitas Esa Unggul, Indonesia

ABSTRACT

This chapter explores the transformative impact of Artificial Intelligence (AI) across four critical sectors healthcare, education, finance, and security while addressing the profound ethical challenges arising from the rise of generative AI. It examines how AI enhances diagnostic precision, personalized learning, financial efficiency, and cyber resilience, yet simultaneously introduces risks such as bias, privacy violations, algorithmic opacity, and misinformation. The chapter emphasizes the growing need for ethical governance frameworks, fairness auditing, and transparency to maintain public trust. Furthermore, it discusses how generative AI technologies, including large language models and deepfakes, complicate issues of authorship, authenticity, and accountability. By proposing governance and mitigation strategies, this chapter contributes to understanding how ethics, trust, and regulation can ensure that AI innovation aligns with human rights, fairness, and societal well-being.

DOI: 10.4018/979-8-3373-7011-8.ch007

ht © 2026, IGI Global Scientific Publishing. Copying or distributing in print or electronic forms without written permission of IGI Global Scientific Publishing is prohibited. Use of this chapter to generative artificial intelligence (AI) technologies is expressly prohibited. The publisher reserves all rights to license its use for generative AI training and machine learning model development.

1. INTRODUCTION

Figure 1. Overview of AI in Critical Sectors and Ethical Challenges

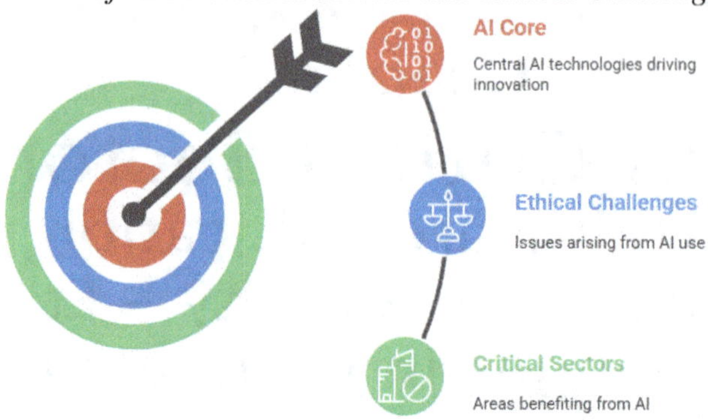

The rapid evolution of Artificial Intelligence (AI) has revolutionized how societies organize and manage critical infrastructures and essential services. Once considered a futuristic concept, AI now underpins decision-making processes across sectors such as healthcare, education, finance, and security. These technologies enhance efficiency, accuracy, and personalization by integrating advanced data analytics, predictive modeling, and machine learning algorithms. From assisting doctors in diagnosing complex diseases to enabling adaptive learning experiences in classrooms, automating credit assessments, and detecting cyber threats in real time, AI has become the backbone of many essential operations. However, this transformation also brings profound ethical and social challenges that demand serious attention, as AI's influence expands into domains that affect fundamental aspects of human life. AI in critical sectors operates within environments that directly impact human welfare, dignity, and trust. Algorithmic decisions influence who receives life-saving treatment first, which students are labeled as at-risk, who qualifies for a loan, and how governments identify and respond to security threats . As a result, errors, biases, or inequities within AI systems are not just technical flaws but moral failures that can perpetuate discrimination, exclusion, and injustice. Machine learning models trained on biased data can replicate existing social inequalities, producing systemic unfairness in domains such as healthcare outcomes, financial accessibility, and educational opportunity. This underscores the need for AI systems to be not only technically sound but ethically accountable ensuring fairness, inclusivity, and respect for human rights. The emergence of generative AI has further intensified these ethical complexities. Unlike traditional rule-based algorithms, generative AI embodied in large language models, image generators, and deepfake systems can autonomously produce text, visuals, and sounds that closely mimic human creativity. While such systems enable innovations in communication, education, and content creation, they also open the door to misinformation, copyright infringement, and identity manipulation. Deepfake videos, for instance, have been weaponized to distort political discourse and defame individuals, eroding public trust and blurring the boundary between truth and fabrication. The dual nature of generative AI its capacity to empower and deceive poses new moral questions regarding authorship, authenticity, and accountability in digital environments. Trust forms the cornerstone of societal acceptance of AI. When AI systems are opaque or produce unjust outcomes, they erode confidence not only in technology but also in the institutions that deploy them. In sensitive domains such as healthcare and finance, maintaining public trust is essential, as individuals must believe that AI-driven decisions uphold fairness and transparency. Consequently, designing AI systems that *deserve* trust through explainability, accountability, and inclusiveness is as important as ensuring their technical robustness. Without a foundation of ethical trust, even the most advanced AI systems risk public resistance and societal backlash. As nations increasingly adopt AI, balancing innovation with ethical governance becomes a global priority. Frameworks such as the European Union's *Artificial Intelligence Act* and UNESCO's *Recommendation on the Ethics of Artificial Intelligence* reflect growing awareness of the need for transparency, fairness, and accountability in AI deployment. Yet these efforts face challenges of implementation, particularly in developing regions where regulatory infrastructure lags behind technological adoption. The absence of consistent oversight risks widening the global digital divide and deepening inequalities between those who create AI technologies and those who are governed by them. Hence, responsible governance must ensure that AI benefits are equitably distributed across societies. This chapter therefore explores the multifaceted role of AI across four critical sectors healthcare, education, finance, and security by examining both its transformative potential and its ethical vulnerabilities. Each sector introduces unique dilemmas: medical AI must balance efficiency with empathy; educational AI must foster inclusion while promoting personalization; financial AI must ensure fairness amid profit-driven motives; and security AI must maintain safety without compromising privacy. The emergence of generative AI amplifies these tensions by creating novel ethical risks misinformation, data exploitation, and intellectual property conflicts that test existing legal and moral frameworks. By investigating these issues, the chapter aims to reveal how ethics, trust, and governance intersect in shaping AI's societal impact. Ultimately, navigating the AI era requires more than technical advancement it requires moral responsibility and the cultivation of social trust. Ethical AI development must transcend compliance and embody shared human values such as justice, dignity, and accountability. The introduction of generative AI challenges societies to rethink not only how technology is created but also how it should be governed and used. The collective task ahead is to ensure that AI serves as an instrument of empowerment rather than manipulation, of equality rather than exclusion. Through ethical stewardship and interdisciplinary collaboration, humanity can guide AI toward a future where innovation coexists harmoniously with integrity and compassion. Quantum Computing (QC) and Artificial Intelligence (AI) stand at the forefront of technological innovation in the Industry 6.0 era, propelling progress in automation, intelligent analytics, and process optimization. The convergence of these two technologies offers transformative potential across domains such as data science, healthcare, finance, and cybersecurity, by harnessing the power of qubits, superposition, and quantum entanglement to achieve significantly faster and more efficient computational performance(Pineda et al., 2026).

2. AI IN HEALTHCARE

2.1 Applications

Artificial Intelligence (AI) has become an indispensable component of modern healthcare systems, transforming both clinical practice and biomedical research. Its integration has led to significant progress in diagnostics, decision support, patient monitoring, and administrative efficiency. In clinical diagnostics, AI-powered image analysis is now widely used in radiology, pathology, and dermatology to detect anomalies that may escape human observation. Convolutional Neural Networks (CNNs) and other deep learning architectures can analyze X-rays, MRIs, and CT scans with accuracy comparable to or even exceeding expert radiologists. For instance, Google's DeepMind successfully developed an AI system capable of detecting over 50 eye diseases from retinal scans, achieving performance on par with clinical specialists

Beyond imaging, AI plays a critical role in predictive analytics, particularly in forecasting disease risks and patient outcomes. Machine learning models are increasingly used for early detection of sepsis, hospital readmission, and treatment response prediction. By integrating data from electronic health records (EHRs), wearable sensors, and laboratory results, AI systems can identify subtle indicators of patient deterioration in real time, allowing for timely interventions that save lives. Predictive models such as gradient boosting or recurrent neural networks help clinicians anticipate complications before they manifest clinically, thus optimizing resource allocation in hospitals. Drug discovery and development have also been revolutionized by AI technologies. Traditional drug design is a costly and time-consuming process; however, AI-driven computational models can accelerate it by predicting molecular interactions, optimizing compounds, and repurposing existing drugs. Generative AI models such as Generative Adversarial Networks (GANs) and transformer-based systems can simulate new molecular structures or synthesize medical data for research purposes, reducing dependency on animal testing and improving data privacy. These technologies not only shorten discovery cycles but also contribute to the emergence of personalized medicine, where AI tailors treatment plans to individual genetic, environmental, and behavioral factors. In clinical documentation and administrative management, AI-based natural language processing (NLP) tools assist healthcare professionals by automatically summarizing clinical notes, generating discharge summaries, and coding diagnoses for billing systems. These tools significantly reduce administrative burden, minimize human error, and allow physicians to devote more time to direct patient care. Furthermore, robotic process automation (RPA) and AI chatbots are increasingly deployed to streamline scheduling, triage patients, and provide preliminary guidance in telemedicine platforms especially relevant during and after the COVID-19 pandemic. At the intersection of clinical care and research, AI driven personalized medicine stands out as one of the most transformative applications. Through the integration of genomic sequencing, biomedical imaging, and real-time biosensor data, AI systems can identify optimal therapeutic pathways tailored to individual patients. For example, machine learning models have been used to predict tumor mutation profiles and select the most effective immunotherapy drugs for oncology patients. This precision-oriented approach marks a paradigm shift from reactive to proactive medicine, emphasizing prevention, prediction, and personalization. Despite its promise, the adoption of AI in healthcare also necessitates attention to ethical, legal, and technical considerations. Issues such as data privacy, algorithmic bias, interpretability, and accountability must be addressed to ensure that AI systems are safe, equitable, and trustworthy. Additionally, medical professionals require proper training to interpret AI-generated insights responsibly. Thus, collaboration between clinicians, data scientists, ethicists, and policymakers is essential for the sustainable integration of AI into healthcare systems. The concept of Trustworthy Artificial Intelligence (TwAI) within the healthcare domain remains inadequately defined, making it challenging for legal manufacturers and developers to effectively interpret and implement the General Safety and Performance Requirements. This ambiguity extends to ensuring the protection of patients' fundamental rights, which are essential for compliance with European regulatory frameworks and for meeting the expectations of diverse stakeholders. Consequently, developers of Medical Device Software (MDS) must determine suitable performance metrics that reflect the robustness and reliability of AI-enabled medical devices, guided by specific use cases and the risk assessments conducted during the development process(Lynch et al., 2026).

Figure 2. AI Applications in Healthcare

Application Area	AI Techniques Used	Example Outcomes
Medical Imaging	CNN, Deep Learning	Tumor detection, retinal scan analysis
Predictive Analytics	Gradient Boosting, RNN	Sepsis, readmission prediction
Drug Discovery	GANs, Reinforcement Learning	New molecule generation, drug repurposing
Personalized Medicine	Genomics + ML	Tailored treatment recommendations
Hospital Management	NLP, RPA, Chatbots	Workflow optimization, triage support

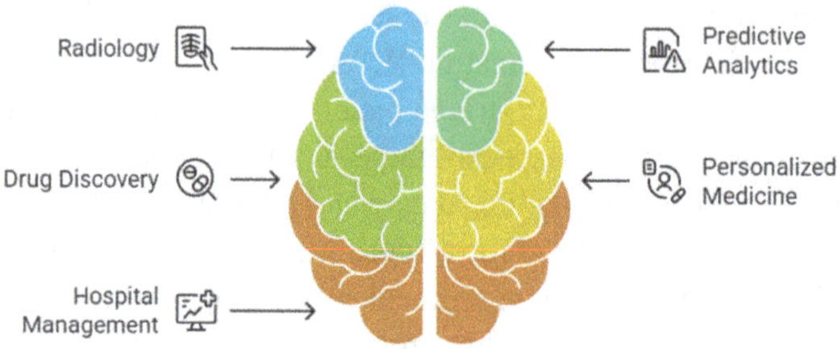

2.2 Benefits

The integration of Artificial Intelligence (AI) in healthcare has produced significant advancements that improve diagnostic accuracy, enhance operational efficiency, and expand accessibility to medical services. Through deep learning and predictive analytics, AI contributes not only to more precise medical decision-making but also to systemic improvements in healthcare delivery. These benefits collectively support a vision of data-driven, equitable, and efficient medical ecosystems.

- **Diagnostic Accuracy:** AI-powered diagnostic systems have demonstrated remarkable capabilities in improving the sensitivity and specificity of disease detection. Deep learning algorithms especially convolutional neural networks (CNNs) analyze complex imaging data such as X-rays, CT scans, or retinal photographs, identifying subtle anomalies that might elude human clinicians. For instance, Google's *DeepMind* algorithm achieved expert-level accuracy in detecting over 50 eye diseases, matching the performance of ophthalmologists. Similarly, AI tools have shown proficiency in classifying skin lesions, predicting cardiovascular diseases, and detecting early-stage cancers. These technologies not only augment physician performance but also facilitate early intervention, potentially reducing mortality rates. Breast cancer persists as a predominant contributor to female mortality globally, highlighting the necessity for timely and accurate diagnostic methodologies to enhance therapeutic effectiveness. While deep learning frameworks have shown promising results in mammogram image classification, their interpretability remains constrained. Moreover, these models are susceptible to diagnostic inconsistencies arising from image variability, noise interference, and the insufficient volume of high-quality annotated data(Ismailova et al., 2026).

- **Operational Efficiency:** Beyond clinical diagnostics, AI substantially enhances hospital operations by automating administrative tasks, optimizing resource allocation, and reducing clinician burnout. Natural Language Processing (NLP) systems, for instance, streamline the documentation process by automatically transcribing and summarizing medical notes. Predictive analytics also supports hospital logistics anticipating patient admissions, managing inventory, and improving scheduling. By minimizing time spent on repetitive, non-clinical activities, AI allows healthcare professionals to focus more on patient care, improving both satisfaction and outcomes. Studies have reported that such automation can reduce waiting times by up to 30% and lower administrative costs by 20%. This study introduces an innovative framework for converting legal language into computational logic that can be directly executed by machines, thereby facilitating the automation of processes within the public sector. Acknowledging the critical impact of artificial intelligence (AI) in legal contexts, the proposed framework prioritizes interpretability by combining explainable AI (XAI) methodologies with natural language processing (NLP) tools. The system utilizes scope-limited pattern recognition and grammatical parsing to ensure transparent and reliable translation of legal provisions into operational logic(Saravanan et al., 2026).
- **Expanded Access to Healthcare:** AI-driven telemedicine and virtual health assistants have transformed access to healthcare, especially in underserved or remote regions. These systems enable real-time consultations, symptom triage, and remote monitoring for chronic diseases using wearable IoT devices and mobile applications. For example, *Babylon Health*'s AI platform provides preliminary diagnostic advice based on patient-reported symptoms, improving healthcare availability in areas with limited medical personnel. Moreover, generative AI models can translate complex medical information into local languages, fostering inclusivity and accessibility for diverse populations. Microstrip patch antennas (MPAs) have become essential components in biomedical technologies due to their compact size, lightweight structure, and suitability for wearable or implantable healthcare devices. This review highlights recent advancements in MPA design, emphasizing the integration of biocompatible materials such as PDMS, Parylene, and graphene. These materials ensure both the safety of human tissues and high antenna

performance during direct interaction with biological environments(Bertl et al., 2026).

Figure 3. Visualization of AI Benefits in Healthcare

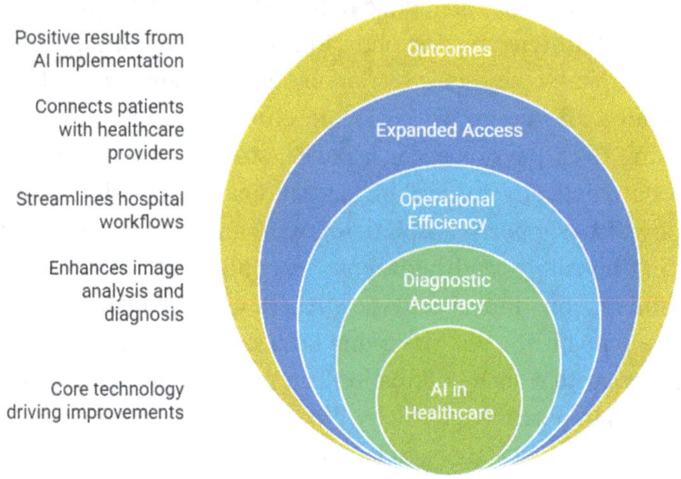

2.3 Ethical Risks

As Artificial Intelligence (AI) becomes increasingly embedded in healthcare, it raises profound ethical and societal questions. While AI systems can enhance diagnostic accuracy, improve operational efficiency, and expand access to medical care, they also introduce risks that threaten patient safety, equity, and trust. Four major ethical challenges dominate discussions in this domain: data bias, privacy and data protection, responsibility and accountability, and hallucination and misinformation in generative AI systems.

- **Data Bias:** Data bias is one of the most pressing ethical risks in medical AI. Machine learning algorithms depend heavily on the quality, diversity, and representativeness of their training data. When datasets disproportionately reflect certain demographics such as primarily Caucasian patients, specific age groups, or urban populations the resulting models tend to perform poorly on underrepresented groups. For instance, discovered that a widely used healthcare risk prediction algorithm in the United States systematically underestimated the medical needs of Black patients because the model used healthcare spending as a proxy for health status. This bias led to discriminatory allocation of medical resources, highlighting how algorithmic inequities can reinforce social disparities in health outcomes. Demonstrated that AI diagnostic systems trained on biased imaging data yielded lower accuracy for minority populations and female patients. The ethical concern extends beyond performance disparity it touches upon the principles of justice and equity in healthcare. When AI-driven diagnostics misclassify or overlook diseases in certain demographic groups, it perpetuates structural inequalities in access and quality of care. Therefore, ensuring dataset diversity, applying bias detection audits, and incorporating fairness-aware machine learning techniques are essential for creating equitable AI healthcare systems. Feature selection (FS) plays a critical role in enhancing model accuracy and efficiency when dealing with high dimensional datasets by isolating the most informative attributes. Concept Factorization (CF), derived from Non negative Matrix Factorization (NMF), has gained attention for its ability to uncover intrinsic data structures and generate interpretable concept representations. Nevertheless, most CF based FS techniques operate in an unsupervised manner, failing to utilize label information, which often results in a preference for features exhibiting high variance rather than high relevance(Sheikhpour et al., 2026).

- **Privacy and Data Security:** AI in healthcare relies on vast amounts of sensitive data electronic health records (EHRs), genetic information, and data collected from wearable sensors or IoT devices. While these data are essential for model training and personalization, they raise serious privacy and data protection concerns. Medical data breaches can have catastrophic consequences, ranging from financial fraud and identity theft to discrimination in employment or insurance coverage. Even anonymized datasets are not entirely secure. Studies have shown that re-identification attacks where anonymized data are cross-referenced with public databases can successfully uncover patient identities. Moreover, with the growing adoption of cloud-based health systems, unauthorized access or cyberattacks can expose sensitive patient information. The ethical challenge lies in balancing data accessibility for innovation with the obligation to safeguard patient confidentiality. Advanced privacy-preserving techniques such as federated learning, homomorphic encryption, and differential privacy have been proposed to mitigate these risks. However, these methods are still evolving and require standardization for widespread adoption. Maintaining transparency in data governance and obtaining informed consent remain central ethical imperatives for building public trust in AI enabled healthcare. Organizations are progressively adopting agentic information systems (agentic IS) to enhance operational efficiency and achieve performance-oriented goals. Despite their advantages, these systems introduce significant ethical challenges, including issues of fairness, bias, autonomy, transparency, accountability, and privacy. Notably, more than 70% of stakeholders particularly end-users have reported apprehension regarding the ethical implications and potential misuse of agentic IS across various business domains(Saeed & Prybutok, 2026) .

- **Responsibility and Accountability:** Determining responsibility when AI systems make medical errors presents a profound ethical and legal dilemma. In traditional healthcare, liability is typically attributed to human professionals; however, AI introduces a shared decision paradigm where outcomes result from collaboration between human clinicians and algorithms. If an AI misdiagnosis leads to patient harm, should responsibility rest with the developer, the clinician, or the institution deploying the system? This issue is exacerbated by the black-box nature of many AI models, especially deep learning systems, which offer limited transparency about how specific decisions are made. Emphasize that explainability and interpretability are essential for accountability. Clinicians must be able to understand and challenge AI recommendations, not merely accept them as authoritative outputs. Establishing ethical governance frameworks including human in the loop oversight, continuous auditing, and transparent documentation can ensure accountability remains traceable and ethical standards are upheld. Open source (OS) software development fundamentally depends on maintaining high code quality, making developers' active engagement in code review a critical component of the improvement process. In contrast to non OS environments where formal mechanisms such as sanctions or rewards are used to enhance developers' sense of accountability open-source projects typically lack such structured incentives. This absence raises important questions regarding how OS developers perceive their accountability for the code they produce and how this perception influences their motivation to maintain and enhance code quality(Bartsch et al., 2026).
- **Hallucination and Misinformation:** The rise of Generative AI has transformed how information is generated and disseminated in medicine but it also brings new risks. Hallucination refers to AI-generated content that is factually incorrect yet presented with high confidence and linguistic fluency. In clinical contexts, this can lead to the dissemination of false medical advice, inaccurate summaries of patient records, or fabricated research interpretations. Demonstrated that while GPT-4 performs impressively on standardized medical exams, it still produces hallucinations that can mislead users if unchecked. warns that generative models trained on unverified medical sources may amplify misinformation, especially when integrated into public health communication systems. These risks underscore the ethical imperative for human verification, source attribution, and regulatory control in deploying

generative AI tools for healthcare applications. Due to the restricted quality and quantity of available training datasets, supervised deep learning approaches for point cloud semantic segmentation frequently suffer from limited generalization capabilities and the occurrence of hallucinations, especially when dealing with unstructured environments in autonomous driving scenarios(Xu et al., 2026).

2.4 Governance Recommendations

The responsible governance of Artificial Intelligence (AI) systems in healthcare requires a multi layered framework that integrates technical, ethical, and regulatory safeguards. As AI continues to influence diagnostic accuracy, treatment personalization, and operational efficiency, implementing robust governance mechanisms becomes essential to ensure fairness, reliability, and accountability.

- **Implement external validation and continual auditing:** External validation is critical for evaluating AI models across diverse populations and healthcare settings. Regular, independent auditing allows stakeholders to detect algorithmic drift, biases, and inconsistencies that might emerge over time due to evolving data distributions. Continuous monitoring and post deployment audits ensure that model performance remains consistent and transparent throughout its lifecycle. Such validation should involve multidisciplinary teams including clinicians, ethicists, and data scientists to maintain alignment between clinical goals and ethical standards. Quantum Computing (QC) and Artificial Intelligence (AI) have become foundational technologies driving the transformation of Industry 6.0, fostering progress in automation, advanced analytics, and process optimization. The convergence of these technologies holds immense potential to revolutionize domains such as data science, healthcare, finance, and cybersecurity by enabling faster and more efficient computation through the principles of qubits, superposition, and quantum entanglement(Pineda et al., 2026).
- **Apply fairness-aware training and debiasing methods:** Bias mitigation must be embedded throughout the AI development process, from data collection to model deployment. Fairness aware algorithms, re-sampling, and re weighting techniques can help reduce representation bias by ensuring that minority and vulnerable groups are not disadvantaged in diagnostic predictions or treatment recommendations. Moreover, incorporating fairness constraints into model objectives encourages equitable performance across demographic subgroups, aligning AI systems with the ethical principle of justice in healthcare. As machine learning continues to be applied in online

and real time settings to handle continuously evolving data streams, algorithmic fairness has become an increasingly critical ethical and legal concern. In many scenarios, class imbalance within the data must also be addressed to maintain reliable predictive accuracy. However, most existing fairness-aware stream learning approaches manage these challenges either through pre or post processing techniques, often concentrating on improving a single bias or discrimination metric, while treating class imbalance as a separate, isolated problem(Lammers et al., 2026).

- **Adhere to strict data governance laws (GDPR, HIPAA):** Compliance with international and national data protection frameworks is essential for preserving patient privacy and preventing data misuse. Regulations such as the General Data Protection Regulation (GDPR) in Europe and the Health Insurance Portability and Accountability Act (HIPAA) in the United States provide legal guidance on data consent, security, and anonymization. Implementing these standards promotes patient trust and transparency in AI driven healthcare systems while ensuring that sensitive medical data are used ethically and responsibly. In the modern digital era, safeguarding personal data has become increasingly vital, with the General Data Protection Regulation (GDPR) standing as a central legal framework for ensuring privacy protection. Nevertheless, many organizations face difficulties in maintaining compliance because of the complexity of legal language, the constant evolution of regulatory requirements, and the challenge of ensuring transparency in their privacy policies(Okonicha & Sadovykh, 2026).
- **Establish shared accountability between developers, clinicians, and regulators:** AI governance in healthcare cannot rely solely on technical controls; it must also clarify roles and responsibilities among stakeholders. Shared accountability frameworks ensure that developers are responsible for algorithmic integrity, clinicians oversee appropriate usage, and regulators provide oversight to safeguard public interest. Collaborative governance fosters transparency and trust, encouraging the responsible adoption of AI innovations without compromising patient welfare. Because large Vision-Language Models (VLMs) possess inherent security vulnerabilities, establishing robust security governance has become increasingly important. These concerns arise mainly from the risks associated with biased or noisy training data and adversarial threats, such as data poisoning and prompt injection attacks, which can compromise model integrity and reliability(Shi et al., 2026).

3. AI IN EDUCATION

3.1 Applications

Artificial Intelligence (AI) has transformed the education sector by enabling personalized, efficient, and data driven learning experiences. One of its main applications is adaptive learning, where AI algorithms adjust the pace and difficulty of lessons according to each learner's ability and progress. This ensures a more tailored and effective learning process. Another major area is automated grading, which uses Natural Language Processing (NLP) to assess assignments and exams automatically, allowing teachers to focus more on mentoring rather than administrative tasks. Student analytics supports educators in identifying learners who may be at risk of underperforming. By analyzing behavioral and performance data, AI enables timely interventions and personalized support strategies. Intelligent Tutoring Systems (ITS) simulate one on one instruction by providing adaptive feedback and personalized learning paths, enhancing understanding and engagement. Finally, generative AI tools such as ChatGPT or educational content generators assist teachers in creating lesson materials, quizzes, and explanations more efficiently, promoting innovation and flexibility in teaching practices.The growing regional inequality in sports education has emerged as a major concern within the educational landscape. Differences in resource allocation, educational quality, and participation levels across regions have resulted in significant gaps in students' physical fitness, health outcomes, and access to developmental opportunities(Li & Zhang, 2026).

3.2 Benefits

Artificial Intelligence (AI) has introduced transformative benefits to the education sector, particularly in enhancing personalization, scalability, and real time learning feedback.

- Personalized learning allows AI-based systems to tailor instruction based on each learner's abilities, interests, and progress. Adaptive algorithms analyze students' interactions and adjust content difficulty or format accordingly, leading to improved engagement, motivation, and long term retention.
- Scalability represents another significant advantage of AI in education. Intelligent platforms can deliver high quality instruction to large groups of learners at lower costs, expanding access to education globally. By automating grading and tutoring, AI helps reduce teacher workload while maintaining consistent instructional quality, especially in regions with limited educational resources.

- Immediate feedback mechanisms enabled by AI powered systems allow learners to receive instant evaluation and personalized suggestions. This not only supports active learning but also accelerates skill acquisition and self directed study. Such timely feedback fosters continuous improvement, helping both students and educators track progress and identify learning gaps efficiently.

3.3 Ethical Risks

While AI offers significant benefits in education, its implementation also introduces a range of ethical risks that must be carefully addressed to maintain fairness, integrity, and inclusivity in learning environments.

- **Academic Integrity:** One of the most pressing concerns is the threat to academic honesty. With the rise of generative AI tools capable of producing essays, solving complex problems, and even generating creative projects, the line between original student work and AI generated content has become blurred. This challenges traditional assessment methods and undermines fairness in academic evaluation. Educators face growing difficulty in distinguishing between genuine student effort and automated assistance, necessitating stronger plagiarism detection and digital literacy education.The growing accessibility of large language models (LLMs) has sparked major concerns regarding the preservation of academic honesty in beginner level programming courses(Esteban Cuellar Argotty & Manrique, 2026).
- **Dependence on AI:** Excessive reliance on AI tools can diminish students' critical thinking, creativity, and problem solving skills. When learners depend heavily on automated tutoring or essay generation systems, they may engage less in cognitive effort and independent reasoning. Moreover, the reduction in human interactionsuch as teacher student dialogue and peer collaborationcan negatively affect social and emotional development, making education overly mechanistic.
- **Digital Divide:** The integration of AI in education also risks deepening the digital divide between students who have access to advanced technologies and those who do not. Learners in under-resourced regions or schools may be excluded from AI based learning tools, widening disparities in educational opportunity and achievement. This inequality threatens the principle of inclusive education, emphasizing the need for equitable access to digital infrastructure and teacher training.
- **Data Privacy and Surveillance:** AI-driven learning analytics collect vast amounts of data about students' behaviors, performance, and even emotional

states. While this data helps personalize learning, it also raises serious privacy and security concerns, especially when involving minors. Unauthorized data sharing or surveillance can expose students to exploitation and breach of confidentiality. Therefore, strict data protection standards and ethical frameworks are needed to ensure that student data is collected and used responsibly.

3.4 Generative AI Challenges

Generative Artificial Intelligence (AI) has transformed educational practices by automating content creation, such as generating quizzes, summaries, essays, and personalized study materials. However, despite these advantages, generative models often face significant challenges related to accuracy, bias, and authorship. First, AI generated content can propagate factual inaccuracies, as models rely on probabilistic predictions rather than verified sources. This issue becomes critical in academic contexts, where misinformation can mislead students and undermine educational credibility. Second, generative systems may reinforce cultural and social biases embedded in their training data. For example, language models trained on internet text can reproduce stereotypes or unequal representations of certain groups, leading to biased educational outcomes. Lastly, AI assisted writing raises authorship and plagiarism concerns. Students may overuse generative tools to produce essays or problem solutions, making it difficult for educators to distinguish between genuine student work and AI-generated output. This challenge necessitates the implementation of AI use policies and plagiarism detection systems to ensure academic integrity. Generative Artificial Intelligence Appropriation (GAIA) refers to the process through which users adopt generative AI technologies, customize them to suit their specific purposes, and incorporate them into their professional workflows(Khatri et al., 2026).

3.5 Recommendations

- Develop transparent institutional AI policies defining acceptable use. Clear institutional policies are vital for guiding the ethical and responsible use of AI in education. These policies should define acceptable and unacceptable uses of AI tools, outline accountability measures, and ensure that educators and students understand the implications of AI-assisted work. Transparent governance frameworks help maintain fairness and trust, preventing misuse such as plagiarism or overreliance on generative systems. Various countries, guided by national and institutional policies, have established repositories of Open Educational Resources (OER) to enhance and support both teaching and learning processes(Drumond et al., 2025).

- Integrate AI ethics and literacy into teacher and student training. Building AI literacy among educators and learners ensures that they can use AI technologies critically and responsibly. Training programs should cover topics like algorithmic bias, data privacy, and the ethical implications of automation in learning. Educators equipped with AI ethics knowledge can guide students in understanding when and how AI should be used as a supportive learning tool rather than a replacement for original thinking.
- Adopt assessment methods emphasizing process and reasoning. Traditional testing methods are increasingly inadequate in the age of AI generated content. Educational institutions should shift toward evaluating students' reasoning processes, problem solving steps, and critical thinking rather than final outputs alone. Process based assessment encourages authentic learning and reduces the temptation to rely on AI generated answers.
- Provide equitable digital infrastructure support for under resourced schools. To prevent widening the digital divide, governments and institutions must ensure equal access to AI based educational tools and digital infrastructure. Support for under resourced schools through funding, teacher training, and affordable connectivity ensures that all students can benefit from AI enhanced education. Equitable access promotes inclusivity and social justice in digital learning ecosystems.

4. AI IN FINANCE

4.1 Applications

Artificial Intelligence (AI) is transforming the financial industry by enhancing security, efficiency, and decision making across multiple domains. One of its most significant contributions lies in fraud detection, where machine learning algorithms analyze vast amounts of transactional data to identify anomalies and suspicious behavior in real time. These systems continuously learn from new fraud patterns, improving their ability to detect and prevent financial crimes more effectively. In the area of credit scoring and risk assessment, AI enables financial institutions to evaluate borrowers more accurately by incorporating diverse data sources such as transaction history, behavioral trends, and social factors. This approach not only reduces default risks but also promotes financial inclusion by extending credit to individuals who lack traditional credit histories. AI also plays a crucial role in algorithmic trading, where deep learning models process massive volumes of market data to predict trends and execute trades within milliseconds. These algorithms enhance profitability, adapt to market volatility, and improve overall market efficiency. In customer service, AI powered chatbots and virtual assistants are reshaping the way banks interact with clients. By utilizing Natural Language Processing (NLP), these systems can understand and respond to customer inquiries, provide personalized financial advice, and operate 24/7, leading to greater satisfaction and reduced operational costs. Finally, predictive analytics empowers financial decision makers with real-time insights into market dynamics, helping them optimize investment portfolios, forecast risks, and identify growth opportunities. Through these data driven approaches, AI ensures that financial institutions remain agile, informed, and resilient in an increasingly complex market environment. In the fast paced advancement of artificial intelligence (AI), establishing strong ethical governance frameworks has become essential, especially as AI technologies are increasingly embedded within sectors such as finance and public administration(Naraganahalli Veerabhadraiah, 2026).

4.2 Benefits

- **Fraud Prevention:** Artificial Intelligence significantly enhances the security of financial transactions by identifying fraudulent activities in real time. Machine learning algorithms analyze millions of data points from customer behavior, transaction histories, and spending patterns to detect irregularities that may indicate fraud. For instance, anomaly detection models can identify deviations from a user's typical activity and trigger alerts within milliseconds, preventing unauthorized transactions before they occur. This proactive defense system strengthens consumer trust and reduces financial loss for institutions.
- **Financial Inclusion:** AI also promotes greater financial inclusion by enabling credit scoring based on alternative data sources such as mobile payment history, social interactions, and digital footprint. This approach allows financial institutions to extend credit to individuals who lack traditional banking records or collateral, especially in developing regions. Such inclusive algorithms help bridge the gap between the banked and unbanked populations, fostering equitable access to financial services.
- **Operational Optimization:** Automation powered by AI improves efficiency across banking and investment operations. Robotic Process Automation (RPA) and predictive analytics streamline repetitive administrative tasks such as compliance reporting, transaction processing, and portfolio monitoring. This reduces operational costs and minimizes human error, while allowing professionals to focus on strategic financial decisions. Studies show that AI driven process automation can increase accuracy by up to 90% and cut operational expenses by 25–30%.

4.3 Ethical Risks

- **Algorithmic Discrimination:** One of the most pressing ethical challenges in AI driven finance is algorithmic discrimination. Biases embedded in training datasets often reflecting historical or structural inequalities can result in discriminatory outcomes against marginalized groups. For instance, automated credit scoring systems may disadvantage women, minorities, or individuals from low-income regions if the training data underrepresents these populations or associates them with higher financial risk. Such biases can perpetuate social inequality rather than promote financial inclusion. Addressing this issue requires fairness aware machine learning frameworks and continuous auditing of AI models to ensure equitable treatment in financial decision making. Unwanted biases embedded within datasets serve as major contributors to algorithmic discrimination. Their significance has been extensively acknowledged in both academic research on algorithmic fairness and in emerging legal and regulatory frameworks addressing anti-discrimination in AI systems(Ceccon et al., 2025).
- **Opacity and Lack of Explainability:** AI systems used for credit scoring, loan approval, and investment recommendations often operate as black boxes, where even developers may not fully understand how specific outputs are generated. This lack of explainability undermines transparency and accountability, especially in cases where users are denied financial access without clear justification. From an ethical standpoint, this opacity conflicts with principles of due process and informed consent, calling for the development of explainable AI (XAI) mechanisms that provide interpretable reasoning for automated financial decisions.
- **Market Instability:** The rise of algorithmic and high frequency trading (HFT) has transformed financial markets, but it also introduces systemic risks. AI driven trading bots can react to market signals at millisecond speeds, amplifying volatility during periods of uncertainty. When multiple algorithms follow similar patterns, cascading effects often termed flash crashes may occur, leading to widespread instability. Ethical governance of AI in trading therefore requires robust oversight, human in the loop mechanisms, and circuit breakers to prevent automated overreactions.
- **Synthetic Fraud and Deepfakes:** The advancement of generative AI technologies introduces a new frontier of financial fraud. Deepfake audio and video can be used to impersonate executives or clients, leading to unauthorized transactions or identity theft. Similarly, AI-generated synthetic identities created by combining real and fake personal data can bypass traditional verification systems, posing major risks for banks and credit institutions. The ethical

implication is profound, as these tools can erode trust within digital financial ecosystems. Mitigating synthetic fraud requires combining AI based authentication systems with human oversight, as well as international cooperation on digital identity standards.

4.4 Recommendations

- **Adopt explainable AI frameworks for decision transparency:** Explainable AI (XAI) ensures that automated financial decisions such as credit approvals or loan assessments are interpretable and justifiable. By making model reasoning transparent, institutions can improve accountability and user trust while enabling regulators to audit decision making processes effectively. Our emphasis is on explainability as an essential requirement for automated decision-making systems rather than solely for individual models. While the field of Explainable Artificial Intelligence (XAI) provides numerous methods to enhance the transparency of automated decisions, most XAI research overlooks the broader social and institutional contexts in which these models function(Buszydlik et al., 2026).
- **Enforce fairness and bias audits:** Regular bias audits are essential to detect and correct algorithmic discrimination embedded in financial models. Continuous monitoring of training data and model outputs helps maintain fairness across demographic groups, aligning with ethical standards and anti discrimination policies.
- **Introduce consumer recourse mechanisms:** Financial systems should provide clear avenues for customers to appeal or question AI driven decisions. Such mechanisms ensure procedural fairness and protect individuals from automated errors or unjust outcomes, reinforcing public confidence in AI powered financial services.
- **Coordinate with regulators to monitor generative fraud risks:** Given the rise of deepfakes and synthetic identity fraud, financial institutions must collaborate with regulatory bodies to establish detection frameworks and reporting standards. Coordinated governance helps mitigate the evolving risks posed by generative AI in digital finance.

5. AI IN SECURITY

5.1 Applications

Artificial Intelligence (AI) plays a transformative role in modern security systems by enhancing threat detection, intrusion response, surveillance analytics, identity management, and counter terrorism analysis. Machine learning algorithms can analyze large scale network traffic and system logs to detect anomalous behaviors that indicate potential cyberattacks. This enables real-time threat detection and rapid incident response, minimizing damage and downtime. AI powered surveillance analytics leverage computer vision to recognize suspicious activities in public spaces, supporting crime prevention and emergency response. In identity management, AI systems employ biometric authentication such as facial recognition or behavioral analysis to strengthen access control and reduce fraud. Furthermore, generative AI contributes to cyber defense by simulating attack scenarios, enabling organizations to test and improve their defensive strategies. These proactive simulations help identify vulnerabilities before real attackers can exploit them, significantly improving overall resilience. The paper explores how Generative Artificial Intelligence (GenAI) is revolutionizing vulnerability assessment (VA) and risk management (RM) throughout their entire lifecycle within the field of cybersecurity (CS)(Mirtaheri et al., 2026).

5.2 Benefits

- **Threat Anticipation:** Artificial Intelligence (AI) significantly enhances the capability of security systems to anticipate and prevent cyberattacks before they occur. Through machine learning and deep learning algorithms, AI continuously analyzes massive amounts of network traffic data to identify subtle anomalies and patterns that may indicate potential intrusions. Predictive models, particularly those based on recurrent neural networks (RNN) and reinforcement learning, can forecast future attack vectors based on historical data trends. For instance, AI powered threat intelligence systems can detect early signs of phishing campaigns, ransomware propagation, or insider threats, allowing organizations to take preemptive countermeasures. This proactive defense approach reduces the time window between threat detection and mitigation, strengthening overall cybersecurity posture.
- **Efficiency:** AI driven automation brings unprecedented efficiency to security operations by handling large-scale and complex data environments. In traditional systems, human analysts manually sift through logs and alerts a process prone to fatigue and error. However, with AI based systems, these tasks are automated through supervised and unsupervised learning models

capable of filtering noise, clustering attack patterns, and prioritizing critical alerts. This dramatically shortens response time and minimizes false positives. Furthermore, Natural Language Processing (NLP) assists in analyzing unstructured data such as threat reports, social media feeds, and dark web communications to detect emerging cyber threats. In national security contexts, AI systems facilitate real time decision making and coordination across agencies, optimizing the allocation of defensive resources.

- **Resilience:** AI enhances the resilience of digital infrastructure by enabling continuous monitoring, adaptive learning, and rapid recovery after incidents. Unlike traditional static defense mechanisms, AI powered cybersecurity frameworks evolve dynamically through reinforcement learning improving their defense strategies with each attack encountered. For example, intrusion detection systems (IDS) integrated with AI can autonomously isolate compromised nodes, restore system integrity, and adapt firewall configurations without human intervention. In critical infrastructures such as defense networks or financial systems, such resilience ensures uninterrupted operations and reduces the potential for cascading system failures. Additionally, AI enables cyber resilience planning through simulation and scenario modeling, using generative models to predict the impact of hypothetical attack scenarios and optimize response strategies.

5.3 Ethical Risks

- **Mass Surveillance:** The deployment of AI driven surveillance systems especially those utilizing computer vision and facial recognition poses profound risks to privacy and civil liberties. Governments and private entities increasingly rely on AI to monitor public spaces, analyze behavioral patterns, and identify individuals in real time. However, such large scale data collection often occurs without explicit consent, enabling potential misuse for political repression, discrimination, or social control. Continuous surveillance blurs the line between security and intrusion, eroding personal autonomy and violating fundamental human rights. Ethical governance must therefore balance the benefits of AI security with the preservation of privacy through transparency, legal oversight, and proportionality in data usage.
- **Misidentification in Facial Recognition:** Facial recognition technologies, although valuable for law enforcement, are prone to significant biases and inaccuracies. Studies have shown that AI models trained on unbalanced datasets tend to misidentify individuals with darker skin tones, women, and other underrepresented demographic groups. These algorithmic disparities can lead to wrongful arrests, false accusations, and public distrust in law

enforcement technologies. The ethical challenge extends beyond technical limitations it raises questions of justice, equality, and the accountability of institutions deploying these tools. Regulatory measures and fairness aware model training are essential to mitigate such harms.

- **Autonomous Weapons and Accountability:** The militarization of AI, particularly in the development of autonomous weapons systems (AWS), introduces complex moral and legal dilemmas. These systems, capable of selecting and engaging targets without direct human intervention, challenge traditional frameworks of accountability and just war theory. Determining responsibility in cases of unintended civilian casualties or unlawful killings becomes highly problematic when lethal decisions are delegated to machines. Ethical and international policy debates increasingly call for strict human oversight, or even bans, on fully autonomous weapons to ensure compliance with humanitarian law and ethical warfare principles.
- **Deepfake Manipulation:** The advent of generative AI has enabled the creation of hyper realistic deepfakes synthetic videos, audio, or images that convincingly mimic real individuals. While generative technologies have legitimate uses in education and entertainment, their misuse poses severe threats to democracy and social trust. Deepfakes can be weaponized for disinformation, political manipulation, blackmail, and identity fraud. The proliferation of manipulated media undermines public confidence in authentic information systems and complicates digital forensics efforts. Addressing these risks requires a combination of technical countermeasures such as watermarking and authenticity verification and legal frameworks that deter malicious creation and distribution.

5.4 Recommendations

- **Establish Strict Oversight and Transparency for Surveillance AI:** AI driven surveillance must be governed through rigorous oversight frameworks to prevent abuse and safeguard civil liberties. Transparent deployment practices, public accountability mechanisms, and independent audits are essential to ensure compliance with ethical standards and privacy laws. Governments should implement clear boundaries on data collection, storage, and use ensuring surveillance remains proportionate to legitimate security objectives. Transparency reports and human rights impact assessments can help rebuild public trust in security technologies. Additionally, algorithmic explainability should be mandated so that affected individuals can challenge or understand surveillance based decisions.

- **Support Global Treaties Restricting Autonomous Weapon Deployment:** The growing development of autonomous weapon systems (AWS) calls for urgent international governance. The United Nations and related bodies must establish global treaties limiting or banning fully autonomous lethal systems to maintain human control over critical combat decisions. Ethical principles such as meaningful human control and adherence to international humanitarian law should underpin all military AI applications. Collaborative regulation can prevent an AI arms race, reduce accidental escalation, and ensure that AI use in warfare aligns with human moral and legal responsibility.
- **Invest in Watermarking and Forensic Deepfake Detection:** The proliferation of deepfakes threatens digital trust and national security, demanding robust technical countermeasures. Investment in AI-based watermarking, provenance verification, and deepfake detection systems is critical to identifying and mitigating maliciously altered content. Forensic tools capable of verifying source authenticity can protect individuals, institutions, and governments from disinformation campaigns and reputational harm. Collaboration between technology companies, researchers, and policymakers can accelerate the adoption of standardized authenticity frameworks to preserve truth in digital communication.
- **Build Cross National Cyberethics Cooperation Frameworks:** Cybersecurity and AI governance transcend national borders; hence, global cooperation is essential. Cross-national cyberethics frameworks can harmonize ethical standards, facilitate information sharing, and coordinate responses to AI-driven cyber threats. International alliances such as the Global Partnership on AI (GPAI) play a crucial role in promoting responsible innovation, human rights compliance, and transparency in AI security. Such collaboration not only enhances collective resilience but also helps establish norms and best practices for the ethical use of AI in defense and surveillance systems.

6. ETHICAL CHALLENGES OF GENERATIVE AI

6.1 Deepfakes and Disinformation

Generative AI tools are now capable of producing ultra-realistic synthetic audio, video, or images often referred to as deepfakes. While these have creative or benign uses, they can also be misused to spread disinformation, impersonate individuals, or manipulate public opinion. Deepfakes erode public trust because it's hard for viewers to distinguish authentic content from fabricated ones. Studies show that exposure to deepfakes doesn't always result in belief in false content, but it fosters distrust and uncertainty toward media in general.

6.2 Intellectual Property

Generative AI often learns from large datasets that include copyrighted texts, images, or other creative works. This raises questions about who owns the AI generated output: the AI developer, the user giving prompts, or the original creator. Legal standards for copyright traditionally require human creativity, which often excludes works generated by AI alone. There are growing concerns that training on copyrighted material without proper licensing or consent may violate intellectual property laws.

6.3 Privacy and Memorization

Large language models and other generative systems have been shown to memorize parts of their training data, including personally identifiable information (PII). Under certain prompts, these models can reproduce sensitive data verbatim, potentially exposing private information. This poses serious privacy risks, especially when models are trained on data with weak privacy protections or no permission. Techniques like differential privacy, model editing, or selective forgetting are being researched to reduce memorization and mitigate risk.

6.4 Hallucination

Generative AI models sometimes generate statements that are factually incorrect or unverifiable known as hallucinations. These errors can emerge even when the model is confident in its output, which is dangerous in domains like law, medicine, or news, where misinformation can have serious consequences. Users may be misled if they assume all AI generated content is accurate.

6.5 Bias and Representation

Bias in the training data (overrepresentation of certain groups, cultural biases, stereotyped media) leads generative AI to perpetuate or even amplify stereotypes and underrepresentation of marginalized groups. The outputs (images, text, etc.) may reflect implicit biases in gender, race, ethnicity, etc., contributing to inequity and reinforcing societal prejudice. Addressing this requires careful dataset curation and fairness aware modeling.

6.6 Accountability

When generative AI causes harm whether via disinformation, privacy breaches, or bias it's often unclear who is legally or ethically responsible: the prompt-giver, the model creator, the deployer, or the platform hosting it. Existing legal frameworks are not always well equipped to assign responsibility, especially where the outcome is emergent and not directly specified by any one actor. This ambiguity complicates recourse for harmed individuals

7. MITIGATION STRATEGIES AND GOVERNANCE

7.1 Technical Measures

- **Apply differential privacy and federated learning:** These techniques enhance data protection by preventing the exposure of individual information during model training. Differential privacy injects statistical noise into data to preserve anonymity, while federated learning allows local model training without transferring raw data to a central server, thus maintaining user privacy.
- **Implement watermarking and content provenance tracking:** Digital watermarking embeds invisible identifiers into AI generated media, while provenance tracking ensures transparency by recording the origin and modification history of digital content. These tools are vital for identifying AI generated materials, combating deepfakes, and preserving content authenticity.
- **Regularly retrain and evaluate models to minimize bias:** AI models must undergo continuous retraining and bias audits to ensure fairness and reliability. Periodic evaluation with diverse datasets reduces discrimination and improves model performance over time.

7.2 Organizational Measures

- **Conduct independent ethics audits pre deployment:** Independent ethics audits ensure that AI systems comply with ethical, legal, and social standards before deployment. These audits evaluate aspects such as fairness, privacy, transparency, and societal impact. Engaging third party evaluators helps prevent internal bias and promotes accountability, especially in high-stakes sectors like healthcare and finance.
- **Establish AI certification for critical applications:** Certification frameworks validate that AI systems meet predefined safety, transparency, and

fairness requirements. Similar to product safety certifications, AI certification provides assurance to users and regulators that the system adheres to trustworthy AI principles. This is particularly vital for AI used in critical areas such as autonomous vehicles, medical diagnosis, or financial decision making.

- **Maintain documentation of decision pipelines and datasets:** Comprehensive documentation covering dataset sources, model design choices, and decision making workflows enhances traceability and accountability. Frameworks like Model Cards and Datasheets for Datasets make AI systems more transparent and interpretable for both regulators and end users.

7.3 Regulatory Approaches

- **Enforce right to explanation laws:** The right to explanation ensures that individuals affected by automated decisions can understand how those decisions were made. This principle, embedded in frameworks like the EU General Data Protection Regulation (GDPR), promotes transparency and accountability in AI systems. By mandating that organizations disclose the rationale behind algorithmic outputs, such laws help prevent opaque decision-making and protect citizens from unjust outcomes.
- **Ban or limit high risk uses (facial recognition, autonomous weapons):** Governments and international organizations increasingly call for restrictions on high-risk AI applications such as real time facial recognition and autonomous weapon systems. These technologies pose severe ethical and human rights risks, including mass surveillance, discrimination, and loss of human control in warfare. Implementing bans or strict regulations ensures that AI development aligns with humanitarian law and democratic values.
- **Develop cross-border agreements for AI misuse prevention:** AI challenges, such as disinformation campaigns, cyberattacks, and data misuse, transcend national borders. Thus, international cooperation and treaties are essential to establish shared norms and enforcement mechanisms. Cross border governance frameworks like the OECD AI Principles and the UNESCO Recommendation on the Ethics of AI foster global accountability, harmonize standards, and promote the safe and ethical use of AI technologies.

8. CASE STUDIES

- **Healthcare:** AI driven diagnostic systems have demonstrated remarkable performance within controlled environments but often fail to generalize across diverse populations. For example, Google's DeepMind model achieved expert level accuracy in detecting eye diseases using UK based datasets but showed reduced accuracy when applied to different demographic groups due to population. This case highlights the ethical and practical necessity of external validation, fairness testing, and continual auditing before clinical deployment.

- **Education:** In education, intelligent tutoring systems and generative AI tools have significantly improved student engagement and personalized learning outcomes. However, these technologies have also led to increased instances of AI assisted cheating and plagiarism, challenging educators to redefine academic integrity frameworks. This illustrates the double edged nature of AI adoption in education enhancing learning while simultaneously demanding stronger ethical oversight and digital literacy training.
- **Finance:** AI based credit scoring systems leveraging alternative data sources such as telecom usage and behavioral analytics have expanded financial access to previously unbanked populations. Yet, these systems raise serious privacy concerns, as continuous data collection blurs the boundaries between financial inclusion and digital surveillance. This case emphasizes the importance of transparent governance and adherence to privacy regulations like GDPR and HIPAA to maintain consumer trust.
- **Security:** In the domain of security, deepfake incidents have become increasingly common, posing a severe threat to public trust and information integrity. The rapid spread of synthetic media has compelled governments and international organizations to introduce emergency policies promoting digital watermarking and forensic verification techniques. This underscores the urgent need for global collaboration in combating AI driven misinformation and strengthening digital authentication systems.

9. POLICY RECOMMENDATIONS

- **Apply risk based regulation according to sector sensitivity:** Regulatory frameworks should adapt to the varying degrees of risk across sectors. For example, AI used in healthcare and law enforcement demands stricter oversight compared to entertainment or marketing applications. The European Union's AI Act adopts this tiered approach, distinguishing between unacceptable, high, and limited risk systems.
- **Ensure dataset transparency and documentation:** Transparent data practices are essential to trace model behavior and biases. Requiring data sheets for datasets allows regulators and researchers to assess fairness, consent, and

representativeness, strengthening accountability and reproducibility in AI systems.

- **Involve multistakeholder governance (public, academic, and industry):** Effective AI governance demands collaboration among governments, researchers, civil society, and private sectors. This inclusive approach ensures diverse ethical perspectives and reduces the risk of regulatory capture or bias.
- **Mandate periodic independent audits:** Independent algorithmic audits enhance trust by verifying model fairness, security, and explainability. Similar to financial audits, they provide external accountability and help detect hidden harms before deployment.
- **Strengthen AI literacy and ethics education:** Embedding AI literacy in education and professional training ensures that users, policymakers, and developers can critically assess AI's social implications. This fosters a culture of ethical awareness and responsible innovation.
- **Foster international cooperation for trust and accountability:** Since AI impacts transcend national borders, global coordination is vital. Initiatives like the OECD AI Principles and the Global Partnership on AI promote shared norms, interoperability, and ethical standards worldwide.

CONCLUSION

Artificial Intelligence (AI) has profoundly transformed critical sectors, redefining how societies deliver essential services in healthcare, education, finance, and security. In healthcare, AI enhances diagnostic accuracy, operational efficiency, and access to care, yet also raises ethical concerns such as data bias, privacy breaches, and accountability gaps. In education, AI driven adaptive learning and generative tools foster personalized instruction and scalability, while simultaneously challenging academic integrity and equitable access. Within finance, predictive analytics, algorithmic trading, and AI based credit scoring improve decision-making and inclusion but risk algorithmic discrimination, opacity, and financial instability. In security, AI strengthens threat detection, surveillance, and cyber defense, yet introduces concerns over mass surveillance, misidentification, autonomous weapons, and the proliferation of deepfakes. Generative AI, in particular, introduces unique ethical and societal challenges. Its ability to produce hyper realistic synthetic content blurs the boundary between truth and fabrication, amplifying misinformation, bias, and potential harm in sensitive domains. Across all sectors, the dual nature of AI its capacity for both innovation and unintended consequences highlights the need for comprehensive governance strategies, including explainability, fairness auditing, robust data governance, stakeholder accountability, and international cooperation.

Ultimately, maximizing AI's benefits while mitigating its risks requires a balanced approach that combines technological safeguards with ethical, legal, and policy frameworks. Societies must cultivate AI literacy, transparency, and trust, ensuring that AI remains a tool for empowerment rather than a source of inequality, manipulation, or systemic harm. The path forward demands continuous vigilance, interdisciplinary collaboration, and proactive policy making to safeguard human rights, social cohesion, and the public good in an AI driven era.

REFERENCES

Bartsch, S. C., Schmidt, J.-H., Adam, M., & Benlian, A. (2026). Increasing developers' code accountability perceptions in open source software development. *International Journal of Information Management*, *86*, 102974. Advance online publication. DOI: 10.1016/j.ijinfomgt.2025.102974

Bertl, M., Price, S., & Draheim, D. (2026). Transforming legal texts into computational logic: Enhancing next generation public sector automation through explainable AI decision support. *International Journal of Cognitive Computing in Engineering*, *7*(1), 40–57. DOI: 10.1016/j.ijcce.2025.07.003

Buszydlik, A., Altmeyer, P., Dobbe, R., & Liem, C. C. S. (2026). Understanding the Affordances and Constraints of Explainable AI in Safety-Critical Contexts: A Case Study in Dutch Social Welfare. *Lecture Notes in Computer Science, 15978 LNCS*, 118–136. DOI: 10.1007/978-3-032-02515-9_8

Ceccon, M., Cornacchia, G., Dalle Pezze, D., Fabris, A., & Susto, G. A. (2025). Underrepresentation, label bias, and proxies: Towards Data Bias Profiles for the EU AI act and beyond. *Expert Systems with Applications*, *292*, 128266. Advance online publication. DOI: 10.1016/j.eswa.2025.128266

Drumond, G. M., Méxas, M. P., & Meza, L. A. (2025). Perception of educators on open educational resources (OER) repositories in higher education. *Encontros Bibli*, *30*, 1–25. DOI: 10.5007/1518-2924.2025.e99827

Esteban Cuellar Argotty, J., & Manrique, R. (2026). AI-Generated Code Detection: An Examination of Current Tools in Education. *Lecture Notes in Computer Science, 15723 LNCS*, 192–201. DOI: 10.1007/978-3-031-98281-1_15

Ismailova, A., Abdikerimova, G., Uzakkyzy, N., Muratkhan, R., Aitimov, M., Tergeusizova, A., & Beissegul, A. (2026). Development of a feature vector for accurate breast cancer detection in mammographic images. *International Journal of Cognitive Computing in Engineering*, *7*, 12–25. DOI: 10.1016/j.ijcce.2025.08.001

Khatri, P., Duggal, H. K., Thomas, A., Corvello, V., Prałat, E., & Shiva, A. (2026). Development and validation of the generative artificial intelligence appropriation (GAIA) Scale: A comprehensive measurement tool for assessing user engagement and utilisation. *Technovation*, *150*, 103379. Advance online publication. DOI: 10.1016/j.technovation.2025.103379

Lammers, K., Vaquet, V., & Hammer, B. (2026). Continuous Fair SMOTE – Fairness-Aware Stream Learning from Imbalanced Data. *Lecture Notes in Computer Science, 16068 LNCS*, 336–348. DOI: 10.1007/978-3-032-04558-4_27

Li, S., & Zhang, Z. (2026). Leveraging Artificial Intelligence Integration in Regional Sports Education to Foster Equitable and Sustainable Development. *Lecture Notes of the Institute for Computer Sciences, Social-Informatics and Telecommunications Engineering, LNICST, 617 LNICST*, 211–220. DOI: 10.1007/978-3-031-92517-7_16

Lynch, N. S. J., Loughran, R., McHugh, M., & McCaffrey, F. (2026). Trustworthy Artificial Intelligence in Healthcare: A Proposed Framework. *Communications in Computer and Information Science, 2657 CCIS*, 69–90. DOI: 10.1007/978-3-032-04288-0_5

Mirtaheri, S. L., Movahed, N., Shahbazian, R., Pascucci, V., & Pugliese, A. (2026). Cybersecurity in the age of generative AI: A systematic taxonomy of AI-powered vulnerability assessment and risk management. *Future Generation Computer Systems, 175*, 108107. Advance online publication. DOI: 10.1016/j.future.2025.108107

Naraganahalli Veerabhadraiah, Y. (2026). Decentralized Blockchain System for Ethical and Responsible AI in Generative Systems. *Lecture Notes in Computer Science, 16159 LNCS*, 87–103. DOI: 10.1007/978-3-032-06323-6_7

Okonicha, O., & Sadovykh, A. (2026). Enhancing GDPR Compliance Through NLP: Automated Policy Evaluation and Legal Document Analysis. *Lecture Notes in Networks and Systems, 1471 LNNS*, 408–423. DOI: 10.1007/978-3-031-94770-4_34

Pineda, V. G., Valencia-Arias, A., Giraldo, F. E. L., & Zapata-Ochoa, E. A. (2026). Integrating artificial intelligence and quantum computing: A systematic literature review of features and applications. *International Journal of Cognitive Computing in Engineering*, *7*, 26–39. DOI: 10.1016/j.ijcce.2025.08.002

Saeed, K., & Prybutok, V. R. (2026). When utility meets ethics: A stakeholder perspective on agentic information systems delegation. *International Journal of Information Management*, *86*, 102976. Advance online publication. DOI: 10.1016/j.ijinfomgt.2025.102976

Saravanan, S., Haimavathi, K. U., & Aafizaa, K. (2026). Biomedical Antenna Design: Micro strip Patch Antennas for Wearable and Implantable Healthcare Applications—A Review. *Biomedical Materials & Devices*, *4*(1), 414–424. DOI: 10.1007/s44174-025-00299-0

Sheikhpour, R., Saberi-Movahed, F., Jalili, M., & Berahmand, K. (2026). Semi-supervised feature selection with concept factorization and robust label learning. *Pattern Recognition*, *172*, 112317. Advance online publication. DOI: 10.1016/j.patcog.2025.112317

Shi, X., Chen, S., Zhang, G., Wei, W., Li, Y., Fan, Z., & Liu, J. (2026). Jailbreak attack with multimodal virtual scenario hypnosis for vision-language models. *Pattern Recognition*, *172*, 112391. Advance online publication. DOI: 10.1016/j.patcog.2025.112391

Xu, F., Xiao, Y., Mei, J., Hu, Y., Fu, Q., & Shi, H. (2026). Domain-adaptive point cloud semantic segmentation via knowledge-augmented deep learning. *Pattern Recognition*, *172*, 112528. Advance online publication. DOI: 10.1016/j.patcog.2025.112528

Chapter 8
AI and Human Dignity for Case Studies and Practical Frameworks for Corporate AI Governance Models

Irna Rismayanti
https://orcid.org/0009-0007-4629-0399
Universitas Esa Unggul, Indonesia

Agung Mulyo Widodo
https://orcid.org/0000-0002-9792-7114
Universitas Esa Unggul, Indonesia

ABSTRACT

This chapter examines the complex interplay between artificial intelligence (AI) and human dignity in the framework of corporate governance and ethical responsibility. This study analyzes the methods by which large technology-driven organizations implement AI systems that significantly influence human lives, social trust, and the ethical dimensions of work. This chapter conducts a multi-layered analysis of corporate practices in automation, labor management, and digital surveillance, demonstrating how these systems challenge conventional notions of respect, fairness, and human autonomy. This analysis utilizes global case studies from prominent corporations including Google, Microsoft, and Amazon to highlight advancements and ethical deficiencies in existing governance models. The discussion highlights

DOI: 10.4018/979-8-3373-7011-8.ch008

ght © 2026, IGI Global Scientific Publishing. Copying or distributing in print or electronic forms without written permission of IGI Global Scientific Publishing is prohibited. Use of this chapter to generative artificial intelligence (AI) technologies is expressly prohibited. The publisher reserves all rights to license its use for generative AI training and machine learning model development.

the ethical conflict between technological efficiency and human-centered values, underscoring the necessity for transparent frameworks that align innovation with moral accountability.

1. INTRODUCTION

The emergence of AI as a significant influence in the global economy, communication, and decision-making represents a pivotal transformation in human history. The assumption that AI would eventually supplant humans in the corporate world is borne out by the fact that AI can mimic human intelligence and carry out tasks that humans aren't capable of (Bariş et al., 2024). AI extends its influence beyond altering production methods and interpersonal interactions; it also impacts cognitive processes and moral decision-making. Agency, accountability, and identity are increasingly distributed across hybrid human-machine systems, extending beyond traditional human actors. In this context, the concept of human dignity representing the intrinsic worth and autonomy of individuals gains significance and relevance. Dignity functions as a moral guide and a standard for evaluating the alignment of AI-driven progress with the core principles of human civilization. The significance of dignity in the era of AI lies in its ability to bridge moral theory and practical governance. Historically, the metrics for assessing technological achievement have included efficiency, accuracy, and optimization. Dignity introduces a novel framework for evaluation. Every new idea must prioritize the preservation of human life, not as a fluctuating factor, but as an ultimate objective. This ethical viewpoint compels businesses, governments, and society to reevaluate their approaches to value creation. The pursuit of automation and algorithmic logic must be continuously assessed concerning the protection of humanity's essential qualities: empathy, agency, and moral self-determination. The increasing prevalence of machine intelligence in various sectors, including the workplace, healthcare, social services, and government, extends its impact beyond economic changes to influence moral and social structures as well. AI systems function as mechanisms for sorting, evaluating, and prioritizing various elements. They determine who is granted visibility, who receives recognition, and who is denied opportunity. The proliferation of AI is a direct outcome of the widespread adoption of new technologies in many different industries. The healthcare business is another major user of AI and related technologies (Demir-Kaymak et al., 2024). The capacity to mediate recognition, which affirms human dignity, renders AI both transformative and perilous. Dehumanization may arise from both technical biases or failures and significant philosophical shifts in societal views regarding the human role in decision-making processes. The delegation of moral authority to autonomous systems may reduce the essence of human dignity to a mere statistical abstraction.

These developments indicate a notable paradox within business structures. Many companies claim to prioritize "ethical AI," yet their daily operations predominantly focus on profit maximization, efficiency, and shareholder satisfaction. In this context, ethics functions more as a rhetorical shield than as a structural constraint. Excluding dignity from the framework of AI governance leads to a scenario where technological advancement occurs without corresponding moral comprehension. AI systems implemented by businesses for purposes such as hiring, credit scoring, or monitoring can yield significant economic advantages; however, they also present risks to the psychological and social foundations of human trust. Trust is essential for the legitimacy of both the technology and the organizations that utilize it. Algorithmic systems diminish dignity through various mechanisms: they generate biased outcomes that exacerbate inequality, infringe upon individual privacy through surveillance, and render interactions less personal, thereby undermining personal freedom (Sekti, 2025b). Each of these strategies diminishes the perception of being recognized as a whole human being rather than simply a data point. The reduction of dignity to a mere criterion for compliance, rather than a lived experience, risks leading civilizations toward a technological utilitarianism in which efficiency justifies various intrusions. This issue reflects a deficiency in governance structures rather than a failure of technology itself, as these structures fail to consider the moral implications of technological advancements. The ethical dimension of machine intelligence should be examined not as a secondary element of AI policy but as a fundamental principle. Developing governance models that incorporate dignity as a fundamental value requires an integration of ethical philosophy, regulatory frameworks, and organizational practices. Businesses must recognize their role not only as economic entities but also as moral institutions that influence the future of society. Incorporating dignity into daily operations allows businesses to restore the ethical framework of a technology-driven society, transforming AI from a potential risk into an instrument for enhancing human well-being.

Furthermore, incorporating dignity into corporate AI governance is not merely idealistic; it is a prudent approach. This is the conviction that people can relate to, comprehend, study, and eventually put to use various forms of artificial intelligence (AI) whenever they so desire (Bewersdorff et al., 2025). The ability of corporations to navigate moral complexity is increasingly critical for establishing trust, legitimacy, and ensuring long-term sustainability within the digital economy. Stakeholders, such as employees, customers, and regulators, evaluate businesses based on operational effectiveness as well as integrity. In a context where data replication is feasible but dignity remains inalienable, enterprises that fail to uphold individual worth are likely to forfeit their legitimacy in the marketplace. In the digital era, human dignity represents the paramount moral value. It determines which organizations can maintain public trust amid rapid technological changes. This introduction situates the chapter within the broader framework of Navigating Social Trust in the AI Era. Trust cannot exist in an environment that continually undermines dignity. The two concepts are interconnected: dignity serves as the moral foundation of trust, whereas trust functions as the social manifestation of dignity. Understanding the influence of AI on human dignity is essential for protecting individual well-being and maintaining societal stability. This chapter introduces the necessity for enterprises to establish governance structures that prioritize human dignity as a guiding principle and measurable objective to restore societal trust in the era of AI.

Figure 1. Human Dignity and the Layers of AI Governance

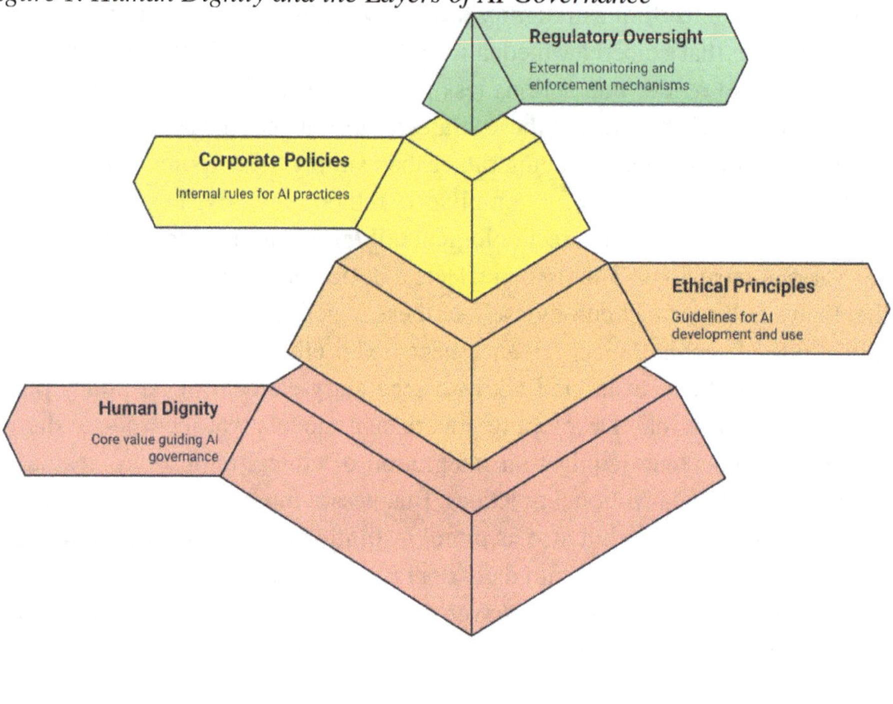

2. CONCEPTUAL FOUNDATIONS: HUMAN DIGNITY AS A GOVERNANCE PRINCIPLE

According to the available evidence, democratic states have traditionally placed a crucial emphasis on human dignity as a fundamental concept. Researchers have paid a lot of attention to human dignity, but they have frequently neglected to address the most basic questions regarding its very existence. Human rights can be interpreted differently depending on one's perspective on human dignity and whether or not it exists (Jafari et al., 2024). This is demonstrated by the fact that it has been included into several legal frameworks, in particular the Universal Declaration of Human Rights. There is still a lack of proper comprehension regarding the application of this notion in the management of artificial intelligence. all a normative idea and a practical constraint, dignity serves all of these duties, performing both of these roles simultaneously. Both carries a lot of weight. This text covers demands that protect autonomy, justice, and respect for individuals, as well as prohibitions that ban activities that degrade, exploit, or dehumanize individuals. It is vital to develop a philosophical foundation that unites moral philosophy with business pragmatism in order to effectively transform abstract principles into code, policy, and management decisions. This foundation must be established in order to achieve this goal. This is truly necessary. When it comes to artificial intelligence, there are three separate sorts of dignity that may be distinguished: intrinsic, relational, and technological respectively. The idea of inherent dignity refers to the fact that every single person have value that is not contingent on their position in society. One's inherent worth is referred to as their "intrinsic dignity," and the word "intrinsic dignity" A concept known as relational dignity refers to the impact that technology has on the degree to which humans acknowledge and respect one another. This is especially important to keep in mind when it comes to different types of client interactions and recruitment processes. The process of ensuring that individuals have the ability to voice their opinions, offer consent, and keep control over procedures that impact them is what is meant by the term "procedural dignity." When some aspects of governance frameworks are ignored, technology can be reduced to instrumentalism, which views persons as only means rather than purposes. This is because instrumentalism views individuals as merely resources. Subject to change, contractual existence is transmitted to objective entities through the mental processes of humans (Jafari et al., 2024). As a consequence, this leads to the reduction of technology to its instrumental capabilities.

It is not unusual for businesses to struggle with comprehending the significance of dignity in regard to the requirements that are associated with compliance. In a similar vein, the security of personal information and intellectual property cannot be assessed using a checklist, and this scenario is difficult to describe in detail. It's possible that this is connected to the fact that simplifying something is difficult because of how significant it is. The inherent quantification bias that is frequently displayed by artificial intelligence systems is mitigated by dignity, which acts as a counterbalance to this natural bias. It is imperative that governance frameworks not only put a stop to the rapid growth of automated processes but also integrate ethical limits prior to their deployment in order to guarantee the preservation of human dignity. It is because of this that human compassion is given precedence over the efficiency of various operations. The concept of human dignity is examined across various disciplines, including law, theology, and ethics. In the realm of human rights and law, dignity is universally fixed and equal for all individuals; however, in theological contexts, it may vary according to human actions. The pinnacle of human achievement is attained through the deliberate choice of virtue (Jafari et al., 2024). Power and dignity are two concepts that are linked to one another in a very tight way. Within the context of corporate environments, a new kind of dependence on artificial intelligence is created as a result of the significant gap in comprehension that exists between data controllers and data subjects. When it comes to the use of artificial intelligence, this is very pertinent. Instead of merely saying that the system is unfair, employees who are evaluated by algorithms are required to show proof to back their assertions of unfairness. There is a widespread problem in which individuals frequently lack a thorough awareness of the influence that recommendation engines exert on their behavior. The formation of ethical norms in the governance of artificial intelligence is insufficient; it requires additional development that goes beyond this concept (Sekti, 2025c). Promoting individuals' participation in decision-making processes and making it easier for them to gain access to educational opportunities related to technology are both extremely important. A governing system that is founded on dignity must take into account the moral relevance of an individual's background. This is a crucial characteristic to take into consideration. When it comes to workplace surveillance, a facial recognition system might be regarded too intrusive, but when it comes to airport security, it might be considered ethically acceptable. The existence of frameworks that are sensitive to context is of the utmost importance. This idea is similar to Amartya Sen's “capability approach,” which maintains that true dignity can be achieved by providing individuals with the resources they need to follow the way of life that they have chosen for themselves. Not only should the outcomes of artificial intelligence (AI) systems in businesses be evaluated, but also the impact that these technologies have on the potential of individuals will be taken into consideration.

Figure 2. Dimensions of Human Dignity in AI Governance

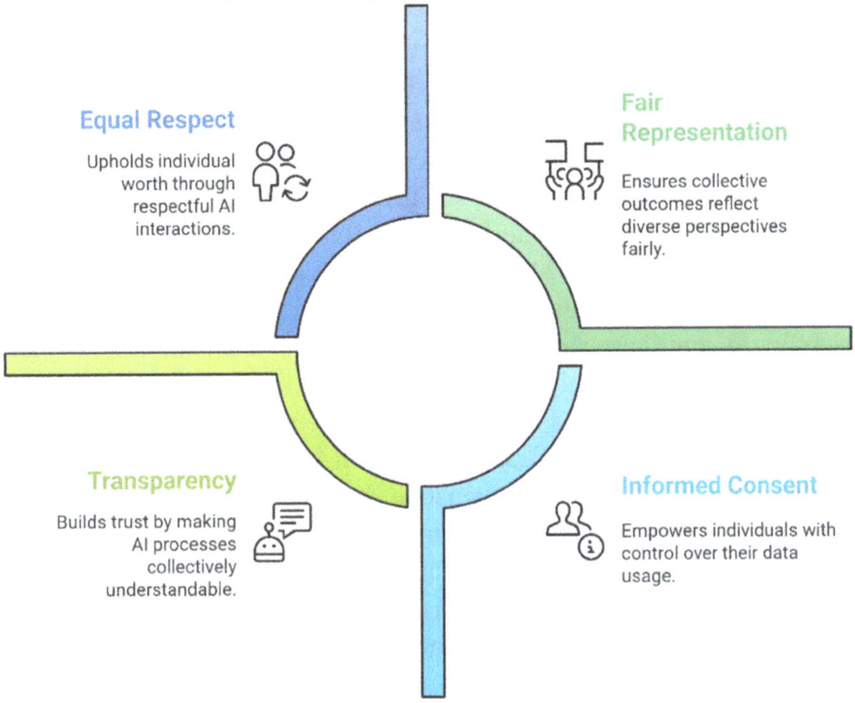

3. THE ETHICAL TENSION BETWEEN EFFICIENCY AND DIGNITY

The rapid integration of artificial intelligence into corporate systems has fundamentally altered the principles of efficiency. Artificial intelligence offers enhancements in speed, precision, and optimization, which have traditionally been key drivers of industrial advancement. Nonetheless, underlying this narrative of progress is a significant ethical conflict: the quest for efficiency frequently conflicts with the maintenance of human dignity. Efficiency, in a limited context, quantifies human activity through metrics and outcomes, whereas dignity represents an inherent human value that cannot be measured. The deployment of AI by corporations to enhance productivity or decrease costs may result in the reconfiguration of individuals as operational variables within algorithmic frameworks. This transition converts workplaces and markets into data-centric ecosystems that prioritize optimization, convenience, and predictive capabilities over empathy, conscience, and comprehension. The ethical inquiry thus centers on the capacity of societies to maintain the moral essence of human labor and identity in an era dominated by machine logic. Automation represents a prominent aspect of this ethical tension. Automation powered by artificial intelligence substitutes repetitive human tasks with self-learning systems capable of continuous operation, free from fatigue, errors, or the need for compensation. The parameters for determining human dignity have been a topic of extensive discussion among scholars for many years. Regardless of the criteria selected for human dignity, each philosophical framework must establish a systematic approach to recognize these attributes in individuals (Jafari, Tavasoli, Tavasoli, Abedi, Navvab, & Darabi, 2024). This efficiency enhances corporate profitability but simultaneously marginalizes millions of workers whose dignity is linked to their ability to contribute meaningfully to social and economic life. The loss of employment signifies not only financial instability but also a profound existential disturbance. Human dignity is derived from engagement in a collective existence, encompassing creation, decision-making, and a sense of belonging. The displacement of human agency by AI can lead to alienation, diminished self-worth, and a reduced sense of purpose among individuals. Corporate decision-making that regards labor reduction solely as a technical optimization neglects the ethical implications of automation, transforming progress into a mechanism of dehumanization. Thus, the ethical governance of AI necessitates more than mere productivity metrics; it calls for a comprehensive examination of the moral dimensions of work itself.

AI-powered surveillance technologies pose a significant ethical challenge. Corporations are increasingly utilizing algorithmic analysis to monitor employee performance, consumer behavior, and customer interactions in the pursuit of efficiency. These systems, presented as instruments for enhancement and individualization, frequently infringe upon privacy and autonomy, which are fundamental to human dignity (Anwar et al., 2025). The pervasive nature of digital surveillance converts individuals into subjects of scrutiny, diminishing their agency regarding personal representation. Michel Foucault's Panopticon metaphor is pertinent in this context: corporate AI systems establish a constant visibility that regulates behavior without the need for coercion. Employees cognizant of ongoing surveillance may align their behaviors with algorithmic standards, thereby diminishing their ability for genuine decision-making. The ethical dilemma involves reconciling operational oversight with the individual's right to privacy the right to not be entirely quantified as data. In the absence of safeguards, surveillance transforms into a tool of domination instead of serving efficiency.

Algorithmic profiling and data-driven personalization exacerbate this tension for consumers and citizens. Corporate AI systems utilize models trained on historical data to predict preferences, evaluate creditworthiness, and ascertain eligibility for services. Although effective for segmentation and marketing purposes, these algorithms may reinforce discrimination and bias, perpetuating social hierarchies while appearing neutral. In these contexts, efficiency serves as a moral facade, justifying practices that prioritize convenience at the expense of justice. Human dignity necessitates the acknowledgment of individuals as ends in themselves, rather than as subjects of algorithmic prediction. Corporate AI governance must ensure that efficiency metrics do not overshadow the ethical obligation to treat all individuals fairly and with respect. Ethical audits, impact assessments, and human-in-the-loop designs can alleviate these tensions, provided they are driven by a sincere commitment to dignity rather than merely risk management (Sekti, 2025a). This ethical conflict also encompasses a psychological dimension. The efficiency ethos of AI cultivates a culture characterized by rapidity and quantification, thereby transforming human self-perception. Employees, consumers, and leaders increasingly internalize algorithmic values, assessing their worth based on measurable outputs and predictive accuracy. In this context, AI efficiency influences human consciousness, redefining value in computational terms. The internalization of technocracy may undermine dignity, as individuals may overlook qualities that surpass mere productivity, such as empathy, creativity, vulnerability, and care. Consequently, corporations face the challenge of not only designing ethical systems but also fostering ethical cultures that counteract this reductionism. Organizations can counteract the machine's drive for acceleration by prioritizing slowness, reflection, and relational integrity.

The ethical trade-off between efficiency and dignity is evident in decision-making processes. AI systems are progressively utilized to inform or supplant human decision-making in recruitment, promotion, and customer service. Decisions that were previously rooted in human relationships are now delegated to algorithms designed for statistical correlation optimization. This outsourcing prompts questions regarding moral agency: who bears responsibility when efficiency leads to injustice? The ethical implications of an algorithm denying employment or suggesting disciplinary measures based on predictive analytics become obscured within the complexity of its code. Accountability becomes obscured by technical abstraction, resulting in a loss of dignity for both the decision-maker and the subject. Reaffirming ethical responsibility in this context necessitates the rehumanization of decision-making, ensuring that corporate actors are held morally accountable for outcomes, even when influenced by machines. A significant aspect of this tension pertains to the commodification of attention and emotion. Corporate AI systems in advertising and social media are designed to enhance behavioral efficiency by optimizing engagement, retention, and monetization. This design conceptualizes human attention as a commodifiable resource, undermining the dignity associated with contemplation and autonomy. The manipulation of emotional responses by algorithms for commercial purposes infringes upon the ethical framework essential for self-determination. This outcome represents a nuanced form of exploitation, wherein human consciousness is treated as a domain for optimization. Ethical corporate AI governance should broaden its focus from data privacy to cognitive dignity, ensuring the protection of human thought integrity from algorithmic manipulation. Moreover, leaders focused on human-centred values, such as dignity, frequently express disappointment regarding the insufficient guidance available to effectively implement this prioritization in technology development (Ruster et al., 2025). A paradigm shift in corporate values is necessary to reconcile efficiency and dignity. Corporations should reconceptualize efficiency not as an ultimate goal, but as a tool for promoting human flourishing. This redefinition incorporates ethical reflection into business strategy, positioning dignity as a criterion of excellence rather than a constraint. Organizations that adopt "dignified efficiency" develop technologies aimed at augmenting human capabilities instead of supplanting them, safeguarding privacy while facilitating understanding, and fostering equity in conjunction with profitability. This balance is practical rather than utopian, as trust and loyalty increasingly serve as the currencies of the AI economy. The moral legitimacy of AI-driven efficiency is contingent upon its alignment with the intrinsic value of the human individual.

4. CORPORATE GOVERNANCE AND AI RESPONSIBILITY MODELS

Corporate governance functions as the institutional framework that enables organizations to convert ethical ideals into practical actions. In the realm of artificial intelligence, governance establishes the framework through which corporations develop, oversee, and address the ethical considerations associated with intelligent systems. Many current governance structures, designed for conventional business risks, are inadequate for addressing the ethical complexities associated with AI. The swift advancement of algorithmic systems exceeds corporate oversight, resulting in discrepancies between intention and execution. This section analyzes the evolution of corporate governance to incorporate AI ethics, emphasizing accountability, transparency, inclusivity, and human-centered design as fundamental principles of responsible innovation. A primary issue in AI governance is the allocation of responsibility. In conventional corporate hierarchies, accountability adheres to a vertical framework, where decision-making occurs in a downward direction and responsibility is assigned in an upward manner. AI systems create distributed agency, where decisions arise from the interactions among data scientists, algorithms, and end-users. Identifying responsibility becomes challenging when harm occurs. AI can enhance transparency, trust, and accountability in democratic processes (Wongmahesak et al., 2025). Governance models must consequently reestablish accountability within a networked context. This necessitates the establishment of clear ethical ownership, specifically identifying responsibility for bias mitigation, model interpretability, and post-deployment monitoring. Ethical accountability cannot be delegated to technology; it must be rooted in human decision-makers who comprehend both the system and its societal implications.

Transparency is essential for restoring trust between corporations and the public. Numerous AI systems function as "black boxes," generating outputs that are often difficult for their developers to elucidate. This lack of transparency compromises regulatory oversight and diminishes user confidence. Thermal modeling of 'black-box' objects presents significant challenges due to the uncertainty of underlying structures and thermophysical properties, resulting in the failure of all conventional methodologies (Gao et al., 2026). Effective governance necessitates the implementation of explainability mechanisms technical, procedural, and communicative that clarify the processes by which AI derives its conclusions. Transparency should not be conflated with total disclosure; it involves a meaningful openness that enables stakeholders to assess fairness and reliability while safeguarding security and intellectual property. Corporate governance boards ought to implement transparency audits, producing accessible reports that illustrate ethical compliance and encourage public engagement. Inclusivity constitutes a fundamental aspect of ethical AI governance. Artificial intelligence systems frequently exhibit the biases inherent in their developers and the imbalances present in data collection processes. To mitigate this issue, governance structures should incorporate diverse perspectives in both design and oversight processes. Multidisciplinary ethics boards, consisting of ethicists, technologists, legal experts, and civil society representatives, can ensure alignment of corporate AI strategies with human rights values. Engaging external stakeholders, including affected communities and advocacy groups, enhances the legitimacy of governance decisions. Inclusivity alters governance from a hierarchical directive to a dialogical process, reflecting the social pluralism of the environments influenced by AI.

Human-centered design serves as the ethical foundation for responsible AI governance. Corporations must prioritize user welfare, psychological safety, and accessibility across the AI lifecycle. This approach reconceptualizes governance as a participatory process instead of merely a compliance activity. It necessitates iterative evaluation ongoing assessment of the impact of systems on human experience, followed by appropriate adjustments. Corporate leaders ought to advocate for design principles that prioritize humanization in AI: systems that assist rather than displace, that inform rather than deceive, and that empower rather than dominate. This design philosophy reinforces the corporate responsibility to uphold dignity as an ethical and operational necessity. Corporate AI governance must navigate the tension between global standards and local contexts. Multinational corporations function within multiple jurisdictions that exhibit diverse legal standards and cultural interpretations of dignity. Ethical governance models must be adaptable, converting universal principles into context-specific practices. Participatory ethical standards highlight the engagement of various stakeholders, seeking to establish a more inclusive and equitable ethical governance framework (Zhang & Pan, 2024). This may entail reconciling Western notions of autonomy with the communal values that are prominent in various societies. A global governance framework that acknowledges local diversity while maintaining fundamental principles of dignity is crucial to avert ethical imperialism and promote authentic inclusivity. Corporate AI governance necessitates institutional courage, which involves prioritizing ethical integrity despite potential conflicts with short-term profitability. Governance boards should avoid using ethics merely as a public relations tool and instead recognize it as essential for establishing corporate legitimacy. This involves the allocation of resources towards ethics training, the integration of moral reflection into performance evaluations, and the association of executive incentives with ethical results. Ethical governance, when properly understood, serves as a facilitator of innovation rather than a hindrance; it establishes the trust conditions essential for sustainable technological advancement. Integrating AI responsibility into corporate governance demonstrates that innovation and the preservation of human dignity are interdependent pillars of the digital age, rather than opposing forces.

5. CASE STUDIES: CORPORATE AI AND HUMAN DIGNITY IN PRACTICE

In analyzing how corporations operationalize artificial intelligence, case studies reveal both the promise and peril inherent in technological innovation. Especially in multinational organizations that have a global reach, the connection between human dignity and the practices of artificial intelligence is particularly manifest. In digital societies, these entities have an impact not only on the dynamics of the market but also on the ethical environment. Their choices, which include information governance and algorithmic openness, have important repercussions from a moral standpoint. The purpose of this section is to investigate a variety of business case studies that illustrate how corporations deal with the ethical imperative of upholding dignity, or how they occasionally fail to do so. The findings suggest that the moral nature of artificial intelligence is not innate to the technology itself, but rather originates from the corporate structures that are responsible for its implementation and operation. An initial case study is conducted to investigate Google, which has been a primary focus of ethical investigation as a result of its considerable involvement in artificial intelligence research through programs such as DeepMind and Google AI. Artificial intelligence principles were formed by Google in 2018 in response to public criticism about the "Project Maven" military contract. The advent of build automation tools equipped with dependency management capabilities has profoundly influenced software development (Yang et al., 2023). These principles promote fairness, accountability, and social benefit. The subsequent internal issues, in particular the leaving of artificial intelligence ethics researchers Timnit Gebru and Margaret Mitchell, bring to light the precarious nature of governance in situations where ethical considerations and commercial interests are in conflict with one another. The events that have transpired have brought to light the fact that corporate institutions that are meant to maximize profits may jeopardize moral commitments to dignity if they are not balanced by independent supervision. There is a lack of institutional mechanisms that protect moral autonomy within corporate structures, which is a sign that artificial intelligence governance is insecure. Despite breakthroughs, Google is having trouble maintaining ethical dissent within the company.

The second scenario examines Amazon, a company that automates labor procedures, improves recommendation engines, and enhances logistics by utilizing a big artificial intelligence infrastructure. In Amazon's massive warehouses, where millions of shelves are stocked with different sized products, automatic object verification is a crucial responsibility. (Rahnemoonfar, 2024) According to detractors, Amazon's warehouse algorithms dehumanize labor by reducing humans to mere components of data-driven logistics networks. However, Amazon's artificial intelligence technologies improve efficiency and allow for greater customisation of the shopping experience for customers. The transformation of persons into measurable measures is one example of how algorithmic optimization diminishes dignity. Excessive surveillance and performance monitoring are similar examples. In the present ethical investigation, the focus is not on the obvious increase in productivity that can be attributed to artificial intelligence (AI), but rather on the question of whether or not this increase in productivity justifies the moral implications of transforming human work into a mechanized process that lacks autonomy. An example of the enormous ethical contradiction that exists between the efficiency of automation and the worker's entitlement to decent treatment is provided by Amazon's model.

On the other hand, Microsoft's Responsible AI Framework is an example of a governance approach that puts more of an emphasis on human interest. Both an Office of Responsible AI and an AI Ethics and Effects in Engineering and Research (AETHER) Committee were established by the corporation in order to guarantee that artificial intelligence systems adhere to a set of principles that include fairness, inclusivity, and transparency. As an example of a governance architecture that values dignity as a design purpose rather than merely a compliance factor, the organizational structure of Microsoft makes it easier for teams to coordinate with one another, including those that are technical, legal, and ethical. Given the limited understanding of AI's impact on corporate entrepreneurship, this study explores how AI resources (AI utilization and AI governance) promote corporate entrepreneurship, especially with top management's involvement (Sekti, 2025b). This exemplifies the potential of ethical frameworks to increase innovation and social legitimacy, given that accountability mechanisms are clearly defined and enforceable. The company's management of AI collaborations, particularly in the fields of healthcare and education, demonstrate this potential.

An example that is both interesting and useful is the IBM Watson project. The integration of diverse datasets within the IBM Watson platform enables scalable, cloud-based processing, where pre-trained deep learning models and visual recognition tools enhance image analysis. (Gurulakshmanan et al., 2025) It was initially acknowledged that Watson's healthcare applications represented a substantial development in cognitive computing; nonetheless, ethical concerns of dependability, bias, and clinical accountability were immediately raised. An acknowledgment of the ethical boundaries of artificial intelligence is reflected in IBM's public statement, which illustrates a transition in Watson's function from that of a diagnostic authority to that of an assisting tool. Maintaining the authority of the physician as the ultimate decision-maker in healthcare is critical to preserving human dignity, and IBM implicitly acknowledged this fact. It is clear from this development that business ethics in artificial intelligence are not static; rather, they must be able to constantly evolve in reaction to shifting social norms and changes in technology breakthroughs.

One other noteworthy example is Facebook, which is now known as Meta. Many students have been compelled to stay at home during this unique epidemic period, receiving their education via social media platforms like Facebook and mobile learning apps (Yu et al., 2023). The algorithms that Facebook uses to curate content and conduct advertising have spurred continuing conversations about autonomy, manipulation, and social trust. Political divisiveness, the spread of false information, and a deterioration in civic dignity have all been linked to the fact that the firm is dependent on engagement-optimizing algorithms. The establishment of ethical governance is the goal of initiatives such as the Oversight Board; nevertheless, detractors argue that these structures are more symbolic than transformative in nature. A fundamental reorganization of incentives that place an emphasis on long-term social trust rather than short-term engagement indicators is required according to the Meta case, which demonstrates that governance that is centered on dignity requires more than just ethics panels that are reactive. The AI industry has systemic trends, which extend beyond the scope of particular firms, as revealed by comparative analysis. Despite the fact that many businesses emphasize ethical concepts such as openness, fairness, and responsibility, these principles typically stay aspirational instead of being put into practice. Different governance cultures, different leadership dynamics, and different stakeholder influences all have a substantial impact on the implementation process. An overview of the most important corporate strategies for artificial intelligence governance is provided in *Table 5.1*, which illustrates how structural differences impact the capacity to safeguard human dignity within technology frameworks.

Table 1. Comparative Overview of Corporate AI Ethics Models

Corporation	AI Ethics Framework/ Principles	Governance Structure	Ethical Focus Areas	Dignity Implications
Google	AI Principles (2018)	Centralized oversight via AI Ethics Board (limited transparency)	Fairness, Safety, Accountability	Internal dissent shows weak protection for researcher autonomy
Amazon	Internal AI Code of Conduct (non-public)	Operational governance under AWS Ethics Team	Efficiency, Privacy, Worker Surveillance	Algorithmic control reduces worker autonomy and dignity
Microsoft	Responsible AI Standard (v2, 2022)	AETHER Committee, Responsible AI Office	Inclusivity, Fairness, Transparency	Ethical design embedded at engineering and policy level
IBM	Everyday Ethics for AI Framework	AI Ethics Board and Chief AI Ethics Officer	Trustworthiness, Reliability, Accountability	Recognizes human oversight as vital to dignity
Meta (Facebook)	Responsible Innovation Principles	Oversight Board (semi-independent)	Harm Reduction, User Control	Algorithmic bias threatens civic dignity and autonomy

The table highlights that the distinction between ethical aspiration and ethical practice is rooted in institutional design. Organizations such as Microsoft and IBM integrate ethical considerations into their engineering processes, whereas Amazon and Meta exemplify the potential moral hazards of treating ethics solely as a public relations strategy. An important observation is that safeguarding human dignity in AI contexts necessitates governance structures capable of resisting economic pressures that prioritize efficiency over moral principles. These cases illustrate a trend in which corporations are transitioning from ethical declarations to operational accountability. Progress remains uneven as corporate AI ethics functions within a capitalist framework, where moral values are often at odds with shareholder interests (Sekti, 2025b). Many ethical measures are thus reactive, initiated by scandals or regulatory pressures rather than by proactive moral commitments. Dignity, within this context, emerges as a contingent virtue recognized in rhetoric yet lacking structural protection.

These case studies underscore the significance of multi-stakeholder governance. Ethical success typically does not stem solely from internal corporate goodwill; rather, it arises from external accountability mechanisms, including civil society advocacy, academic collaboration, and government regulation. Transparency reports, ethics audits, and open AI research partnerships have demonstrated greater efficacy than voluntary codes in sustaining public trust. In the absence of enforceable governance, corporations may prioritize dignity as a reputational asset instead of recognizing it as an intrinsic moral obligation. The comparative perspective highlights a paradox inherent to the AI era: corporations that adopt dignity as a guiding principle frequently experience enhanced innovation rather than limitations. Ethical design fosters trust, thereby enhancing adoption and contributing to market stability. The challenge is not in selecting between innovation and dignity, but in creating systems that allow both to mutually reinforce each other. Section 6 will build upon this analysis by proposing a governance framework that operationalizes human dignity as a measurable and actionable standard within corporate AI ecosystems.

6. BUILDING PRACTICAL FRAMEWORKS FOR CORPORATE AI GOVERNANCE

Corporations face significant ethical challenges regarding artificial intelligence, highlighting the urgent necessity for effective governance frameworks. Ethics statements and codes of conduct are essential; however, they are inadequate in the absence of corresponding structural instruments. A dignity-centered governance model transforms ethics from a mere moral embellishment to an essential operational requirement. It positions human welfare as the primary standard for AI success, guaranteeing that technical performance is inherently linked to moral accountability. Frameworks should be principled and pragmatic, effectively guiding decisions in contexts characterized by uncertainty, scale, and economic pressure. Effective governance of artificial intelligence necessitates the incorporation of ethical oversight throughout all phases of the AI lifecycle, including design, data collection, model training, deployment, and monitoring. This integration must be anticipatory rather than reactive, incorporating dignity protection prior to the occurrence of harm. Algorithmic impact assessments can evaluate risks to autonomy, privacy, and equality in advance. Dignity audits, akin to financial audits, can assess the compliance of AI applications with respect-based principles. These mechanisms convert abstract ethical concepts into quantifiable performance metrics.

AI corporate governance should prioritize interdisciplinary inclusion. Governments around the globe are facing complex challenges in governance, and the incorporation of AI brings forth a dual-edged scenario that impacts democratic principles such as transparency, accountability, and public trust (Wongmahesak et al., 2025). Ethical oversight teams should include engineers, ethicists, sociologists, and legal experts who can identify systemic risks. This pluralism promotes a comprehensive understanding of the impact of AI systems on human experience. Dignity, as a fundamentally social and moral concept, cannot be protected solely through technical expertise. Organizations that incorporate varied epistemic viewpoints exhibit increased resilience to ethical blind spots and public criticism. A vital aspect of practical frameworks is the governance accountability chains. Ethical responsibility should be traceable, allowing for accountability of decision-makers regarding the moral implications of AI operations. This involves the creation of Chief AI Ethics Officers or similar positions with the power to suspend projects that present risks to dignity. Furthermore, external advisory boards and independent audits enhance the legitimacy of governance frameworks by ensuring alignment with societal expectations rather than solely internal priorities. The implementation of dignity-centered AI frameworks necessitates alignment with global regulatory ecosystems. Initiatives like the EU's Artificial Intelligence Act, the OECD AI Principles, and UNESCO's Recommendation on the Ethics of AI serve as normative frameworks for corporate adaptation. Aligning internal policies with international ethical standards enables corporations to establish cross-border coherence, thereby enhancing public trust. Regulation serves as a framework for moral innovation, safeguarding dignity within transnational digital markets rather than acting as a constraint.

The internal culture is a fundamental factor influencing the success of governance. Ethical infrastructure requires an organizational culture that prioritizes transparency, empathy, and moral courage for effective functioning. This entails the establishment of internal reporting systems, fostering psychological safety for ethical dissent, and implementing reward structures that acknowledge moral decision-making in conjunction with technical proficiency. A dignity-centered framework reconceptualizes success as the optimization of systems not solely for accuracy or profit, but for the preservation of agency and respect for all stakeholders, including employees, users, and affected communities. With AI constantly evolving and software startups adopting it at a rapid pace, it is crucial to incorporate governance mechanisms during the design and development phases to address concerns about AI governance (Agbese et al., 2023). The sustainability of corporate AI governance in the long term relies on ongoing learning. The rapid evolution of AI outpaces legal and policy frameworks, necessitating governance models that can adapt and improve iteratively. Feedback loops between deployment outcomes and policy adjustments are critical. This reflects the process of human learning, which involves recognizing errors, assessing their consequences, and continuously improving principles over time. Ethical maturity, akin to technological maturity, evolves through systematic experimentation, thorough evaluation, and transparent practices.

Figure 3. Framework for Dignity-Centered AI Governance in Corporations

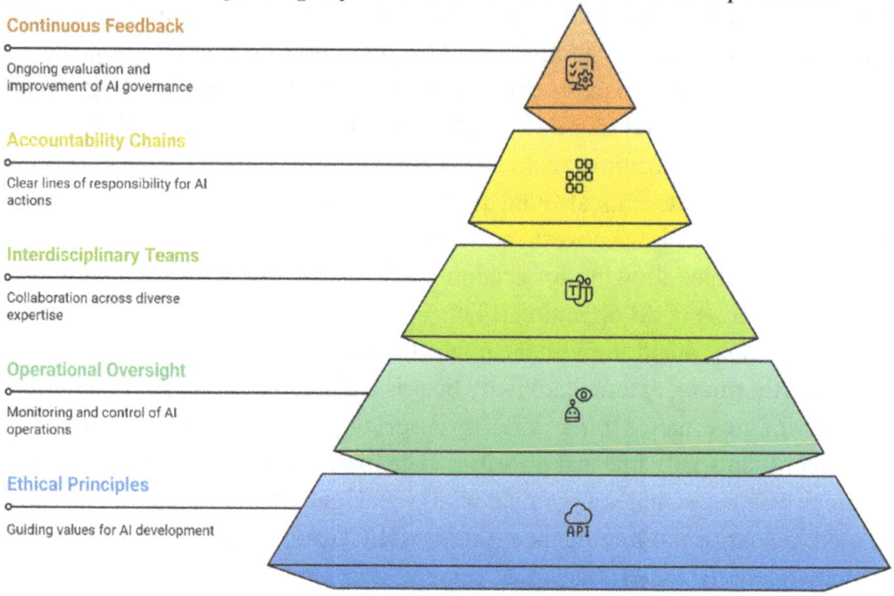

7. CHALLENGES AND FUTURE DIRECTIONS IN AI AND HUMAN DIGNITY

Although advancements have been made in ethical AI governance, corporations encounter significant difficulties in translating theoretical principles into practical implementation. The primary challenge is translating moral imperatives into measurable metrics suitable for integration into business models. Dignity, while universally acknowledged in theory, presents challenges in practical definition. This concept includes respect, autonomy, and recognition; however, these values frequently defy simplification into computational terms. Corporate AI systems, designed for optimization and efficiency, inherently prioritize quantifiable results. The initial challenge is epistemic: determining how to render dignity perceptible to systems that prioritize calculable values over those that possess moral significance. A significant challenge emerges from the fragmentation of accountability in complex AI supply chains. Most AI ethical design and development tools primarily depend on AI ethics principles as the principal governance and regulatory framework for creating ethical AI that guides AI governance (Agbese et al., 2023). Contemporary AI systems seldom arise from a singular source; they consist of open-source code, outsourced datasets, and cloud-based infrastructures that are distributed across various jurisdictions. Ethical breaches, such as algorithmic discrimination, privacy violations, and labor exploitation, raise questions regarding the assignment of responsibility. The diffusion of responsibility undermines the moral integrity of AI governance and reveals the shortcomings of current corporate frameworks. Protecting true dignity necessitates accountability frameworks that extend beyond contractual and national limits, thereby reinforcing moral obligations even after legal jurisdiction ceases.

Third, a cultural dissonance exists between ethical rhetoric and corporate reality. Despite public commitments to AI ethics, internal incentives frequently prioritize speed, innovation, and revenue growth at the expense of ethical considerations. Employees may be reluctant to express concerns due to fears of retaliation or potential hindrance to career advancement. Underfunded or marginalized ethical teams may transform into symbolic entities instead of functioning as agents of change. Dignity-centered governance necessitates a fundamental transformation in corporate culture, emphasizing reflection, empathy, and moral dialogue as critical elements of innovation. In the absence of such a transformation, even the most effectively articulated ethical codes tend to be performative rather than transformative. A fourth challenge pertains to the global asymmetry of artificial intelligence capabilities. Major technology companies lead in the development and implementation of AI, whereas smaller enterprises and developing countries frequently lack the resources to establish effective governance frameworks. This imbalance perpetuates digital colonialism, concentrating moral and technological authority among a limited number of global actors. Centralizing dignity in AI development could offer a solution in the face of algorithms that dehumanize, disenfranchise, discriminate, and disempower humans. There are growing demands to put humans at the center of AI development processes and to humanize AI development in practice. Despite the fact that many AI ethics frameworks include dignity as one of their cornerstones, there is still a lack of practical knowledge regarding how dignity might manifest in algorithm development (Ruster et al., 2022). Dignity is a universal concept that cannot be monopolized by individuals or entities with greater resources or geopolitical power. Corporate governance models must evolve to promote inclusivity, ensuring representation of global South perspectives and marginalized communities in ethical deliberations.

Fifth, an ethical risk exists in excessive dependence on automation. As corporations implement automation in both manual labor and decision-making processes, they may undermine the moral agency essential for maintaining dignity. When algorithms are employed in hiring, healthcare, policing, or finance, human lives are governed by opaque systems that function devoid of empathy. Automation enhances efficiency but simultaneously fosters moral detachment, rendering detrimental outcomes as technical certainties instead of ethical shortcomings. Reinstating dignity involves reaffirming the importance of human judgment, especially in situations where moral complexity cannot be simplified to data patterns. A sixth significant challenge pertains to the economic framework of surveillance capitalism. Corporations dependent on behavioral data encounter a fundamental conflict between upholding privacy and optimizing profit. The transformation of user data into an economic asset results in the commodification of individual autonomy and dignity. Despite the existence of ethical principles, corporate reliance on data-driven revenue continues to instrumentalize human experience. Resolving this tension necessitates the reconfiguration of business models to ensure that dignity is not only maintained through regulation but also integrated as a fundamental source of value creation.

The seventh challenge addresses ethical pluralism and variations across cultures. Dignity is understood variably among societies, grounded in unique moral, religious, and philosophical traditions. A universal corporate governance model may impose Western-centric values that do not necessarily align with local interpretations of justice or respect. Corporations must establish AI governance frameworks that are coherent on a global scale while remaining adaptable to local contexts, ensuring moral sensitivity. Dignity, as a collective human value, ought to promote unity without enforcing uniformity. The eighth point is that technological opacity persists in obstructing public comprehension and trust. AI models, especially those based on deep learning architectures, function as "black boxes," rendering their internal logic frequently opaque, even to their developers. Lack of transparency inhibits informed consent, thereby compromising dignity through epistemic exclusion (Anwar et al., 2025). Corporate frameworks should prioritize explainability as both a technical objective and an ethical obligation. Comprehending the mechanisms and rationale behind a system's outcomes reinstates a sense of agency for individuals impacted by its decisions. The ninth challenge pertains to ethical fatigue, characterized by the gradual normalization of ethical violations in rapidly evolving innovation contexts. The proliferation of AI may diminish moral sensitivity, resulting in corporations perceiving minor compromises as acceptable trade-offs for advancement. This desensitization represents a significant threat to dignity, as it converts ethics into a negotiable commodity. Addressing ethical fatigue necessitates ongoing moral education, active leadership involvement, and systems for reflective practice that maintain ethical awareness in the face of operational demands.

A tenth dimension of challenge pertains to regulatory fragmentation. Regions like the European Union have developed comprehensive AI regulations, while others remain behind, resulting in inconsistent ethical frameworks. Global corporations must manage divergent standards, frequently opting for the least restrictive environments. This regulatory inconsistency facilitates ethical arbitrage, allowing corporations to relocate or structure operations to circumvent moral constraints. A coherent global framework for AI governance would reduce these disparities, ensuring that the protection of dignity is not dependent on geographic location. The eleventh challenge pertains to the assessment of ethical success. Compliance metrics, including the frequency of audits or violations, may assess procedural adherence; however, they seldom reflect the actual experience of dignity. What methods can be employed to assess if an algorithm upholds autonomy or validates human dignity? Creating qualitative indicators, including user perception studies and employee morale assessments, can provide a more human-centered evaluation of ethical performance. The point where human ethics, dignity, and AI cross has become an important topic of conversation in this AI era. There are clear concerns regarding the need to establish ethical boundaries and safeguard human dignity as AI systems have an increasing impact on decision-making, social dynamics, and human interactions (Chakraborty, 2025). Metrics should advance beyond mere efficiency and compliance to encompass the complexity of moral impact. The twelfth and arguably most enduring challenge involves maintaining trust in the context of technological advancement. The emergence of self-learning and adaptive AI systems poses a threat to the relevance of existing governance models. Static ethics are inadequate for guiding dynamically evolving systems. Protecting dignity necessitates governance frameworks that can evolve morally mechanisms that enable ethical norms to develop in tandem with technological advancement. Thus, human dignity is not a static doctrine but a dynamic framework that directs innovation through continuous reflection.

8. GLOBAL COOPERATION AND MULTI-STAKEHOLDER GOVERNANCE

To protect human dignity in an AI-driven environment, corporate governance must extend beyond organizational and national limits. Global cooperation is essential from both ethical and practical perspectives, as AI technologies function across digital boundaries. An ethical lapse by a single corporation can have widespread implications, influencing employment, privacy, and social cohesion. The future of AI governance relies on a multi-stakeholder model in which governments, corporations, civil society, and academia collaboratively establish and uphold ethical standards. This cooperative vision embodies the principle that dignity is not possessed by any single entity; rather, it is a collective responsibility. International institutions are progressing towards this collaborative framework. The OECD AI Principles, the UNESCO Recommendation on the Ethics of Artificial Intelligence, and the EU AI Act together constitute a developing ethical framework. The frameworks emphasize the necessity of transparency, accountability, and adherence to human rights in all AI systems. Nonetheless, their efficacy is contingent upon corporate engagement and alignment. A global consensus on AI ethics should be integrated into both policy frameworks and the daily operations of corporate design, engineering, and management. International law must be implemented through internal corporate governance. A multi-stakeholder model enhances moral legitimacy through the integration of diverse perspectives. Civil society organizations contribute insights regarding social impact, academia offers theoretical rigor, governments ensure accountability, and corporations provide technical expertise. The collaboration of these voices yields a governance framework that is both ethically sound and pragmatically viable. This collaboration shifts ethics from an exclusive discussion to a democratic practice that is open, inclusive, and attuned to the realities of individuals impacted by AI (Sekti, 2025b).

The incorporation of employee perspectives in AI governance warrants significant consideration. Labor unions and advocacy groups are essential in recognizing dignity risks linked to automation, surveillance, and algorithmic management. Incorporating worker representation in governance boards safeguards employee rights and bolsters the credibility of corporate ethical claims. Ensuring dignity in AI environments necessitates that individuals affected by its outcomes participate in the formulation of its regulations. Corporate collaboration should encompass cross-industry alliances. Environmental sustainability necessitates collaborative commitments across sectors; similarly, AI ethics requires such cooperation. Initiatives such as the Partnership on AI illustrate the potential for competitors to collaborate in the establishment of ethical norms. Collaborative research, established transparency standards, and adherence to best practices foster a collective responsibility framework, preventing any corporation from ethically undermining others for competitive gain. Dignity is conceptualized as a public good instead of a private asset. An important aspect of global cooperation is capacity-building for the Global South. Numerous developing countries primarily consume AI technologies instead of producing them, which exposes them to ethical risks associated with imports. Research and practice in the area of artificial intelligence (AI) governance aims to maximize the positive and reduce the negative effects of AI systems (Attard-Frost, 2025). Equitable AI governance necessitates investments in education, infrastructure, and regulatory capacity to guarantee the global distribution of dignity protection. Corporate social responsibility should transform into a model of ethical solidarity, wherein companies facilitate the moral and technical empowerment of disadvantaged regions.

Advancing multi-stakeholder governance necessitates the implementation of data democratization. Open data initiatives, participatory audits, and citizen oversight mechanisms can reinforce public governance of algorithmic systems. Transparency serves to deter abuse and restore dignity by acknowledging citizens as co-owners of digital ecosystems, rather than as passive subjects. This democratization reconfigures the relationship between corporations and society, transitioning from paternalistic control to mutual accountability. The establishment of global ethical certification systems for AI presents a significant opportunity. Environmental and labor certifications indicate corporate adherence to sustainability standards; similarly, AI ethics certifications may serve as reputational indicators for technologies that respect human dignity. These certifications would establish market incentives for ethical behavior, incentivizing companies that integrate dignity as a quantifiable business value. Consequently, consumers and investors would be enabled to make ethical decisions through informed purchasing and investment choices.

9. CONCLUSION

This chapter has examined the progression of corporate AI governance from theoretical ethical principles to established institutional frameworks focused on human dignity. The exploration highlights the transformative capacity and ongoing vulnerability of moral reasoning in the context of technological capitalism. Dignity serves as the ethical framework that underpins responsible innovation; it is not a limitation on advancement but rather the essential element that imparts significance to progress. Lacking dignity, efficiency transforms into exploitation; in the absence of respect, intelligence devolves into domination. Corporate case studies, such as Google's ethical challenges and Microsoft's structured accountability, illustrate that governance based on dignity produces both ethical and strategic benefits. Organizations that integrate ethical considerations into their design and management practices foster trust, drive innovation, and ensure long-term legitimacy. In contrast, the commodification of human experience undermines dignity and social trust, leading to reputational and existential risks that cannot be mitigated by technological advancements.

The future of AI governance relies on transitioning from a focus on compliance to an emphasis on ethical considerations. The rise of AI-enabled applications has highlighted the necessity for AI governance (Sidorova & Saeed, 2022). Codes, audits, and regulations serve as essential frameworks; however, they cannot substitute for the intrinsic moral compass that informs decision-making. A dignity-first governance model operationalizes ethics through a continuous dialogue between human judgment and technological capabilities. It requires corporations to exhibit humility, acknowledging that intelligence devoid of empathy lacks ethical substance. Furthermore, as AI systems increasingly mediate social reality, corporations are taking on roles that were traditionally the responsibility of public institutions. Algorithms influence perception, discourse, and opportunities. In this broadened moral framework, corporate ethics should transform into a model of digital citizenship, wherein corporations serve as guardians of collective dignity instead of merely private beneficiaries of public data. This redefinition obscures the distinction between business and society, rendering ethical responsibility integral to operational success.

An approach to AI governance that prioritizes dignity has significant implications for labor and democracy. Preserving human agency in automated systems demonstrates that technology is designed to serve humanity, rather than the opposite. Workers should retain their role as decision-makers rather than being reduced to mere data points. Algorithms should enhance moral reasoning rather than supplant it. When governance frameworks incorporate this principle, they transform automation from a potential threat into a means for enhancing human well-being. Future challenges will involve maintaining ethical vigilance in the context of rapid change. The ability of AI to self-learn and adapt will consistently challenge the limits of ethical foresight. Consequently, governance systems must evolve into adaptive entities learning institutions that can undergo moral development. Dignity-centered design should encompass both corporate policy and technical architecture, embedding empathy, transparency, and justice within the code. The future of corporate AI governance can be conceptualized as a pursuit of technological humanism, representing a synthesis of innovation and ethical considerations. This vision does not idealize humanity or demonize technology; instead, it aims to integrate them within a common ethical framework. Dignity serves as the moral framework that facilitates alignment between machine intelligence and human values.

As society progresses through the complexities of the AI era, the safeguarding of human dignity will serve as the paramount measure of our collective wisdom. Corporations possess significant authority in shaping the nature of the contemporary era. The potential of AI as a means of liberation or alienation hinges not on its algorithms, but rather on the ethical framework established around them. The governance models presented are not final solutions but rather prompts for ongoing ethical reflection, shared responsibility, and the reaffirmation of human values in the context of technological advancement.

REFERENCES

Agbese, M., Alanen, H.-K., Antikainen, J., Halme, E., Isomaki, H., Jantunen, M., Kemell, K.-K., Rousi, R., Vainio-Pekka, H., & Vakkuri, V. (2023). Governance in Ethical and Trustworthy AI Systems: Extension of the ECCOLA Method for AI Ethics Governance Using GARP. *E-Informatica Software Engineering Journal, 17*(1), 230101. Advance online publication. DOI: 10.37190/e-Inf230101

Anwar, N., Sekti, B. A., Widodo, A. M., Erzed, N., Gunawan, H., Tangkudung, R. R. S., Muchlis, M., & Budhisantosa, N. (2025). *Emerging Innovations in AI and Green Computing for Cybersecurity.*, DOI: 10.4018/979-8-3693-8034-5.ch002

Attard-Frost, B. (2025). Transfeminist AI governance. *First Monday, 30*(4). Advance online publication. DOI: 10.5210/fm.v30i4.14121

Bariş, Ö., Yeşilyurt, S., & Ün, O. (2024). Professions transformed by artificial intelligence. In *Generating Entrepreneurial Ideas With AI* (pp. 19–40). DOI: 10.4018/979-8-3693-3498-0.ch002

Bewersdorff, A., Hornberger, M., Nerdel, C., & Schiff, D. S. (2025). AI advocates and cautious critics: How AI attitudes, AI interest, use of AI, and AI literacy build university students' AI self-efficacy. *Computers and Education: Artificial Intelligence, 8*, 100340. DOI: 10.1016/j.caeai.2024.100340

Chakraborty, S. (2025). Human values, ethics, and dignity in the age of artificial intelligence. In *Human Values.* Ethics, and Dignity in the Age of Artificial Intelligence., DOI: 10.4018/979-8-3693-9035-1

Demir-Kaymak, Z., Turan, Z., Unlu-Bidik, N., & Unkazan, S. (2024). Effects of midwifery and nursing students' readiness about medical Artificial intelligence on Artificial intelligence anxiety. *Nurse Education in Practice, 78*, 103994. DOI: 10.1016/j.nepr.2024.103994 PMID: 38810350

Gao, Y., Li, B., Zhao, J., & Dong, S. (2026). Boundary conditions treatment strategies for black-box objects thermal modeling using thermal response function method. *International Journal of Heat and Mass Transfer, 255*, 127852. DOI: 10.1016/j.ijheatmasstransfer.2025.127852

Gurulakshmanan, G., Bini Marin, V., Channapragada, R. S. R., Ajit, S., Srinivasan, C., & Ayushma, K. (2025). Advancing Medical Imaging with Machine Learning Techniques by Utilising IBM Watson Studio. *Proceedings of the 2025 11th International Conference on Communication and Signal Processing, ICCSP 2025*, 1867–1872. DOI: 10.1109/ICCSP64183.2025.11088799

Jafari, S. A., Araminia, B., Tavasoli, H., Tavasoli, N., Abedi, S., & Bakhsh, A. F. (2024). Human dignity: A contract or an abstract? *Journal of Medical Ethics and History of Medicine, 17*. Advance online publication. DOI: 10.18502/jmehm.v17i6.17105 PMID: 40395479

Jafari, S. A., Araminia, B., Tavasoli, H., Tavasoli, N., Abedi, S., & Bakhshe, A. F. (2024). Human dignity, minimum and maximum: What is the justification for the difference between male and female Diyah" in Islam? *Journal of Medical Ethics and History of Medicine, 17*. Advance online publication. DOI: 10.18502/jmehm.v17i7.17106 PMID: 40395476

Jafari, S. A., Tavasoli, N., Tavasoli, H., Abedi, S., Navvab, S. A., & Darabi, B. T. (2024). Existence and Manifestations of human dignity: Can a person be deprived of dignity? *Journal of Medical Ethics and History of Medicine, 17*. Advance online publication. DOI: 10.18502/jmehm.v17i8.17107 PMID: 40395477

Rahnemoonfar, M. (2024). DEEP SPECTRAL SIAMESE NETWORK FOR HETEROGENEOUS OBJECT VERIFICATION IN AMAZON ROBOTIC WAREHOUSE. *Proceedings - International Conference on Image Processing, ICIP*, 922–928. DOI: 10.1109/ICIP51287.2024.10647558

Ruster, L. P., Oliva-Altamirano, P., & Daniell, K. A. (2022). Centring dignity in algorithm development: testing a Dignity Lens. *ACM International Conference Proceeding Series*, 1–8. DOI: 10.1145/3572921.3572938

Ruster, L. P., Oliva-Altamirano, P., & Daniell, K. A. (2025). The Dignity Lens: Advancing Human-Centred Protective and Proactive Algorithmic Responsibility. *Information Systems Journal*, isj.12601. Advance online publication. DOI: 10.1111/isj.12601

Sekti, B. A. (2025a). *Adversarial Machine Learning in Industrial Cybersecurity*., DOI: 10.4018/979-8-3373-3241-3.ch018

Sekti, B. A. (2025b). Information Security Awareness. In *User-Centric Cybersecurity Implications for Sustainable Digital Transformation* (pp. 111–146). IGI Global Scientific Publishing., DOI: 10.4018/979-8-3373-3171-3.ch004

Sekti, B. A. (2025c). Machine Learning and Artificial Intelligence (AI) in Manufacturing. In *Integrating Digital Innovation and Integrated Frameworks in Manufacturing* (pp. 255–292). IGI Global Scientific Publishing. DOI: 10.4018/979-8-3373-1082-4.ch011

Sidorova, A., & Saeed, K. (2022). Incorporating Stakeholder enfranchisement, Risks, Gains, and AI decisions in AI Governance Framework. *Proceedings of the Annual Hawaii International Conference on System Sciences, 2022-January*, 5943–5952. DOI: 10.24251/HICSS.2022.722

Wongmahesak, K., Singh, B., Arora, M. K. K., Lal, S., Malviya, R., & Chandra, S. (2025). AI-Driven Solutions for Transparent Governance. In *Democracy and Democratization in the Age of AI* (pp. 153–166). IGI Global., DOI: 10.4018/979-8-3693-8749-8.ch009

Yang, H., Chen, L., Cao, Y., Li, Y., & Zhou, Y. (2023). Towards Better Dependency Scope Settings in Maven Projects. *ACM International Conference Proceeding Series*, 90–100. DOI: 10.1145/3609437.3609447

Yu, L., Xu, W., Sukjairungwattana, P., & Yu, Z. (2023). A Meta-Analysis of Facebook-Assisted Learning Outcomes in Different Countries or Regions. *International Journal of Information Technology and Web Engineering*, *18*(1), 1–18. Advance online publication. DOI: 10.4018/IJITWE.319312

Zhang, C., & Pan, L. (2024). Participatory ethical regulations: Risk challenges of artificial intelligence era and construction of governance logic. *Bulletin of Chinese Academy of Sciences*, *39*(11), 1860–1870. DOI: 10.16418/j.issn.1000-3045.20240417002

Chapter 9
Ai in Critical Sectors:
AI in Healthcare, Education, Finance, and Security – Ethical Challenges in Generative AI

R. Velmurugan
https://orcid.org/0000-0002-7925-9757
Karpagam Academy of Higher Education, Coimbatore, India

R. Bhuvaneswari
https://orcid.org/0009-0003-9396-6129
Dr. Mahalingam College of Engineering and Technology, Pollachi, India

Maksud A. Madraswale
https://orcid.org/0000-0001-9565-0775
Presidency University, Bangalore, India

S. Senthilkumar
https://orcid.org/0000-0003-1968-6877
Skyline University, Nigeria

ABSTRACT

Artificial Intelligence (AI) is transforming sectors like healthcare, education, finance, and security by enhancing efficiency, personalization, and decision-making. In healthcare, AI supports diagnostics, predictive care, and resource optimization, though privacy and bias remain concerns. Education benefits from adaptive learning and automation but faces challenges in equity and data ethics. Finance leverages AI for fraud detection, trading, and risk analysis, yet regulatory oversight is vital to prevent discrimination and instability. In security, AI enhances surveillance and

DOI: 10.4018/979-8-3373-7011-8.ch009

ght © 2026, IGI Global Scientific Publishing. Copying or distributing in print or electronic forms without written permission of IGI Global Scientific Publishing is prohibited. Use of this chapter to generative artificial intelligence (AI) technologies is expressly prohibited. The publisher reserves all rights to license its use for generative AI training and machine learning model development.

cyber defense but raises ethical issues around privacy and autonomy. Generative AI fuels creativity but risks misinformation and copyright breaches. Ensuring fairness, transparency, and ethical governance is crucial for sustainable, inclusive AI adoption.

INTRODUCTION

The development of textual content, language translation, and a custom learning path can be generated with the use of advanced natural language processing and machine learning methods, which can satisfy a wide range of linguistic and cognitive needs (Ranga, 2024). These AI-based utilities add accessibility and inclusivity, making learning resources to be tuned to a broader group of learners, such as persons with a particular learning disability, and those in remote locations (Singh and Gibu, 2023). Educational applications of AI go beyond digitization; the spectrum of applications includes systems of adaptive assessment and the provision of dynamically changing curriculum (Chetry, 2024). Furthermore, AI-based inclusive learning is being designed to translate learning content into different languages, thus, eliminating linguistic barriers and promoting an equal opportunity to obtain knowledge, which is especially relevant to developing nations (Dahal, 2024). Automation of the grading and administrative tasks is also part of this paradigm shift, so the teachers are set free to focus on more advanced pedagogical activities (Dey, 2025). To simplify these developments, the shift towards machine learning (from rigidity, rule-based system, to fluid, data-driven model) represents a positive feedback in society, a shift towards intellectual and analytical labour (Fabregas Alvarez et al., 2024). However, these educational changes also bring in some issues of data privacy, algorithm fairness, and the possible widening of digital disparities in case the access to AI technologies is unequal. The essential explainable AI in education, similar to the paramount role of explainable AI in healthcare, would be critical in guaranteeing the transparency of the algorithms and prevent the risks of biased results that may harm the specific patient demographics (Wani et al., 2023). As a result, effective regulatory frameworks are necessary to regulate the ethical use of AI in education and promote responsible innovation by eliminating socio-economic inequality that might be caused by unequal technology accessibility (Chetry, 2024; Zhang, 2023).

AI algorithms are transforming market prediction, algorithmic trading, and fraud detection in the financial sector by processing complex information and, thus, discovering its patterns and abnormalities at an unprecedented rate and accuracy (Bahroun et al., 2023). This analytical skill allows financial institutions to handle risk better, customize customer experience and best operational efficiency through automated processes and predictive analytics (Panda, 2025). To give an example, AI-based systems have the capability to predict emerging trends and investment opportunities after analyzing large amounts of financial data, thus enabling more informed decision-making and potentially better returns (Proceedings of the 19th Conference on Computer Science and Intelligence Systems (FedCSIS)), 2024). Moreover, chatbots and other virtual assistants with AI are improving customer services by providing immediate support and personalized financial recommendations, whereas machine learning models are good at preventing fraudulent activities in real-time, thus improving security (Imran et al., 2024). This preemptive security approach takes advantage of deep learning capabilities to identify subtle differences that may not be detected by traditional rule based detection controls and therefore protect assets and maintain consumer trust (Shatnabi et al., 2024). Although these are the advantages, the widespread use of AI in financial technologies requires strict governance frameworks and responsible AI use to mitigate ethical and regulatory issues, such as transparency and accountability (Kumar, 2024; Anang et al., 2024). The complexity of AI systems, and in particular, the critical financial decisions, is opaque and highlights the necessity of explainable AI that could assure regulatory legal violations and maintain consumer trust (Anang et al., 2024). This call has triggered an increased emphasis on explainable AI in financial services, where the stakeholders will be able to understand the logic of AI-based decisions and reduce the risk of harmful algorithmic bias (Anang et al., 2024). Besides, the use of AI in financial markets also raises the concerns of market manipulation and systemic risks that is rooted in the speed of following the algorithmic strategies of trading (Rawas, 2024). The rising complexity of AI-based financial models also requires a constant surveillance and regulation development to avoid flash crashes or other destabilising market events caused by interconnected algorithmic behaviours (Anang et al., 2024; Qayoumi et al., 2025).

AI IN HEALTHCARE: REVOLUTIONIZING DIAGNOSTICS AND PATIENT CARE

The application of artificial intelligence (AI) in the healthcare industry involves the optimisation of the administrative side of the hospital, resource distribution, and prediction of patient flow, thus improving efficiency in operations by relying on data-driven conclusions. An example of this is that AI is able to forecast patient admissions and discharges, thus, enabling dynamic staffing and bed management to assist in shortening waiting times and enhancing the overall patient experience. In addition, deep-learning algorithms, especially, demonstrate impressive effectiveness in cancer detection as they train the complex patterns in multimodal data sets including medical images, clinical reports, and genomics, and then provide more accurate and personalised diagnoses (Gayap & Akhloufi, 2024). This increased diagnostic accuracy is central to early diagnosis and much more effective in patient outcomes in cancer care (Wani et al., 2023). In addition to diagnostics, AI will help in drug discovery and development with the ability to simulate molecular interactions and predict the efficacy of compounds to speed up the process of research and development of new drugs (Weng et al., 2024). The implementation of AI also enables personalised medicine as the data on individual patients is analysed by customising the treatment plans, anticipating responses to therapies, and optimizing dosages, thus leaving the one-size-fits-all approach. The individualised nature of this is augmented by AI ability to remotely monitor the patients, where biometric data is analysed and the health care giver is informed of any possible health decline as well as the ability to take proactive measures.

These developments, though promising, need to be supported by strong ethical principles to ensure fair access to AI-based healthcare as well as address the potential bias of AI-based decision-making, especially when it comes to vulnerable groups (Weng et al., 2024). More specifically, deep learning in clinical diagnostics, including the examination of radiographs and medical scans, is gradually developing and globally provides better quality and safety of care in a healthcare facility (Rawat, 2023). As an illustration, deep-learning-based systems play a key role in early lung cancer detection with the ability to detect subtle tumour patterns in diagnostic images that conventional methods may fail to detect (Rawat et al., 2023; Gayap and Akhloufi, 2024). The ability allows defining the tumours more accurately and staging them, which is essential in planning the treatment (Gayap & Akhloufi, 2024). These diagnostic models are further optimized with the help of multimodal data, such as genomic and clinical responses, and result in more detailed information about disease progression and treatment response (Gayap & Akhloufi, 2024). In addition, deep convolutional neural networks are also more accurate in identifying tumours in medical images, including mammograms and MRI scans, than human radiologists, which makes them much faster to diagnose (Sinha, 2024; Waqas et al., 2024). This feature not only helps to make the initial diagnosis and identify the spheres that require further pathological examination but also serves as a confirmatory measure, which in turn will help to make a definitive diagnosis and avoid the use of additional therapeutic measures (Faria et al., 2023; Tiwari et al., 2025). Integration of deep learning with conventional medical care will entail the development of well-thought workflows, infrastructure planning, and policy formulation that will allow to maximize its transformative potential in patient care (Gayap & Akhloufi, 2024). Such developments must pay close attention to the problem of data privacy and security since the processing of sensitive patient data is a priority (Nguyen, 2024).

Also, AI models entry into clinical practice requires strict validation to be conducted on a wide range of patients to enable generalisability and overcome the implicit biases that may emerge due to non-representative training samples (SHARIFF et al., 2023). Overcoming such issues as data heterogeneity, model interpretability, and regulatory compliance is a necessity to the smooth adoption of deep-learning solutions into the daily clinical routine (Thakur et al., 2024). Current studies center on the issue, and a partnership between clinicians, data scientists and industry representatives has been instrumental in achieving the full capabilities of deep learning in the next stage of development of medical image analysis and diagnosis (Thakur et al., 2024). An example of such a promising course of action is federated learning, which would allow addressing the problem of privacy issues by training models on decentralised clinical data yet only transmit model updates, preventing the sensitive patient data from being shared (Nguyen, 2024).

AI IN EDUCATION: PERSONALIZING LEARNING AND ENHANCING PEDAGOGY

val applications of AI in education include automated content creation, intelligent tutoring systems, and predictive analytics for student performance, all designed to make learning more accessible and effective. For example, AI algorithms can analyze student interactions with course materials to identify optimal learning pathways, recommending tailored resources and interventions to address individual comprehension gaps. Furthermore, AI-powered systems can provide real-time feedback on assignments, enabling students to correct misconceptions immediately and reinforce their understanding. Additionally, AI facilitates the development of dynamic curricula that adapt to evolving educational needs and industry demands, ensuring graduates possess relevant skills for future employment. ational boundaries by enabling remote learning and providing access to quality educational resources for underserved populations worldwide. This global reach extends educational opportunities, thereby contributing to the reduction of educational disparities and fostering a more inclusive learning environment. However, the ethical deployment of AI in education necessitates careful consideration of data privacy, algorithmic bias in assessment, and the potential for over-reliance on technology, which could diminish critical thinking skills and human interaction. Therefore, establishing robust ethical frameworks and governance structures is imperative to ensure AI complements, rather than supplants, human pedagogical expertise and critical intellectual development (Yekaterina, 2024). Furthermore, interdisciplinary collaboration between AI developers, educators, and ethicists is vital to design and implement AI tools that are pedagogically sound, equitable, and privacy-preserving (Knopp et al., 2023). AI-driven platforms can also support educators by automating routine administrative tasks and providing sophisticated analytics on student progress, allowing teachers to dedicate more time to personalized instruction and mentorship. ative learning platforms, and intelligent tutoring systems highlight its potential to revolutionize traditional pedagogical approaches and enhance academic outcomes (Eden et al., 2024) (Zaman, 2023). Nonetheless, challenges such as data privacy, ethical considerations in decision-making processes like grading, and the necessity for professional development for educators persist (Ellegaard et al., 2024) (Angwaomaodoko, 2023). Moreover, the implementation of AI in educational settings demands significant investment in infrastructure, comprehensive training for staff, and ongoing technical support to ensure successful integration and utilization (Chetry, 2024). Moreover, ensuring equitable access to these technologies across diverse socioeconomic backgrounds is crucial to prevent the exacerbation of existing educational inequalities (Khan et al., 2025) (Eden et al., 2024). Furthermore, the rapid growth of AI in education, including the emergence of generative AI, necessitates a critical examination of potential pitfalls such as the generation of incorrect information and persistent privacy concerns (Ifenthaler et al., 2024). ural language processing models, and computer vision applications are becoming increasingly sophisticated, enabling the automation of tasks that previously required human cognitive effort (Willet & Na, 2024).

AI IN FINANCE: RESHAPING BANKING, INVESTMENT, AND SECURITY

The financial sector is undergoing a profound transformation driven by the integration of AI, which enhances efficiency, optimizes decision-making, and strengthens security protocols across various operations. From algorithmic trading and fraud detection to personalized financial advice and credit risk assessment, AI applications are redefining the landscape of modern finance (Eden et al., 2024). This integration of AI is not merely technological but socio-economic, impacting decision-making processes, operational efficiency, human welfare, and governance frameworks (Weng et al., 2024). In particular, AI-powered systems are revolutionizing fraud detection by analyzing transactional data in real-time to identify anomalous patterns indicative of illicit activities, significantly reducing financial crime (Soomro et al., 2025). Furthermore, machine learning algorithms can predict market trends with greater accuracy, aiding investors in making more informed decisions and optimizing portfolio performance (Weng et al., 2024). AI also plays a crucial role in risk management by evaluating vast datasets to assess creditworthiness and predict potential defaults with enhanced precision (Baloda et al., 2025). Beyond these applications, AI-driven chatbots and virtual assistants are transforming customer service by providing instant support and personalized financial guidance, improving client engagement and accessibility. Moreover, AI facilitates the development of sophisticated financial models for stress testing and scenario analysis, enabling institutions to better navigate economic uncertainties and regulatory changes. These advancements are further bolstered by the application of deep learning and machine learning, which are critical for processing and interpreting complex financial data to provide actionable insights (Qayoumi et al., 2025). Its use extends to areas such as customer service enhancements, fraud detection, risk management, credit assessments, and high-frequency trading, showcasing its comprehensive impact across the financial sector (Maple et al., 2023). Specifically, AI technologies such as machine learning and deep learning are being leveraged to refine processes in banking, insurance, and payment systems, enhancing their efficiency and service delivery (Purwar, 2025). AI's capacity to process extensive data, identify complex patterns, and generate predictions has led to substantial advancements in areas such as risk management, fraud detection, personalized financial services, and financial inclusion (Alemu, 2024). Notably, AI significantly enhances fraud detection by leveraging advanced machine learning techniques to identify real-time anomalies and patterns indicative of illicit activities, thereby reducing false positives and accelerating detection (Patil, 2025). This technological advancement allows financial institutions to process vast quantities of data, identify complex patterns, and make decisions with unprecedented speed and accuracy, thereby fundamentally reimagining core financial processes (Obbu, 2025). These capabilities enable more precise fraud detection, improved risk assessments, and the optimization of trading strategies, contributing to greater financial stability and operational efficiency within the sector (Patil, 2025) (Patil, 2025). AI-powered predictive analytics are also transforming how financial organizations identify and mitigate risks, enabling institutions to forecast credit defaults, market fluctuations, and operational vulnerabilities through the analysis of extensive datasets (Patil, 2025). For example, machine learning models, including support vector machines and neural networks, are extensively used for predictive modeling, fraud detection, and portfolio management (Paramesha et al., 2024) (Liu et al., 2024). Moreover, AI-driven approaches enable real-time detection of anomalies, predictive risk assessment, and adaptive learning mechanisms that continuously evolve to counteract new fraudulent tactics (Paul & Ogburie, 2025). This continuous adaptation is vital for staying ahead of sophisticated cyber threats and evolving fraud schemes (Anang et al., 2024) (Purwar, 2025). Such advancements in AI for financial security not only protect assets but also enhance consumer trust and regulatory compliance (Dakalbab et al., 2024) (Patil, 2025). The efficacy of these AI systems is continually being refined through advancements in computational power, sophisticated algorithms, and the availability of extensive datasets (Baduge et al., 2022). The integration of AI in financial fraud detection, for instance, has significantly improved the ability to identify anomalous patterns and detect fraudulent behavior in real-time, thereby reducing financial losses across banking, insurance, and healthcare sectors (Adhikari et al., 2024) (Paul & Ogburie, 2025).

AI IN SECURITY: ENHANCING THREAT DETECTION AND LAW ENFORCEMENT

In the security domain, AI is revolutionizing threat detection, predictive policing, and cybersecurity by analyzing vast datasets from various sources to identify potential risks and anomalous activities with high precision. This includes leveraging machine learning algorithms to sift through surveillance footage, network traffic, and open-source intelligence for proactive identification of security breaches and emerging threats. AI-driven analytics are also crucial for predicting potential criminal activities and optimizing resource deployment for law enforcement agencies, thereby enhancing public safety and operational efficiency. Furthermore, AI systems are increasingly deployed in cybersecurity to identify sophisticated malware, detect intrusion attempts, and automate responses to cyberattacks, thereby strengthening digital infrastructures against evolving threats. Moreover, artificial intelligence is pivotal in forensic analysis, facilitating the rapid processing of digital evidence and enhancing the accuracy of crime scene investigations. AI's role extends to smart building security, where vision systems and sensors leverage AI to improve the safety of occupants by detecting unusual behavior or unauthorized access (Baduge et al., 2022). Its widespread adoption across critical infrastructures, from autonomous vehicles to financial markets, highlights AI's potential societal benefits while underscoring the urgent need to address its security vulnerabilities (Roshanaei et al., 2024). This includes developing robust ethical guidelines and regulatory frameworks to ensure responsible AI deployment, particularly concerning privacy, bias, and accountability (Patil, 2025). However, the rapid progress in algorithmic machine learning and autonomous decision-making in AI presents both opportunities to address societal challenges, such as cybercrime, and risks that require careful consideration (Fulton et al., 2024). Indeed, the ethical deployment of AI in security applications necessitates rigorous attention to issues such as data privacy, algorithmic transparency, and potential biases that could disproportionately affect certain populations (Zhang, 2023). In cybersecurity, AI systems offer a proactive stance against threats by leveraging machine learning to identify patterns in attack behavior and predict new vulnerabilities (Swetha et al., 2025) (Kunle-Lawanson, 2022). This enables a shift from reactive defense mechanisms to proactive threat intelligence and real-time mitigation strategies against sophisticated cyber threats (Achuthan et al., 2024). This proactive capability is critical as AI also enables the development of more advanced and adaptive cyberattack vectors, necessitating continuous innovation in defense mechanisms (Homaei et al., 2024). Consequently, the integration of AI into cybersecurity frameworks significantly reduces response times to threats and enhances the accuracy of vulnerability identification, fostering more proactive risk management strategies (Uzoka et al., 2024). This includes leveraging AI and ML to enhance detection and response capabilities, enabling quicker and more effective management of security incidents, including novel malware and zero-day exploits (Roshanaei et al., 2024). This advanced capability is particularly vital given the increasing sophistication of cyber threats and the expanding attack surface presented by interconnected systems (Hamid & Rahman, 2025). The proactive detection of anomalies and potential threats is further bolstered by AI's capacity for real-time data analysis across vast networks, enabling security systems to learn and adapt to new threat landscapes dynamically (Sarker et al., 2024). This adaptive learning is crucial for identifying and mitigating sophisticated cyber threats, such as advanced persistent threats and polymorphic malware, which continuously evolve their attack signatures to evade traditional security measures (Roshanaei et al., 2024) (Roshanaei et al., 2024). The application of AI in cybersecurity extends to the automation of security operations, including automated threat hunting, incident response, and vulnerability management, thereby reducing the manual burden on security analysts (Achuthan et al., 2024). AI-powered systems can anticipate cyber assaults by utilizing data analytics, behavioral analysis, and machine learning, which allows for more efficient and rapid threat detection (Patel et al., 2024).

GENERATIVE AI: OPPORTUNITIES AND ETHICAL CHALLENGES

The rapid evolution of generative AI presents a dual-edged sword, offering unprecedented capabilities for innovation while simultaneously introducing complex ethical dilemmas that demand rigorous examination and policy responses. Specifically, these models, capable of producing highly realistic text, images, and other media, raise concerns regarding the potential for misuse in generating disinformation, deepfakes, and automated social engineering attacks (Gilbert & Gilbert, 2025). This ability to synthesize new content, while powerful for creative and analytical tasks, also poses significant risks for cybersecurity, enabling malicious actors to create highly convincing phishing attempts or manipulate data (Palani et al., 2024). Furthermore, the emergence of generative AI, particularly large language models, significantly impacts the cybersecurity landscape by enabling both innovative defense mechanisms and novel forms of attack, which nation-state actors are leveraging to enhance cyberattack sophistication (Orpak, 2025). This rapid advancement necessitates a parallel evolution in defensive strategies to counteract the escalating threat landscape (Achuthan et al., 2024). As generative artificial intelligence outpaces existing cybersecurity protocols and regulatory frameworks, it inadvertently provides cybercriminals with enhanced tools, creating a paradox where advancements in AI also escalate potential threats (Metta et al., 2024). However, these systems also offer the potential to create new defense mechanisms, such as AI-driven threat intelligence and automated anomaly detection, which are crucial for combating increasingly sophisticated cyberattacks. The development of robust and generalizable AI models remains a key challenge, particularly in ensuring their reliability and adaptability across diverse and evolving threat landscapes (Qayoumi et al., 2025). This includes the generation of synthetic data, which, while beneficial for training AI models and testing systems, can also inadvertently violate privacy laws and facilitate new cyberattack methods, posing questions about consent, anonymization, and data ownership (Verma et al., 2025). The intersection of generative AI and cybersecurity, therefore, presents a complex landscape fraught with legal issues and technical challenges that necessitate careful consideration (Verma et al., 2025) (Metta et al., 2024). This necessitates the development of sophisticated detection mechanisms to differentiate between AI-generated synthetic content and authentic data, a task complicated by the increasing realism of generative models (Fang & P.V. Maldague, 2021). This complexity is further exacerbated by the potential for generative AI to craft polymorphic malware and sophisticated social engineering campaigns that bypass traditional security filters (Ibrar et al., 2025) (Neupane et al., 2023). Such AI-created evasion and camouflage techniques pose significant challenges for filtering out malicious content (Schmitt & Fléchais, 2024). The evolving capabilities of generative AI offer both attackers and defenders powerful new tools, creating an unpredictable and uncertain security landscape for the foreseeable future (Barrett et al., 2023). Moreover, the dual-use dilemma of generative AI—where the same capabilities can be exploited for both beneficial and nefarious purposes—underscores the urgent need for comprehensive ethical guidelines and regulatory frameworks (Barrett et al., 2023). This includes addressing issues such as accountability for AI-generated harms, intellectual property rights for AI-created content, and the prevention of AI weaponization (Kurtović et al., 2025).

ETHICAL AND SOCIETAL IMPLICATIONS OF AI INTEGRATION

The widespread deployment of AI across various sectors invariably introduces a myriad of profound ethical and societal implications that extend beyond technological concerns to influence human autonomy, social equity, and economic structures. This pervasive integration necessitates a thorough examination of AI's potential to amplify existing societal biases, create new forms of discrimination, and concentrate power in the hands of a few (Qayoumi et al., 2025). For example, biases encoded within AI models, often inherited from the datasets on which they are trained, can perpetuate or even exacerbate existing societal inequalities across various domains, including employment, credit assessment, and criminal justice (Al-kfairy et al., 2024). Such algorithmic bias, if left unaddressed, could undermine trust in AI systems and lead to significant social unrest (Al-kfairy et al., 2024) (Calzada et al., 2025). Moreover, the increasing sophistication of generative AI, particularly in creating convincing deepfakes and misinformation, highlights the critical need for advanced detection mechanisms and media literacy initiatives to preserve informational integrity and public trust (Ferrara, 2024) (Barrett et al., 2023). The ethical considerations also extend to data privacy and security, as AI systems often rely on vast datasets that can contain sensitive personal information, making robust anonymization and continuous monitoring crucial (Zhang, 2023). Furthermore, the economic implications of AI, particularly concerning job displacement and the transformation of labor markets, demand proactive policy interventions to mitigate negative impacts and foster a smooth transition for the workforce (Akhtar, 2024). These considerations highlight the urgent need for interdisciplinary collaboration among technologists, ethicists, and policymakers to establish comprehensive regulations and transparent AI frameworks (Li, 2023) (Kanbach et al., 2023). This includes exploring the practical implementation of regulatory requirements, such as those outlined in the EU AI Act, to ensure accountability and transparency in AI deployment (Jedličková, 2024) (Sridhar, 2025). Explainable AI is emerging as a critical field to address these concerns by developing models that not only perform effectively but also provide transparent and understandable insights into their decision-making processes, thereby fostering greater trust and enabling human oversight in sensitive applications like medicine and defense (Wani et al., 2023). This emphasis on explainability is crucial given that many advanced AI models, particularly deep learning networks, function as "black boxes," making it difficult for users to understand or validate their predictions, thereby hindering adoption in critical fields like healthcare (Wani et al., 2023) (Radanliev, 2025). The inherent opacity of these complex algorithms, often referred to as "black box" models, impedes accountability and the identification of biased decision-making, particularly in high-stakes domains such as medical diagnostics and legal sentencing (Chellappan, 2024) (Olatoye et al., 2024). Consequently, there is a growing imperative for Explainable AI to demystify these opaque processes, offering insights into how AI arrives at specific conclusions and enabling human users to scrutinize, understand, and trust these systems (Wani et al., 2023) (He et al., 2023). This shift towards transparent AI aligns with global regulatory initiatives, such as the proposed EU AI Act, which increasingly mandate explainability and ethical considerations for high-impact AI applications (Petković, 2023).

THE FUTURE OF AI: EXPLAINABLE AI, GOVERNANCE, AND ETHICAL OVERSIGHT

This demand for transparency and interpretability in AI systems was notably underscored by the Defense Advanced Research Projects Agency in 2016, which officially coined the term "Explainable AI" to promote methods that allow humans to comprehend and justify AI decisions (Shabbir et al., 2024). This initiative aims to transform complex "black-box" models into more transparent systems, thereby increasing user trust and facilitating the responsible deployment of AI in critical applications (Rane et al., 2024) (Chellappan, 2024). The overarching goal of XAI is to provide human-understandable explanations for AI-driven outcomes, enabling stakeholders to evaluate the trustworthiness, fairness, and potential biases embedded within these systems (Chellappan, 2024). This is particularly crucial in sensitive sectors like structural engineering, where AI's analytical capabilities must be balanced with clear interpretability for safety and regulatory compliance (Qayoumi et al., 2025). Such interpretability is paramount for bridging the gap between technological advancement and societal acceptance, especially as AI systems become more autonomous and pervasive (Chellappan, 2024) (Thirunagalingam, 2025). Moreover, XAI techniques are vital for auditing AI systems, ensuring compliance with ethical guidelines, and enabling continuous refinement of models by identifying limitations or erroneous decision pathways (Qayoumi et al., 2025). These techniques often involve methods such as feature attribution, rule-based explanations, and surrogate models, all designed to illuminate the internal workings of complex algorithms (Patil, 2025). However, the implementation of XAI faces challenges, including trade-offs between accuracy and interpretability, and difficulties in creating comprehensive frameworks for real-world engineering systems (Shabbir et al., 2024). The integration of XAI into safety-critical aerospace applications, for example, demands not only model-agnostic and fuzzy logic approaches but also white-box and knowledge graph methodologies to enhance understanding and trustworthiness among developers, guarantors, and interpreters (Cohen, 2023). This necessity for robust interpretability stems from the high-stakes nature of such applications, where understanding the rationale behind an AI's decision is crucial for preventing catastrophic failures and ensuring human oversight (Mersha et al., 2024) (Zorita et al., 2024). This emphasis on transparent AI models is particularly pertinent when dealing with scenarios where the model's predictions can have significant real-world consequences, necessitating an understanding of the decision-making process rather than merely the outcome (Tapeh & Naser, 2022) (Roeslin et al., 2022). This allows for the validation of AI reasoning and promotes greater acceptance and reliance on AI systems across diverse industries (Mir & Perinpanayagam, 2022). Furthermore, for high-stakes applications like healthcare and finance, the necessity for stakeholders to comprehend the rationale behind AI decisions is paramount, driving the demand for inherently interpretable models or methods to explain their behavior (Mumuni & Mumuni, 2025). This is especially true in finance, where regulatory compliance and investor trust necessitate clear insights into algorithmic trading and credit scoring decisions (Anang et al., 2024). The General Data Protection Regulation further incentivizes XAI by recognizing the right of individuals not to be subject to decisions based solely on automated processing, thereby demanding transparency in AI decision-making (Afroogh et al., 2024) (Hossain et al., 2025). This underscores the foundational role of explainability in fostering trust and facilitating the responsible integration of AI, especially in domains where misclassification carries substantial risk (Wani et al., 2023). Therefore, the development and adoption of robust XAI methods are not merely technical enhancements but fundamental requirements for ethical AI deployment, mitigating the "black-box" problem that hinders adoption in critical domains such as healthcare and autonomous vehicles (Mersha et al., 2024) (Gerlach et al., 2022). In healthcare, for instance, the lack of transparency in AI models can lead to diagnostic errors or suboptimal treatment plans, underscoring the critical need for explanations that medical professionals can comprehend and validate (Saranya & Subhashini, 2023) (Wani et al., 2023). Similarly, in finance, regulatory bodies are increasingly demanding explainable AI to ensure accountability, transparency, and compliance with ethical standards in areas like credit scoring and fraud detection (Rane et al., 2023). Such interpretability is crucial for financial institutions to justify their decisions to customers and regulators, particularly when dealing with loan approvals, risk assessments, or identifying suspicious transactions (Chellappan, 2024).

EDUCATION AND WORKFORCE READINESS FOR AN AI-AUGMENTED SOCIETY

While AI offers transformative potential for educational paradigms, its successful integration necessitates a comprehensive approach to workforce readiness, preparing individuals to adapt to evolving job markets and to leverage AI tools effectively across various professions. This includes developing curricula that not only teach AI concepts but also foster critical thinking, problem-solving, and ethical reasoning skills essential for navigating an AI-driven world. Furthermore, a strong emphasis on digital literacy and data science fundamentals is crucial to equip the future workforce with the necessary competencies to interact with and manage AI technologies (Arsenault et al., 2025). This comprehensive preparation extends beyond technical skills, encompassing the cultivation of socio-emotional intelligence and adaptability to ensure individuals can thrive in collaborative human-AI ecosystems (Raza et al.,

2025) (Shamsuddin et al., 2025). This educational transformation also entails retraining and upskilling existing workforces to mitigate job displacement and leverage AI as a tool for augmentation rather than replacement in various sectors. nalysis of educational data offers insights into learning patterns and pedagogical effectiveness, guiding institutions in curriculum development and resource allocation (Chellappan, 2024). This is further supported by the need for globally consistent regulations and guidelines in the AI in education field, which require practical examples for educational needs (Banu, 2024). In financial services, AI is transforming how institutions manage risk, detect fraud, and personalize customer experiences. Algorithmic models enhance fraud detection through advanced pattern recognition, while machine learning algorithms optimize credit scoring and investment strategies (Anang et al., 2024). Personalized financial advice, automated trading, and robo-advisors leverage AI to provide tailored services, improving accessibility and efficiency for clients. Moreover, AI applications in finance extend to regulatory compliance, utilizing natural language processing to analyze complex legal documents and ensure adherence to evolving financial regulations (Bahroun et al., 2023). This integration has led to an anticipated doubling of financial institutions' AI expenditure, projected to reach $97 billion by 2027, underscoring its significant role in reshaping modern finance (Vuković et al., 2025). Beyond these direct applications, AI also plays a crucial role in enabling financial institutions to analyze vast market data for predictive insights, thereby supporting strategic decision-making and enhancing competitive advantage. In the realm of security solutions, AI significantly bolsters capabilities for threat detection, predictive policing, and cybersecurity defense by analyzing vast datasets to identify anomalous behaviors and potential vulnerabilities (Shatnawi et al., 2024). This allows for the proactive identification of cyber threats, optimization of surveillance systems, and rapid response to security incidents across both digital and physical domains (Weng et al., 2024). In this context, AI models are employed for facial recognition in access control, anomaly detection in video surveillance, and sophisticated data analysis to prevent financial crimes, thus enhancing overall security infrastructure (Minssen et al., 2025). However, ethical concerns regarding surveillance, privacy, and potential biases in predictive policing algorithms necessitate careful consideration and the development of robust ethical guidelines for AI deployment in security contexts. In the financial sector, AI-driven operations are revolutionizing customer interaction, analytics, decision support, and the prevention of money laundering and fraud through pattern identification (Ridzuan et al., 2024). These capabilities extend to refining credit scoring and risk management, allowing financial institutions to process extensive data and detect subtle correlations that enhance predictive accuracy and decision-making speed (Obbu, 2025) (Buchanan, 2019) (Fabregas Alvarez et al., 2024). This enhanced analytical capability allows for real-time adjustments to investment strategies and more precise valuation of financial instruments, leading to optimized portfolio performance and reduced exposure to market volatility (Onabowale, 2025) (Truby et al., 2020). Furthermore, AI applications in finance include advanced algorithmic trading models that analyze extensive datasets to identify patterns and make informed trading decisions, often outperforming human traders even during market crises (Liu et al., 2024).

CONCLUSION: NAVIGATING THE FUTURE OF AI FOR COLLECTIVE WELL-BEING

The pervasive integration of AI across these critical sectors underscores its multifaceted impact, necessitating a balanced approach that leverages its transformative potential while meticulously addressing ethical, societal, and regulatory challenges to ensure equitable and sustainable development. This requires ongoing interdisciplinary dialogue, robust policy frameworks, and continuous innovation in AI governance to harness its benefits responsibly and inclusively for collective well-being. This holistic perspective ensures that AI development aligns with broader societal goals, fostering a future where technological advancement genuinely contributes to human flourishing and global stability (Weng et al., 2024). Moreover, the development of intelligent systems in smart cities and buildings, as well as advancements in construction, will further drive resource efficiency and promote sustainable practices (Baduge et al., 2022) (Zhang, 2023). These applications demonstrate AI's capacity to revolutionize urban infrastructure and improve the quality of life for citizens, offering solutions for enhanced mobility, improved public services, and optimized resource management (Hamedani et al., 2025). In the energy sector, AI and machine learning optimize generation, distribution, and consumption through smart grids, reducing waste and carbon emissions (Akavova et al., 2023). Such applications leverage AI to analyze complex energy data, predict demand fluctuations, and manage renewable energy sources more effectively, contributing to a more resilient and sustainable energy infrastructure (Akavova et al., 2023). This integration allows for dynamic load balancing and predictive maintenance, thereby enhancing grid stability and reducing operational costs while accelerating the transition to net-zero sustainability (Olawade et al., 2024) (Akavova et al., 2023). AI's critical role in energy conservation in smart buildings highlights its importance in achieving sustainability goals (Baduge et al., 2022). For instance, AI-driven smart manufacturing processes have demonstrated the potential to decrease energy consumption and waste by 30-50%, while intelligent transportation systems can cut emissions by approximately 60% (Olawade et al., 2024). These significant reductions underscore AI's profound potential to mitigate environmental impacts and drive sustainable development across various industries, complementing efforts in carbon reduction and energy optimization (Pimenow et al., 2024). Furthermore, AI is instrumental in advancing structural engineering, particularly in seismic design and damage assessment, where machine learning algorithms improve the accuracy of predictions and guide adaptive strategies for more resilient infrastructure (Qayoumi et al., 2025). This includes leveraging AI for structural health monitoring to detect early signs of material degradation and stress, ensuring timely interventions and extending the lifespan of critical assets (Anjum et al., 2024). Such applications, including those predicting bond strength in corroded steel and optimizing concrete mixtures, utilize advanced computational techniques to enhance material science and structural engineering practices (Qayoumi et al., 2025). AI can also facilitate the creation of regenerative systems and accelerate the transition to a circular economy by optimizing processes for reuse, repair, and recycling (Baduge et al., 2022). In civil engineering, AI optimizes building designs for energy efficiency and minimal environmental impact, aligning with rigorous green building standards and fostering innovation in construction materials and technologies (Regona et al., 2024) (Shukla, 2024). This optimization extends to leveraging AI for predictive maintenance in infrastructure, where it can analyze sensor data to forecast potential failures and recommend timely interventions, thereby preventing costly repairs and extending asset longevity (Zhang, 2023) (Anjum et al., 2024). This includes leveraging AI for structural health monitoring to detect early signs of material degradation and stress, ensuring timely interventions and extending the lifespan of critical assets (Rajpoot & Tiwari, 2025). Similarly, AI applications contribute to smarter, more sustainable construction practices by streamlining project management and optimizing resource allocation (Regona et al., 2024). This approach allows for real-time adjustments in construction schedules and material procurement, significantly reducing waste and improving overall project efficiency (Baduge et al., 2022).

REFERENCES

Achuthan, K., Ramanathan, S., Srinivas, S., & Raman, R. (2024). Advancing cybersecurity and privacy with artificial intelligence: current trends and future research directions [Review of *Advancing cybersecurity and privacy with artificial intelligence: current trends and future research directions*]. *Frontiers in Big Data, 7*. Frontiers Media. DOI: 10.3389/fdata.2024.1497535

Adhikari, P., Hamal, P., & Baidoo, F. (2024). Artificial Intelligence in fraud detection: Revolutionizing financial security. *International Journal of Science and Research Archive, 13*(1), 1457–1472. DOI: 10.30574/ijsra.2024.13.1.1860

Afroogh, S., Akbari, A., Malone, E., Kargar, M., & Alambeigi, H. (2024). Trust in AI: Progress, challenges, and future directions. *Humanities & Social Sciences Communications, 11*(1), 1568. Advance online publication. DOI: 10.1057/s41599-024-04044-8

Akavova, A., Beguyev, S., & Zaripova, R. (2023). How AI and machine learning can drive sustainable development. *E3S Web of Conferences, 460*, 4018. DOI: 10.1051/e3sconf/202346004018

Akhtar, Z. B. (2024). Unveiling the evolution of generative AI (GAI): A comprehensive and investigative analysis toward LLM models (2021–2024) and beyond. *Journal of Electrical Systems and Information Technology, 11*(1). Advance online publication. DOI: 10.1186/s43067-025-00196-y

Al-kfairy, M., Mustafa, D., Kshetri, N., Insiew, M., & Alfandi, O. (2024). Ethical Challenges and Solutions of Generative AI: An Interdisciplinary Perspective. *Informatics (MDPI), 11*(3), 58. DOI: 10.3390/informatics11030058

Alemu, M. D. (2024). Financial Technology (FinTech), Artificial Intelligence (AI), ICT, Institutional Quality, and Financial Sector Development: International Evidence. *Research Square (Research Square)*. DOI: 10.21203/rs.3.rs-5712330/v1

Anang, A. N., Ajewumi, O. E., Sonubi, T., Nwafor, K. C., Arogundade, J. B., & Akinbi, I. J. (2024). Explainable AI in financial technologies: Balancing innovation with regulatory compliance. *International Journal of Science and Research Archive, 13*(1), 1793–1806. DOI: 10.30574/ijsra.2024.13.1.1870

Angwaomaodoko, E. A. (2023). The Re-examination of the Dangers and Implications of Artificial Intelligence for the Future of Scholarship and Learning. *Traektoriâ Nauki, 9*(10), 3021–3028. DOI: 10.22178/pos.97-24

Anjum, A., Hrairi, M., Aabid, A., Yatim, N. H. M., & Ali, M. (2024). Civil Structural Health Monitoring and Machine Learning: A Comprehensive Review [Review of *Civil Structural Health Monitoring and Machine Learning: A Comprehensive Review*]. *Frattura Ed Integrità Strutturale, 18*(69), 43. Gruppo Italiano Frattura. DOI: 10.3221/IGF-ESIS.69.04

Arsenault, P.-D., Wang, S., & Patenaude, J.-M. (2025). A Survey of Explainable Artificial Intelligence (XAI) in Financial Time Series Forecasting [Review of *A Survey of Explainable Artificial Intelligence (XAI) in Financial Time Series Forecasting*]. *ACM Computing Surveys*. Association for Computing Machinery. DOI: 10.1145/3729531

Baduge, S. K., Thilakarathna, S., Perera, J. S., Arashpour, M., Sharafi, P., Teodosio, B., Shringi, A., & Mendis, P. (2022). *Artificial intelligence and smart vision for building and construction 4.0: Machine and deep learning methods and applications*.

Bahroun, Z., Anane, C., Ahmed, V., & Zacca, A. (2023). Transforming Education: A Comprehensive Review of Generative Artificial Intelligence in Educational Settings through Bibliometric and Content Analysis [Review of *Transforming Education: A Comprehensive Review of Generative Artificial Intelligence in Educational Settings through Bibliometric and Content Analysis*]. *Sustainability, 15*(17), 12983. Multidisciplinary Digital Publishing Institute. DOI: 10.3390/su151712983

Baloda, S., Sharma, M., & Kumar, M. (2025). Future of humanity in an artificial intelligence centric world. *Engineering Applications of Artificial Intelligence, 162*, 112405. DOI: 10.1016/j.engappai.2025.112405

Banu, J. T. (2024). AI in Learning: Designing the Future. *Technical Communication Quarterly, 1*. Advance online publication. DOI: 10.1080/10572252.2024.2428400

Barrett, C., Boyd, B., Bursztein, E., Carlini, N., Chen, B., Choi, J., Chowdhury, A. R., Christodorescu, M., Datta, A., Feizi, S., Fisher, K., Hashimoto, T., Hendrycks, D., Jha, S., Kang, D., Kerschbaum, F., Mitchell, E., Mitchell, J. C., Ramzan, Z., … Yang, D. (2023). Identifying and Mitigating the Security Risks of Generative AI. *Foundations and Trends® in Privacy and Security, 6*(1), 1. DOI: 10.1561/3300000041

Buchanan, B. (2019). Artificial intelligence in finance. In Zenodo *(CERN European Organization for Nuclear Research)*. European Organization for Nuclear Research. DOI: 10.5281/zenodo.2612537

Calzada, I., Németh, G., & Al-Radhi, M. S. (2025). Trustworthy AI for Whom? GenAI Detection Techniques of Trust Through Decentralized Web3 Ecosystems. *Big Data and Cognitive Computing*, *9*(3), 62. DOI: 10.3390/bdcc9030062

Chellappan, R. B. (2024). From Algorithms to Accountability: The Societal and Ethical Need for Explainable AI. *Research Square (Research Square)*. DOI: 10.21203/rs.3.rs-5277731/v1

Chetry, K. K. (2024). Transforming Education: How AI is Revolutionizing the Learning Experience. *International Journal of Research Publication and Reviews*, *5*(5), 6352–6356. DOI: 10.55248/gengpi.5.0524.1277

Cohen, K. (2023). Grand challenges in intelligent aerospace systems. *Frontiers in Aerospace Engineering*, *2*, 1281522. Advance online publication. DOI: 10.3389/fpace.2023.1281522

Dahal, C. (2024). Revolutionizing Education through AI-Powered Inclusive Learning Systems. *Proceedings of the AAAI Conference on Artificial Intelligence*, *38*(21), 23736–23737. DOI: 10.1609/aaai.v38i21.30546

Dakalbab, F., Talib, M. A., Nasir, Q., & Saroufil, T. (2024). Artificial intelligence techniques in financial trading: A systematic literature review. *Journal of King Saud University. Computer and Information Sciences*, *36*(3), 102015. DOI: 10.1016/j.jksuci.2024.102015

Dey, D. (2025). *Enhancing Educational Tools Through Artificial Intelligence in Perspective of Need of AI*. DOI: 10.2139/ssrn.5031275

Eden, C. A., Chisom, O. N., & Adeniyi, I. S.Chima Abimbola EdenOnyebuchi Nneamaka ChisomIdowu Sulaimon Adeniyi. (2024). Integrating AI in education: Opportunities, challenges, and ethical considerations. *Magna Scientia Advanced Research and Reviews*, *10*(2), 6. DOI: 10.30574/msarr.2024.10.2.0039

Ellegaard, M., Johannsen, B. F., & Jacobsen, D. (2024). Peer feedback as a professional competence: Students' experiences of practicing feedback literacy in professional settings. *Research Portal Denmark*, 71. https://local.forskningsportal.dk/local/dki-cgi/ws/cris-link?src=kp&id=kp-9835e9f2-446a-4c9f-8bfb-562839456927&ti=Peer%20feedback%20as%20a%20professional%20competence%3A%20Students%2019%20experiences%20of%20practicing%20feedback%20literacy%20in%20professional%20settings

Fabregas Alvarez, A., Bertolin, C., Gonizzi, S., & Califano, A. (2024). *Development of an Automated Procedure for the Damage Pattern Recognition Via Infrared Thermography and Machine Learning*.

Fang, Q., & Maldague, P. V. (2021). *X*. DEFECT DETECTION IN INFRARED THERMOGRAPHY BY DEEP LEARNING ALGORITHMS.

Faria, N., Campelos, S., & Carvalho, V. (2023). A Novel Convolutional Neural Network Algorithm for Histopathological Lung Cancer Detection. *Applied Sciences (Basel, Switzerland)*, *13*(11), 6571. DOI: 10.3390/app13116571

Ferrara, E. (2024). GenAI against humanity: Nefarious applications of generative artificial intelligence and large language models. *Journal of Computational Social Science*, *7*(1), 549–569. DOI: 10.1007/s42001-024-00250-1

Fulton, R., Fulton, D., Hayes, N., & Kaplan, S. (2024). *The Transformation Risk-Benefit Model of Artificial Intelligence: Balancing Risks and Benefits Through Practical Solutions and Use Cases. arXiv*. Cornell University., DOI: 10.5121/ijaia.15201

Gayap, H. T., & Akhloufi, M. A. (2024). Deep Machine Learning for Medical Diagnosis, Application to Lung Cancer Detection: A Review [Review of Deep Machine Learning for Medical Diagnosis, Application to Lung Cancer Detection: A Review]. *BioMedInformatics*, *4*(1), 236–284. DOI: 10.3390/biomedinformatics4010015

Gerlach, J., Hoppe, P., Jagels, S., Licker, L., & Breitner, M. H. (2022). Decision support for efficient XAI services - A morphological analysis, business model archetypes, and a decision tree. *Electronic Markets*, *32*(4), 2139–2158. DOI: 10.1007/s12525-022-00603-6

Gilbert, C., & Gilbert, M. A. (2025). The Impact of AI on Cybersecurity Defense Mechanisms: Future Trends and Challenges. SSRN *Electronic Journal*. DOI: 10.2139/ssrn.5258783

Hamedani, S. S., Aslam, S., & Hamedani, S. S. (2025). AI in business operations: Driving urban growth and societal sustainability. *Frontiers in Artificial Intelligence*, *8*, 1568210. Advance online publication. DOI: 10.3389/frai.2025.1568210 PMID: 40196185

Hamid, I., & Rahman, M. M. H. (2025). AI, machine learning and deep learning in cyber risk management. *Discover Sustainability*, *6*(1), 389. Advance online publication. DOI: 10.1007/s43621-025-01012-3

He, Z., Zhang, R., Diallo, G., Huang, Z., & Glicksberg, B. S. (2023). Editorial: Explainable artificial intelligence for critical healthcare applications. *Frontiers in Artificial Intelligence*, *6*, 1282800. Advance online publication. DOI: 10.3389/frai.2023.1282800 PMID: 37771610

Homaei, M., Mogollón-Gutiérrez, Ó., Núñez, J. C. S., Ávila, M., & Caro, A. (2024). A review of digital twins and their application in cybersecurity based on artificial intelligence [Review of *A review of digital twins and their application in cybersecurity based on artificial intelligence*]. *Artificial Intelligence Review, 57*(8). Springer Science+Business Media. DOI: 10.1007/s10462-024-10805-3

Hossain, I., Ahmad, R., Amin, S., Sultana, N., & Chowdhury, S. (2025). Risk assessment in financial services: Advancing transparency and trust through explainable AI models. *International Journal of Science and Research Archive, 16*(1), 1409–1419. DOI: 10.30574/ijsra.2025.16.1.2150

Ibrar, W., Mahmood, D., Al-Shamayleh, A. S., Ahmed, G., Zayed, S. B., & Akhunzada, A. (2025). Generative AI: A double-edged sword in the cyber threat landscape. *Artificial Intelligence Review, 58*(9), 285. Advance online publication. DOI: 10.1007/s10462-025-11285-9

Ifenthaler, D., Majumdar, R., Gorissen, P., Judge, M., Mishra, S., Raffaghelli, J. E., & Shimada, A. (2024). *Artificial Intelligence in Education: Implications for Policymakers, Researchers, and Practitioners*. Technology Knowledge and Learning., DOI: 10.1007/s10758-024-09747-0

Imran, M. A. U., Aziz, M. B., Tiwari, A., Saha, S., & Ghimire, A. (2024). Exploring the Latest Trends in AI Technologies: A Study on Current State, Application and Individual Impacts. *Journal of Computer and Communications, 12*(8), 21–36. DOI: 10.4236/jcc.2024.128002

Jedličková, A. (2024). Ethical approaches in designing autonomous and intelligent systems: A comprehensive survey towards responsible development. *AI & Society*. Advance online publication. DOI: 10.1007/s00146-024-02040-9

Kanbach, D. K., Heiduk, L., Blueher, G., Schreiter, M., & Lahmann, A. (2023). The GenAI is out of the bottle: Generative artificial intelligence from a business model innovation perspective. *Review of Managerial Science, 18*(4), 1189–1220. DOI: 10.1007/s11846-023-00696-z

Khan, S., Mazhar, T., Shahzad, T., Khan, M. A., Rehman, A. U., Saeed, M. M., & Hamam, H. (2025). Harnessing AI for sustainable higher education: Ethical considerations, operational efficiency, and future directions. *Discover Sustainability, 6*(1), 23. Advance online publication. DOI: 10.1007/s43621-025-00809-6

Knopp, M., Warm, E. J., Weber, D., Kelleher, M., Kinnear, B., Schumacher, D. J., Santen, S. A., Mendonça, E. A., & Turner, L. (2023). AI-Enabled Medical Education: Threads of Change, Promising Futures, and Risky Realities Across Four Potential Future Worlds. *JMIR Medical Education*, *9*, e50373. Advance online publication. DOI: 10.2196/50373 PMID: 38145471

Kumar, A. (2024). Redefining Finance: The Influence of Artificial Intelligence (AI) and Machine Learning (ML). *arXiv*. DOI: 10.48550/ARXIV.2410.15951

Kunle-Lawanson, O. (2022). The role of AI in information security risk management. *World Journal of Advanced Engineering Technology and Sciences*, *7*(2), 308–319. DOI: 10.30574/wjaets.2022.7.2.0128

Kurtović, H., Šabanović, E., Almisreb, A. A., Saleh, M. A., & Ismail, N. (2025). Exploring the Dark Side: A Systematic Review of Generative AI's Role in Network Attacks and Breaches [Review of *Exploring the Dark Side: A Systematic Review of Generative AI's Role in Network Attacks and Breaches*]. *Lecture Notes in Networks and Systems*, 27. Springer International Publishing. DOI: 10.1007/978-3-031-82881-2_3

Li, N. (2023). Ethical Considerations in Artificial Intelligence: A Comprehensive Disccusion from the Perspective of Computer Vision. *SHS Web of Conferences, 179*, 4024. DOI: 10.1051/shsconf/202317904024

Liu, L. X., Sun, Z., Xu, K., & Chen, C. (2024). AI-Driven Financial Analysis: Exploring ChatGPT's Capabilities and Challenges. *International Journal of Financial Studies, 12*(3), 60. DOI: 10.3390/ijfs12030060

Maple, C., Szpruch, Ł., Epiphaniou, G., Staykova, K., Singh, S. B., Penwarden, W., Wen, Y., Wang, Z., Hariharan, J., & Avramović, P. (2023). The AI Revolution: Opportunities and Challenges for the Finance Sector. *arXiv (Cornell University)*. https://doi.org//arxiv.2308.16538DOI: 10.48550

Mersha, M., Lâm, K. N., Wood, J., AlShami, A. K., & Kalita, J. (2024). Explainable artificial intelligence: A survey of needs, techniques, applications, and future direction. *Neurocomputing*, *599*, 128111. DOI: 10.1016/j.neucom.2024.128111

Metta, S., Chang, I., Parker, J., Roman, M. P., & Ehuan, A. F. (2024). *Generative AI in Cybersecurity*. DOI: 10.48550/ARXIV.2405.01674

Minssen, T., Smith, H. J., Mann, S. P., García, A. M., & Negrete, J. (2025). THE EUROPEAN AI ACT : PROMISES, PERILS & TRADE-OFFS IN A COMPLEX REGULATORY ECOSYSTEM. *Research Portal Denmark, 1*, 330. https://local.forskningsportal.dk/local/dki-cgi/ws/cris-link?src=ku&id=ku-2fbecc26-4adb-487a-92d7-469ae5a7b774&ti=THE%20EUROPEAN%20AI%20ACT%20%3A%20PROMISES%2C%20PERILS%20%26amp%3B%20TRADE-OFFS%20IN%20A%20COMPLEX%20REGULATORY%20ECOSYSTEM

Mir, H. E., & Perinpanayagam, S. (2022). Certification of machine learning algorithms for safe-life assessment of landing gear. *Frontiers in Astronomy and Space Sciences, 9*, 896877. Advance online publication. DOI: 10.3389/fspas.2022.896877

Mumuni, F., & Mumuni, A. (2025). *Explainable artificial intelligence (XAI): from inherent explainability to large language models*. DOI: 10.48550/ARXIV.2501.09967

Neupane, S., Fernandez, I., Mittal, S., & Rahimi, S. (2023). Impacts and Risk of Generative AI Technology on Cyber Defense. *arXiv (Cornell University)*. https://doi.org//arxiv.2306.13033DOI: 10.48550

Nguyen, M. (2024). A scoping review of deep learning approaches for lung cancer detection using chest radiographs and computed tomography scans [Review of *A scoping review of deep learning approaches for lung cancer detection using chest radiographs and computed tomography scans*]. *Biomedical Engineering Advances, 9*, 100138. Elsevier BV. DOI: 10.1016/j.bea.2024.100138

Obbu, S. (2025). AI in finance: Transforming risk management and fraud detection. *World Journal of Advanced Engineering Technology and Sciences, 15*(1), 747–756. DOI: 10.30574/wjaets.2025.15.1.0281

Olatoye, F. O., Awonuga, K. F., Mhlongo, N. Z., Ibeh, C. V., Elufioye, O. A., & Ndubuisi, N. L.Funmilola Olatundun OlatoyeKehinde Feranmi AwonugaNoluthando Zamanjomane MhlongoChidera Victoria IbehOluwafunmi Adijat ElufioyeNdubuisi Leonard Ndubuisi. (2024). AI and ethics in business: A comprehensive review of responsible AI practices and corporate responsibility [Review of AI and ethics in business: A comprehensive review of responsible AI practices and corporate responsibility]. *International Journal of Science and Research Archive, 11*(1), 1433–1443. DOI: 10.30574/ijsra.2024.11.1.0235

Olawade, D. B., Wada, O. Z., David-Olawade, A. C., Fapohunda, O., Ige, A. O., & Ling, J. (2024). Artificial intelligence potential for net zero sustainability: Current evidence and prospects. *Next Sustainability, 4*, 100041. DOI: 10.1016/j.nxsust.2024.100041

Onabowale, O. (2025). The Rise of AI and Robo-Advisors: Redefining Financial Strategies in the Digital Age. *International Journal of Research Publication and Reviews*, *6*(6), 4832. DOI: 10.55248/gengpi.6.0125.0640

Orpak, K. (2025). Generative AI and cybersecurity: Exploring opportunities and threats at their intersection. *Maandblad Voor Accountancy en Bedrijfseconomie*, *99*(4), 221–230. DOI: 10.5117/mab.99.149299

Palani, K., Kethar, J., Prasad, S., & Torremocha, V. (2024). Impact of AI and Generative AI in transforming Cybersecurity. *Journal of Student Research*, *13*(2). Advance online publication. DOI: 10.47611/jsrhs.v13i2.6710

Panda, S. N. (2025). The Role of Artificial Intelligence in Healthcare, Finance, and Education. SSRN *Electronic Journal*. DOI: 10.2139/ssrn.5258064

Paramesha, M., Rane, N., & Rane, J. (2024). Artificial intelligence, machine learning, deep learning, and blockchain in financial and banking services: a comprehensive review [Review of *Artificial intelligence, machine learning, deep learning, and blockchain in financial and banking services: a comprehensive review*]. SSRN *Electronic Journal*. RELX Group (Netherlands). DOI: 10.2139/ssrn.4855893

Patel, B., Bhagavanbhai, P. K., & Dhameliya, N. (2024). Revolutionizing Cybersecurity with AI: Predictive Threat Intelligence and Automated Response Systems. *Deleted Journal*, *12*(4), 1–5. DOI: 10.36676/dira.v12.i4.126

Patil, D. (2025a). *Artificial Intelligence In Financial Risk Assessment And Fraud Detection: Opportunities And Ethical Concerns*. DOI: 10.2139/ssrn.5057434

Patil, D. (2025b). *Artificial Intelligence In Financial Services: Advancements In Fraud Detection, Risk Management, And Algorithmic Trading Optimization*. DOI: 10.2139/ssrn.5057412

Patil, D. (2025c). *Explainable Artificial Intelligence (XAI): Enhancing Transparency And Trust In Machine Learning Models*. DOI: 10.2139/ssrn.5057400

Paul, A. A., & Ogburie, C. P. (2025). The Role of AI in preventing financial fraud and enhancing compliance. *GSC Advanced Research and Reviews*, *22*(3), 269–282. DOI: 10.30574/gscarr.2025.22.3.0086

Petković, D. (2023). It is Not "Accuracy vs. Explainability"—We Need Both for Trustworthy AI Systems. *IEEE Transactions on Technology and Society*, *4*(1), 46–53. DOI: 10.1109/TTS.2023.3239921

Pimenow, S., Pimenowa, O., & Prus, P. (2024). Challenges of Artificial Intelligence Development in the Context of Energy Consumption and Impact on Climate Change. *Energies*, *17*(23), 5965. DOI: 10.3390/en17235965

Proceedings of the 19th Conference on Computer Science and Intelligence Systems (FedCSIS). (2024). *Annals of Computer Science and Information Systems, 39*. https://doi.org/DOI: 10.15439/978-83-969601-6-0

Purwar, P. (2025). The Transformational Impact of AI Across Financial Services. *Journal of Computer Science and Technology Studies*, *7*(3), 461–469. DOI: 10.32996/jcsts.2025.7.3.52

Qayoumi, A. S., Shalizi, H., & Dhankot, M. A. (2025). Review on artificial intelligence application in structural earthquake engineering. *International Journal of Science and Research Archive*, *14*(1), 83. DOI: 10.30574/ijsra.2025.14.1.2659

Radanliev, P. (2025). AI Ethics: Integrating Transparency, Fairness, and Privacy in AI Development. *Applied Artificial Intelligence*, *39*(1), 2463722. Advance online publication. DOI: 10.1080/08839514.2025.2463722

Rajpoot, A., & Tiwari, S. (2025). Predictive Modeling of Structural Performance Using Machine Learning: A Comprehensive Review [Review of Predictive Modeling of Structural Performance Using Machine Learning: A Comprehensive Review]. *Deleted Journal*, *3*(1), 25–30. DOI: 10.47392/IRJAEH.2025.0005

Rane, J., Kaya, Ö., Mallick, S. K., & Rane, N. L. (2024). *Enhancing black-box models: Advances in explainable artificial intelligence for ethical decision-making*. DOI: 10.70593/978-81-981271-0-5_4

Rane, N. L., Choudhary, S., & Rane, J. (2023). Explainable Artificial Intelligence (XAI) Approaches for Transparency and Accountability in Financial Decision-Making. SSRN *Electronic Journal*. DOI: 10.2139/ssrn.4640316

Ranga, M. (2024). ARTIFICIAL INTELLIGENCE AND ITS IMPACT ON SOCIETY. *International Journal of Engineering Science & Humanities.*, *14*(Special Issue 1), 170–177. DOI: 10.62904/9fmpr623

Rawas, S. (2024). AI: The future of humanity. *Discover Artificial Intelligence*, *4*(1), 25. Advance online publication. DOI: 10.1007/s44163-024-00118-3

Rawat, D., Sharma, S., & Bhadula, S. (2023). Deep Learning Techniques in Digital Clinical Diagnostic System for Lung Cancer. *2022 8th International Conference on Advanced Computing and Communication Systems (ICACCS)*, 1232. DOI: 10.1109/ICACCS57279.2023.10113055

Raza, S., Qureshi, R., Zahid, A., Fioresi, J., Sadak, F., Saeed, M. A., Sapkota, R., Jain, A., Zafar, A., Hassan, M., Zafar, A., Maqbool, H., Vayani, A., Wu, J., & Shoman, M. (2025). *Who is Responsible? The Data, Models, Users or Regulations? Responsible Generative AI for a Sustainable Future*. DOI: 10.36227/techrxiv.173834932.29831105/v1

Regona, M., Yiğitcanlar, T., Hon, C. K. H., & Teo, M. (2024). Artificial intelligence and sustainable development goals: Systematic literature review of the construction industry. *Sustainable Cities and Society, 108*, 105499. DOI: 10.1016/j.scs.2024.105499

Ridzuan, N. N., Masri, M., Anshari, M., Fitriyani, N. L., & Syafrudin, M. (2024). AI in the Financial Sector: The Line between Innovation, Regulation and Ethical Responsibility. *Information (Basel), 15*(8), 432. DOI: 10.3390/info15080432

Roeslin, S., Ma, Q., Chigullapally, P., Wicker, J., & Wotherspoon, L. (2022). *Development of a Seismic Loss Prediction Model for Residential Buildings using Machine Learning – Christchurch, New Zealand*. DOI: 10.5194/nhess-2022-227

Roshanaei, M., Khan, M. R., & Sylvester, N. N. (2024a). Enhancing Cybersecurity through AI and ML: Strategies, Challenges, and Future Directions. *Journal of Information Security, 15*(3), 320–339. DOI: 10.4236/jis.2024.153019

Roshanaei, M., Khan, M. R., & Sylvester, N. N. (2024b). Navigating AI Cybersecurity: Evolving Landscape and Challenges. *Journal of Intelligent Learning Systems and Applications, 16*(3), 155–174. DOI: 10.4236/jilsa.2024.163010

Saranya, A., & Subhashini, R. (2023). A systematic review of Explainable Artificial Intelligence models and applications: Recent developments and future trends [Review of *A systematic review of Explainable Artificial Intelligence models and applications: Recent developments and future trends*]. *Decision Analytics Journal, 7*, 100230. Elsevier BV. DOI: 10.1016/j.dajour.2023.100230

Sarker, I. H., Janicke, H., Mohammad, N., Watters, P., & Nepal , Surya. (2024). AI Potentiality and Awareness: A Position Paper from the Perspective of Human-AI Teaming in Cybersecurity. In *Lecture notes in networks and systems* (p. 140). Springer International Publishing. DOI: 10.1007/978-3-031-50887-5_14

Schmitt, M., & Fléchais, I. (2024). Digital deception: Generative artificial intelligence in social engineering and phishing. *Artificial Intelligence Review, 57*(12), 324. Advance online publication. DOI: 10.1007/s10462-024-10973-2

Shabbir, K., Noureldin, M., & Sim, S. (2024). Data-driven model for seismic assessment, design, and retrofit of structures using explainable artificial intelligence. *Computer-Aided Civil and Infrastructure Engineering*. Advance online publication. DOI: 10.1111/mice.13338

Shamsuddin, R., Tabrizi, H. B., & Gottimukkula, P. R. (2025). Towards responsible AI: An implementable blueprint for integrating explainability and social-cognitive frameworks in AI systems. *AI Perspectives & Advances*, *7*(1), 1. Advance online publication. DOI: 10.1186/s42467-024-00016-5

SHARIFF, V., PARITALA, C., & ANKALA, K. (2023). *AN ANALYSIS ON ADVANCES IN LUNG CANCER DIAGNOSIS WITH MEDICAL IMAGING AND DEEP LEARNING TECHNIQUES: CHALLENGES AND OPPORTUNITIES.*

Shatnawi, M. Q., Abuein, Q., & Al-Quraan, R. (2024). Deep Learning-Based Approach to Diagnose Lung Cancer Using CT-Scan Images. *Intelligence-Based Medicine*, *100188*. Advance online publication. DOI: 10.1016/j.ibmed.2024.100188

Shukla, S. K. (2024). AI for Sustainable Ground Infrastructure. *International Journal of Geosynthetics and Ground Engineering*, *10*(6), 90. Advance online publication. DOI: 10.1007/s40891-024-00600-z

Singh, R., & Gibu, S. M. (2023). Exploring the Transformative Potential and the Challenges of Artificial Intelligence in Vauhini Vara's The Immortal King Rao. *Rupkatha Journal on Interdisciplinary Studies in Humanities*, *15*(4). Advance online publication. DOI: 10.21659/rupkatha.v15n4.06

Sinha, R. K. (2024). The role and impact of new technologies on healthcare systems. *Discover Health Systems*, *3*(1), 96. Advance online publication. DOI: 10.1007/s44250-024-00163-w

Soomro, R. B., Al-Rahmi, W. M., Dahri, N. A., Almuqren, L., Almogren, A. S., & Aldaijy, A. (2025). A SEM–ANN analysis to examine impact of artificial intelligence technologies on sustainable performance of SMEs. *Scientific Reports*, *15*(1), 5438. Advance online publication. DOI: 10.1038/s41598-025-86464-3 PMID: 39948417

Sridhar, U. (2025). Ethical frameworks for responsible ai development: Challenges and implementation strategies. *World Journal of Advanced Engineering Technology and Sciences*, *15*(1), 2028–2038. DOI: 10.30574/wjaets.2025.15.1.0420

Swetha, T., Kumaran, U., Meena, V. P., & Hameed, I. A. (2025). Leveraging AI for enhanced cybersecurity: A comprehensive review [Review of Leveraging AI for enhanced cybersecurity: a comprehensive review]. *Discover Applied Sciences*, *7*(6), 584. Advance online publication. DOI: 10.1007/s42452-025-06773-0

Tapeh, A. T. G., & Naser, M. Z. (2022). Discovering Graphical Heuristics on Fire-Induced Spalling of Concrete Through Explainable Artificial Intelligence. *Fire Technology, 58*(5), 2871–2898. DOI: 10.1007/s10694-022-01290-7 PMID: 35910785

Thakur, G. K., Thakur, A., Kulkarni, S., Khan, N., & Khan, S. (2024). Deep Learning Approaches for Medical Image Analysis and Diagnosis. *Cureus*. Advance online publication. DOI: 10.7759/cureus.59507 PMID: 38826977

Thirunagalingam, A. (2025). Enhancing Data Governance Through Explainable AI: Bridging Transparency and Automation. SSRN *Electronic Journal*. DOI: 10.2139/ssrn.5047713

Tiwari, A., Mishra, S. N., & Kuo, T. (2025). Current AI technologies in cancer diagnostics and treatment [Review of *Current AI technologies in cancer diagnostics and treatment*]. *Molecular Cancer, 24*(1). BioMed Central. DOI: 10.1186/s12943-025-02369-9

Truby, J., Brown, R. D., & Dahdal, A. (2020). Banking on AI: Mandating a proactive approach to AI regulation in the financial sector. *Law and Financial Markets Review, 14*(2), 110–120. DOI: 10.1080/17521440.2020.1760454

Uzoka, A., Cadet, E., & Ojukwu, P. U. (2024). Applying artificial intelligence in Cybersecurity to enhance threat detection, response, and risk management. *Computer Science & IT Research Journal, 5*(10), 2511–2538. DOI: 10.51594/csitrj.v5i10.1677

Verma, A., Sankhyayan, S., Jawanda, K., & Tandon, S. N. (2025). Generative Artificial Intelligence and Cybersecurity Risks: Issues and Challenges. In *Lecture notes in networks and systems* (p. 321). Springer International Publishing. DOI: 10.1007/978-981-97-8602-2_29

Vuković, D., Dekpo-Adza, S., & Matović, S. (2025). AI integration in financial services: a systematic review of trends and regulatory challenges [Review of *AI integration in financial services: a systematic review of trends and regulatory challenges*]. *Humanities and Social Sciences Communications, 12*(1). Palgrave Macmillan. DOI: 10.1057/s41599-025-04850-8

Wani, N. A., Kumar, R., & Bedi, J. (2023). DeepXplainer: An interpretable deep learning based approach for lung cancer detection using explainable artificial intelligence. *Computer Methods and Programs in Biomedicine, 243*, 107879. DOI: 10.1016/j.cmpb.2023.107879 PMID: 37897989

Waqas, A., Tripathi, A., Ramachandran, R. P., Stewart, P. A., & Rasool, G. (2024). Multimodal data integration for oncology in the era of deep neural networks: a review [Review of *Multimodal data integration for oncology in the era of deep neural networks: a review*]. *Frontiers in Artificial Intelligence, 7*. Frontiers Media. DOI: 10.3389/frai.2024.1408843

Weng, Y., Wu, J., Kelly, T., & Johnson, W. (2024). *Comprehensive Overview of Artificial Intelligence Applications in Modern Industries*. DOI: 10.20944/preprints202409.1638.v1

Willet, K. B. S., & Na, H. (2024). Generative AI Generating Buzz: Volume, Engagement, and Content of Initial Reactions to ChatGPT in Discussions Across Education-Related Subreddits. *Online Learning : the Official Journal of the Online Learning Consortium, 28*(2). Advance online publication. DOI: 10.24059/olj.v28i2.4434

Yekaterina, K. (2024). Challenges and Opportunities for AI in Healthcare. *International Journal of Law and Policy, 2*(7), 11–15. DOI: 10.59022/ijlp.203

Zaman, B. U. (2023). *Transforming Education Through AI, Benefits, Risks, and Ethical Considerations*. DOI: 10.36227/techrxiv.24231583.v1

Zhang, S. (2023). Artificial Intelligence and Applications in Structural and Material Engineering. *Highlights in Science Engineering and Technology, 75*, 240–245. DOI: 10.54097/9qknfc57

Zorita, F. J. C., Galafate, M., Moguerza, J. M., de Diego, I. M., González, M., & Peña, G. G. (2024). The Role of XAI in Transforming Aeronautics and Aerospace Systems. *arXiv (Cornell University)*. https://doi.org//arxiv.2412.17440DOI: 10.48550

Chapter 10
Demystifying Deepfakes: Understanding Its Technological Landscape

Pooja Dehankar
Ajeenkya D.Y. Patil School of Engineering, India

Kashvi Chaturvedi
https://orcid.org/0009-0005-3192-3400
Ajeenkya D.Y. Patil University, India

Susanta Das
https://orcid.org/0000-0002-9314-3988
Ajeenkya D.Y. Patil University, India

ABSTRACT

Deepfakes are emerging topic at the nexus of multimedia & AI that have experienced a significant surge in recent years. AI is experiencing a technical upsurge with the creation of hyper-realistic video, audio, & images produced by algorithms known as deepfakes. The world was enthralled by the introduction of deepfake, a new method of media manipulation. Deep learning algorithms enable the manipulation & creation of digital information that is incredibly realistic & difficult to distinguish from actual content, leading to the creation of fake media. Although deepfakes can be useful for study, education, & entertainment, they also present a number of serious issues in a number of different fields, including fraud, political manipulation, disinformation, & reputational harm. This chapter examines how deepfakes are created & detected. It investigates ways to counteract deepfake's adversarial purposes. It provide readers a better grasp of the trends & breakthroughs that are currently occurring in this field, & the areas that still need to be researched/addressed.

DOI: 10.4018/979-8-3373-7011-8.ch010

ght © 2026, IGI Global Scientific Publishing. Copying or distributing in print or electronic forms without written permission of IGI Global Scientific Publishing is prohibited. Use of this chapter to generative artificial intelligence (AI) technologies is expressly prohibited. The publisher reserves all rights to license its use for generative AI training and machine learning model development.

1. INTRODUCTION

Deep learning-based Artificial Intelligence (AI) technologies have advanced significantly over the past few years, improving both the form and quality of content production as well as automatic content generating. With deepfake technology, images, sounds, and movies can be automatically generated, manipulated, and forged to create incredibly realistic and challenging-to-distinguish effects. The public news, democracy, and human society are now seriously threatened by fake information (Borges et al., 2019).

Among the DL-powered apps that have been making an appearance lately is Deepfake. Therefore, the main way that deepfake systems can produce fake visuals is by substituting scenes or videos, images and sounds which are indistinguishable from genuine ones by people. Our fingertips now have the ability to manipulate artificial speech, images, and videos thanks to a variety of technologies. Today, video and image forgeries can be indistinguishable from genuine work with the naked eye. This could result in several problems, from portraying fake evidence in court to influencing public perception. Given these considerations, we need to have some tools in order to determine reality (Heidari et al., 2024). With the evolving technology, it is possible to create forgeries or altered images, which are nearly identical to real images, but undetectable to naked eye. The generative adversarial network (GAN) is most popular and trusted artificial intelligence models for creating fake images. It modifies and reorders pixels in unique ways, making images that have never been created before. Initially intended to produce fake images, these models are becoming more and more popular. Two neural networks, discriminator network and generator network, support GAN approaches; the discriminator is the one that tells the difference between the generated images (from generator) & original images (used for training the discriminators). The generator's objective is to minimize the chance of being wrong, while the discriminator's is to maximize the chance of being right, in a minimax game. Resulting fake images have propagated misinformation online and violated our privacy. Majority of these images are posted on social media in order to help their false validity and create misinformation. This illegal and immoral method can also be used to carry out a lot of frauds (Arora & Soni, 2021).

Deep learning algorithms are causing a rapid revolution in the production of audiovisual material. The term "deepfakes" refers to the term used to refer to artificial audiovisual media produced by deep learning. These media are characterized by their remarkable qualities, including being incredibly easy to create and having the ability to blend in with actual sounds and images captured by sensors. This technological progress has brought up ethical issues that have received a lot of attention (Millière, 2022).

Artificial intelligence-generated audiovisual materials known as "deepfakes" imitate incredibly lifelike portrayals of real people speaking & doing things they haven't said/done. As a result, they can do harm to both the public and private spheres. Deepfakes are just one technique used to create and disseminate false material online. They have the potential to undermine public confidence in political and cultural institutions, particularly when they feature well-known and easily identifiable individuals. Deepfakes of people who are not well-known characters can seriously harm the autonomy, integrity, and dignity of those who are wrongly portrayed, which can have a negative impact on their reputations both personally and professionally. It is reasonable to anticipate a rise in deepfake injuries to non-famous individuals as the software used to generate deepfakes becomes more widely available, more reasonably priced, and yields more lifelike outcomes (Judge & Korhani, 2021).

Many difficult problems, such as computer vision, human-level control, and big data analytics, have been successfully solved by deep learning. But DL advancements have also been used to create software that jeopardizes privacy, democracy, & national security. One of the recently popular deep learning apps is called Deepfake. Deepfake algorithms have the ability to produce films and images that are so realistic-looking that people will be unable to tell the difference between them and real ones. It is consequently essential to propose solutions that are capable of automatically detecting and evaluating the integrity of digital visual material (Nguyen et al., 2022).

2. LITERATURE SURVEY

Deepfake technology is a disruptive change, challenging the integrity of information, personal privacy, and trust in our society in the digital age. This technology uses advances in generative adversarial networks (GANs) as well as applications of other AI based algorithms. Fundamentally, deepfakes disrupt our understanding of what constituted authentic visual and audio information that is being shared through digital communication, and compared to traditional forms of modifying images or videos, deepfakes create images and sounds that are highly realistic but completely fabricated. Deepfakes are often framed and made with malicious intent (Kietzmann et al, 2020; Navarro Martínez et al, 2024; Patterson 2023), but it can be utilized in a prosocial way in various contexts, including education, entertainment, accessibility, and medical communication. For example, deepfake technology could be used to create an even more advanced lipsyncing tool for use in language based translation services (Suwajanakorn et al 2017), or create convincingly authentic voiceovers for a film (Chesney & Citron, 2019).

The Sopranos are impact of deepfakes is evident in their increasing prevalence, as well as a gaping role in their replacement of focused regulatory responses, public awareness efforts, and strategies to address deepfakes effectively and safely. Past research has raised serious issues with Rupa's (2018) organizations' "disruptive potential" to further develop levels of uncertainty within social media (Vaccari & Chadwick 2020), which will challenge democratic processes and civic culture. The nation's more recent incidents of fake propaganda or fake videos of political figures sent into the 2022 mafia between Russia and Ukraine, and surveillance Cain and raises Kevin (2022) appeal unregulated laid the model for need our public regulation and legislation governing deepfakes.

The idea of researching the "digital divide" is that differences in access to and use of digital technologies result from differences in socioeconomic status (Hargittai, 2002). This field of study explores personal characteristics (e.g., age, gender, or health), positional characteristics (e.g., income or education), as well as access to technology, in relation to the use of technology (Helsper, 2017a; Van Deursen & Van Dijk, 2019; Van Dijk, 2005). Exclusion from access to digital technologies is an issue because it manifests itself as a limited socioeconomic opportunity (Van Deursen et al., 2017; Van Deursen & Helsper, 2018). One of the emerging new forms of digital inequality as technologies evolve is called the "AI divide" (Carter et al., 2020) (Lutz, 2019; Vartanova & Gladkova, 2019). Any artificial media generated through deep learning technologies, including generative AI technologies, is called a "deepfake." The distinction between generative AI and deepfake is notable, however, when you consider the two together. While the primary goal of deepfakes is to create realistic-looking material that aims to trick media users into believing it is real, generative AI primarily uses patterns found in real data to create synthetic content. The first time deepfakes gained attention was in 2017, when a Reddit user posted phony celebrity pornographic movies made with deepfake technology (Fernando et al, 2025).

Advances in ML and AI technologies are extending capabilities of computers and influencing our daily interactions with visual media. Even though audio and video recordings are frequently regarded as reliable proof, modern software that manipulates digital data using deep learning algorithms creates new difficulties in determining authenticity. "Deepfakes" are highly realistic audio, video, or image files created using DL and AI techniques that mislead users about statements or events. High-quality deepfakes utilize advanced machine-learning algorithms, such as Generative Adversarial Networks (GANs) (Singh & Dhiman, 2023). Algorithms of this type rely on extensive datasets to recognize how to alter, merge, and synthesize video that depicts a person doing or saying something they never said or attempted.

In 2017, a user on Reddit shared an altered video of a celebrity rendering them in a predicament; this was the first deepfake video to be shared publicly (Chadha et al., 2021; Deshmukh & Wankhade, 2020; Rana et al., 2022). Deepfake technology has also been applied as a constructive tool for educational purposes and cultural institutions. For instance, face-swapping applications have been utilized in interactive museum exhibits and to reenact significant historical events. Also, the media and film industries also have potential benefit from the utilization of deepfakes (Westerlund, 2019). Nonetheless, this technology can mostly be used for malicious purposes. Deepfakes can generate sexual photographs of someone famous or blackmail them (Harris, 2018; Kugler & Pace, 2021). Similarly, for entertainment or retribution purposes, employees can use phonied-up photographs or audio/video recordings of co-workers (Albahar & Almalki, 2019). Deepfakes may represent a new kind of content production to spread misinformation that could lead to significantly dangerous consequences like political interference, propaganda, fraud, and reputational harm. The production of various forms of deepfakes has also become easier using AI applications. This kind of technology requires no access to expensive equipment and the developer does not need any learned skills or inherent skillset (Matern et al., 2019; Mirsky & Lee, 2021; Venema & Geradts, 2020). For example, a computer system titled Sora utilizes text prompts to generate brand new video footages. Sora produces complex scenes, featuring multiple performers, unique movements or action patterns, and the added features of mapping the subject and setting accurately. In addition, the model is stable on the actual portrayal of the subjects being requested within the physical world. The same team of engineers, researchers and ethical policies staff at OpenAI that developed Sora are also developing tools to assess if material is misleading or even prompts entering the text chat beyond capacity and/or usage policies. Their text classifier will identify and reject prompts and content that contain excessive violence, sexual content, aggressive images, celebrity likenesses, or intellectual property (OpenAI, 2023).

2.1. Deepfake creation

Using deep learning techniques, deepfakes are made with the intention of substituting another person's face for the targets in a picture/video. Developers and online communities refined this technology to produce remarkably user-friendly applications like FaceSwap and FakeApp that are easily accessible online. In various contexts, such as the preservation of privacy, appearance modification in portraits, video compositing, and other artistic uses, face replacement or face swapping is pertinent.

A pipeline of autoencoders and decoders powers deepfake. Encoders, which use deep neural networks to compress images, are commonly used in image compression. Introducing a bottleneck into the network produces a compressed form of the input

(Ballé et al., 2016). If more sophisticated encoders are released, deepfake tasks may become less difficult as they provide high-quality image compression at a reduced processing power cost (Cheng et al., 2019). Two autoencoders are trained to create deepfakes. In this case, both autoencoders share parameters, so one autoencoder examines the features of the source image, and the other autoencoder examines the features of the target image. When the target image is reconstructed using the source image decoder, the produced image contains features of the source (Punnappurath & Brown, 2019). DeepFaceLab and numerous other platforms use this technique, which is the most popular means of producing deepfake images (Perov et al., 2020; Tewari et al., 2018).

Effectiveness of this method directly depends on how large the dataset is that is used to train deep neural network. Luckily, platforms such as Instagram and YouTube have vast amounts of public images and videos of public figures and celebrities. As a result, these individuals are frequently the targets of deepfakes and suffer the most from them (Dack, 2019). Numerous datasets for deepfake are also made available by the scientific community.

2.2. DeepFake detection

DeepFakes are a growing concern for consumers these days. Videos like these can be made to pose a risk to privacy, commit fraud, and other crimes. It can occasionally be difficult for human eyes to discern between high-quality DeepFake films. For this reason, scientists must create algorithms to find them. Several readily apparent indicators of the "fakeness" of a video or photo can be found while discussing Deepfake detection. It might be prudent to investigate a few common signs.

One issue with DeepFake algorithms is the low resolution of synthetic faces, which results in signs such as excessively smooth skin and lack of skin features. However, there are situations when detection is extremely difficult, particularly when one of the two faces has makeup on it. A few common indicators are temporal flashing, visible portions of the original face, color differences between the synthetic and original faces, head position, small moving components artifacts, eye blink rate, face warping artifacts, individual behavior patterns, etc. (Maksutov et al., 2020).

Deepfake can have negative effects on political and social forces when technology is employed maliciously. These effects can include lowering public faith in institutions, harming the reputations of well-known people, and swaying public opinion. Since there is currently no legislation specifically designed to combat deepfakes, deepfake detection—a method of distinguishing between pristine and deepfake media—is essential to detecting and combating deepfakes (Seow et al., 2022).

In addition to detecting whether a video has been processed, DL is utilized to produce fake videos. Videos can have their facial expressions and movements altered with Deepfake. Deepfake uses a similar tactic to fake video, while Face2Face also uses traditional computer vision techniques to achieve the same goal without using DL. In a video, Deepfake can replace a character's face with someone else's. The ability of DeepFake to swiftly produce a large number of falsified photos sets it apart from manual image forgery techniques. Counterfeiters need to have advanced image editing skills and manually process each image if they want to manually create a big number of forged photos. Manual forging can provide more realistic results and leave less noticeable traces than Deepfake. The technical bar to do this degree of fake is really high, though.

Without expert forgery or editing abilities, a counterfeiter can quickly create a falsified video using DeepFake, given enough training data. Likewise, for an AI model to identify a movie or image produced with Deepfake, it needs to be trained with the characteristics of facial forgeries. After extensive training, the AI model will be able to identify the ideal weight distribution. As a result, the AI model must learn how to correlate vast volumes of data. Because of this, such detection approaches demand very high technology requirements as data volumes increase. On the Internet, however, it is simple to find fake photos for training (Yu et al., 2019).

Modern state-of-the-art techniques for identifying AI-generated facial material in films rely on convolutional neural networks counterfeit vids from authentic ones (Afchar et al., 2018; Amerini et al., 2019; Li & Lyu, 2018; Rahmouni et al., 2017; Rossler et al., 2019).

These techniques treat the DeepFake identification challenge as a classification problem that occurs once every frame. Typically, they use image classification networks that function on either the entire frame or a cropped piece of the frame that contains information specific to a given domain.

Modern DeepFake classification algorithms begin with face tracking and then send the cropped face to a CNN-based classifier to determine if it is real or fake (Chollet, 2017). Typically, the final label of a video is the result of combining the labels for a few candidate frames.

2.3. Ways to counteract deepfake's adversarial purposes

Organizations and individuals can use tactics like employee education, multi-factor authentication, deepfake detection tool investments, crisis communication plans, and media literacy and awareness promotion to combat deepfakes used for adversarial purposes (Keerthana et al., 2025). Increase knowledge of deepfakes and the dangers they may present by promoting skepticism and putting strict verification procedures in place for private correspondence (Alanazi et al., 2025). Encourage mechanisms for critical thinking for the identification and verification of information, especially in the digital space (Lissitsa, 2025). Use and invest in AI processes that can identify and label possibly compromised media (Olanipekun, 2025). Use methods to monitor the provenance tracking and validation of media effectively to support validations of media authenticity (Amerini et al., 2025). Promote the creation of AI laws that ensure ethical use of AI while restricting malicious uses of deepfake technology in media (Judijanto et al., 2025). Battle requests to find ways to differentiate AI from authentic media using methods such as watermarks or other identifiers (Fernandez, 2025). Investigate blockchain technology - use to help reduce tampering and provide proof of authenticity (Jain et al., 2025).

Deepfake detector systems are growing in importance for maintaining the authenticity of digital content, but they too face threats from adversarial attacks that change the inputs to affect the detection properties. To enhance the resilience of deepfake detectors against external attacks, an end-to-end approach is proposed to improve deepfake detection systems. Two adversarial attack techniques include Projected Gradient Descent & the Fast Gradient Sign Method. Both adversarial attack methods generate adversarial samples by incorporating perturbations into the inputs in order to deceive the detection system. A multi-faceted defense approach comprising randomized smoothing, defensive distillation, input preprocessing and adversarial training is employed. Adversarial training enhances the model performance with the addition of adversarial samples to the training data, while preprocessing is used for filtering disturbances (through denoising or similar approaches). Randomized smoothing applies noisy inputs to the model and averages the predictions, thus serving as a defensible method to adversarial perturbations, while defensive distillation adds resiliency to the model via softening the output predictions. The proposed improvements will contribute to the general adversarial defense space in deep learning models and/or enhance the defensive properties of deepfake detection systems. The literature shows that image-based classification models, like XceptionNet and MesoNet, have solid performance in applications like deepfake detection. XceptionNet, has been established as computationally efficient without sacrificing accuracy given its use of depthwise separable convolutions. On the other hand, because MesoNet is designed to detect manipulated media, it is a good fit for this application (Abed et al., 2025).

3. CURRENT TRENDS AND BREAKTHROUGHS

By employing deep learning techniques (in particular GANs), deepfake technology can create incredibly realistic synthetic material (audio, video, photo) (Babaei et al., 2025). Furthermore, artificial intelligence (AI) is now capable of producing persuasive text and speech, making it more difficult to tell real from forgery. Deepfakes have gone beyond solely visual manipulation (Nasiri & Hashemzadeh, 2025).

Academics are responding to this moving forward by developing detection methods that are artificial intelligence based, which analyzes the minor imperfections or artifacts present in creating deepfake material (Basyoni et al., 2025). With the advent of many open-source deepfake tools and applications, even those without any technical background, present or prior, can now hopefully produce and disseminate deepfakes, (Obioha et al., 2025). Additionally, users can create deepfake avatars in real time for applications such as teleconferencing, which raise impersonation and misuse issues (Nannaware et al., 2025). Deepfake technology can create videos that look real or seem that they could be real, by mapping another person's actions and facial expression onto another body, or by they completely swap the person's face with another person (Kaushik et al., 2025). Finally, researchers are looking into creative uses of deepfake technology, such as using the deepfake technology to recreate a deceased actor in a film for such as normally producing deepfakes and using the deepfake actors to recreate virtual concerts (Ginsburg & Austin, 2025).

4. AREAS REQUIRING FURTHER RESEARCH AND ADDRESSING

As the production of deepfakes is rapidly improving (Goyal et al., 2025), the need for algorithms with greater reliability and generalizability is urgent, as current algorithms are incapable of keeping pace with deepfake production capabilities. The rapid improvement of deepfakes has ethical implications like potential misuse, deception, and injury—all of which will necessitate the development of policies and rules (Alanazi et al., 2025). The emergence of deepfakes will have significant social and legal consequences, such as the decrease of trust in the media, the potential for political interference, and the need for a policy framework for the prosecution of deepfake crimes (Alanazi et al., 2025). We must take a multi-pronged approach when creating a policy to combat deepfakes, which should center around policy, educational components about developing technology, and ethical practices, as media and technology practitioners (Folorunsho & Boamah, 2025). It will be necessary to create protocols to address how to establish reliability in verifying digital information and validating identity in online media (Alrawahneh et al., 2025). Deepfakes will be (and already are) used to spread propaganda and misinformation, so we need to create mechanisms for reliably detecting and deterring deepfakes (Davis, 2025). We should focus on deepfakes, as well as developing protocols for their detection, as part of educating the public on critical thinking and media literacy during "digital age" (Lee et al., 2025).

5. CONCLUSION

Synthetic media can be both creative and destructive, as demonstrated by deepfake technology. Learning about deepfake technology, including its definition, functions, and expectations, is necessary to reflect its dual characteristics. Since it can be challenging to tell fact from fiction in the digital age, the rise of deepfakes is a serious problem. As we've seen, deepfake technology uses sophisticated ML methods, such as GAN and Convolution Neural Networks, to produce remarkably lifelike, but phony, audio, video, and images. The technology's dual nature—its capacity for both creative and destructive purposes—makes it even more urgent to comprehend its significance. Stakeholders from a wide range of industries, including media, technology, law, and others, will need to work together to create solutions that reduce the risks while maximizing the potential and opportunity of deepfake technology. Among other things, this entails making investments in detection tools, encouraging media literacy, and creating high-quality ethical and legal standards. We can strive toward a future where digital content is both imaginative and reliable by comprehending and resolving the issues that come up when handling deepfakes. Even though deepfakes may seem very realistic, you can spot them by looking for specific warning signs, like strange gestures, erratic facial expressions, or issues with the audio or video.

REFERENCES

Abed, A. D., Najim, B., Sarab Hussien, S. A., & Majeed, S. H. (2025). Adversarial Attacks on Deepfake Detectors and Defence Mechanisms: A Cyber Security Model. *International Journal of Intelligent Engineering & Systems*, *18*(3).

Afchar, D., Nozick, V., Yamagishi, J., & Echizen, I. (2018, December). Mesonet: a compact facial video forgery detection network. In 2018 IEEE international workshop on information forensics and security (WIFS) (pp. 1-7). IEEE.

Alanazi, S., Asif, S., Caird-daley, A., & Moulitsas, I. (2025). Unmasking deepfakes: a multidisciplinary examination of social impacts and regulatory responses. Human-Intelligent Systems Integration, 1-23.

Albahar, M., & Almalki, J. (2019). Deepfakes: Threats and countermeasures systematic review. *Journal of Theoretical and Applied Information Technology*, *97*(22), 3242–3250.

Alrawahneh, A. A. M., Abdullah, S. N. A. S., Abdullah, S. N. H. S., Kamarudin, N. H., & Taylor, S. K. (2025). Video authentication detection using deep learning: A systematic literature review. *Applied Intelligence*, *55*(3), 239.

Amerini, I., Barni, M., Battiato, S., Bestagini, P., Boato, G., Bruni, V., Caldelli, R., De Natale, F., De Nicola, R., Guarnera, L., & Vitulano, D. (2025). Deepfake Media Forensics: Status and Future Challenges. *Journal of Imaging*, *11*(3), 73.

Amerini, I., Galteri, L., Caldelli, R., & Del Bimbo, A. (2019). Deepfake video detection through optical flow based cnn. In *Proceedings of the IEEE/CVF international conference on computer vision workshops.*

Arora, T., & Soni, R. (2021). A review of techniques to detect the GAN-generated fake images. Generative Adversarial Networks for Image-to-Image Translation, 125-159.

Babaei, R., Cheng, S., Duan, R., & Zhao, S. (2025). Generative Artificial Intelligence and the Evolving Challenge of Deepfake Detection: A Systematic Analysis. *Journal of Sensor and Actuator Networks*, *14*(1), 17.

Ballé, J., Laparra, V., & Simoncelli, E. P. (2016). End-to-end optimized image compression. arXiv preprint arXiv:1611.01704.

Basyoni, L., Qayyum, A., Shaban, K., Elmahjub, E., Al-Ali, A., Halabi, O., & Qadir, J. (2025). Generative AI-Driven Metaverse: The Promises and Challenges of AI-Generated Content. *Authorea Preprints.*

Borges, L., Martins, B., & Calado, P. (2019). Combining similarity features and deep representation learning for stance detection in the context of checking fake news. [JDIQ]. *Journal of Data and Information Quality*, *11*(3), 1–26.

Carter, L., Liu, D., & Cantrell, C. (2020). Exploring the intersection of the digital divide and artificial intelligence: A hermeneutic literature review. *AIS Transactions on Human-Computer Interaction*, *12*(4), 253–275. DOI: 10.17705/1thci.00138

Chadha, A., Kumar, V., Kashyap, S., & Gupta, M. (2021). Deepfake: An overview. In Singh P. K., Wierzchoń S. T., Tanwar S., Ganzha M., & Rodrigues J. J. P. C. (Eds), Proceedings of second international conference on computing, communications, and cyber-security: IC4S 2020 (pp. 557–566). Springer.

Cheng, Z., Sun, H., Takeuchi, M., & Katto, J. (2019). Energy compaction-based image compression using convolutional autoencoder. IEEE Transactions on Multimedia, 22(4), 860-873. Punnappurath, A., & Brown, M. S. (2019). Learning raw image reconstruction-aware deep image compressors. *IEEE Transactions on Pattern Analysis and Machine Intelligence*, *42*(4), 1013–1019.

Chesney, B., & Citron, D. (2019). Deep fakes: A looming challenge for privacy, democracy, and national security. *California Law Review*, *107*(6), 1753–1820. DOI: 10.15779/Z38RV0D15J

Chollet, F. (2017). Xception: Deep learning with depthwise separable convolutions. In *Proceedings of the IEEE conference on computer vision and pattern recognition* (pp. 1251-1258).

Dack, S. (2019). *Deep fakes, fake news, and what comes next. The Henry M.* Jackson School of International Studies.

Davis, J. (2025). Disinformation in the Era of Generative AI: Challenges, Detection Strategies, and Countermeasures. In Public Relations and the Rise of AI (pp. 242-269). Routledge.

Deshmukh, A., & Wankhade, S. B. (2020). Deepfake detection approaches using deep learning: A systematic review. In Balas V. E., Semwal V. B., Khandare A., & Patil M. (Eds), Intelligent computing and networking: Proceedings of IC-ICN 2020 (pp. 293–302). Springer.

Fernandez, P., Elsahar, H., Rebuffi, S. A., Soucek, T., Lacatusu, V., Tran, T., & Mourachko, A. (2025). A Taxonomy of Watermarking Methods for AI-Generated Content. In The 1st Workshop on GenAI Watermarking.

Fernando, T., Priyasad, D., Sridharan, S., Ross, A., & Fookes, C. (2025). Face Deepfakes-A Comprehensive Review. arXiv preprint arXiv:2502.09812.

Folorunsho, F., & Boamah, B. F. (2025). Deepfake technology and its impact: Ethical considerations, societal disruptions, and security threats in ai-generated media. *Management, 16*(1), 1060–1080.

Ginsburg, J. C., & Austin, G. W. (2025). Regulating Deepfakes at Home and Abroad. Forthcoming, Columbia Journal of Law & the Arts, 48.

Goyal, H., Wajid, M. S., Wajid, M. A., Khanday, A. M. U. D., Neshat, M., & Gandomi, A. (2025). State-of-the-art AI-based Learning Approaches for Deepfake Generation and Detection, Analyzing Opportunities, Threading through Pros, Cons, and Future Prospects. arXiv preprint arXiv:2501.01029.

Hargittai, E. (2002). Second-level digital divide: Differences in people's online skills. *First Monday*, *7*(4), 1–18. DOI: 10.5210/fm.v7i4.942

Harris, D. (2018). Deepfakes: False pornography is here and the law cannot protect you. *Duke Law & Technology Review*, *17*, 99.

Heidari, A., Jafari Navimipour, N., Dag, H., & Unal, M. (2024). Deepfake detection using deep learning methods: A systematic and comprehensive review. *Wiley Interdisciplinary Reviews. Data Mining and Knowledge Discovery*, *14*(2), e1520.

Helsper, E. J. (2017a). The social relativity of digital exclusion: Applying relative deprivation theory to digital inequalities. *Communication Theory*, *27*(3), 223–242. DOI: 10.1111/comt.12110

Jain, A., Gaur, A., Gupta, G., Mishra, S., Johari, R., & Vidyarthi, D. P. (2025). Securing Digital Integrity: Proposed Comprehensive Framework for Deepfake Detection and Blockchain Validation. In *International Conference on Cognitive Computing and Cyber Physical Systems* (pp. 579-589). Springer, Singapore.

Judge, E. F., & Korhani, A. M. (2021). *Deepfakes*. Counterfeits, and Personality.

Judijanto, L., Utama, A. S., & Setiyawan, H. (2025). Implementation of Ethical Artificial Intelligence Law to Prevent the Use of AI in Spreading False Information (Deepfake) in Indonesia. *The Easta Journal Law and Human Rights*, *3*(02), 101–109.

Kaushik, P., Garg, V., Priya, A., & Kant, S. (2025). Financial Fraud and Manipulation: The Malicious Use of Deepfakes in Business. In Deepfakes and Their Impact on Business (pp. 173-196). IGI Global Scientific Publishing.

Keerthana, N. V., Suresh, P., Kulandaivel, M., & Kulandaivel, S. (2025). Critical Strategies for Phishing Defense and Digital Asset Protection: A Case Study Approach. In Critical Phishing Defense Strategies and Digital Asset Protection (pp. 221-244). IGI Global Scientific Publishing.

Kietzmann, J., Lee, L. W., McCarthy, I. P., & Kietzmann, T. C. (2020). Deepfakes: Trick or treat? In Business horizons (Vol. 63, Issue 2, pp. 135–146). Elsevier Ltd. https://doi.org/DOI: 10.1016/j.bushor.2019.11.006

Kugler, M. B., & Pace, C. (2021). Deepfake privacy: Attitudes and regulation. *Northwestern University Law Review, 116*, 611.

Lee, F. Y., Kumaresan, S. P., Anaam, E. A., & Kong, W. C. (2025). Social Platforms in the Deepfake Age: Navigating Media Trust through Media Literacy. *JOIV: International Journal on Informatics Visualization*, *9*(1), 176–183.

Li, Y., & Lyu, S. (2018). Exposing deepfake videos by detecting face warping artifacts. arXiv preprint arXiv:1811.00656.

Lissitsa, S. (2025). Generations X, Y, Z: The effects of personal and positional inequalities on critical thinking digital skills. *Online Information Review*, *49*(1), 35–54.

Lutz, C. (2019). Digital inequalities in the age of artificial intelligence and bit data. *Human Behavior and Emerging Technologies*, *1*(2), 141–148. DOI: 10.1002/hbe2.140

Maksutov, A. A., Morozov, V. O., Lavrenov, A. A., & Smirnov, A. S. (2020, January). Methods of deepfake detection based on machine learning. In 2020 IEEE conference of russian young researchers in electrical and electronic engineering (EIConRus) (pp. 408-411). IEEE.

Matern, F., Riess, C., & Stamminger, M. (2019). Exploiting visual artifacts to expose deepfakes and face manipulations. In IEEE winter applications of computer vision workshops (WACVW) (pp. 83–92). IEEE. https://doi.org/DOI: 10.1109/WACVW.2019.00020

Millière, R. (2022). Deep learning and synthetic media. *Synthese*, *200*(3), 231.

Mirsky, Y., & Lee, W. (2021). The creation and detection of deepfakes: A survey. *ACM Computing Surveys*, *54*(1), 1–41.

Nannaware, S. C., Pillai, R., & Kate, N. (2025). Deepfakes in Action: Exploring Use Cases Across Industries. In Deepfakes and Their Impact on Business (pp. 71-98). IGI Global Scientific Publishing.

Nasiri, S., & Hashemzadeh, A. (2025). The Evolution of Disinformation from Fake News Propaganda to AI-driven Narratives as Deepfake. *Journal of Cyberspace Studies*, *9*(1), 203–222.

Navarro Martínez, O., Fernández-García, D., Cuartero Monteagudo, N., & Forero-Rincón, O. (2024). Possible health benefits and risks of deepfake videos: A qualitative study in nursing students. *Nursing Reports*, *14*(4), 2746–2757. DOI: 10.3390/nursrep14040203

Nguyen, T. T., Nguyen, Q. V. H., Nguyen, D. T., Nguyen, D. T., Huynh-The, T., Nahavandi, S., Nguyen, T. T., Pham, Q. V., & Nguyen, C. M. (2022). Deep learning for deepfakes creation and detection: A survey. *Computer Vision and Image Understanding*, *223*, 103525.

Obioha Val, O., Gbadebo, M. O., Olaniyi, O. O., Chinye, N. C., & Balogun, A. Y. (2025). Innovative regulation of open source intelligence and deepfakes AI in managing public trust. Michael Olayinka and Olaniyi, Oluwaseun Oladeji and Chinye, Noah Chukwufumnanya and Balogun, Adebayo Yusuf, Innovative Regulation of Open Source Intelligence and Deepfakes AI in Managing Public Trust (January 30, 2025).

Olanipekun, S. O. (2025). Computational propaganda and misinformation: AI technologies as tools of media manipulation.

Open, A. I. (2023). Creating video from text. Sora is an AI model that can create realistic and imaginative scenes from text instructions. OpenAI. https://openai.com/sora

Patterson, D. (2023). Deepfakes for good? How synthetic media is transforming business. https://techinformed.com/deepfakes-for-good-how-synthetic-media-is-transforming-business/

Perov, I., Gao, D., Chervoniy, N., Liu, K., Marangonda, S., Umé, C., . . . Zhang, W. (2020). DeepFaceLab: Integrated, flexible and extensible face-swapping framework. arXiv preprint arXiv:2005.05535.

Rahmouni, N., Nozick, V., Yamagishi, J., & Echizen, I. (2017, December). Distinguishing computer graphics from natural images using convolution neural networks. In 2017 IEEE workshop on information forensics and security (WIFS) (pp. 1-6). IEEE.

Rana, M. S., Nobi, M. N., Murali, B., & Sung, A. H. (2022). Deepfake detection: A systematic literature review. *IEEE Access : Practical Innovations, Open Solutions*, *10*, 25494–25513.

Rossler, A., Cozzolino, D., Verdoliva, L., Riess, C., Thies, J., & Nießner, M. (2019). Faceforensics++: Learning to detect manipulated facial images. In Proceedings of the IEEE/CVF international conference on computer vision (pp. 1-11).

Seow, J. W., Lim, M. K., Phan, R. C., & Liu, J. K. (2022). A comprehensive overview of Deepfake: Generation, detection, datasets, and opportunities. *Neurocomputing*, *513*, 351–371.

Singh, P., & Dhiman, B. (2023, December 27). Exploding AI-generated deepfakes and misinformation: A threat to global concern in the 21st century. https://shorturl.at/pffhV

Suwajanakorn, S., Seitz, S. M., & Kemelmacher-Shlizerman, I. (2017). Synthesizing obama: Learning lip sync from audio. [ToG]. *ACM Transactions on Graphics*, *36*(4), 1–13.

Tewari, A., Zollhoefer, M., Bernard, F., Garrido, P., Kim, H., Perez, P., & Theobalt, C. (2018). High-fidelity monocular face reconstruction based on an unsupervised model-based face autoencoder. *IEEE Transactions on Pattern Analysis and Machine Intelligence*, *42*(2), 357–370.

Vaccari, C., & Chadwick, A. (2020). Deepfakes and disinformation: Exploring the impact of synthetic political video on deception, uncertainty, and trust in news. *Social Media + Society*, *6*(1). Advance online publication. DOI: 10.1177/2056305120903408

Van Deursen, A. J., & Van Dijk, J. A. (2019). The first-level digital divide shifts from inequalities in physical access to inequalities in material access. *New Media & Society*, *21*(2), 354–375. DOI: 10.1177/1461444818797082

Van Deursen, A., Helsper, E., Eynon, R., & Van Dijk, J. (2017). The compoundness and sequentiality of digital inequality. *International Journal of Communication*, *11*, 452–473.

Van Dijk, J. A. (2005). The deepening divide. *Sage (Atlanta, Ga.)*.

Vartanova, E., & Gladkova, A. (2019). New forms of the digital divide. In Trappel, J. (Ed.), *Digital media inequalities: Policies against divides, distrust and discrimination* (pp. 193–213). Nordicom., https://urn.kb.se/resolve?urn=urn:nbn:se:norden:org:diva-11846

Venema, A. E., & Geradts, Z. J. (2020). Digital forensics, deepfakes, and the legal process. *The SciTech Lawyer*, *16*(4), 14–23.

Westerlund, M. (2019). The emergence of deepfake technology: A review. *Technology Innovation Management Review*, *9*(11), 40–53.

Yu, C. M., Chang, C. T., & Ti, Y. W. (2019). Detecting deepfake-forged contents with separable convolutional neural network and image segmentation. arXiv preprint arXiv:1912.12184

ADDITIONAL READING

Balasubramanian, M., Varun, S. G. A., Pranav, R. A., Gnanamoorthi, P. V., & Chitra, P. (2025). A Comparative Analysis of Deepfake Detection Mechanism Using AI Architecture Models: ResNext-LSTMArchitecture and MesoNet Architecture. In *Recent Advances in Computing Sciences* (pp. 180–184). CRC Press.

Abhinandhan, S., Sreedevi, A. G., & Saranya, G. (2025). From Pixels to Truth: Unveiling Deepfakes with a Meso-5 and XceptionNet Fusion Network. In *International Conference on Cognitive Computing and Cyber Physical Systems* (pp. 67-79). Springer, Singapore.

Chiang, C. Y., Chua, H. N., Jasser, M. B., Wong, R. T., & Issa, B. (2025, February). Transformer-Based Ensemble Approach for Robust Deepfake Detection in Low-Resolution Short Videos. In 2025 21st IEEE International Colloquium on Signal Processing & Its Applications (CSPA) (pp. 307-312). IEEE.

Arshath, B., Balaji, M., Surya, A. B., & Hariprasath, L. (2025). Deepfake detection over different media types using deep learning algorithms. In Challenges in Information, Communication and Computing Technology (pp. 353-358). CRC Press.

Ilhan, I., & Karaköse, M. (2025, February). MesoNet-ViT: Meso Network and Vision Transformer for Deepfake Detection. In 2025 29th International Conference on Information Technology (IT) (pp. 1-4). IEEE.

KEY TERMS AND DEFINITIONS

Deepfakes: Deepfakes are synthetic media, including images, videos, and audio, generated by AI to portray something that does not exist in reality or events that have never occurred, often used for deceptive purposes.

Digital Impersonation: Deepfakes can be used to impersonate individuals, potentially leading to harm, blackmail, or cyberbullying.

FaceSwap: Faceswap is the leading free and Open Source multi-platform Deepfakes software.

FakeApp: apps in mobile devices that trick users into downloading them by using legitimate companies or popular references.

MesoNet: MesoNet is a neural network built primarily to identify deep fakes, but it would also be used for other purposes. MesoNet manages the noise produced by low-quality video processing, which impedes analysis.

Misinformation and Propaganda: Deepfakes can be used to spread false information, manipulate public opinion, and undermine trust in institutions.

XceptionNet: XceptionNet is a Deep Learning Algorithm that Detects Face Swaps in Videos.

Chapter 11
Societal and Human Rights Implications to AI and Democracy, Labor, Automation, and the Future of Work

Irna Rismayanti
https://orcid.org/0009-0007-4629-0399
Universitas Esa Unggul, Indonesia

Mohammad Norman Gaza Laksono
https://orcid.org/0009-0005-2863-5483
Uppsala Universitet, Sweden

ABSTRACT

This chapter per author explores the societal and human rights implications of Artificial Intelligence within the evolving dynamics of democracy, labor, and automation. This analysis explores the dual impact of AI technologies, highlighting their potential to enhance efficiency and innovation while simultaneously exacerbating structural inequalities, undermining human dignity, and altering governance frameworks. The discourse initiates with the convergence of artificial intelligence and democratic principles, examining aspects of transparency and representation, subsequently addressing the socioeconomic implications of labor automation. The discussion subsequently explores global inequality, surveillance ethics, and the diminishing of privacy in the algorithmic era. This chapter examines regulatory responses and emphasizes the necessity for reliable AI based on accountability and fairness.

DOI: 10.4018/979-8-3373-7011-8.ch011

ght © 2026, IGI Global Scientific Publishing. Copying or distributing in print or electronic forms without written permission of IGI Global Scientific Publishing is prohibited. Use of this chapter to generative artificial intelligence (AI) technologies is expressly prohibited. The publisher reserves all rights to license its use for generative AI training and machine learning model development.

1. INTRODUCTION: THE INTERSECTION OF AI, SOCIETY, AND HUMAN RIGHTS

Artificial intelligence is one of the most significant shifts in human history. The pervasive impact of this phenomenon extends far beyond the realm of technology and has an effect on the basic foundations of society, economics, and democratic societies. Artificial intelligence has becoming more widely used in numerous fields as a result of technological advancements. Another industry that makes extensive use of artificial intelligence technologies is the health sector (Demir-Kaymak et al., 2024). The equilibrium between innovation and ethics is becoming increasingly hazardous as a result of the influence that algorithms have on political ideas, the automatic judgments they make, and the changes they bring about in the employment market. As the use of artificial intelligence (AI) grows more prevalent in our everyday lives, we need to question ourselves: how can we maintain our values, fairness, and dignity while simultaneously accepting the progression of technology? Because we need to know not just what artificial intelligence is capable of doing technically, but also how it impacts society and human rights, we can develop a solution. A conversation on the ways in which artificial intelligence (AI) affects democracy, work, and the future of human activity and agency in general will be facilitated by this introduction. From the mechanization of the Industrial Revolution to the digital transformation of the Information Age, technology has always changed the way people work together. This change has been brought about by technological advancements. However, artificial intelligence represents a different turning point. Not only does technology have the ability to replace labor or equipment, but it also has the ability to replace decision-making, creativity, and even perception. Increased growth in the use of AI is lacking a cybersecurity and privacy framework In the paper AI secure development is introduced along with AI Dev/Sec/Ops which leads into the creation and understanding of having an AI cybersecurity framework for ML, DNN and CC systems (Darraj et al., 2019). Due to the fact that the distinctions between people and machines are becoming increasingly blurry, there is a need for a moral framework that can address not only the increase in productivity but also more fundamental issues about identity, fairness, and purpose. The intersection of artificial intelligence and human rights has emerged as an important subject for governance in the 21st century. In contrast, the proliferation of artificial intelligence technology across the globe demonstrates how unjust things are. When it comes to artificial intelligence (AI), nations with high incomes are at the forefront of the field. On the other hand, underdeveloped countries typically only use algorithms that were developed in other countries, which demonstrates how economic inequality already exists. The term “digital colonialism” refers to the situation in which a small number of multinational corporations hold a significant amount of power over data and algorithms. This kind of imbalance may make the situation even more severe. In light of this, privacy, consent, and autonomy have emerged as significant concerns all over the world, establishing a direct connection between the administration of artificial intelligence and democratic involvement on a worldwide scale.

Artificial intelligence's capacity to automate decision-making also results in the emergence of new social dangers that have never been seen before. As artificial intelligence (AI) becomes more common in our daily lives and workplaces, college students need to build their AI self-efficacy. This is the belief that they can connect with, understand, learn about, and use (when they want to) AI technologies and applications (Bewersdorff et al., 2025). Whether it be credit-scoring algorithms, automated recruitment systems, or predictive policing, there is a possibility that these systems will have prejudice built into them. When a large number of people utilize these approaches, discrimination shifts from being based on individual bias to being based on systemic exclusion, which is a powerful but difficult to manifest phenomenon. The legal and moral principles that were previously used to guide human judgment need to be updated in order to incorporate the agency of algorithms. The implication of this is that we require methods to guarantee that the decisions that are made by computers are just and accountable. However, as societies become increasingly reliant on AI systems to do tasks in a more expedient manner, the manner in which individuals interact with one another is undergoing subtle shifts. Information and news are curated by recommendation systems, workplaces are transformed into algorithmic ecosystems, and communication channels that are powered by data make it simpler for citizens to participate in civic life. People are concerned about an increase in espionage, manipulation, and the loss of human cognition as a result of these changes. When it comes to the subject of artificial intelligence, democracy and labor cannot be seen to be two distinct spheres; rather, they are inextricably intertwined. The future of work is one that is both exciting and terrifying. The promise of automation is that it will make labor more productive and liberate us from dull chores; yet, it also puts at danger the stability of the economy, the cohesiveness of society, and the security of jobs (Anwar et al., 2025). The fact that artificial intelligence can act as both a facilitator and a disruptor makes it necessary to take into account ethical considerations that go beyond simple economic metrics. In the process of technological innovation, the fundamental human right to meaningful employment and social involvement must continue to be of the utmost importance. In conclusion, the purpose of this chapter is to investigate the myriad of ways in which artificial intelligence (AI) impacts democracy, work, automation, and human rights. In the next sections, we will examine a variety of significant topics, including the state of democratic institutions, the evolution of the labor market, the widening of socioeconomic divides, the dangers posed by monitoring and invasions of privacy, and the emergence of new policy solutions. A critical perspective on how to cope with trust, fairness, and dignity in a world that is becoming increasingly defined by smart machines is presented by each of them each individually (Sekti, 2025b).

Figure 1. Global AI Integration Across Societal Domains

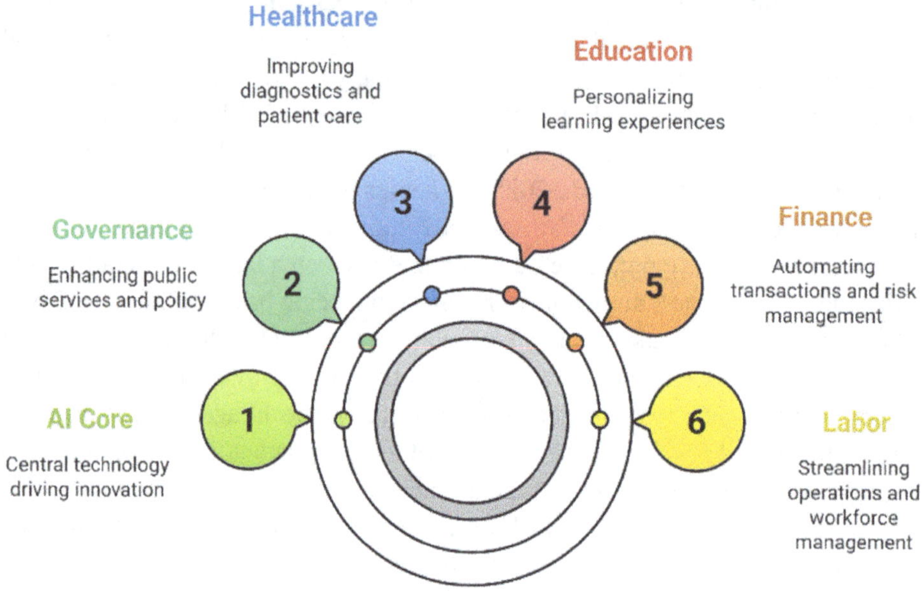

2. AI AND DEMOCRATIC GOVERNANCE: THE CHALLENGE OF REPRESENTATION AND TRANSPARENCY

Through the use of artificial intelligence, the connections that exist between citizens and the governments of their separate countries are undergoing a revolutionary change. Artificial intelligence (AI) has the potential to revolutionize many different industries, including government. In democratic processes, AI has the potential to increase openness, confidence, and responsibility (Lal et al., 2025). Representation, participation, and accountability are the core tenets upon which democratic institutions are constructed. These are the pillars around which democratic systems are created. The application of technology that utilizes artificial intelligence has the potential to either advance or undermine these fundamental principles. Platforms that are driven by information have the potential to improve the design of policies, the solicitation of feedback from the public, and the delivery of services. On the other side, the use of algorithms for decision-making may make accountability more difficult, lead to gaps in knowledge, and reduce the openness of democratic systems. These are all potential outcomes. In order to guarantee that the deployment of artificial intelligence into public administration, law enforcement, and electoral institutions does not undermine democratic governance but rather supports it, it is necessary to conduct a comprehensive review following the installation of this technology. Through the implementation of algorithms in political communication practices, artificial intelligence (AI) has the potential to have a substantial impact on democratic processes. This is one of the most significant ways that AI could use AI. Given the limited understanding of AI's impact on corporate entrepreneurship, this study explores how AI resources (AI utilization and AI governance) promote corporate entrepreneurship, especially with top management's involvement (Fang et al., 2024). It is more critical for recommendation systems and social media bots to prioritize the transmission of information based on engagement metrics than it is for the content to be accurate. The public discourse is affected as a result of this logic of virality, which places a focus on anger and division rather than reasoned discussion. This logic of virality is responsible for altered public conversation. Individuals now have the opportunity to inhabit a mediated environment, which has the capacity to affect their ideas of political consensus. This opportunity has been made possible by the expansion of algorithmic platforms into contemporary public squares. This tendency is frequently referred to as "algorithmic populism," and it is characterized by the substitution of emotional amplification for intellectual communication as well as a drop in public faith in government. In addition, it may be characterized by a decrease in public trust in the government.

The use of artificial intelligence is becoming an increasingly important consideration in the context of electoral procedures and discussions. It is possible to improve the strategic efficiency of campaign advertising by utilizing artificial intelligence. This can be accomplished by targeting certain demographic groups and predicting the voting behavior of voters in advance. A significant number of ethical questions are raised as a result of this circumstance. Top management beliefs positively moderate the impact of AI utilization and AI governance on corporate entrepreneurship (Fang et al., 2024). The use of psychographic profiling in order to exercise influence on voters is a violation of the fundamental democratic ideal of informed consent, which makes it a violation of the democratic process. Democracy runs the risk of deteriorating into a marketplace of attention rather than acting as a platform for collaborative and reasonable debate when voters are considered solely as data points rather than as moral actors. This risks the democracy from working as a platform for reasonable conversation. In order to maintain the integrity of the legitimacy and fairness of algorithmic governance, it is very necessary to have transparency. Applications that make use of artificial intelligence have been welcomed with both praise and criticism within the realm of public administration. By utilizing predictive analytics, it is possible to ascertain the requirements of individuals, enhance the efficiency of governmental organizations, and recognize fraudulent acts on the part of individuals. The distribution of assistance, the screening of immigration, and the enforcement of laws are all examples of procedures that can be affected by algorithmic bias, which can lead to inequitable treatment by the system.

However, despite the fact that insights are generated from existing data, algorithms have the potential to perpetuate preconceptions that already exist. Governments may better monitor spending of public funds, spot anomalies, and guarantee policy compliance with the use of AI-powered systems that enable real-time data analytics (Lal et al., 2025). As a result of the absence of instruments that allow for explanation or contestation, citizens are unable to oppose judgments that are made by automated systems that are regarded as being unfair. This results in the erosion of the procedural justice that is essential to the functioning of a democratic government. Regulatory oversight of artificial intelligence extends beyond the borders of individual nations. When it comes to the process of influencing public information environments, firms that operate on the internet operate on a worldwide scale and hold influence that is comparable to that of international governments. As a result of the impact that private algorithms have on the perspectives and ideas of billions of people, there are questions that have been raised questioning the clarity of sovereignty. The conventional notions of democratic governance, which are predicated on the existence of distinct centers of power, are called into question for the purpose of this proposition. It looks at how AI affects government, voting, and public participation, showing the difficulties and chances of promoting democratic values in the digital era (Wongmahesak et al., 2025). It is vital to develop innovative methods for international cooperation on digital governance that include democratic ideals into algorithmic systems in order to successfully address this topic. This is necessary in order to effectively address this matter. Concerns regarding privacy and surveillance are closely related to the ethical challenges that artificial intelligence puts forward for democratic institutions. There is a direct relationship between the two kinds of issues.

The purpose of governments employing surveillance techniques that are based on artificial intelligence is to enhance public safety and advance the prevention of criminal behavior. On the other hand, comparable technologies might likewise be utilized to exert control over persons. When it comes to democratic resilience in this age of artificial intelligence, one of the most important aspects to consider is the connection between individual liberty and the safety of the general people. It is vital to have institutional safeguards, human monitoring, and transparency measures that empower citizens rather than restrict their voices in order to maintain this equilibrium. Governments around the globe are facing complex challenges in governance, and the incorporation of AI brings forth a dual-edged scenario that impacts democratic principles such as transparency, accountability, and public trust (Wongmahesak et al.,

2025). These measures should be implemented. Taking all of this into consideration, the establishment of democratic governance over artificial intelligence encompasses not only technological concerns but also cultural aspects. Individuals should have a knowledge of the influence that algorithms have on their decision-making processes; legislators should be educated on the ethical considerations that are associated with data governance; and businesses should make a commitment to transparency and accountability. It is essential for individuals to have this knowledge. It is necessary for citizens to be educated on the application of technology, ethical issues in civic technology, and the creation of artificial intelligence that is user-friendly in order to bring about the formation of viable democracies in a world that is driven by data. It is very necessary for the technological systems of ancient civilizations to be in conformity with democratic principles in order for those civilizations to be able to maintain both their freedom and their creativity.

3. AI, LABOR TRANSFORMATION, AND AUTOMATION: DISPLACEMENT OR OPPORTUNITY?

One of the most contentious implications of AI is its revolutionary impact on employment. In a period defined by industrialization, globalisation, and societal change, this chapter discusses how artificial intelligence (AI) is altering agriculture, quickly shifting from old approaches to data-driven practices (Gupta et al., 2025). AI-driven automation has transformed the concepts of employment, production, and societal contribution. Machines previously supplanted physical labor; now they are progressively substituting cognitive labor. The automation frontier now encompasses both blue-collar and white-collar professions, ranging from manufacturing robots to generative AI systems that can write, design, or analyze data. This transition offers productivity and efficiency but also induces worry regarding mass displacement, increasing income inequality, and the diminishing role of work as a social foundation. Economic history demonstrates that technology revolutions have consistently disrupted employment while ultimately generating new types of work. The period of artificial intelligence, however, varies in magnitude and velocity. Automation increasingly focuses on intricate cognitive and creative tasks areas formerly deemed exclusively human. Recent breakthroughs in AI allow it to exceed human capabilities, especially in agriculture, where enhanced production methods and interactive communication are essential (Gupta et al., 2025). This transition prompts fundamental inquiries: if machines possess the capacity to understand, anticipate, and even "create," what is left for human labor? The change necessitates both economic adjustment and intellectual contemplation regarding purpose and dignity in labor. The influence of AI on employment differs among industries at the structural level. Industries characterized by routine tasks, such as manufacturing, logistics, and banking, are at the greatest danger of automation. However, industries that prioritize empathy, critical thinking, and creativity such as education, healthcare, and design exhibit resilience. Nonetheless, even these domains are being restructured as AI enhances rather than supplants human labor. The difficulty resides in overseeing a hybrid workforce where human discernment and machine intelligence function collaboratively.

Consequently, reskilling and lifelong learning have emerged as crucial governmental concerns. As artificial intelligence hastens the obsolescence of skills, educational systems must transition from mere rote knowledge dissemination to the cultivation of adaptive skills. Governments and corporations must allocate resources to training programs that equip workers for multidisciplinary, technology-driven positions. Access to such programs frequently corresponds with socioeconomic position, potentially exacerbating inequality. Inclusive education and social protection measures are crucial to guarantee that automation advantages rather than marginalizes the majority. The societal significance of labor necessitates reevaluation. Labor is not solely a mechanism for subsistence but a foundation of identity and social cohesion. Temporary mass displacement might undermine social cohesion and intensify mental health crises. Policymakers must thus conceptualize automation not merely as an economic efficiency initiative but as a societal upheaval necessitating empathy, involvement, and collaborative governance. Ethical considerations arise at each phase of AI-driven automation. The development of reliable AI and its use in practical settings, however, are still very far off. In order to solve this problem, we looked into the viewpoints of AI engineers and the difficulties they encounter when building reliable AI systems (Cousineau et al., 2025). The use of autonomous systems prompts inquiries regarding accountability who has responsibility when an AI-driven process inflicts harm or exhibits bias? Transparency and employee involvement in AI implementation decisions can alleviate opposition and foster trust. Furthermore, ongoing discussions regarding universal basic income and job guarantee initiatives indicate society's effort to separate survival from employment in expectation of extensive automation.

Table 1. Comparative Effects of AI Automation Across Sectors

Sector	Automation Risk Level	Nature of Transformation	Example Application	Human Role Remaining
Manufacturing	Very High	Replacement of repetitive tasks	Robotic assembly lines	Quality supervision, creative problem-solving
Finance	High	Algorithmic trading, risk analysis	Fraud detection AI	Strategic oversight, client relations
Healthcare	Moderate	Diagnostic and administrative AI	Radiology, scheduling systems	Empathy, ethical judgment, patient care
Education	Moderate	Adaptive learning platforms	Intelligent tutoring systems	Mentorship, creativity, moral guidance
Arts and Media	Variable	Generative content creation	AI music and art generation	Curation, originality, cultural interpretation

In the future, the composition of labor will be significantly influenced by the choices that civilizations make over how to react to the technological advancements that are occurring. In the event that technology is utilized as a liberating tool that encourages inventiveness and eliminates monotony, then there is a possibility that artificial intelligence will be able to maintain human dignity. Therefore, this is the case provided that technology is utilized to its full potential. However, if it is not regulated, it has the potential to make unfairness, alienation, and a lack of purpose much worse. This is because it has the ability to compound these problems. Consequently, the question that arises is not whether artificial intelligence will replace employment; rather, the question that arises is how humans will redefine the value of labor itself. This is because of the fact that this is the result of what has occurred. Within the context of the adaptation process, artificial intelligence (AI) should be exploited as a tool for inclusion rather than exclusion in order to achieve sustainable adaptation. This is for the purpose of achieving sustainable adaptation. An artificial intelligence (AI) system is a particular kind of software system with certain standards for reliability because of its unique data and algorithmic features (Liu et al., 2025). When social justice and technological innovation are brought together, there is the possibility that the intended outcomes will be achieved.

4. SOCIOECONOMIC INEQUALITY AND THE ETHICS OF TECHNOLOGICAL DISTRIBUTION

The concept of artificial intelligence does not exist in a vacuum; rather, it improves the frameworks into which it is integrated. Recent research on socioeconomic health inequality has investigated potential determinants; however, empirical evidence regarding the relationship between environmental pollution and socioeconomic health inequality remains insufficient (Liao et al., 2023). The use of artificial intelligence technology is becoming increasingly widespread in both enterprises and governments; as a consequence, these technologies both disclose and worsen the socioeconomic inequities that already exist. People who have access to computers, those who have access to good data, and those who have skilled individuals are the ones who are able to take benefit of artificial intelligence. Human oversight is being considered as a possible defense against some of the drawbacks of high-risk AI applications. This leads to a critical analysis of the function and prerequisites for what is commonly referred to as meaningful or effective human supervision of these systems (Sterz et al., 2024). Those persons who are missing in these things are the ones who are lacking in these things. This gap has resulted in the emergence of a new form of inequality, which is currently being referred to as the "AI divide." equivalent to earlier disparities in terms of income, education, and power, this division is equivalent to those discrepancies. As a result, the ethical dilemma includes not only the question of how to make effective use of artificial intelligence (AI), but also the question of who can use it, for what reasons, and under what conditions. This mismatch is made much more apparent by the panorama of investments in artificial intelligence that all over the world are currently seeing. Only a handful of nations are in control of artificial intelligence research, patents, and infrastructure. These nations are responsible for these things. The majority of these nations can be found between the continents of North America, Europe, and East Asia. Poor countries, on the other hand, continue to be dependent customers since they do not possess the financial means and the technical capabilities that are required to participate in sophisticated artificial intelligence innovation in a big way. Because of this structural mismatch, local economies are dependent on foreign technologies that may not correspond with their cultural, linguistic, or moral values. This scenario is referred to as "algorithmic dependency," and it exists when local economies are dependent on foreign technology. When countries and communities are placed in these conditions, they lose their independence because they do not have complete control over the decisions and facts that concern to them. This is because they did not have the ability to make their own decisions.

The borders of individual nations exhibit a pattern that is comparable to the one described above. In order to boost output, maximize revenue, and anticipate the actions of customers, wealthy individuals and organizations are turning to artificial intelligence (AI) for assistance. On the other hand, people who have low incomes can regard artificial intelligence as a way to keep an eye on them, not include them in activities, or take advantage of them. Because AI-specific competencies are absent from current digital literacy frameworks, assessments of AI competency are inconsistent (S. C. Lee et al., 2026). For instance, workers on platforms that are a part of the gig economy and use algorithmic management have very little control over the algorithms that determine how much they are paid and what jobs they are given to accomplish. This is because the algorithms determine how much they are paid and why they are paid. Both a source of economic growth and a covert means of classifying workers into clusters, artificial intelligence (AI) is a technology that classifies workers into clusters. For the purpose of ensuring that technology is distributed in a manner that is fair to all, it is vital to enact rules that prohibit artificial intelligence from becoming a tool that is used by a select few individuals to achieve control. Education and access to digital technology are both of equal relevance within the framework of this condition for the reasons stated above. Participation in the digital economy is defined as the capacity to comprehend and make use of technology that are powered by artificial intelligence. In the event that students are not taught how to think in a rational and ethical manner while they are in school, they run the risk of missing out on possibilities in the future. Because of this, governments are obligated to ensure that they commit funds not just to the development of infrastructure but also to the promotion of digital citizenship. Providing individuals with the knowledge and skills necessary to analyze, question, and adjust artificial intelligence systems that have an impact on their lives is a vital step in this process. Empowering individuals with the capacity to acquire knowledge is the initial step toward the establishment of ethical guidelines for artificial intelligence. The fact that the private sector is in charge of the development of artificial intelligence makes things a great deal more complicated than they would otherwise be.

Machine learning systems are built on the foundation of massive datasets, which are owned by tech businesses (Sekti, 2025a). These datasets serve as the core components of these systems. When these datasets are used to produce algorithms, those algorithms have a propensity to duplicate the preconceptions of the dominant population. This, in turn, leads to the marginalization of groups that are considered to be among the minority. Typically, these datasets do not contain a great deal of variation, which is the reason behind this. Additionally, the transformation of personal data into a commodity changes the human experience into a method of creating financial advantage. This is a significant change. In order to discover answers to these ethical problems, it is essential to have data governance that is open and transparent, to provide equal access to the benefits of artificial intelligence, and to make innovation ecosystems accessible to all individuals through open innovation. Resolving these inequalities could be accomplished through a number of different approaches, one of which is through global collaboration. It is possible for individuals to become less reliant on one another and to become more involved in the affairs of the world by promoting open-source technologies for artificial intelligence, partnerships for the sharing of data, and ethical technology transfer. On the other hand, these programs need to ensure that the local community maintains its autonomy and cultural sovereignty through their implementation. Without taking into account the myriad of various moral traditions and aspects that society lays value on, it is hard to make a generalization regarding the ethics of technical advancements. A more successful method for the creation of artificial intelligence would be to adopt a pluralistic approach that takes into account the values of a variety of situations. This would be a more effective strategy.

On a cultural level, there is a need to present a fresh story about the prosperity that has been brought about by artificial intelligence. It is not possible for economic development to be the sole criterion for success if there is a correlation between economic advancement and inequality and exclusion. In this day and age of artificial intelligence, the pursuit of justice necessitates a reassessment of the social compact. In order to accomplish this, it is necessary to make certain that the advantages of innovation are dispersed in an equitable manner and that the quest of efficiency does not come at the sacrifice of human dignity. We need redistribution mechanisms, inclusive design principles, and participatory policymaking in order to bridge the expanding gap that exists between the people who are at the vanguard of technology and the general public. This gap is getting wider all the time. In addition, the ethics of the spread of technology incorporates the conservation of the environment as a component. There is a huge difficulty for places that do not have access to renewable energy sources since machine learning models, particularly large neural networks, demand a significant amount of energy (Sekti, 2025a). This provides a significant obstacle for states and regions. Consequently, inequality is a phenomenon that can be observed in both the material world and the natural world. It is imperative that responsible innovation takes into consideration the effects on carbon, the equitable distribution of resources, and the entitlement of future generations to reside on a world that is capable of supporting life. This is a significant factor to take into account because nations are vying with one another to improve their capabilities in the field of artificial intelligence. A different way of putting it is that the fight for environmental justice and the fight for equality in this age of artificial intelligence are two sides of the same coin.

Figure 2. Global Distribution of AI Investment and Workforce Automation Risk

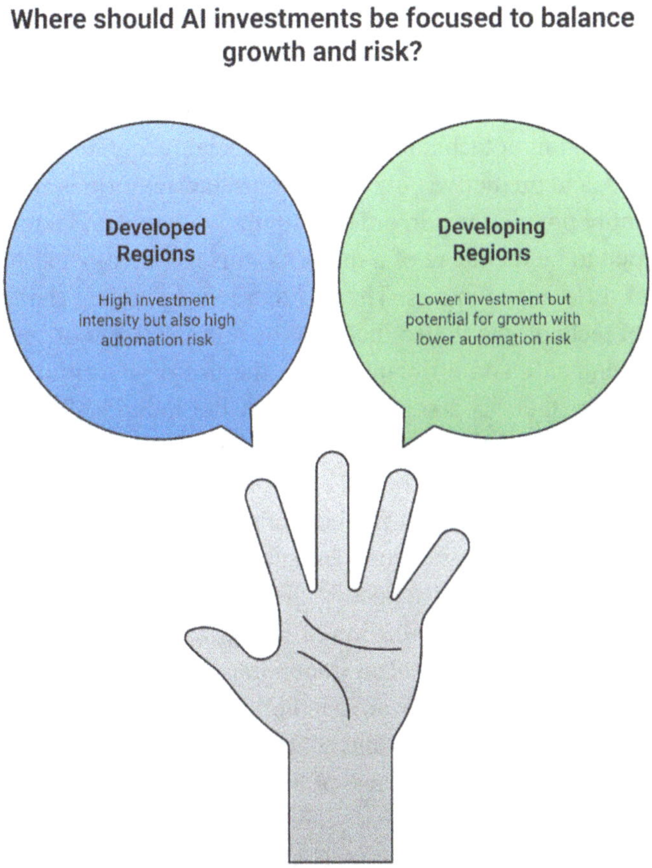

5. HUMAN RIGHTS, DIGNITY, AND SURVEILLANCE IN THE ALGORITHMIC AGE

The human rights movement is currently facing a new level of vulnerability as a result of the advent of the algorithmic era. AI has touched human rights through literature and law, providing modern society both possibilities and challenges. AI has major human rights issues as it spreads (Chattopadhyay et al., 2025). There are significant concerns over the blurring of the lines between surveillance and service that are brought up by the increasing use of artificial intelligence technologies into government, security, and commercial settings. Currently, governments and businesses have the power to monitor, analyze, and forecast the behavior of individuals on a scale that has never been seen before. This capability has never been seen before. In times past, involvement in digital systems was a question of personal preference; nevertheless, in the modern world, it has evolved into a fundamental component of citizenship. As the century progresses, one of the most significant issues that pertains to human rights is the constantly shrinking value of privacy. Through the utilization of technologies such as facial recognition technology, biometric databases, and predictive policing systems, the authorities are able to keep a close eye on entire populations. In order to suppress dissent and target populations that are regarded to be members of a minority, this technology has been deployed in a number of different countries. There is more to the ethical challenge than the mere misuse of technology; it also includes the normalization of surveillance that is framed as being safe and efficient. When the use of algorithmic examination becomes the norm, there is a subtle erosion of the individuality and dignity of people. A fundamental concern in this topic is the right to human dignity, which asserts that people should not be treated as if they were nothing more than figures. This is one of the most important implications of this matter. When it comes to forecasting behavior, giving risk scores, or automating social judgments, artificial intelligence systems invariably objectify the individuals they are attempting to anticipate. As a result of the automation of identification, there is a dilemma that arises from a philosophical and ethical standpoint: is it possible for dignity to exist in a time where personhood is measured and predicted? Concerns have been raised by researchers over the potential for algorithmic methods to reduce moral agents to simple statistical entities in the absence of human monitoring. This, in turn, could lead to a reduction in empathy and individual identity.

The technique of predictive policing is a perfect illustration of this moral hazard, as it provides a perfectly obvious example of it. These algorithms make use of historical crime data, which frequently exhibit inherent biases based on social classification and racial identity. These biases manifest themselves in a variety of ways. As a result of this, communities that are already already at a disadvantage are subjected to artificial intelligence surveillance at a disproportionately larger rate, which in turn perpetuates cycles of bias. There are ramifications for human rights that transcend beyond the concept of bias. These consequences include the institutionalization of prejudice through the application of computational logic, which ultimately results in the transfer of bias into policy views. Consumer analytics, smart gadgets, and workplace monitoring are all examples of areas that fall under the purview of algorithmic surveillance, which has expanded beyond the realm of police enforcement and into the private sector. In order to infer patterns of behavior, feelings, and health issues, continuous analysis is performed on the data obtained from wearables, home assistants, and digital platforms. This analysis is undertaken in order to gather information. The persistent surveillance makes it significantly more challenging to express oneself and to preserve one's right to freedom of opinion. The persistent monitoring of individuals results in the accumulation of a psychological burden that undermines both mental integrity and emotional security. Both of these aspects of human well-being are susceptible to the burden that is imposed by the surveillance. The proliferation of artificial intelligence (AI) systems and technologies that are aimed to discern whether a person is being honest or dishonest based on their facial expressions is extremely worrying. These systems and technologies are designed to analyze facial expressions. In spite of the fact that their scientific validity is currently being called into doubt, these systems are increasingly being utilized in other areas, such as education, recruitment, and border control. There is a possibility that such approaches might oversimplify complex human emotions into basic data models, so neglecting the significance of cultural diversity and additional contextual variables. The epistemological problem that is presented is a challenge to ethics; when robots declare that they have a "understanding" of human conduct, they impose a mechanical view of humanity on the world.

As a consequence of the process of commodifying data, the scenario is made more complicated than it would have been otherwise. When it comes to the global digital economy of today, personal information, which was once considered to be private, has transformed into a commodity. People have a limited level of control over the collecting, processing, and monetization of their data. This is because individuals have limited influence over these aspects of their data. Citizens are transformed into commodities rather than active participants in the environment that is offered by artificial intelligence as a result of the imbalance of power, which contributes to the undermining of the concepts of informed consent and autonomy. One of the greatest concepts humanity has ever developed, human rights are the rights that every human being has simply by virtue of being human. They are outlined in the Universal Declaration of Human Rights (UDHR) as principles pertaining to special treatment for members of particular (human) species (Cobansoy Hizel, 2023). Protecting human rights in this day and age of artificial intelligence demands not only the application of rules, but also a rearrangement of the ethical framework that was previously developed for technology. This is because the framework was originally established for technology. When it comes to the development of artificial intelligence, there are three concepts that ought to be incorporated into each and every part of the process. These principles are privacy-by-design, algorithmic transparency, and digital rights charters. To ensure that ethical issues are prioritized before to deployment, rather than as a response to scandals that have already occurred, it is vital that these measures be preventative rather than reactive. The purpose of this precautionary measure is to ensure that ethical considerations are emphasized. When it comes to bringing itself into alignment with technological advancements, international human rights law faces challenges, notwithstanding the fact that it is a broad concept. Examples of frameworks that are now in use include the Universal Declaration of Human Rights. These frameworks were designed in a context that did not make use of digital technologies. The long-term advancement of universal human rights is reversing course. Digital domains that were previously seen as the pillars of a new age in human rights are where this decline is most noticeable (Brantly, 2022). When it comes to adapting these principles to algorithmic settings, unique interpretations are required in order to guarantee the protection of rights such as freedom of expression, privacy, and equality in digital environments. This is because these principles are suited to algorithmic situations.

Within the context of this process, the function that civil society performs is of the utmost significance. In their capacity as defenders of digital accountability, advocacy groups, investigative journalists, and academics from universities all play a vital role. When unethical surveillance techniques are brought to light and advocates for openness are campaigned for, the democratic function of critique is preserved in a society that is more dominated by code. This is because, in this world, code is becoming increasingly prevalent. In this day and age of algorithmic systems, it is necessary to refocus technology in a humanistic direction in order to safeguard human dignity. In order to facilitate empowerment rather than tyranny, the objective of artificial intelligence should be to act as a tool for emancipation rather than dominance: this would be the ideal application of AI. If it is built with respect, empathy, and agency, artificial intelligence has the ability to coexist with human rights rather than undermine them. This is the case if it is developed.

6. POLICY, REGULATION, AND INSTITUTIONAL RESPONSES: TOWARD TRUSTWORTHY AI

The rapid incorporation of artificial intelligence into governance, commerce, and social life has outgrown the capacity of legal and institutional frameworks to effectively control it. This issue has been brought about by the rapid integration of AI. Systems that are compliant with laws, conform to ethical norms, and demonstrate robustness are receiving the term "trustworthy artificial intelligence" (AI), which is a notion that is currently gaining popularity in talks regarding policy. Within the framework of the modern government, the process of transforming these concepts into frameworks that are capable of being implemented remains a significant challenge. inherent limitations to stakeholders. in the context of AI, the role of trust attributes has been redefined. Transparency is divided into accuracy, clarity, and disclosure, whereas trust in AI is identified through functionality, helpfulness, and predictability (C. Lee & Cha, 2025). Governments in every region of the world have used a variety of different strategies. A legislative framework that is oriented on rights is offered by the Artificial Intelligence Act of the European Union. This act serves as an example of such a framework. Because of this legislation, systems are classified according to the level of risk they pose, and stringent compliance requirements are imposed on applications that pose a high level of risk. However, the United States of America is growing increasingly dependent on industry-specific norms and self-regulation within specific industries. This trend is expected to continue in the foreseeable future. Not only do these opposing methods shed light on political culture, but they also bring to light the numerous ways in which trust and responsibility are perceived in the context of technology governance. The Organization for Economic Cooperation and Development (OECD), the United Nations Educational, Scientific, and Cultural Organization (UNESCO), and the Group of Seven (G7) have all established principles that emphasize the value of transparency, justice, and accountability. These principles have been endorsed by all three organizations. On the other hand, these frameworks frequently lack the legal enforceability that is required to guarantee conformity with the requirements of the law. Regulation, governance, and organizational issues are critical factors in the public utilities market, particularly when these markets seek to initiate homogenization processes (Tomo et al., 2024). As a consequence of this, the landscape of governance is fragmented, and it is marked by the presence of ethical aims in addition to substantial supervision deficiencies.

With algorithmic auditing as one of its components, policy innovation is a crucial field that is becoming increasingly important. It is essential to carry out audits of artificial intelligence systems on a consistent basis and in an independent manner in order to identify biases, assess robustness, and evaluate the influence that artificial intelligence has on society. Through the institutionalization of audit procedures, politicians are afforded the opportunity to integrate ethical ideals with technical execution, which is a capability that was previously unavailable to them. On the other hand, in order to carry out these audits, a significant number of firms do not currently possess the level of expertise and transparency that is necessary for the task. As a consequence of the introduction of artificial intelligence into the public sector, new problems regarding accountability have been brought to light. In instances such as the distribution of assistance, the administration of criminal justice, and immigration, it is essential necessary for citizens to have clear methods for contesting and appealing judgments that are made by algorithms. The technologies that we today refer to as artificial intelligence (AI), including computer vision, deep learning, machine learning, and natural language processing, are evolving into all-purpose instruments that have a big influence on social and economic structures in organizations. That influence hasn't always been favorable, either (Sharma et al., 2024). These processes must be in place. As a consequence of this topic, the implementation of new procedural rights, which are often referred to as algorithmic due process, is necessary in order to guarantee that individuals will not be subjected to unjust punishments by means of systems that are devoid of transparency. The relevance of corporate commitments continues to be the same regardless of the context. When compared to political agencies, organizations that create and implement artificial intelligence systems have a significant amount of influence and have an effect on public life. This is akin to the way that political agencies operate. Accountability can be effectively fostered by the adoption of essential instruments such as organizational ethics programs, impact evaluations, and open data regulations. The implementation of effective monitoring mechanisms is a fundamental must; there is no way that self-regulation can serve as a substitute for legislative responsibilities.

The option of forming partnerships with other countries opens up the door to further opportunities for progress. It is necessary to have transnational cooperation in the field of artificial intelligence ethics, just as it is necessary to have international collaboration in order to effectively administer environmental policy. Through the harmonization of standards for data protection, algorithmic transparency, and human rights safeguards, it is possible to reduce the risk of regulatory arbitrage and increase the level of trust that people around the world have in artificial intelligence systems. The reliability of artificial intelligence is not only dependent on legislation, but also on the culture that is prominent within the organization whose artificial intelligence is being used. It is required to embrace a worldview that incorporates moral reflection into the processes of policymaking and technical application in order to achieve ethical government. This adoption is necessary in order to accomplish ethical governance. In this particular environment, it is very necessary for individuals from different departments and fields of study, such as engineers, ethicists, attorneys, and social scientists, to collaborate with one another. However, AI still encounters significant challenges related to explainability, privacy protection, ethics, and accountability, all of which are crucial for establishing trustworthy AI systems (Otaegui et al., 2026).

Figure 3. Multi-Level AI Governance Ecosystem

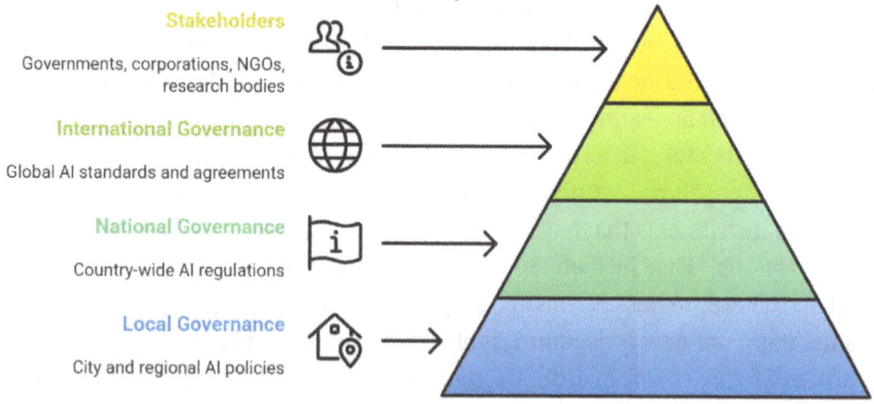

7. CONCLUSION

This chapter demonstrates that the implications of artificial intelligence for society and human rights extend well beyond the technological aspects that are taken into consideration. This is proved by the facts that are presented in this chapter. During the course of their conversation, the fundamental principles of democracy, labor, and human dignity are taken into consideration. The most significant question for the 21st century is not whether or whether artificial intelligence will necessarily have an effect on our world; rather, it is whether or not we will be able to lead that transformation in a way that will conform to ideals of justice, freedom, and equality. This is the question that will determine the ultimate significance of the 21st century. The first step toward a future that is centered on artificial intelligence is to reclaim agency. This is the beginning of the process. To ensure that the design of technological systems is in agreement with the collective moral priorities of a society, rather than being driven by limited profit or control aims, societies should make certain that the design of technology systems is in compliance with these priorities. To be successful in this endeavor, it is vital to incorporate ethical considerations throughout the course of the process of developing artificial intelligence. This includes the collection of data, the training of models, the deployment of the system, and the evaluation of the system. Within the context of the present era of digital technology, the presence of human oversight is a vital component of moral accountability.

In the second place, there is an imperative that is associated with inclusiveness. When it comes to democracy, it is absolutely necessary that the advantages of artificial intelligence be spread in a fair and equitable manner. Consequently, this will ensure that marginalized populations as well as technologically privileged groups are given the opportunity to gain power. In order to guarantee that artificial intelligence (AI) embodies humanity's collective intelligence rather than preserving societal inequities, it is vital to implement efforts that encourage digital literacy, equitable access to innovation, and public participation in the decision-making process regarding policy. Concerning the third point, it is imperative that societies address the ethical issues that are connected to the use of automation. On the other hand, despite the fact that efficiency is typically regarded as a virtue, it should not be permitted to diminish the value of human beings. It is not possible to conduct an evaluation of the goal of advancement based merely on the metrics of productivity or the precision of algorithmic procedures. The maintenance of meaning, dignity, and purpose within the context of human labor and the presence of civilization is the foundation upon which genuine progress is built. Last but not least, it is of the utmost importance that the governance of artificial intelligence incorporate, as core components, the principles of transparency and accountability. Given the lack of transparency that occurs inside the decision-making process of algorithms, there is a significant risk that the general public's trust in these systems may be undermined. There are a number of approaches to ensure that automation will not undermine democracy but rather strengthen it. Some of these strategies include the insertion of interpretability into artificial intelligence systems, the providing of individuals with the right to explanation, and the development of independent oversight agencies.

There will be an urgent requirement for unity on a worldwide scale. It is essential to recognize that the ethical and human rights concerns that are associated with artificial intelligence are inherently global in scope. Due to the fact that data may be transferred beyond national boundaries, it is essential to establish accountability mechanisms that are compatible with this situation. Through the deployment of cooperative governance frameworks that are focused on shared goals and reciprocal accountability, it is possible to reduce the impact of technological supremacy and to encourage innovation that is equitable.The principles of human rights ought to be implemented as the basis for the ethics of artificial intelligence. In order to accommodate the digital era, governments need not establish new ethical frameworks but rather reinforce notions that have been around for a long time and have proven to be effective. The inviolability of human dignity, the universality of justice, and the necessity of freedom are all principles that fall under this category. These ideas serve as essential guiding principles for humanity, which is particularly important given the unpredictability of technology progress. Consistent nurturing is required in order to successfully navigate the junction between democracy and artificial intelligence. There are aspects of democratic government that cannot be recreated by mathematical algorithms, such as transparency, deliberation, and collaborative decision-making. These are characteristics that distinguish democratic government from other forms of government. Through the employment of artificial intelligence to enhance involvement rather than to completely replace it, it is possible to design systems that enhance the human voice rather than lessen it. This is made possible by the fact that the human voice is not diminished.

In the field of education, there is an urgent requirement for a fundamental reform. To be successful in the workforce of the future, one must not only possess technical abilities but also have a strong foundation in ethical literacy. This knowledge is essential for success. It is imperative that the fields of philosophy, law, and social science be incorporated into the curriculum of artificial intelligence programs at educational institutions and universities. This will allow for the cultivation of responsible innovators who are able to strike a healthy balance between efficiency and empathy.In order to be successful in the field of technological design, it is essential required to revitalize one's sense of morality. It is important for engineers and data scientists to not only consider themselves to be the creators of tools, but also to consider themselves to be the protectors of the digital future of humanity. There are a variety of ethical ramifications associated with each and every line of code, and each and every trained model reflects a unique point of view on the world. It is crucial to the long-term development of artificial intelligence to establish trust, which is not built by rhetoric but rather through a consistent commitment to justice, transparency, and shared human values. While there is a large amount of potential, there is also a number of challenges. If humanity is able to successfully combine the advancement of science with an awareness of ethical issues, the era of artificial intelligence will not be a sign of the loss of human sovereignty but rather of the resuscitation of human sovereignty.

REFERENCES

Anwar, N., Sekti, B. A., Widodo, A. M., Erzed, N., Gunawan, H., Tangkudung, R. R. S., Muchlis, M., & Budhisantosa, N. (2025). *Emerging Innovations in AI and Green Computing for Cybersecurity.*, DOI: 10.4018/979-8-3693-8034-5.ch002

Bewersdorff, A., Hornberger, M., Nerdel, C., & Schiff, D. S. (2025). AI advocates and cautious critics: How AI attitudes, AI interest, use of AI, and AI literacy build university students' AI self-efficacy. *Computers and Education: Artificial Intelligence, 8*. Advance online publication. DOI: 10.1016/j.caeai.2024.100340

Brantly, A. (2022). Utopia Lost – Human Rights in a Digital World. *Applied Cybersecurity and Internet Governance, 1*(1). Advance online publication. DOI: 10.5604/01.3001.0016.1238

Chattopadhyay, S., Choudhury, R. R., & Chakraborty, P. (2025). Evolution of human rights through literature and law: Role of AI in its exploration in modern ages. In *Human Values* (pp. 73–93). Ethics, and Dignity in the Age of Artificial Intelligence., DOI: 10.4018/979-8-3693-9035-1.ch004

Cobansoy Hizel, G. (2023). Metaverse and Human Rights: Do We Need Metaversal Declaration of Human Rights? In Studies in Big Data (Vol. 133, pp. 219–229). DOI: 10.1007/978-981-99-4641-9_15

Cousineau, C., Dara, R., & Chowdhury, A. (2025). Trustworthy AI: AI developers' lens to implementation challenges and opportunities. *Data and Information Management, 9*(2), 100082. DOI: 10.1016/j.dim.2024.100082

Darraj, E., Sample, C., & Justice, C. (2019). Artificial intelligence cybersecurity framework: Preparing for the here and now with ai. European Conference on Information Warfare and Security, ECCWS, 2019-July, 132–141. https://www.scopus.com/inward/record.uri?eid=2-s2.0-85070023435&partnerID=40&md5=acc5ea96e58e66c866982fac029066c6

Demir-Kaymak, Z., Turan, Z., Unlu-Bidik, N., & Unkazan, S. (2024). Effects of midwifery and nursing students' readiness about medical Artificial intelligence on Artificial intelligence anxiety. *Nurse Education in Practice, 78*, 103994. DOI: 10.1016/j.nepr.2024.103994 PMID: 38810350

Fang, C., Li, H., & Wang, Y. (2024). AI Utilization and Governance in Corporate Entrepreneurship: Investigating the Moderating Influence of Top Management. Proceedings of the International Conference on Electronic Business (ICEB), 24, 32–43. https://www.scopus.com/inward/record.uri?eid=2-s2.0-85213324449&partnerID=40&md5=00bd2124fc46444e9d35238a5a788d18

Gupta, M., Mishra, G., Bajpai, S., Bhardwaj, A., & Gautam, M. (2025). AI in Agriculture: A Comprehensive Exploration of Technological Transformation. In Emerging Smart Agricultural Practices Using Artificial Intelligence (pp. 105–132). DOI: 10.1002/9781394274277.ch6

Lal, S., Malviya, R., Chandra, S., Wongmahesak, K., Singh, B., & Arora, M. K. K. (2025). AI-driven solutions for transparent governance: Enhancing trust and accountability in modern democratic systems. In Democracy and Democratization in the Age of AI (pp. 153–166). DOI: 10.4018/979-8-3693-8749-8.ch009

Lee, C., & Cha, K. (2025). Toward the Dynamic Relationship Between AI Transparency and Trust in AI: A Case Study on ChatGPT. *International Journal of Human-Computer Interaction*, *41*(13), 8086–8103. DOI: 10.1080/10447318.2024.2405266

Lee, S. C., Baby, T., Vongvit, R., Lee, J., Kim, Y. W., Cha, M. C., & Yoon, S. H. (2026). Development and validation of Generative AI Competence Scale (GenAIComp) among university students. *Technology in Society*, *84*, 103059. DOI: 10.1016/j.techsoc.2025.103059

Liao, L., Du, M., & Chen, Z. (2023). Environmental pollution and socioeconomic health inequality: Evidence from China. *Sustainable Cities and Society*, *95*. Advance online publication. DOI: 10.1016/j.scs.2023.104579

Liu, B., Li, G., Zhang, H., Jin, Y., Wang, Z., & Shao, D. (2025). The Gap Between Trustworthy AI Research and Trustworthy Software Research: A Tertiary Study. *ACM Computing Surveys*, *57*(3), 1–40. DOI: 10.1145/3694964

Otaegui, O., Nieto, M., Rasca, S. I., den Ouden, J., Ubach, C., Stolz, M., & Beckmann, J. (2026). AITHENA: Towards a Trustworthy AI for CCAM Development (pp. 483–489). DOI: 10.1007/978-3-031-88974-5_71

Sekti, B. A. (2025a). *Adversarial Machine Learning in Industrial Cybersecurity.*, DOI: 10.4018/979-8-3373-3241-3.ch018

Sekti, B. A. (2025b). Information Security Awareness. In User-Centric Cybersecurity Implications for Sustainable Digital Transformation (pp. 111–146). IGI Global Scientific Publishing. DOI: 10.4018/979-8-3373-3171-3.ch004

Sharma, M., Biros, D., Baham, C., & Biros, J. (2024). What Went Wrong? Identifying Risk Factors for Popular Negative Consequences in AI. *AIS Transactions on Human-Computer Interaction*, *16*(2), 139–176. 10.17705/1thci.00203

Sterz, S., Baum, K., Biewer, S., Hermanns, H., Lauber-Rönsberg, A., Meinel, P., & Langer, M. (2024). On the Quest for Effectiveness in Human Oversight: Interdisciplinary Perspectives. The 2024 ACM Conference on Fairness Accountability and Transparency, 2495–2507. DOI: 10.1145/3630106.3659051

Tomo, A., Iacono, M. P., Mercurio, L., Mangia, G., & Todisco, L. (2024). Regulation, governance and organisational issues in European Railway Regulation Authorities. Journal of Rail Transport Planning & Management, 29, 100428.

Wongmahesak, K., Wekke, I. S., Seftyono, C., & Nurdin, N. H. (2025). Democracy and democratization in the age of AI. In Democracy and Democratization in the Age of AI. DOI: 10.4018/979-8-3693-8749-8

Compilation of References

Abed, A. D., Najim, B., Sarab Hussien, S. A., & Majeed, S. H. (2025). Adversarial Attacks on Deepfake Detectors and Defence Mechanisms: A Cyber Security Model. *International Journal of Intelligent Engineering & Systems*, *18*(3).

Achuthan, K., Ramanathan, S., Srinivas, S., & Raman, R. (2024). Advancing cybersecurity and privacy with artificial intelligence: current trends and future research directions [Review of *Advancing cybersecurity and privacy with artificial intelligence: current trends and future research directions*]. *Frontiers in Big Data*, *7*. Frontiers Media. DOI: 10.3389/fdata.2024.1497535

Adhikari, P., Hamal, P., & Baidoo, F. (2024). Artificial Intelligence in fraud detection: Revolutionizing financial security. *International Journal of Science and Research Archive*, *13*(1), 1457–1472. DOI: 10.30574/ijsra.2024.13.1.1860

Afchar, D., Nozick, V., Yamagishi, J., & Echizen, I. (2018, December). Mesonet: a compact facial video forgery detection network. In 2018 IEEE international workshop on information forensics and security (WIFS) (pp. 1-7). IEEE.

Afroogh, S., Akbari, A., Malone, E., Kargar, M., & Alambeigi, H. (2024). Trust in AI: Progress, challenges, and future directions. *Humanities & Social Sciences Communications*, *11*(1), 1568. Advance online publication. DOI: 10.1057/s41599-024-04044-8

Agbese, M., Alanen, H.-K., Antikainen, J., Halme, E., Isomäki, H., Jantunen, M., Kemell, K.-K., Rousi, R., Vainio-Pekka, H., & Vakkuri, V. (2023). Governance in Ethical and Trustworthy AI Systems: Extension of the ECCOLA Method for AI Ethics Governance Using GARP. *E-Informatica Software Engineering Journal*, *17*(1), 230101. Advance online publication. DOI: 10.37190/e-Inf230101

Ahmad, N., Anshari, M., Hamdan, M., & Ali, E. (2024). Ethics and public trust in ai governance: A literature review. International Journal of Law. *Government and Communication*, *9*(37), 296–305. DOI: 10.35631/IJLGC.937025

Aiyankovil, K. G., Hernandez, J., & Lewis, D. (2024). Mapping Data Governance Requirements Between the European Union's AI Act and ISO/IEC 5259: A Semantic Analysis. B. Esteves, H. J. Pandit, & R. Verborgh (Eds.), CEUR Workshop Proceedings (Vol. 3891). CEUR-WS. Retrieved from https://www.scopus.com/inward/record.uri?eid=2-s2.0-85215996698&partnerID=40&md5=0d067b89e4658ec87460b581416df0be

Akavova, A., Beguyev, S., & Zaripova, R. (2023). How AI and machine learning can drive sustainable development. *E3S Web of Conferences, 460*, 4018. DOI: 10.1051/e3sconf/202346004018

Akhtar, Z. B. (2024). Unveiling the evolution of generative AI (GAI): A comprehensive and investigative analysis toward LLM models (2021–2024) and beyond. *Journal of Electrical Systems and Information Technology, 11*(1). Advance online publication. DOI: 10.1186/s43067-025-00196-y

Al Jadaan, O., Zaidi, H., Al Faress, M. Y., & Jabas, A. O. (2024). Ethics in AI and Computation in Automated Decision-Making. Advances in Computational Intelligence and Robotics Book Series, 397–424. DOI: 10.4018/979-8-3693-6230-3.ch012

Alanazi, S., Asif, S., Caird-daley, A., & Moulitsas, I. (2025). Unmasking deepfakes: a multidisciplinary examination of social impacts and regulatory responses. Human-Intelligent Systems Integration, 1-23.

Albahar, M., & Almalki, J. (2019). Deepfakes: Threats and countermeasures systematic review. *Journal of Theoretical and Applied Information Technology, 97*(22), 3242–3250.

Alemu, M. D. (2024). Financial Technology (FinTech), Artificial Intelligence (AI), ICT, Institutional Quality, and Financial Sector Development: International Evidence. *Research Square (Research Square)*. DOI: 10.21203/rs.3.rs-5712330/v1

Al-Hattami, H. M. (2025). Empowering business research with ChatGPT: Academic and student insights through the UTAUT lens. *Discover Computing, 28*(1), 179. Advance online publication. DOI: 10.1007/s10791-025-09692-1

Al-kfairy, M., Mustafa, D., Kshetri, N., Insiew, M., & Alfandi, O. (2024). Ethical Challenges and Solutions of Generative AI: An Interdisciplinary Perspective. *Informatics (MDPI), 11*(3), 58. DOI: 10.3390/informatics11030058

Alrawahneh, A. A. M., Abdullah, S. N. A. S., Abdullah, S. N. H. S., Kamarudin, N. H., & Taylor, S. K. (2025). Video authentication detection using deep learning: A systematic literature review. *Applied Intelligence, 55*(3), 239.

Amerini, I., Barni, M., Battiato, S., Bestagini, P., Boato, G., Bruni, V., Caldelli, R., De Natale, F., De Nicola, R., Guarnera, L., & Vitulano, D. (2025). Deepfake Media Forensics: Status and Future Challenges. *Journal of Imaging*, *11*(3), 73.

Amerini, I., Galteri, L., Caldelli, R., & Del Bimbo, A. (2019). Deepfake video detection through optical flow based cnn. In *Proceedings of the IEEE/CVF international conference on computer vision workshops*.

Anang, A. N., Ajewumi, O. E., Sonubi, T., Nwafor, K. C., Arogundade, J. B., & Akinbi, I. J. (2024). Explainable AI in financial technologies: Balancing innovation with regulatory compliance. *International Journal of Science and Research Archive*, *13*(1), 1793–1806. DOI: 10.30574/ijsra.2024.13.1.1870

Angwaomaodoko, E. A. (2023). The Re-examination of the Dangers and Implications of Artificial Intelligence for the Future of Scholarship and Learning. *Traektoriâ Nauki*, *9*(10), 3021–3028. DOI: 10.22178/pos.97-24

Anjum, A., Hrairi, M., Aabid, A., Yatim, N. H. M., & Ali, M. (2024). Civil Structural Health Monitoring and Machine Learning: A Comprehensive Review [Review of *Civil Structural Health Monitoring and Machine Learning: A Comprehensive Review*]. *Frattura Ed Integrità Strutturale, 18*(69), 43. Gruppo Italiano Frattura. DOI: 10.3221/IGF-ESIS.69.04

Anwar, N., Sekti, B. A., Widodo, A. M., Erzed, N., Gunawan, H., Tangkudung, R. R. S., Muchlis, M., & Budhisantosa, N. (2025). *Emerging Innovations in AI and Green Computing for Cybersecurity.*, DOI: 10.4018/979-8-3693-8034-5.ch002

Arbelaez Ossa, L., Lorenzini, G., Milford, S. R., Shaw, D., Elger, B. S., & Rost, M. (2024). Integrating ethics in AI development: A qualitative study. *BMC Medical Ethics*, *25*(1), 10. DOI: 10.1186/s12910-023-01000-0 PMID: 38262986

Arora, T., & Soni, R. (2021). A review of techniques to detect the GAN-generated fake images. Generative Adversarial Networks for Image-to-Image Translation, 125-159.

Arora, A. S., Marshall, A., Arora, A., & McIntyre, J. R. (2025). Virtuous integrative social robotics for ethical governance. *Discover Artificial Intelligence*, *5*(1), 8. Advance online publication. DOI: 10.1007/s44163-025-00228-6

Arsenault, P.-D., Wang, S., & Patenaude, J.-M. (2025). A Survey of Explainable Artificial Intelligence (XAI) in Financial Time Series Forecasting [Review of *A Survey of Explainable Artificial Intelligence (XAI) in Financial Time Series Forecasting*]. *ACM Computing Surveys*. Association for Computing Machinery. DOI: 10.1145/3729531

Artemova, I. (2025). Exploring responsible technology through archetypal responses: Uncertainty analysis in Leave the World Behind. *Journal of Responsible Technology*, *23*, 100134. Advance online publication. DOI: 10.1016/j.jrt.2025.100134

Asghar, M. Z., Duah, K. A., Iqbal, J., & Järvenoja, H. (2025). Evidence from West Africa on the interplay of affective behavioral cognitive and ethical dimensions of AI literacy in Ghanaian and Nigerian Universities. *Discover Computing*, *28*(1), 169. Advance online publication. DOI: 10.1007/s10791-025-09691-2

Attard-Frost, B. (2025). Transfeminist AI governance. *First Monday*, *30*(4). Advance online publication. DOI: 10.5210/fm.v30i4.14121

Babaei, R., Cheng, S., Duan, R., & Zhao, S. (2025). Generative Artificial Intelligence and the Evolving Challenge of Deepfake Detection: A Systematic Analysis. *Journal of Sensor and Actuator Networks*, *14*(1), 17.

Badawy, W. (2025). AI ethics: A textbook by Paula Boddington. *AI and Ethics*, *5*(5), 5607–5609. DOI: 10.1007/s43681-025-00769-7

Baduge, S. K., Thilakarathna, S., Perera, J. S., Arashpour, M., Sharafi, P., Teodosio, B., Shringi, A., & Mendis, P. (2022). *Artificial intelligence and smart vision for building and construction 4.0: Machine and deep learning methods and applications*.

Bahroun, Z., Anane, C., Ahmed, V., & Zacca, A. (2023). Transforming Education: A Comprehensive Review of Generative Artificial Intelligence in Educational Settings through Bibliometric and Content Analysis [Review of *Transforming Education: A Comprehensive Review of Generative Artificial Intelligence in Educational Settings through Bibliometric and Content Analysis*]. *Sustainability*, *15*(17), 12983. Multidisciplinary Digital Publishing Institute. DOI: 10.3390/su151712983

Bakiner, O. (2023). Pluralistic sociotechnical imaginaries in Artificial Intelligence (AI) law: The case of the European Union's AI Act. *Law, Innovation and Technology*, *15*(2), 558–582. DOI: 10.1080/17579961.2023.2245675

Ballé, J., Laparra, V., & Simoncelli, E. P. (2016). End-to-end optimized image compression. arXiv preprint arXiv:1611.01704.

Baloda, S., Sharma, M., & Kumar, M. (2025). Future of humanity in an artificial intelligence centric world. *Engineering Applications of Artificial Intelligence*, *162*, 112405. DOI: 10.1016/j.engappai.2025.112405

Banu, J. T. (2024). AI in Learning: Designing the Future. *Technical Communication Quarterly*, *1*. Advance online publication. DOI: 10.1080/10572252.2024.2428400

Bariş, Ö., Yeşilyurt, S., & Ün, O. (2024). Professions transformed by artificial intelligence. In *Generating Entrepreneurial Ideas With AI* (pp. 19–40). DOI: 10.4018/979-8-3693-3498-0.ch002

Barredo Arrieta, A., Díaz-Rodríguez, N., Del Ser, J., Bennetot, A., Tabik, S., Barbado, A., Garcia, S., Gil-Lopez, S., Molina, D., Benjamins, R., Chatila, R., & Herrera, F. (2020). Explainable Artificial Intelligence (XAI): Concepts, taxonomies, opportunities and challenges toward responsible AI. *Information Fusion*, *58*, 82–115. DOI: 10.1016/j.inffus.2019.12.012

Barrett, C., Boyd, B., Bursztein, E., Carlini, N., Chen, B., Choi, J., Chowdhury, A. R., Christodorescu, M., Datta, A., Feizi, S., Fisher, K., Hashimoto, T., Hendrycks, D., Jha, S., Kang, D., Kerschbaum, F., Mitchell, E., Mitchell, J. C., Ramzan, Z., ... Yang, D. (2023). Identifying and Mitigating the Security Risks of Generative AI. *Foundations and Trends® in Privacy and Security*, *6*(1), 1. DOI: 10.1561/3300000041

Barry, S. E., Sullivan, O., & Wooldridge, M. (n.d.). *Artificial Intelligence: Foundations*. Theory, and Algorithms.

Bartneck, C., Lütge, C., Wagner, A., & Welsh, S. (n.d.). *SPRINGER BRIEFS IN ETHICS*. https://www.springer.com/series/10184

Bartsch, S. C., Schmidt, J.-H., Adam, M., & Benlian, A. (2026). Increasing developers' code accountability perceptions in open source software development. *International Journal of Information Management*, *86*, 102974. Advance online publication. DOI: 10.1016/j.ijinfomgt.2025.102974

Basyoni, L., Qayyum, A., Shaban, K., Elmahjub, E., Al-Ali, A., Halabi, O., & Qadir, J. (2025). Generative AI-Driven Metaverse: The Promises and Challenges of AI-Generated Content. *Authorea Preprints*.

Becker, S. J., Nemat, A. T., Lucas, S., Heinitz, R. M., Klevesath, M., & Charton, J. E. (2023). A Code of Digital Ethics: Laying the foundation for digital ethics in a science and technology company. *AI & Society*, *38*(6), 2629–2639. DOI: 10.1007/s00146-021-01376-w

Bélisle-Pipon, J.-C., Powell, M., English, R., Malo, M.-F., Ravitsky, V., & Bensoussan, Y. (2024). Stakeholder perspectives on ethical and trustworthy voice AI in health care. *Digital Health*, *10*, 20552076241260407. Advance online publication. DOI: 10.1177/20552076241260407 PMID: 39055787

Beltrán, M. (2025). AI algorithms under scrutiny: GDPR, DSA, AI Act and CRA as pillars for algorithmic security and privacy in the European Union. *Computers & Security*, *158*, 104628. Advance online publication. DOI: 10.1016/j.cose.2025.104628

Bertl, M., Price, S., & Draheim, D. (2026). Transforming legal texts into computational logic: Enhancing next generation public sector automation through explainable AI decision support. *International Journal of Cognitive Computing in Engineering*, *7*(1), 40–57. DOI: 10.1016/j.ijcce.2025.07.003

Bewersdorff, A., Hornberger, M., Nerdel, C., & Schiff, D. S. (2025). AI advocates and cautious critics: How AI attitudes, AI interest, use of AI, and AI literacy build university students' AI self-efficacy. *Computers and Education: Artificial Intelligence*, *8*, 100340. DOI: 10.1016/j.caeai.2024.100340

Bleher, H., & Braun, M. (2023a). Reflections on Putting AI Ethics into Practice: How Three AI Ethics Approaches Conceptualize Theory and Practice. *Science and Engineering Ethics*, *29*(3), 21. DOI: 10.1007/s11948-023-00443-3 PMID: 37237246

Borges, L., Martins, B., & Calado, P. (2019). Combining similarity features and deep representation learning for stance detection in the context of checking fake news. [JDIQ]. *Journal of Data and Information Quality*, *11*(3), 1–26.

Boris, D. (2022). *Grozdanoff*. Rationality and Ethics in Artificial Intelligence.

Bossert, L. N., & Hagendorff, T. (2023). The ethics of sustainable AI: Why animals (should) matter for a sustainable use of AI. *Sustainable Development (Bradford)*, *31*(5), 3459–3467. DOI: 10.1002/sd.2596

Bouderhem, R. (2024). Shaping the future of AI in healthcare through ethics and governance. *Humanities & Social Sciences Communications*, *11*(1), 1–12. DOI: 10.1057/s41599-024-02894-w

Brantly, A. (2022). Utopia Lost – Human Rights in a Digital World. *Applied Cybersecurity and Internet Governance*, *1*(1). Advance online publication. DOI: 10.5604/01.3001.0016.1238

Buchanan, B. (2019). Artificial intelligence in finance. In Zenodo *(CERN European Organization for Nuclear Research)*. European Organization for Nuclear Research. DOI: 10.5281/zenodo.2612537

Buszydlik, A., Altmeyer, P., Dobbe, R., & Liem, C. C. S. (2026). Understanding the Affordances and Constraints of Explainable AI in Safety-Critical Contexts: A Case Study in Dutch Social Welfare. *Lecture Notes in Computer Science, 15978 LNCS*, 118–136. DOI: 10.1007/978-3-032-02515-9_8

Calzada, I., Németh, G., & Al-Radhi, M. S. (2025). Trustworthy AI for Whom? GenAI Detection Techniques of Trust Through Decentralized Web3 Ecosystems. *Big Data and Cognitive Computing*, *9*(3), 62. DOI: 10.3390/bdcc9030062

Camilleri, M. A. (2024). Artificial intelligence governance: Ethical considerations and implications for social responsibility. *Expert Systems: International Journal of Knowledge Engineering and Neural Networks*, *41*(7), e13406. Advance online publication. DOI: 10.1111/exsy.13406

Cao, Y. (2025, April 3). C: Unifying programming and verification in C. arXiv. https://doi.org//arXiv.2504.02246DOI: 10.48550

Carter, L., Liu, D., & Cantrell, C. (2020). Exploring the intersection of the digital divide and artificial intelligence: A hermeneutic literature review. *AIS Transactions on Human-Computer Interaction*, *12*(4), 253–275. DOI: 10.17705/1thci.00138

Carter, M. (2007). *Minds and computers: an introduction to the philosophy of artificial intelligence*. Edinburgh University Press. DOI: 10.1515/9780748629305

Casiraghi, S. (2023). Anything new under the sun? Insights from a history of institutionalized AI ethics. *Ethics and Information Technology*, *25*(2), 28. DOI: 10.1007/s10676-023-09702-0

Ceccon, M., Cornacchia, G., Dalle Pezze, D., Fabris, A., & Susto, G. A. (2025). Underrepresentation, label bias, and proxies: Towards Data Bias Profiles for the EU AI act and beyond. *Expert Systems with Applications*, *292*, 128266. Advance online publication. DOI: 10.1016/j.eswa.2025.128266

Cecez-Kecmanovic, D. (2025). Ethics in the world of automated algorithmic decision-making – A Posthumanist perspective. *Information and Organization*, *35*(3), 100587. Advance online publication. DOI: 10.1016/j.infoandorg.2025.100587

Chadha, A., Kumar, V., Kashyap, S., & Gupta, M. (2021). Deepfake: An overview. In Singh P. K., Wierzchoń S. T., Tanwar S., Ganzha M., & Rodrigues J. J. P. C. (Eds), Proceedings of second international conference on computing, communications, and cyber-security: IC4S 2020 (pp. 557–566). Springer.

Chakraborty, S. (2025). Human values, ethics, and dignity in the age of artificial intelligence. In *Human Values*. Ethics, and Dignity in the Age of Artificial Intelligence., DOI: 10.4018/979-8-3693-9035-1

Chatzichristofis, S. A., Tsopozidis, A., Kyriakidou-Zacharoudiou, A., Evripidou, S., & Amanatiadis, A. (2025). Designing an AI-Supported Framework for Literary Text Adaptation in Primary Classrooms. *AI*, *6*(7), 150. Advance online publication. DOI: 10.3390/ai6070150

Chellappan, R. B. (2024). From Algorithms to Accountability: The Societal and Ethical Need for Explainable AI. *Research Square (Research Square)*. DOI: 10.21203/rs.3.rs-5277731/v1

Chen, F., Zhou, J., Holzinger, A., Fleischmann, K. R., & Stumpf, S. (2023). Artificial Intelligence Ethics and Trust: From Principles to Practice. *IEEE Intelligent Systems, 38*(6), 5–8. DOI: 10.1109/MIS.2023.3324470

Cheng, Z., Sun, H., Takeuchi, M., & Katto, J. (2019). Energy compaction-based image compression using convolutional autoencoder. IEEE Transactions on Multimedia, 22(4), 860-873. Punnappurath, A., & Brown, M. S. (2019). Learning raw image reconstruction-aware deep image compressors. *IEEE Transactions on Pattern Analysis and Machine Intelligence, 42*(4), 1013–1019.

Chesney, B., & Citron, D. (2019). Deep fakes: A looming challenge for privacy, democracy, and national security. *California Law Review, 107*(6), 1753–1820. DOI: 10.15779/Z38RV0D15J

Chetry, K. K. (2024). Transforming Education: How AI is Revolutionizing the Learning Experience. *International Journal of Research Publication and Reviews, 5*(5), 6352–6356. DOI: 10.55248/gengpi.5.0524.1277

Chollet, F. (2017). Xception: Deep learning with depthwise separable convolutions. In *Proceedings of the IEEE conference on computer vision and pattern recognition* (pp. 1251-1258).

Chong, H., Shah, R., & Kulkarni, K. (2023). The Emergence of AI Tools in Academia: Potential and Limitations. *The Bulletin of the Royal College of Surgeons of England, 105*(8), 400–402. DOI: 10.1308/rcsbull.2023.125

Chong, K. C. M., Tan, Y.-K., & Zhou, X. (2025). Impacts of Artificial Intelligence Development on Humanity and Social Values. *Information (Basel), 16*(9), 810. Advance online publication. DOI: 10.3390/info16090810

Choung, H., David, P., & Ross, A. (2023). Trust and ethics in AI. *AI & Society, 38*(2), 733–745. DOI: 10.1007/s00146-022-01473-4

Churi, P., Joshi, S., Elhoseny, M., & Omrane, A. (n.d.). *Artificial Intelligence in Higher Education: A Practical Approach.*

Cobansoy Hizel, G. (2023). Metaverse and Human Rights: Do We Need Metaversal Declaration of Human Rights? In Studies in Big Data (Vol. 133, pp. 219–229). DOI: 10.1007/978-981-99-4641-9_15

Cohen, K. (2023). Grand challenges in intelligent aerospace systems. *Frontiers in Aerospace Engineering, 2*, 1281522. Advance online publication. DOI: 10.3389/fpace.2023.1281522

Cousineau, C., Dara, R., & Chowdhury, A. (2025). Trustworthy AI: AI developers' lens to implementation challenges and opportunities. *Data and Information Management*, *9*(2), 100082. DOI: 10.1016/j.dim.2024.100082

Dack, S. (2019). *Deep fakes, fake news, and what comes next. The Henry M.* Jackson School of International Studies.

Dahal, C. (2024). Revolutionizing Education through AI-Powered Inclusive Learning Systems. *Proceedings of the AAAI Conference on Artificial Intelligence*, *38*(21), 23736–23737. DOI: 10.1609/aaai.v38i21.30546

Dakalbab, F., Talib, M. A., Nasir, Q., & Saroufil, T. (2024). Artificial intelligence techniques in financial trading: A systematic literature review. *Journal of King Saud University. Computer and Information Sciences*, *36*(3), 102015. DOI: 10.1016/j.jksuci.2024.102015

Dameski, A. (2018). A Comprehensive Ethical Framework for AI Entities. *Lecture Notes in Computer Science*, *10999*, 42–51. DOI: 10.1007/978-3-319-97676-1_5

Darraj, E., Sample, C., & Justice, C. (2019). Artificial intelligence cybersecurity framework: Preparing for the here and now with ai. European Conference on Information Warfare and Security, ECCWS, 2019-July, 132–141. https://www.scopus.com/inward/record.uri?eid=2-s2.0-85070023435&partnerID=40&md5=acc5ea96e58e66c866982fac029066c6

Dattathrani, S., & De', R. (2023). The Concept of Agency in the Era of Artificial Intelligence: Dimensions and Degrees. *Information Systems Frontiers*, *25*(1), 29–54. DOI: 10.1007/s10796-022-10336-8

Davis, J. (2025). Disinformation in the Era of Generative AI: Challenges, Detection Strategies, and Countermeasures. In Public Relations and the Rise of AI (pp. 242-269). Routledge.

De Rose, L., Andresini, G., Appice, A., & Malerba, D. (2025). OLIVANDER: A counterfactual-based method to generate adversarial Windows PE malware. *Data Mining and Knowledge Discovery*, *39*(5), 46. Advance online publication. DOI: 10.1007/s10618-025-01127-1

Degen, P.-B. (2025). Revisiting generalizability theory in the age of artificial intelligence: Implications for empirical educational research. *Computers and Education Open*, *9*, 100278. Advance online publication. DOI: 10.1016/j.caeo.2025.100278

Demir-Kaymak, Z., Turan, Z., Unlu-Bidik, N., & Unkazan, S. (2024). Effects of midwifery and nursing students' readiness about medical Artificial intelligence on Artificial intelligence anxiety. *Nurse Education in Practice*, *78*, 103994. DOI: 10.1016/j.nepr.2024.103994 PMID: 38810350

Deng, Z., Song, D., & Liu, S. (2025). How does AI-assisted diagnosis decision support systems influence doctors' coping styles and work outcomes? Bright and dark sides of AI in the workplace. *Decision Support Systems*, *197*, 114512. Advance online publication. DOI: 10.1016/j.dss.2025.114512

Deric, E., Frank, D., & Milković, M. (2025). Trust in Generative AI Tools: A Comparative Study of Higher Education Students, Teachers, and Researchers. *Information (Basel)*, *16*(7), 622. Advance online publication. DOI: 10.3390/info16070622

Deshmukh, A., & Wankhade, S. B. (2020). Deepfake detection approaches using deep learning: A systematic review. In Balas V. E., Semwal V. B., Khandare A., & Patil M. (Eds), Intelligent computing and networking: Proceedings of IC-ICN 2020 (pp. 293–302). Springer.

Dey, D. (2025). *Enhancing Educational Tools Through Artificial Intelligence in Perspective of Need of AI*. DOI: 10.2139/ssrn.5031275

Díaz-Rodríguez, N., Del-Ser-Lorente, J., Coeckelbergh, M., de Prado, M., Herrera-Viedma, E., & Herrera, F. (2023). Connecting the dots in trustworthy Artificial Intelligence: From AI principles, ethics, and key requirements to responsible AI systems and regulation. *Information Fusion*, *99*, 101896. Advance online publication. DOI: 10.1016/j.inffus.2023.101896

Ding, X., Liu, M., & Hu, S. (2024). Exploration of Teaching Reform in C Language Programming Course under the Background of New Engineering. *Frontiers in Humanities and Social Sciences*, *4*(7), 56–59. DOI: 10.54691/tp1vv609

Drumond, G. M., Méxas, M. P., & Meza, L. A. (2025). Perception of educators on open educational resources (OER) repositories in higher education. *Encontros Bibli*, *30*, 1–25. DOI: 10.5007/1518-2924.2025.e99827

Eden, C. A., Chisom, O. N., & Adeniyi, I. S.Chima Abimbola EdenOnyebuchi Nneamaka ChisomIdowu Sulaimon Adeniyi. (2024). Integrating AI in education: Opportunities, challenges, and ethical considerations. *Magna Scientia Advanced Research and Reviews*, *10*(2), 6. DOI: 10.30574/msarr.2024.10.2.0039

El Arab, R. A., Al Moosa, O. A., & Sagbakken, M. (2025). Economic, ethical, and regulatory dimensions of artificial intelligence in healthcare: An integrative review. *Frontiers in Public Health, 13*, 1617138. Advance online publication. DOI: 10.3389/fpubh.2025.1617138 PMID: 40951387

Ellegaard, M., Johannsen, B. F., & Jacobsen, D. (2024). Peer feedback as a professional competence: Students' experiences of practicing feedback literacy in professional settings. *Research Portal Denmark*, 71. https://local.forskningsportal.dk/local/dki-cgi/ws/cris-link?src=kp&id=kp-9835e9f2-446a-4c9f-8bfb-562839456927&ti=Peer%20feedback%20as%20a%20professional%20competence%3A%20Students%2019%20experiences%20of%20practicing%20feedback%20literacy%20in%20professional%20settings

Erfani, F. (2025). Not "just a language model": AI's ideological functions. *AI & Society*. Advance online publication. DOI: 10.1007/s00146-025-02623-0

Esteban Cuellar Argotty, J., & Manrique, R. (2026). AI-Generated Code Detection: An Examination of Current Tools in Education. *Lecture Notes in Computer Science, 15723 LNCS*, 192–201. DOI: 10.1007/978-3-031-98281-1_15

Etienne, H. (2022). When AI Ethics Goes Astray: A Case Study of Autonomous Vehicles. *Social Science Computer Review, 40*(1), 236–246. DOI: 10.1177/0894439320906508

Fabregas Alvarez, A., Bertolin, C., Gonizzi, S., & Califano, A. (2024). *Development of an Automated Procedure for the Damage Pattern Recognition Via Infrared Thermography and Machine Learning*.

Falvo, F., & Cannataro, M. (2024). Ethics of Artificial Intelligence: challenges, opportunities and future prospects. 5860–5867. DOI: 10.1109/BIBM62325.2024.10822112

Fang, C., Li, H., & Wang, Y. (2024). AI Utilization and Governance in Corporate Entrepreneurship: Investigating the Moderating Influence of Top Management. Proceedings of the International Conference on Electronic Business (ICEB), 24, 32–43. https://www.scopus.com/inward/record.uri?eid=2-s2.0-85213324449&partnerID=40&md5=00bd2124fc46444e9d35238a5a788d18

Fang, Q., & Maldague, P. V. (2021). *X*. DEFECT DETECTION IN INFRARED THERMOGRAPHY BY DEEP LEARNING ALGORITHMS.

Faria, N., Campelos, S., & Carvalho, V. (2023). A Novel Convolutional Neural Network Algorithm for Histopathological Lung Cancer Detection. *Applied Sciences (Basel, Switzerland), 13*(11), 6571. DOI: 10.3390/app13116571

Ferhataj, A., Memaj, F., Sahatcija, R., Ora, A., & Koka, E. (2025). Ethical concerns in AI development: Analyzing students' perspectives on robotics and society. *Journal of Information. Communication and Ethics in Society*, *23*(2), 165–187. DOI: 10.1108/JICES-08-2024-0111

Fernandez, P., Elsahar, H., Rebuffi, S. A., Soucek, T., Lacatusu, V., Tran, T., & Mourachko, A. (2025). A Taxonomy of Watermarking Methods for AI-Generated Content. In The 1st Workshop on GenAI Watermarking.

Fernando, T., Priyasad, D., Sridharan, S., Ross, A., & Fookes, C. (2025). Face Deepfakes-A Comprehensive Review. arXiv preprint arXiv:2502.09812.

Ferrara, E. (2024). GenAI against humanity: Nefarious applications of generative artificial intelligence and large language models. *Journal of Computational Social Science*, *7*(1), 549–569. DOI: 10.1007/s42001-024-00250-1

Floridi, L. (2023). *The ethics of artificial intelligence: Principles, challenges, and opportunities.*

Floridi, L., Cowls, J., Beltrametti, M., Chatila, R., Chazerand, P., Dignum, V., Luetge, C., Madelin, R., Pagallo, U., Rossi, F., Schafer, B., Valcke, P., & Vayena, E. (2018). AI4People—An Ethical Framework for a Good AI Society: Opportunities, Risks, Principles, and Recommendations. *Minds and Machines*, *28*(4), 689–707. DOI: 10.1007/s11023-018-9482-5 PMID: 30930541

Folorunsho, F., & Boamah, B. F. (2025). Deepfake technology and its impact: Ethical considerations, societal disruptions, and security threats in ai-generated media. *Management*, *16*(1), 1060–1080.

Fulton, R., Fulton, D., Hayes, N., & Kaplan, S. (2024). *The Transformation Risk-Benefit Model of Artificial Intelligence: Balancing Risks and Benefits Through Practical Solutions and Use Cases. arXiv*. Cornell University., DOI: 10.5121/ijaia.15201

Gao, Y., Li, B., Zhao, J., & Dong, S. (2026). Boundary conditions treatment strategies for black-box objects thermal modeling using thermal response function method. *International Journal of Heat and Mass Transfer*, *255*, 127852. DOI: 10.1016/j.ijheatmasstransfer.2025.127852

Gayap, H. T., & Akhloufi, M. A. (2024). Deep Machine Learning for Medical Diagnosis, Application to Lung Cancer Detection: A Review [Review of Deep Machine Learning for Medical Diagnosis, Application to Lung Cancer Detection: A Review]. *BioMedInformatics*, *4*(1), 236–284. DOI: 10.3390/biomedinformatics4010015

Gerlach, J., Hoppe, P., Jagels, S., Licker, L., & Breitner, M. H. (2022). Decision support for efficient XAI services - A morphological analysis, business model archetypes, and a decision tree. *Electronic Markets*, *32*(4), 2139–2158. DOI: 10.1007/s12525-022-00603-6

Gesser da Costa, P., de Bem Machado, A., Antunes Vieira Willerding, I., & Mafra Lápolli, É. (2025). Governance and Ethics in the Use of Artificial Intelligence in Health. 377–392. DOI: 10.4018/979-8-3693-7630-0.ch015

Gilbert, C., & Gilbert, M. A. (2025). The Impact of AI on Cybersecurity Defense Mechanisms: Future Trends and Challenges. SSRN *Electronic Journal*. DOI: 10.2139/ssrn.5258783

Ginsburg, J. C., & Austin, G. W. (2025). Regulating Deepfakes at Home and Abroad. Forthcoming, Columbia Journal of Law & the Arts, 48.

Gioiosa, S., Chiavarini, B., D'Antonio, M., Trotta, G., Chandramouli, B., Mata Naranjo, J., Muscianisi, G., Cestari, M., & Rossi, E. (2025). A GDPR-compliant solution for analysis of large-scale genomics datasets on HPC cloud infrastructure. *Journal of Big Data*, *12*(1), 31. Advance online publication. DOI: 10.1186/s40537-024-01047-9

Giovanola, B., & Tiribelli, S. (2023). Beyond bias and discrimination: Redefining the AI ethics principle of fairness in healthcare machine-learning algorithms. *AI & Society*, *38*(2), 549–563. DOI: 10.1007/s00146-022-01455-6 PMID: 35615443

Göksal, S. I., Solarte-Vásquez, M. C. S., & Chochia, A. (2024). The EU AI Act's Alignment within the European Union's Regulatory Framework on Artificial Intelligence. *International and Comparative Law Review*, *24*(2), 25–53. DOI: 10.2478/iclr-2024-0017

Gorski, L., & Ramakrishna, S. (2025). Right to Explanation in Large Language Models: Lessons from the European Union AI Act and General Data Protection Regulation. *IT Professional*, *27*(1), 34–40. DOI: 10.1109/MITP.2024.3518917

Goyal, H., Wajid, M. S., Wajid, M. A., Khanday, A. M. U. D., Neshat, M., & Gandomi, A. (2025). State-of-the-art AI-based Learning Approaches for Deepfake Generation and Detection, Analyzing Opportunities, Threading through Pros, Cons, and Future Prospects. arXiv preprint arXiv:2501.01029.

Gundu, S. R., Charanarur, P., Chandelkar, K. K., Samanta, D., Poonia, R. C., & Chakraborty, P. (2022). Sixth-generation (6G) mobile cloud security and privacy risks for AI system using high-performance computing implementation. *Wireless Communications and Mobile Computing*, *2022*(1), 4397610. Advance online publication. DOI: 10.1155/2022/4397610

Gupta, M., Mishra, G., Bajpai, S., Bhardwaj, A., & Gautam, M. (2025). AI in Agriculture: A Comprehensive Exploration of Technological Transformation. In Emerging Smart Agricultural Practices Using Artificial Intelligence (pp. 105–132). DOI: 10.1002/9781394274277.ch6

Gurulakshmanan, G., Bini Marin, V., Channapragada, R. S. R., Ajit, S., Srinivasan, C., & Ayushma, K. (2025). Advancing Medical Imaging with Machine Learning Techniques by Utilising IBM Watson Studio. *Proceedings of the 2025 11th International Conference on Communication and Signal Processing, ICCSP 2025*, 1867–1872. DOI: 10.1109/ICCSP64183.2025.11088799

Hagendorff, T. (2020). The Ethics of AI Ethics: An Evaluation of Guidelines. *Minds and Machines*, *30*(1), 99–120. DOI: 10.1007/s11023-020-09517-8

Hagendorff, T. (2022a). A Virtue-Based Framework to Support Putting AI Ethics into Practice. *Philosophy & Technology*, *35*(3), 55. DOI: 10.1007/s13347-022-00553-z

Hagendorff, T. (2022b). Blind spots in AI ethics. *AI and Ethics*, *2*(4), 851–867. DOI: 10.1007/s43681-021-00122-8

Hallamaa, J., & Kalliokoski, T. (2022). AI Ethics as Applied Ethics. *Frontiers of Computer Science*, *4*, 776837. Advance online publication. DOI: 10.3389/fcomp.2022.776837

Hamedani, S. S., Aslam, S., & Hamedani, S. S. (2025). AI in business operations: Driving urban growth and societal sustainability. *Frontiers in Artificial Intelligence*, *8*, 1568210. Advance online publication. DOI: 10.3389/frai.2025.1568210 PMID: 40196185

Hamid, I., & Rahman, M. M. H. (2025). AI, machine learning and deep learning in cyber risk management. *Discover Sustainability*, *6*(1), 389. Advance online publication. DOI: 10.1007/s43621-025-01012-3

Hanna, R., & Kazim, E. (2021a). Philosophical foundations for digital ethics and AI Ethics: A dignitarian approach. *AI and Ethics*, *1*(4), 405–423. DOI: 10.1007/s43681-021-00040-9 PMID: 34790944

Hargittai, E. (2002). Second-level digital divide: Differences in people's online skills. *First Monday*, *7*(4), 1–18. DOI: 10.5210/fm.v7i4.942

Harris, D. (2018). Deepfakes: False pornography is here and the law cannot protect you. *Duke Law & Technology Review*, *17*, 99.

Harrison, D. E., Ajjan, H., Ferrell, O. C., Ferrell, L., Hochstein, B. W., & Johnson, R. (2025). Bridging the gap: Aligning developers and managers in implementing AI ethics. *Journal of Marketing Theory and Practice*, •••, 1–20. DOI: 10.1080/10696679.2025.2552275

Heidari, A., Jafari Navimipour, N., Dag, H., & Unal, M. (2024). Deepfake detection using deep learning methods: A systematic and comprehensive review. *Wiley Interdisciplinary Reviews. Data Mining and Knowledge Discovery*, *14*(2), e1520.

Helsper, E. J. (2017a). The social relativity of digital exclusion: Applying relative deprivation theory to digital inequalities. *Communication Theory*, *27*(3), 223–242. DOI: 10.1111/comt.12110

He, X., Song, Y., Du, Y., Huang, Y., Yin, X., & Long, X. (2022). Research on teaching reform of C programming language course for deep integration of professional fields. *Open Journal of Social Sciences*, *10*(1), 267–275. DOI: 10.4236/jss.2022.101022

He, Z., Zhang, R., Diallo, G., Huang, Z., & Glicksberg, B. S. (2023). Editorial: Explainable artificial intelligence for critical healthcare applications. *Frontiers in Artificial Intelligence*, *6*, 1282800. Advance online publication. DOI: 10.3389/frai.2023.1282800 PMID: 37771610

Homaei, M., Mogollón-Gutiérrez, Ó., Núñez, J. C. S., Ávila, M., & Caro, A. (2024). A review of digital twins and their application in cybersecurity based on artificial intelligence [Review of *A review of digital twins and their application in cybersecurity based on artificial intelligence*]. *Artificial Intelligence Review, 57*(8). Springer Science+Business Media. DOI: 10.1007/s10462-024-10805-3

Hossain, I., Ahmad, R., Amin, S., Sultana, N., & Chowdhury, S. (2025). Risk assessment in financial services: Advancing transparency and trust through explainable AI models. *International Journal of Science and Research Archive*, *16*(1), 1409–1419. DOI: 10.30574/ijsra.2025.16.1.2150

Huang, C., Zhang, Z., Mao, B., & Yao, X. (2023). An Overview of Artificial Intelligence Ethics. *IEEE Transactions on Artificial Intelligence*, *4*(4), 799–819. DOI: 10.1109/TAI.2022.3194503

Hultin, L., & Mähring, M. (2025). Reimagining AI for sustainability: Cultivating imagination, hope, and response-ability. *Information and Organization*, *35*(3), 100586. Advance online publication. DOI: 10.1016/j.infoandorg.2025.100586

Ibrar, W., Mahmood, D., Al-Shamayleh, A. S., Ahmed, G., Zayed, S. B., & Akhunzada, A. (2025). Generative AI: A double-edged sword in the cyber threat landscape. *Artificial Intelligence Review*, *58*(9), 285. Advance online publication. DOI: 10.1007/s10462-025-11285-9

Ifenthaler, D., Majumdar, R., Gorissen, P., Judge, M., Mishra, S., Raffaghelli, J. E., & Shimada, A. (2024). *Artificial Intelligence in Education: Implications for Policymakers, Researchers, and Practitioners*. Technology Knowledge and Learning., DOI: 10.1007/s10758-024-09747-0

Imran, M. A. U., Aziz, M. B., Tiwari, A., Saha, S., & Ghimire, A. (2024). Exploring the Latest Trends in AI Technologies: A Study on Current State, Application and Individual Impacts. *Journal of Computer and Communications*, *12*(8), 21–36. DOI: 10.4236/jcc.2024.128002

Ishkhanyan, A. (2025). The sovereignty-internationalism paradox in AI governance: Digital federalism and global algorithmic control. *Discover Artificial Intelligence*, *5*(1), 123. Advance online publication. DOI: 10.1007/s44163-025-00374-x

Ismail, O. H., & Ahmad, N. (2025). Ethical and Governance Frameworks for Artificial Intelligence: A Systematic Literature Review. *International Journal of Interactive Mobile Technologies*, *19*(14), 121–136. DOI: 10.3991/ijim.v19i14.56981

Ismailova, A., Abdikerimova, G., Uzakkyzy, N., Muratkhan, R., Aitimov, M., Tergeusizova, A., & Beissegul, A. (2026). Development of a feature vector for accurate breast cancer detection in mammographic images. *International Journal of Cognitive Computing in Engineering*, *7*, 12–25. DOI: 10.1016/j.ijcce.2025.08.001

Jafari, S. A., Araminia, B., Tavasoli, H., Tavasoli, N., Abedi, S., & Bakhsh, A. F. (2024). Human dignity: A contract or an abstract? *Journal of Medical Ethics and History of Medicine*, *17*. Advance online publication. DOI: 10.18502/jmehm.v17i6.17105 PMID: 40395479

Jafari, S. A., Araminia, B., Tavasoli, H., Tavasoli, N., Abedi, S., & Bakhshe, A. F. (2024). Human dignity, minimum and maximum: What is the justification for the difference between male and female Diyah" in Islam? *Journal of Medical Ethics and History of Medicine*, *17*. Advance online publication. DOI: 10.18502/jmehm.v17i7.17106 PMID: 40395476

Jafari, S. A., Tavasoli, N., Tavasoli, H., Abedi, S., Navvab, S. A., & Darabi, B. T. (2024). Existence and Manifestations of human dignity: Can a person be deprived of dignity? *Journal of Medical Ethics and History of Medicine*, *17*. Advance online publication. DOI: 10.18502/jmehm.v17i8.17107 PMID: 40395477

Jain, A., Gaur, A., Gupta, G., Mishra, S., Johari, R., & Vidyarthi, D. P. (2025). Securing Digital Integrity: Proposed Comprehensive Framework for Deepfake Detection and Blockchain Validation. In *International Conference on Cognitive Computing and Cyber Physical Systems* (pp. 579-589). Springer, Singapore.

Jedličková, A. (2024). Ethical approaches in designing autonomous and intelligent systems: A comprehensive survey towards responsible development. *AI & Society*. Advance online publication. DOI: 10.1007/s00146-024-02040-9

Jiang, Y. (2021). Design optimization and application analysis of embedded C program. *Journal of Networking and Telecommunications*, *3*(1), 5–7. DOI: 10.18282/jnt.v3i1.1943

Judge, E. F., & Korhani, A. M. (2021). *Deepfakes*. Counterfeits, and Personality.

Judijanto, L., Utama, A. S., & Setiyawan, H. (2025). Implementation of Ethical Artificial Intelligence Law to Prevent the Use of AI in Spreading False Information (Deepfake) in Indonesia. *The Easta Journal Law and Human Rights*, *3*(02), 101–109.

Kalodanis, K., Feretzakis, G., Rizomiliotis, P., Verykios, V. S., Papapavlou, C., Skrekas, A., & Anagnostopoulos, D. (2025). Assessing the Readiness of European Healthcare Institutions for EU AI Act Compliance. J. Mantas, A. Hasman, E. Zoulias, K. Karitis, P. Gallos, M. Diomidous, S. Zogas, & M. Charalampidou (Eds.), Studies in Health Technology and Informatics (Vol. 323, pp. 50–54). IOS Press BV. DOI: 10.3233/SHTI250047

Kanbach, D. K., Heiduk, L., Blueher, G., Schreiter, M., & Lahmann, A. (2023). The GenAI is out of the bottle: Generative artificial intelligence from a business model innovation perspective. *Review of Managerial Science*, *18*(4), 1189–1220. DOI: 10.1007/s11846-023-00696-z

Karmakar, D., Das, A., & Khati, A. (2025). *Building Ethical Foundations*., DOI: 10.4018/979-8-3693-9035-1.ch008

Kartika, A. N., & Vic, B. J. (2025). Bridging Innovation and Governance: A Systematic Literature Review of Artificial Intelligence. *Electronic Medical Records, and Legal Protection in Healthcare.*, *3*(2), 173–181. DOI: 10.38035/gijlss.v3i2.411

Kasar, P. (2025). There is a problem, but not a responsibility gap. *Ethics and Information Technology*, *27*(4), 47. Advance online publication. DOI: 10.1007/s10676-025-09851-4

Kaushik, P., Garg, V., Priya, A., & Kant, S. (2025). Financial Fraud and Manipulation: The Malicious Use of Deepfakes in Business. In Deepfakes and Their Impact on Business (pp. 173-196). IGI Global Scientific Publishing.

Kaushik, S., Poonia, R. C., Khatri, S. K., Samanta, D., & Chakraborty, P. (2022). Transmit range adjustment using artificial intelligence for enhancement of location privacy and data security in service location protocol of VANET. *Wireless Communications and Mobile Computing*, *2022*(1), 9642774. Advance online publication. DOI: 10.1155/2022/9642774

Kazim, E., & Koshiyama, A. S. (2021). A high-level overview of AI ethics. *Patterns (New York, N.Y.)*, *2*(9), 100314. DOI: 10.1016/j.patter.2021.100314 PMID: 34553166

Keerthana, N. V., Suresh, P., Kulandaivel, M., & Kulandaivel, S. (2025). Critical Strategies for Phishing Defense and Digital Asset Protection: A Case Study Approach. In Critical Phishing Defense Strategies and Digital Asset Protection (pp. 221-244). IGI Global Scientific Publishing.

Khan, S., Mazhar, T., Shahzad, T., Khan, M. A., Rehman, A. U., Saeed, M. M., & Hamam, H. (2025). Harnessing AI for sustainable higher education: Ethical considerations, operational efficiency, and future directions. *Discover Sustainability*, *6*(1), 23. Advance online publication. DOI: 10.1007/s43621-025-00809-6

Khatri, P., Duggal, H. K., Thomas, A., Corvello, V., Prałat, E., & Shiva, A. (2026). Development and validation of the generative artificial intelligence appropriation (GAIA) Scale: A comprehensive measurement tool for assessing user engagement and utilisation. *Technovation*, *150*, 103379. Advance online publication. DOI: 10.1016/j.technovation.2025.103379

Khorshidi, M. S., Merigó, J. M., & Beydoun, G. (2025). Half a Century of Information Processing & Management: A bibliometric retrospective. *Information Processing & Management*, *62*(6), 104238. Advance online publication. DOI: 10.1016/j.ipm.2025.104238

Kietzmann, J., Lee, L. W., McCarthy, I. P., & Kietzmann, T. C. (2020). Deepfakes: Trick or treat? In Business horizons (Vol. 63, Issue 2, pp. 135–146). Elsevier Ltd. https://doi.org/DOI: 10.1016/j.bushor.2019.11.006

Kim, S.-E., Kim, K., Lee, J., Ko, Y., Wang, Y., & So, H.-J. (2025). *Dilemmas in AI Ethics: A Digital Game for Moral Reasoning and Collective Decision-Making*., DOI: 10.1007/978-3-031-98417-4_31

Knopp, M., Warm, E. J., Weber, D., Kelleher, M., Kinnear, B., Schumacher, D. J., Santen, S. A., Mendonça, E. A., & Turner, L. (2023). AI-Enabled Medical Education: Threads of Change, Promising Futures, and Risky Realities Across Four Potential Future Worlds. *JMIR Medical Education*, *9*, e50373. Advance online publication. DOI: 10.2196/50373 PMID: 38145471

Knoth, N., Decker, M., Laupichler, M. C., Pinski, M., Buchholtz, N., Bata, K., & Schultz, B. (2024). Developing a holistic AI literacy assessment matrix – Bridging generic, domain-specific, and ethical competencies. *Computers and Education Open*, *6*, 100177. Advance online publication. DOI: 10.1016/j.caeo.2024.100177

Kong, S. C., & Zhu, J. (2025). Developing and validating an artificial intelligence ethical awareness scale for secondary and university students: Cultivating ethical awareness through problem-solving with artificial intelligence tools. *Computers and Education: Artificial Intelligence*, *9*, 100447. Advance online publication. DOI: 10.1016/j.caeai.2025.100447

Küçükuncular, A., & Ertugan, A. (2025). Teaching in the AI Era: Sustainable Digital Education Through Ethical Integration and Teacher Empowerment. *Sustainability (Basel)*, *17*(16), 7405. Advance online publication. DOI: 10.3390/su17167405

Kugler, M. B., & Pace, C. (2021). Deepfake privacy: Attitudes and regulation. *Northwestern University Law Review*, *116*, 611.

Kumar, A. (2024). Redefining Finance: The Influence of Artificial Intelligence (AI) and Machine Learning (ML). *arXiv*. DOI: 10.48550/ARXIV.2410.15951

Kumar, A., Upadhyay, U., Sharma, G., Sharma, R. S., Mishra, N., & Kumawat, J. (2024). Strengthening AI Governance through Advanced Cryptographic Techniques. *International Journal of Intelligent Systems and Applications in Engineering*, *12*(17s), 553–560. https://www.scopus.com/inward/record.uri?eid=2-s2.0-85185915901&partnerID=40&md5=368e0138a40c2e6d797e0de992a39a90

Kunle-Lawanson, O. (2022). The role of AI in information security risk management. *World Journal of Advanced Engineering Technology and Sciences*, *7*(2), 308–319. DOI: 10.30574/wjaets.2022.7.2.0128

Kurtović, H., Šabanović, E., Almisreb, A. A., Saleh, M. A., & Ismail, N. (2025). Exploring the Dark Side: A Systematic Review of Generative AI's Role in Network Attacks and Breaches [Review of *Exploring the Dark Side: A Systematic Review of Generative AI's Role in Network Attacks and Breaches*]. *Lecture Notes in Networks and Systems*, 27. Springer International Publishing. DOI: 10.1007/978-3-031-82881-2_3

Lammers, K., Vaquet, V., & Hammer, B. (2026). Continuous Fair SMOTE – Fairness-Aware Stream Learning from Imbalanced Data. *Lecture Notes in Computer Science, 16068 LNCS*, 336–348. DOI: 10.1007/978-3-032-04558-4_27

Lee, C., & Cha, K. (2025). Toward the Dynamic Relationship Between AI Transparency and Trust in AI: A Case Study on ChatGPT. *International Journal of Human-Computer Interaction*, *41*(13), 8086–8103. DOI: 10.1080/10447318.2024.2405266

Lee, F. Y., Kumaresan, S. P., Anaam, E. A., & Kong, W. C. (2025). Social Platforms in the Deepfake Age: Navigating Media Trust through Media Literacy. *JOIV: International Journal on Informatics Visualization*, *9*(1), 176–183.

Lee, S. C., Baby, T., Vongvit, R., Lee, J., Kim, Y. W., Cha, M. C., & Yoon, S. H. (2026). Development and validation of Generative AI Competence Scale (GenAIComp) among university students. *Technology in Society*, *84*, 103059. DOI: 10.1016/j.techsoc.2025.103059

Lei, S., Xie, L., & Peng, J. (2025). Unethical Consumer Behavior Following Artificial Intelligence Agent Encounters: The Differential Effect of AI Agent Roles and its Boundary Conditions. *Journal of Service Research*, *28*(4), 598–613. DOI: 10.1177/10946705241278837

Lewis, D., Hogan, L., Filip, D., & Wall, P. J. (2020). Global challenges in the standardization of ethics for trustworthy AI. *Journal of ICT Standardisation*, *8*(2), 123–150. DOI: 10.13052/jicts2245-800X.823

Li, N. (2023). Ethical Considerations in Artificial Intelligence: A Comprehensive Disccusion from the Perspective of Computer Vision. *SHS Web of Conferences, 179*, 4024. DOI: 10.1051/shsconf/202317904024

Li, S., & Zhang, Z. (2026). Leveraging Artificial Intelligence Integration in Regional Sports Education to Foster Equitable and Sustainable Development. *Lecture Notes of the Institute for Computer Sciences, Social-Informatics and Telecommunications Engineering, LNICST, 617 LNICST*, 211–220. DOI: 10.1007/978-3-031-92517-7_16

Li, Y., & Lyu, S. (2018). Exposing deepfake videos by detecting face warping artifacts. arXiv preprint arXiv:1811.00656.

Liao, L., Du, M., & Chen, Z. (2023). Environmental pollution and socioeconomic health inequality: Evidence from China. *Sustainable Cities and Society*, *95*. Advance online publication. DOI: 10.1016/j.scs.2023.104579

Li, F., Ruijs, N., & Lu, Y. (2022). Ethics & AI: A Systematic Review on Ethical Concerns and Related Strategies for Designing with AI in Healthcare. *AI*, *4*(1), 28–53. DOI: 10.3390/ai4010003

Lim, T. (2024). Environmental, social, and governance (ESG) and artificial intelligence in finance: State-of-the-art and research takeaways. *Artificial Intelligence Review*, *57*(4), 76. Advance online publication. DOI: 10.1007/s10462-024-10708-3

Lissitsa, S. (2025). Generations X, Y, Z: The effects of personal and positional inequalities on critical thinking digital skills. *Online Information Review*, *49*(1), 35–54.

Liu, B., Li, G., Zhang, H., Jin, Y., Wang, Z., & Shao, D. (2025). The Gap Between Trustworthy AI Research and Trustworthy Software Research: A Tertiary Study. *ACM Computing Surveys*, *57*(3), 1–40. DOI: 10.1145/3694964

Liu, D. (2024). Application of neuroscience in C language teaching research. *Applied & Educational Psychology*, *5*(5), 158–162. DOI: 10.23977/appep.2024.050522

Liu, D., & Li, X. (2025). AI vs. Human: Reconciling Autonomy and Governance in Decision-Making. *Lecture Notes in Education Psychology and Public Media*, *114*(1), 82–87. DOI: 10.54254/2753-7048/2025.LC19101

Liu, L. X., Sun, Z., Xu, K., & Chen, C. (2024). AI-Driven Financial Analysis: Exploring ChatGPT's Capabilities and Challenges. *International Journal of Financial Studies*, *12*(3), 60. DOI: 10.3390/ijfs12030060

Lu, Q., Zhu, L., Xu, X., Whittle, J., Zowghi, D., & Jacquet, A. (2024). Responsible AI Pattern Catalogue: A Collection of Best Practices for AI Governance and Engineering. *ACM Computing Surveys*, *56*(7), 1–35. Advance online publication. DOI: 10.1145/3626234

Lutz, C. (2019). Digital inequalities in the age of artificial intelligence and bit data. *Human Behavior and Emerging Technologies*, *1*(2), 141–148. DOI: 10.1002/hbe2.140

Lynch, N. S. J., Loughran, R., McHugh, M., & McCaffrey, F. (2026). Trustworthy Artificial Intelligence in Healthcare: A Proposed Framework. *Communications in Computer and Information Science, 2657 CCIS*, 69–90. DOI: 10.1007/978-3-032-04288-0_5

Madanchian, M., & Taherdoost, H. (2025). Ethical theories, governance models, and strategic frameworks for responsible AI adoption and organizational success. *Frontiers in Artificial Intelligence*, *8*, 1619029. Advance online publication. DOI: 10.3389/frai.2025.1619029 PMID: 40741285

Maksutov, A. A., Morozov, V. O., Lavrenov, A. A., & Smirnov, A. S. (2020, January). Methods of deepfake detection based on machine learning. In 2020 IEEE conference of russian young researchers in electrical and electronic engineering (EIConRus) (pp. 408-411). IEEE.

Matern, F., Riess, C., & Stamminger, M. (2019). Exploiting visual artifacts to expose deepfakes and face manipulations. In IEEE winter applications of computer vision workshops (WACVW) (pp. 83–92). IEEE. https://doi.org/DOI: 10.1109/WACVW.2019.00020

McIntosh, T. R., Susnjak, T., Liu, T., Watters, P., Xu, D., Liu, D., Nowrozy, R., & Halgamuge, M. N. (2024). From COBIT to ISO 42001: Evaluating cybersecurity frameworks for opportunities, risks, and regulatory compliance in commercializing large language models. *Computers & Security*, *144*, 103964. Advance online publication. DOI: 10.1016/j.cose.2024.103964

Mersha, M., Lâm, K. N., Wood, J., AlShami, A. K., & Kalita, J. (2024). Explainable artificial intelligence: A survey of needs, techniques, applications, and future direction. *Neurocomputing*, *599*, 128111. DOI: 10.1016/j.neucom.2024.128111

Metta, S., Chang, I., Parker, J., Roman, M. P., & Ehuan, A. F. (2024). *Generative AI in Cybersecurity*. DOI: 10.48550/ARXIV.2405.01674

Millière, R. (2022). Deep learning and synthetic media. *Synthese*, *200*(3), 231.

Minssen, T., Smith, H. J., Mann, S. P., García, A. M., & Negrete, J. (2025). THE EUROPEAN AI ACT : PROMISES, PERILS & TRADE-OFFS IN A COMPLEX REGULATORY ECOSYSTEM. *Research Portal Denmark*, *1*, 330. https://local.forskningsportal.dk/local/dki-cgi/ws/cris-link?src=ku&id=ku-2fbecc26-4adb-487a-92d7-469ae5a7b774&ti=THE%20EUROPEAN%20AI%20ACT%20%3A%20PROMISES%2C%20PERILS%20%26amp%3B%20TRADE-OFFS%20IN%20A%20COMPLEX%20REGULATORY%20ECOSYSTEM

Mir, H. E., & Perinpanayagam, S. (2022). Certification of machine learning algorithms for safe-life assessment of landing gear. *Frontiers in Astronomy and Space Sciences*, *9*, 896877. Advance online publication. DOI: 10.3389/fspas.2022.896877

Mirsky, Y., & Lee, W. (2021). The creation and detection of deepfakes: A survey. *ACM Computing Surveys*, *54*(1), 1–41.

Mirtaheri, S. L., Movahed, N., Shahbazian, R., Pascucci, V., & Pugliese, A. (2026). Cybersecurity in the age of generative AI: A systematic taxonomy of AI-powered vulnerability assessment and risk management. *Future Generation Computer Systems*, *175*, 108107. Advance online publication. DOI: 10.1016/j.future.2025.108107

Mittelstadt, B. (2019). Principles alone cannot guarantee ethical AI. *Nature Machine Intelligence*, *1*(11), 501–507. DOI: 10.1038/s42256-019-0114-4

Mohan, N., Singla, R., Kaushal, P., & Kadry, S. (2021). Artificial Intelligence, Machine Learning, and Data Science Technologies: Future Impact and Well-Being for Society 5.0. In *Artificial Intelligence, Machine Learning, and Data Science Technologies: Future Impact and Well-Being for Society 5.0*. CRC Press., DOI: 10.1201/9781003153405

Mooghali, M., Stroud, A. M., Yoo, D. W., Barry, B. A., Grimshaw, A. A., Ross, J. S., Zhu, X., & Miller, J. E. (2024). Trustworthy and ethical AI-enabled cardiovascular care: A rapid review. *BMC Medical Informatics and Decision Making*, *24*(1), 247. Advance online publication. DOI: 10.1186/s12911-024-02653-6 PMID: 39232725

Muloor, K., Sahu, S. K., Behera, T. K., & Samanta, D. (2024). Computational intelligence in communication networks: Classification, clustering, reinforcement learning, deep learning. In Patnaik, S. K., Gao, X.-Z., & Biswal, B. (Eds.), *Intelligent communication networks* (pp. 221–236). CRC Press., DOI: 10.1201/9781003303114-10

Mumuni, F., & Mumuni, A. (2025). *Explainable artificial intelligence (XAI): from inherent explainability to large language models*. DOI: 10.48550/ARXIV.2501.09967

Mussgnug, A. M. (2025). Technology as Uncharted Territory: Integrative AI Ethics as a Response to the Notion of AI as New Moral Ground. *Philosophy & Technology*, *38*(3), 106. DOI: 10.1007/s13347-025-00938-w

Nannaware, S. C., Pillai, R., & Kate, N. (2025). Deepfakes in Action: Exploring Use Cases Across Industries. In Deepfakes and Their Impact on Business (pp. 71-98). IGI Global Scientific Publishing.

Naraganahalli Veerabhadraiah, Y. (2026). Decentralized Blockchain System for Ethical and Responsible AI in Generative Systems. *Lecture Notes in Computer Science, 16159 LNCS*, 87–103. DOI: 10.1007/978-3-032-06323-6_7

Naripeddy, S. C. B., & Thotakura, V. R. (2025). Ethical Challenges and Solutions in the Deployment of Artificial Intelligence Sys-tems. *Deleted Journal*, *8*(02), 81–110. DOI: 10.60087/jaigs.v8i02.392

Nasiri, S., & Hashemzadeh, A. (2025). The Evolution of Disinformation from Fake News Propaganda to AI-driven Narratives as Deepfake. *Journal of Cyberspace Studies*, *9*(1), 203–222.

Navarro Martínez, O., Fernández-García, D., Cuartero Monteagudo, N., & Forero-Rincón, O. (2024). Possible health benefits and risks of deepfake videos: A qualitative study in nursing students. *Nursing Reports*, *14*(4), 2746–2757. DOI: 10.3390/nursrep14040203

Nguyen, M. (2024). A scoping review of deep learning approaches for lung cancer detection using chest radiographs and computed tomography scans [Review of *A scoping review of deep learning approaches for lung cancer detection using chest radiographs and computed tomography scans*]. *Biomedical Engineering Advances*, *9*, 100138. Elsevier BV. DOI: 10.1016/j.bea.2024.100138

Nguyen, T. T., Nguyen, Q. V. H., Nguyen, D. T., Nguyen, D. T., Huynh-The, T., Nahavandi, S., Nguyen, T. T., Pham, Q. V., & Nguyen, C. M. (2022). Deep learning for deepfakes creation and detection: A survey. *Computer Vision and Image Understanding*, *223*, 103525.

Nunes, J. R., Rita, P., Costa Pinto, D., Gonzalez-Jimenez, H., Akdim, K., & Wagner, R. L. (2025). Moral appraisals of generative AI: How mindset framing shapes moral judgments, emotional appraisals and privacy behavior. *International Journal of Information Management*, *84*, 102940. Advance online publication. DOI: 10.1016/j.ijinfomgt.2025.102940

Obbu, S. (2025). AI in finance: Transforming risk management and fraud detection. *World Journal of Advanced Engineering Technology and Sciences*, *15*(1), 747–756. DOI: 10.30574/wjaets.2025.15.1.0281

Obioha Val, O., Gbadebo, M. O., Olaniyi, O. O., Chinye, N. C., & Balogun, A. Y. (2025). Innovative regulation of open source intelligence and deepfakes AI in managing public trust. Michael Olayinka and Olaniyi, Oluwaseun Oladeji and Chinye, Noah Chukwufumnanya and Balogun, Adebayo Yusuf, Innovative Regulation of Open Source Intelligence and Deepfakes AI in Managing Public Trust (January 30, 2025).

Okonicha, O., & Sadovykh, A. (2026). Enhancing GDPR Compliance Through NLP: Automated Policy Evaluation and Legal Document Analysis. *Lecture Notes in Networks and Systems, 1471 LNNS*, 408–423. DOI: 10.1007/978-3-031-94770-4_34

Olanipekun, S. O. (2025). Computational propaganda and misinformation: AI technologies as tools of media manipulation.

Olatoye, F. O., Awonuga, K. F., Mhlongo, N. Z., Ibeh, C. V., Elufioye, O. A., & Ndubuisi, N. L.Funmilola Olatundun OlatoyeKehinde Feranmi AwonugaNoluthando Zamanjomane MhlongoChidera Victoria IbehOluwafunmi Adijat ElufioyeNdubuisi Leonard Ndubuisi. (2024). AI and ethics in business: A comprehensive review of responsible AI practices and corporate responsibility [Review of AI and ethics in business: A comprehensive review of responsible AI practices and corporate responsibility]. *International Journal of Science and Research Archive*, *11*(1), 1433–1443. DOI: 10.30574/ijsra.2024.11.1.0235

Olawade, D. B., Wada, O. Z., David-Olawade, A. C., Fapohunda, O., Ige, A. O., & Ling, J. (2024). Artificial intelligence potential for net zero sustainability: Current evidence and prospects. *Next Sustainability*, *4*, 100041. DOI: 10.1016/j.nxsust.2024.100041

Onabowale, O. (2025). The Rise of AI and Robo-Advisors: Redefining Financial Strategies in the Digital Age. *International Journal of Research Publication and Reviews*, *6*(6), 4832. DOI: 10.55248/gengpi.6.0125.0640

Open, A. I. (2023). Creating video from text. Sora is an AI model that can create realistic and imaginative scenes from text instructions. OpenAI. https://openai.com/sora

Orpak, K. (2025). Generative AI and cybersecurity: Exploring opportunities and threats at their intersection. *Maandblad Voor Accountancy en Bedrijfseconomie*, *99*(4), 221–230. DOI: 10.5117/mab.99.149299

Otaegui, O., Nieto, M., Rasca, S. I., den Ouden, J., Ubach, C., Stolz, M., & Beckmann, J. (2026). AITHENA: Towards a Trustworthy AI for CCAM Development (pp. 483–489). DOI: 10.1007/978-3-031-88974-5_71

Palani, K., Kethar, J., Prasad, S., & Torremocha, V. (2024). Impact of AI and Generative AI in transforming Cybersecurity. *Journal of Student Research*, *13*(2). Advance online publication. DOI: 10.47611/jsrhs.v13i2.6710

Palladino, N. (2023). A 'biased' emerging governance regime for artificial intelligence? How AI ethics get skewed moving from principles to practices. *Telecommunications Policy*, *47*(5), 102479. Advance online publication. DOI: 10.1016/j.telpol.2022.102479

Panda, S. N. (2025). The Role of Artificial Intelligence in Healthcare, Finance, and Education. SSRN *Electronic Journal*. DOI: 10.2139/ssrn.5258064

Paraman, P., & Anamalah, S. (2023). Ethical artificial intelligence framework for a good AI society: Principles, opportunities and perils. *AI & Society*, *38*(2), 595–611. DOI: 10.1007/s00146-022-01458-3

Paramesha, M., Rane, N., & Rane, J. (2024). Artificial intelligence, machine learning, deep learning, and blockchain in financial and banking services: a comprehensive review [Review of *Artificial intelligence, machine learning, deep learning, and blockchain in financial and banking services: a comprehensive review*]. SSRN *Electronic Journal*. RELX Group (Netherlands). DOI: 10.2139/ssrn.4855893

Patel, B., Bhagavanbhai, P. K., & Dhameliya, N. (2024). Revolutionizing Cybersecurity with AI: Predictive Threat Intelligence and Automated Response Systems. *Deleted Journal*, *12*(4), 1–5. DOI: 10.36676/dira.v12.i4.126

Patil, D. (2025a). *Artificial Intelligence In Financial Risk Assessment And Fraud Detection: Opportunities And Ethical Concerns*. DOI: 10.2139/ssrn.5057434

Patil, D. (2025b). *Artificial Intelligence In Financial Services: Advancements In Fraud Detection, Risk Management, And Algorithmic Trading Optimization*. DOI: 10.2139/ssrn.5057412

Patil, D. (2025c). *Explainable Artificial Intelligence (XAI): Enhancing Transparency And Trust In Machine Learning Models*. DOI: 10.2139/ssrn.5057400

Patterson, D. (2023). Deepfakes for good? How synthetic media is transforming business. https://techinformed.com/deepfakes-for-good-how-synthetic-media-is-transforming-business/

Paul, A. A., & Ogburie, C. P. (2025). The Role of AI in preventing financial fraud and enhancing compliance. *GSC Advanced Research and Reviews*, *22*(3), 269–282. DOI: 10.30574/gscarr.2025.22.3.0086

Perez-Cerrolaza, J., Abella, J., Borg, M., Donzella, C., Cerquides, J., Cazorla, F. J., Englund, C., Tauber, M., Nikolakopoulos, G., & Flores, J. L. (2024). Artificial Intelligence for Safety-Critical Systems in Industrial and Transportation Domains: A Survey. *ACM Computing Surveys*, *56*(7), 1–40. Advance online publication. DOI: 10.1145/3626314

Perov, I., Gao, D., Chervoniy, N., Liu, K., Marangonda, S., Umé, C., . . . Zhang, W. (2020). DeepFaceLab: Integrated, flexible and extensible face-swapping framework. arXiv preprint arXiv:2005.05535.

Petković, D. (2023). It is Not "Accuracy vs. Explainability"—We Need Both for Trustworthy AI Systems. *IEEE Transactions on Technology and Society*, *4*(1), 46–53. DOI: 10.1109/TTS.2023.3239921

Phan, T., & Goldenfein, J. (n.d.). Repositorium für die Medienwissenschaft Economies of Virtue-The Circulation of "Ethics" in AI 2022 Erstmalig hier erschienen / Initial publication here: https://networkcultures.org/blog/publication/economies-of-virtue-the-circulation-of-ethics-in-ai. DOI: 10.25969/mediarep/19267

Pimenow, S., Pimenowa, O., & Prus, P. (2024). Challenges of Artificial Intelligence Development in the Context of Energy Consumption and Impact on Climate Change. *Energies*, *17*(23), 5965. DOI: 10.3390/en17235965

Pineda, V. G., Valencia-Arias, A., Giraldo, F. E. L., & Zapata-Ochoa, E. A. (2026). Integrating artificial intelligence and quantum computing: A systematic literature review of features and applications. *International Journal of Cognitive Computing in Engineering*, *7*, 26–39. DOI: 10.1016/j.ijcce.2025.08.002

Podder, S. K., Thomas, B., & Samanta, D. (2022). Impact of innovative technology on quality education: The resourceful intelligence for smart society development. In A. Kumar & N. R. Das (Eds.), *Machine intelligence and data science applications: Proceedings of MIDAS 2021* (Vol. 132, pp. 293–304). Springer. https://doi.org/DOI: 10.10054/MIDA.2022.293

Proceedings of the 19th Conference on Computer Science and Intelligence Systems (FedCSIS). (2024). *Annals of Computer Science and Information Systems, 39.* https://doi.org/DOI: 10.15439/978-83-969601-6-0

Pruski, M. (2025). Ethical Challenges to the Adoption of AI in Healthcare: A Review. The New Bioethics, 1–17. DOI: 10.1080/20502877.2025.2541438

Purwar, P. (2025). The Transformational Impact of AI Across Financial Services. *Journal of Computer Science and Technology Studies*, *7*(3), 461–469. DOI: 10.32996/jcsts.2025.7.3.52

Qayoumi, A. S., Shalizi, H., & Dhankot, M. A. (2025). Review on artificial intelligence application in structural earthquake engineering. *International Journal of Science and Research Archive*, *14*(1), 83. DOI: 10.30574/ijsra.2025.14.1.2659

Radanliev, P. (2025). AI Ethics: Integrating Transparency, Fairness, and Privacy in AI Development. *Applied Artificial Intelligence*, *39*(1), 2463722. Advance online publication. DOI: 10.1080/08839514.2025.2463722

Rahmouni, N., Nozick, V., Yamagishi, J., & Echizen, I. (2017, December). Distinguishing computer graphics from natural images using convolution neural networks. In 2017 IEEE workshop on information forensics and security (WIFS) (pp. 1-6). IEEE.

Rahnemoonfar, M. (2024). DEEP SPECTRAL SIAMESE NETWORK FOR HETEROGENEOUS OBJECT VERIFICATION IN AMAZON ROBOTIC WAREHOUSE. *Proceedings - International Conference on Image Processing, ICIP*, 922–928. DOI: 10.1109/ICIP51287.2024.10647558

Rajpoot, A., & Tiwari, S. (2025). Predictive Modeling of Structural Performance Using Machine Learning: A Comprehensive Review [Review of Predictive Modeling of Structural Performance Using Machine Learning: A Comprehensive Review]. *Deleted Journal*, *3*(1), 25–30. DOI: 10.47392/IRJAEH.2025.0005

Rajwade, S., Yadaw, P. K., & Ingle, A. (2025). Ethics and legal dimensions of artificial intelligence in healthcare: technical, business, and educational perspectives. DOI: 10.52152/801158

Rana, M. S., Nobi, M. N., Murali, B., & Sung, A. H. (2022). Deepfake detection: A systematic literature review. *IEEE Access : Practical Innovations, Open Solutions, 10*, 25494–25513.

Rane, J., Kaya, Ö., Mallick, S. K., & Rane, N. L. (2024). *Enhancing black-box models: Advances in explainable artificial intelligence for ethical decision-making*. DOI: 10.70593/978-81-981271-0-5_4

Rane, N. L., Choudhary, S., & Rane, J. (2023). Explainable Artificial Intelligence (XAI) Approaches for Transparency and Accountability in Financial Decision-Making. SSRN *Electronic Journal*. DOI: 10.2139/ssrn.4640316

Ranga, M. (2024). ARTIFICIAL INTELLIGENCE AND ITS IMPACT ON SOCIETY. *International Journal of Engineering Science & Humanities., 14*(Special Issue 1), 170–177. DOI: 10.62904/9fmpr623

Ratti, E., & Graves, M. (2025). A Capability Approach to AI Ethics. *American Philosophical Quarterly, 62*(1), 1–16. DOI: 10.5406/21521123.62.1.01

Rawas, S. (2024). AI: The future of humanity. *Discover Artificial Intelligence, 4*(1), 25. Advance online publication. DOI: 10.1007/s44163-024-00118-3

Rawat, D., Sharma, S., & Bhadula, S. (2023). Deep Learning Techniques in Digital Clinical Diagnostic System for Lung Cancer. *2022 8th International Conference on Advanced Computing and Communication Systems (ICACCS)*, 1232. DOI: 10.1109/ICACCS57279.2023.10113055

Raza, S., Qureshi, R., Zahid, A., Fioresi, J., Sadak, F., Saeed, M. A., Sapkota, R., Jain, A., Zafar, A., Hassan, M., Zafar, A., Maqbool, H., Vayani, A., Wu, J., & Shoman, M. (2025). *Who is Responsible? The Data, Models, Users or Regulations? Responsible Generative AI for a Sustainable Future*. DOI: 10.36227/techrxiv.173834932.29831105/v1

Regona, M., Yiğitcanlar, T., Hon, C. K. H., & Teo, M. (2024). Artificial intelligence and sustainable development goals: Systematic literature review of the construction industry. *Sustainable Cities and Society, 108*, 105499. DOI: 10.1016/j.scs.2024.105499

Reinhardt, K. (2023). Trust and trustworthiness in AI ethics. *AI and Ethics, 3*(3), 735–744. DOI: 10.1007/s43681-022-00200-5

Ricon, T. (2025). AI and adolescent Relationships: Bridging emotional intelligence and practical guidance. *Computers in Human Behavior Reports, 19*, 100752. Advance online publication. DOI: 10.1016/j.chbr.2025.100752

Ridzuan, N. N., Masri, M., Anshari, M., Fitriyani, N. L., & Syafrudin, M. (2024). AI in the Financial Sector: The Line between Innovation, Regulation and Ethical Responsibility. *Information (Basel), 15*(8), 432. DOI: 10.3390/info15080432

Riti, R. I., Abrudan, C. I., Bacali, L., & Balc, N. (2025). Command Redefined: Neural-Adaptive Leadership in the Age of Autonomous Intelligence. *AI, 6*(8), 176. Advance online publication. DOI: 10.3390/ai6080176

Robbins, P. (2025). Of machines and men: Attributions of moral responsibility in AI-assisted warfare. *Ethics and Information Technology, 27*(3), 35. Advance online publication. DOI: 10.1007/s10676-025-09844-3

Roeslin, S., Ma, Q., Chigullapally, P., Wicker, J., & Wotherspoon, L. (2022). *Development of a Seismic Loss Prediction Model for Residential Buildings using Machine Learning – Christchurch, New Zealand.* DOI: 10.5194/nhess-2022-227

Rojas Contreras, M., & Portilla Jaimes, J. O. (2024). AI Ethics in the Fields of Education and Research: A Systematic Literature Review. 1–6. DOI: 10.1109/ICACIT62963.2024.10788651

Roshanaei, M., Khan, M. R., & Sylvester, N. N. (2024a). Enhancing Cybersecurity through AI and ML: Strategies, Challenges, and Future Directions. *Journal of Information Security, 15*(3), 320–339. DOI: 10.4236/jis.2024.153019

Roshanaei, M., Khan, M. R., & Sylvester, N. N. (2024b). Navigating AI Cybersecurity: Evolving Landscape and Challenges. *Journal of Intelligent Learning Systems and Applications, 16*(3), 155–174. DOI: 10.4236/jilsa.2024.163010

Rossler, A., Cozzolino, D., Verdoliva, L., Riess, C., Thies, J., & Nießner, M. (2019). Faceforensics++: Learning to detect manipulated facial images. In Proceedings of the IEEE/CVF international conference on computer vision (pp. 1-11).

Rubeis, G. (2024). *Ethical Foundations: Medical Ethics and Data Ethics* (pp. 55–87). DOI: 10.1007/978-3-031-55744-6_4

Ruster, L. P., Oliva-Altamirano, P., & Daniell, K. A. (2022). Centring dignity in algorithm development: testing a Dignity Lens. *ACM International Conference Proceeding Series*, 1–8. DOI: 10.1145/3572921.3572938

Ruster, L. P., Oliva-Altamirano, P., & Daniell, K. A. (2025). The Dignity Lens: Advancing Human-Centred Protective and Proactive Algorithmic Responsibility. *Information Systems Journal*, isj.12601. Advance online publication. DOI: 10.1111/isj.12601

Saeed, K., & Prybutok, V. R. (2026). When utility meets ethics: A stakeholder perspective on agentic information systems delegation. *International Journal of Information Management, 86*, 102976. Advance online publication. DOI: 10.1016/j.ijinfomgt.2025.102976

Salim, S., Jayasudha, J. S., & Soniya, B. (2024). *Ensuring Ethical AI: Unpacking the Significance of Risk Analysis Under the European Union's Artificial Intelligence Act*. DOI: 10.1109/TENSYMP61132.2024.10752133

Saranya, A., & Subhashini, R. (2023). A systematic review of Explainable Artificial Intelligence models and applications: Recent developments and future trends [Review of *A systematic review of Explainable Artificial Intelligence models and applications: Recent developments and future trends*]. *Decision Analytics Journal, 7*, 100230. Elsevier BV. DOI: 10.1016/j.dajour.2023.100230

Saravanan, S., Haimavathi, K. U., & Aafizaa, K. (2026). Biomedical Antenna Design: Micro strip Patch Antennas for Wearable and Implantable Healthcare Applications—A Review. *Biomedical Materials & Devices, 4*(1), 414–424. DOI: 10.1007/s44174-025-00299-0

Sarker, I. H., Janicke, H., Mohammad, N., Watters, P., & Nepal , Surya. (2024). AI Potentiality and Awareness: A Position Paper from the Perspective of Human-AI Teaming in Cybersecurity. In *Lecture notes in networks and systems* (p. 140). Springer International Publishing. DOI: 10.1007/978-3-031-50887-5_14

Schmitt, M., & Fléchais, I. (2024). Digital deception: Generative artificial intelligence in social engineering and phishing. *Artificial Intelligence Review, 57*(12), 324. Advance online publication. DOI: 10.1007/s10462-024-10973-2

Securities and Exchange Board of India. (2019, May 15). Reporting for artificial intelligence (AI) and machine learning (ML) applications and systems offered and used by mutual funds (Circular No. SEBI/HO/IMD/DF2/CIR/P/2019/56). https://www.sebi.gov.in/legal/circulars/may-2019/reporting-for-artificial-intelligence-ai-and-machine-learn-ing-ml-applications-and-systems-offered-and-used-by-mutual-funds_42932.html

Sekti, B. A. (2025). Information Security Awareness. In *User-Centric Cybersecurity Implications for Sustainable Digital Transformation* (pp. 111–145). DOI: 10.4018/979-8-3373-3171-3.ch004

Sekti, B. A. (2025c). Machine Learning and Artificial Intelligence (AI) in Manufacturing. In *Integrating Digital Innovation and Integrated Frameworks in Manufacturing* (pp. 255–292). IGI Global Scientific Publishing. DOI: 10.4018/979-8-3373-1082-4.ch011

Sekti, B. A. (2025a). *Adversarial Machine Learning in Industrial Cybersecurity.*, DOI: 10.4018/979-8-3373-3241-3.ch018

Şenocak, D., Koçdar, S., Bozkurt, A., & Professor, A. (2023). Historical, Philosophical and Ethical Roots of Artificial Intelligence. In *Pakistan Journal of Education* (Vol. 40, Issue 1). https://orcid.org/0000-0001-9099-6312

Seow, J. W., Lim, M. K., Phan, R. C., & Liu, J. K. (2022). A comprehensive overview of Deepfake: Generation, detection, datasets, and opportunities. *Neurocomputing, 513*, 351–371.

Shabbir, K., Noureldin, M., & Sim, S. (2024). Data-driven model for seismic assessment, design, and retrofit of structures using explainable artificial intelligence. *Computer-Aided Civil and Infrastructure Engineering*. Advance online publication. DOI: 10.1111/mice.13338

Shamsuddin, R., Tabrizi, H. B., & Gottimukkula, P. R. (2025). Towards responsible AI: An implementable blueprint for integrating explainability and social-cognitive frameworks in AI systems. *AI Perspectives & Advances, 7*(1), 1. Advance online publication. DOI: 10.1186/s42467-024-00016-5

Shanker, S. (n.d.). *WITTGENSTEIN'S REMARKS ON THE FOUNDATIONS OF AI.*

SHARIFF, V., PARITALA, C., & ANKALA, K. (2023). *AN ANALYSIS ON ADVANCES IN LUNG CANCER DIAGNOSIS WITH MEDICAL IMAGING AND DEEP LEARNING TECHNIQUES: CHALLENGES AND OPPORTUNITIES.*

Sharma, M., Biros, D., Baham, C., & Biros, J. (2024). What Went Wrong? Identifying Risk Factors for Popular Negative Consequences in AI. *AIS Transactions on Human-Computer Interaction, 16*(2), 139–176. 10.17705/1thci.00203

Shatnawi, M. Q., Abuein, Q., & Al-Quraan, R. (2024). Deep Learning-Based Approach to Diagnose Lung Cancer Using CT-Scan Images. *Intelligence-Based Medicine, 100188*. Advance online publication. DOI: 10.1016/j.ibmed.2024.100188

Sheikhpour, R., Saberi-Movahed, F., Jalili, M., & Berahmand, K. (2026). Semi-supervised feature selection with concept factorization and robust label learning. *Pattern Recognition, 172*, 112317. Advance online publication. DOI: 10.1016/j.patcog.2025.112317

Shi, X., Chen, S., Zhang, G., Wei, W., Li, Y., Fan, Z., & Liu, J. (2026). Jailbreak attack with multimodal virtual scenario hypnosis for vision-language models. *Pattern Recognition, 172*, 112391. Advance online publication. DOI: 10.1016/j.patcog.2025.112391

Shukla, S. K. (2024). AI for Sustainable Ground Infrastructure. *International Journal of Geosynthetics and Ground Engineering, 10*(6), 90. Advance online publication. DOI: 10.1007/s40891-024-00600-z

Shuster, L. A. (2024). European Union AI Act Aims to Lower the Risks. *SWE Magazine, 70*(4), 12–13. Retrieved from https://www.scopus.com/inward/record.uri?eid=2-s2.0-85201044389&partnerID=40&md5=b81d63d872437a6b6d9e61a13d006001

Sidorova, A., & Saeed, K. (2022). Incorporating Stakeholder enfranchisement, Risks, Gains, and AI decisions in AI Governance Framework. *Proceedings of the Annual Hawaii International Conference on System Sciences, 2022-January*, 5943–5952. DOI: 10.24251/HICSS.2022.722

Singh, P., & Dhiman, B. (2023, December 27). Exploding AI-generated deepfakes and misinformation: A threat to global concern in the 21st century. https://shorturl.at/pffhV

Singhal, A., Neveditsin, N., Tanveer, H., & Mago, V. (2024). Toward Fairness, Accountability, Transparency, and Ethics in AI for Social Media and Health Care: Scoping Review. *JMIR Medical Informatics, 12*, e50048. DOI: 10.2196/50048 PMID: 38568737

Singh, B., Rahim, M. A. B. U., Hussain, S., Rizwan, M. A., & Zhao, J. (2023). AI Ethics in Healthcare -. *Survey (London, England)*, •••, 826–833. DOI: 10.1109/QRS-C60940.2023.00086

Singh, D. P., Gupta, S., Ganesh, D., Sharma, S., Kalnawat, A., Pramanik, S., & Samanta, D. (2024). Technologies that Work Together for Precision Agriculture. In *Data Driven Mathematical Modeling in Agriculture* (pp. 367–388). River Publishers. DOI: 10.1201/9781003515883-17

Singh, R., & Gibu, S. M. (2023). Exploring the Transformative Potential and the Challenges of Artificial Intelligence in Vauhini Vara's The Immortal King Rao. *Rupkatha Journal on Interdisciplinary Studies in Humanities, 15*(4). Advance online publication. DOI: 10.21659/rupkatha.v15n4.06

Sinha, R. K. (2024). The role and impact of new technologies on healthcare systems. *Discover Health Systems, 3*(1), 96. Advance online publication. DOI: 10.1007/s44250-024-00163-w

Smuha, N. A. (2025). *The Cambridge Handbook ofTHE LAW, ETHICS AND POLICY OF ARTIFICIAL INTELLIGENCE*. https://www.cambridge.org/core/terms.https://www.cambridge.org/core/product/0AD007641DE27F837A3A16DBC0888DD1Downloadedfromhttps://www.cambridge.org/core

Solaiman, B., & Malik, A. (2025). Regulating algorithmic care in the European Union: Evolving doctor–patient models through the Artificial Intelligence Act (AI-Act) and the liability directives. *Medical Law Review*, *33*(1), fwae033. Advance online publication. DOI: 10.1093/medlaw/fwae033 PMID: 39257157

Soomro, R. B., Al-Rahmi, W. M., Dahri, N. A., Almuqren, L., Almogren, A. S., & Aldaijy, A. (2025). A SEM–ANN analysis to examine impact of artificial intelligence technologies on sustainable performance of SMEs. *Scientific Reports*, *15*(1), 5438. Advance online publication. DOI: 10.1038/s41598-025-86464-3 PMID: 39948417

Sridhar, U. (2025). Ethical frameworks for responsible ai development: Challenges and implementation strategies. *World Journal of Advanced Engineering Technology and Sciences*, *15*(1), 2028–2038. DOI: 10.30574/wjaets.2025.15.1.0420

Sterz, S., Baum, K., Biewer, S., Hermanns, H., Lauber-Rönsberg, A., Meinel, P., & Langer, M. (2024). On the Quest for Effectiveness in Human Oversight: Interdisciplinary Perspectives. The 2024 ACM Conference on Fairness Accountability and Transparency, 2495–2507. DOI: 10.1145/3630106.3659051

Struniawski, K., Kozera, R., & Konopka, A. (2025). Analyzing LLM Sentencing Variability in Theft Indictments Across Gender, Family Status and the Value of the Stolen Item. *Applied Sciences (Basel, Switzerland)*, *15*(16), 8860. Advance online publication. DOI: 10.3390/app15168860

Suter, V., Ma, C., Pöhlmann, G., & Meckel, M. (2025). When Politicians Talk AI: Issue-Frames in Parliamentary Debates Before and After ChatGPT. *Policy and Internet*, *17*(3), e70010. Advance online publication. DOI: 10.1002/poi3.70010

Suwajanakorn, S., Seitz, S. M., & Kemelmacher-Shlizerman, I. (2017). Synthesizing obama: Learning lip sync from audio. [ToG]. *ACM Transactions on Graphics*, *36*(4), 1–13.

Swetha, T., Kumaran, U., Meena, V. P., & Hameed, I. A. (2025). Leveraging AI for enhanced cybersecurity: A comprehensive review [Review of Leveraging AI for enhanced cybersecurity: a comprehensive review]. *Discover Applied Sciences*, *7*(6), 584. Advance online publication. DOI: 10.1007/s42452-025-06773-0

Tapeh, A. T. G., & Naser, M. Z. (2022). Discovering Graphical Heuristics on Fire-Induced Spalling of Concrete Through Explainable Artificial Intelligence. *Fire Technology*, *58*(5), 2871–2898. DOI: 10.1007/s10694-022-01290-7 PMID: 35910785

Telkamp, J. B., & Anderson, M. H. (2022). The Implications of Diverse Human Moral Foundations for Assessing the Ethicality of Artificial Intelligence. *Journal of Business Ethics*, *178*(4), 961–976. DOI: 10.1007/s10551-022-05057-6

Teng, Z., Xia, H., & He, Y. (2025). Algorithmic Fairness and Digital Financial Stress: Evidence from AI-Driven E-Commerce Platforms in OECD Economies. *Journal of Theoretical and Applied Electronic Commerce Research, 20*(3), 213. Advance online publication. DOI: 10.3390/jtaer20030213

Tewari, A., Zollhoefer, M., Bernard, F., Garrido, P., Kim, H., Perez, P., & Theobalt, C. (2018). High-fidelity monocular face reconstruction based on an unsupervised model-based face autoencoder. *IEEE Transactions on Pattern Analysis and Machine Intelligence, 42*(2), 357–370.

Thakur, G. K., Thakur, A., Kulkarni, S., Khan, N., & Khan, S. (2024). Deep Learning Approaches for Medical Image Analysis and Diagnosis. *Cureus*. Advance online publication. DOI: 10.7759/cureus.59507 PMID: 38826977

Thi Nguyet Trang, T. T. N., Thang, P. C., & Vo, T. A. (2025). Moderating the AI Revolution: Perceived threat and generative AI implementation in Vietnamese hospitals. *Computers in Human Behavior Reports, 19*, 100774. Advance online publication. DOI: 10.1016/j.chbr.2025.100774

Thirunagalingam, A. (2025). Enhancing Data Governance Through Explainable AI: Bridging Transparency and Automation. SSRN *Electronic Journal*. DOI: 10.2139/ssrn.5047713

Thomsen, K. (2019). Ethics for Artificial Intelligence, Ethics for All. *Paladyn : Journal of Behavioral Robotics, 10*(1), 359–363. DOI: 10.1515/pjbr-2019-0029

Tiwari, A., Mishra, S. N., & Kuo, T. (2025). Current AI technologies in cancer diagnostics and treatment [Review of *Current AI technologies in cancer diagnostics and treatment*]. *Molecular Cancer, 24*(1). BioMed Central. DOI: 10.1186/s12943-025-02369-9

Tomo, A., Iacono, M. P., Mercurio, L., Mangia, G., & Todisco, L. (2024). Regulation, governance and organisational issues in European Railway Regulation Authorities. Journal of Rail Transport Planning & Management, 29, 100428.

Truby, J., Brown, R. D., & Dahdal, A. (2020). Banking on AI: Mandating a proactive approach to AI regulation in the financial sector. *Law and Financial Markets Review, 14*(2), 110–120. DOI: 10.1080/17521440.2020.1760454

Uzoka, A., Cadet, E., & Ojukwu, P. U. (2024). Applying artificial intelligence in Cybersecurity to enhance threat detection, response, and risk management. *Computer Science & IT Research Journal, 5*(10), 2511–2538. DOI: 10.51594/csitrj.v5i10.1677

Vaccari, C., & Chadwick, A. (2020). Deepfakes and disinformation: Exploring the impact of synthetic political video on deception, uncertainty, and trust in news. *Social Media + Society*, *6*(1). Advance online publication. DOI: 10.1177/2056305120903408

Van Deursen, A. J., & Van Dijk, J. A. (2019). The first-level digital divide shifts from inequalities in physical access to inequalities in material access. *New Media & Society*, *21*(2), 354–375. DOI: 10.1177/1461444818797082

Van Deursen, A., Helsper, E., Eynon, R., & Van Dijk, J. (2017). The compoundness and sequentiality of digital inequality. *International Journal of Communication*, *11*, 452–473.

Van Dijk, J. A. (2005). The deepening divide. *Sage (Atlanta, Ga.)*.

van Toorn, G., Scully, J. L., & Gendera, S. (2025). "This robot is dictating her next steps in life": Disability justice and relational AI ethics. *AI & Society*, *40*(6), 4473–4483. DOI: 10.1007/s00146-025-02224-x

Vartanova, E., & Gladkova, A. (2019). New forms of the digital divide. In Trappel, J. (Ed.), *Digital media inequalities: Policies against divides, distrust and discrimination* (pp. 193–213). Nordicom., https://urn.kb.se/resolve?urn=urn:nbn:se:norden:org:diva-11846

Vascelli, L. (2025). From philosophy to algorithms: A commentary on the evolution of human behavior and the role of artificial intelligence. *Discover Artificial Intelligence*, *5*(1), 138. Advance online publication. DOI: 10.1007/s44163-025-00394-7

Venema, A. E., & Geradts, Z. J. (2020). Digital forensics, deepfakes, and the legal process. *The SciTech Lawyer*, *16*(4), 14–23.

Verma, A., Sankhyayan, S., Jawanda, K., & Tandon, S. N. (2025). Generative Artificial Intelligence and Cybersecurity Risks: Issues and Challenges. In *Lecture notes in networks and systems* (p. 321). Springer International Publishing. DOI: 10.1007/978-981-97-8602-2_29

Vuković, D., Dekpo-Adza, S., & Matović, S. (2025). AI integration in financial services: a systematic review of trends and regulatory challenges [Review of *AI integration in financial services: a systematic review of trends and regulatory challenges*]. *Humanities and Social Sciences Communications, 12*(1). Palgrave Macmillan. DOI: 10.1057/s41599-025-04850-8

Wagner, M., Borg, M., & Runeson, P. (2024). Navigating the Upcoming European Union AI Act. *IEEE Software*, *41*(1), 19–24. DOI: 10.1109/MS.2023.3322913

Walawalkar, A. KUMAR, S., Moslehpour, M., & Moslehpour, M. (2025). Foundations of AI Ethics. SSRN *Electronic Journal*. DOI: 10.2139/ssrn.5187641

Wani, N. A., Kumar, R., & Bedi, J. (2023). DeepXplainer: An interpretable deep learning based approach for lung cancer detection using explainable artificial intelligence. *Computer Methods and Programs in Biomedicine, 243*, 107879. DOI: 10.1016/j.cmpb.2023.107879 PMID: 37897989

Waqas, A., Tripathi, A., Ramachandran, R. P., Stewart, P. A., & Rasool, G. (2024). Multimodal data integration for oncology in the era of deep neural networks: a review [Review of *Multimodal data integration for oncology in the era of deep neural networks: a review*]. *Frontiers in Artificial Intelligence, 7*. Frontiers Media. DOI: 10.3389/frai.2024.1408843

Waser, M. R. (2008). *Discovering The Foundations Of A Universal System of Ethics As A Road To Safe Artificial Intelligence*. www.aaai.org

Weng, Y., Wu, J., Kelly, T., & Johnson, W. (2024). *Comprehensive Overview of Artificial Intelligence Applications in Modern Industries*. DOI: 10.20944/preprints202409.1638.v1

Westerlund, M. (2019). The emergence of deepfake technology: A review. *Technology Innovation Management Review*, *9*(11), 40–53.

Westerstrand, S. (2024). Reconstructing AI Ethics Principles: Rawlsian Ethics of Artificial Intelligence. *Science and Engineering Ethics*, *30*(5), 46. DOI: 10.1007/s11948-024-00507-y PMID: 39384600

Westerstrand, S. (2025). Fairness in AI systems development: EU AI Act compliance and beyond. *Information and Software Technology*, *187*, 107864. Advance online publication. DOI: 10.1016/j.infsof.2025.107864

White, G. R. T., Samuel, A., Jones, P., Madhavan, N., Afolayan, A., Abdullah, A., & Kaushik, T. (2024). Mapping the ethical-theoretical foundations of artificial intelligence research. *Thunderbird International Business Review*, *66*(2), 171–183. DOI: 10.1002/tie.22368

Willet, K. B. S., & Na, H. (2024). Generative AI Generating Buzz: Volume, Engagement, and Content of Initial Reactions to ChatGPT in Discussions Across Education-Related Subreddits. *Online Learning : the Official Journal of the Online Learning Consortium*, *28*(2). Advance online publication. DOI: 10.24059/olj.v28i2.4434

Wongmahesak, K., Wekke, I. S., Seftyono, C., & Nurdin, N. H. (2025). Democracy and democratization in the age of AI. In Democracy and Democratization in the Age of AI. DOI: 10.4018/979-8-3693-8749-8

Wongmahesak, K., Singh, B., Arora, M. K. K., Lal, S., Malviya, R., & Chandra, S. (2025). AI-Driven Solutions for Transparent Governance. In *Democracy and Democratization in the Age of AI* (pp. 153–166). IGI Global., DOI: 10.4018/979-8-3693-8749-8.ch009

Wu, Y., & Liu, X. M. (2023). Navigating the Ethical Landscape of AI in Healthcare: Insights From a Content Analysis. *IEEE Technology and Society Magazine*, *42*(3), 76–87. DOI: 10.1109/MTS.2023.3306543

Xiong, S., Gu, H., Liang, W., & Yin, L. (2025). Moral Judgment with a Large Language Model-Based Agent. *Electronics (Basel)*, *14*(13), 2580. Advance online publication. DOI: 10.3390/electronics14132580

Xu, F., Xiao, Y., Mei, J., Hu, Y., Fu, Q., & Shi, H. (2026). Domain-adaptive point cloud semantic segmentation via knowledge-augmented deep learning. *Pattern Recognition*, *172*, 112528. Advance online publication. DOI: 10.1016/j.patcog.2025.112528

Yang, H., Chen, L., Cao, Y., Li, Y., & Zhou, Y. (2023). Towards Better Dependency Scope Settings in Maven Projects. *ACM International Conference Proceeding Series*, 90–100. DOI: 10.1145/3609437.3609447

Yan, Y., Liu, H., Zhang, H., Chau, T., & Li, J. (2025). Designing a Generalist Education AI Framework for Multimodal Learning and Ethical Data Governance. *Applied Sciences (Basel, Switzerland)*, *15*(14), 7758. Advance online publication. DOI: 10.3390/app15147758

Yao, D., Zhang, X., & Liu, Y. (2022). Teaching Reform in C Programming Course from the Perspective of Sustainable Development: Construction and 9-Year Practice of "Three Classrooms–Four Integrations–Five Combinations" Teaching Model. *Sustainability (Basel)*, *14*(22), 15226. DOI: 10.3390/su142215226

Yekaterina, K. (2024). Challenges and Opportunities for AI in Healthcare. *International Journal of Law and Policy*, *2*(7), 11–15. DOI: 10.59022/ijlp.203

Yu, C. M., Chang, C. T., & Ti, Y. W. (2019). Detecting deepfake-forged contents with separable convolutional neural network and image segmentation. arXiv preprint arXiv:1912.12184

Yu, L., Xu, W., Sukjairungwattana, P., & Yu, Z. (2023). A Meta-Analysis of Facebook-Assisted Learning Outcomes in Different Countries or Regions. *International Journal of Information Technology and Web Engineering*, *18*(1), 1–18. Advance online publication. DOI: 10.4018/IJITWE.319312

Yu, M., & Ming, Z. (2024). Research on the reform of C language programming teaching based on the training of new engineering talents. *Advances in Vocational and Technical Education*, *6*(2), 1–8. DOI: 10.23977/avte.2024.060201

Yu, S., & Lu, Y. (2021). *An Introduction to Artificial Intelligence in Education*. Springer Singapore., DOI: 10.1007/978-981-16-2770-5

Zaman, B. U. (2023). *Transforming Education Through AI, Benefits, Risks, and Ethical Considerations*. DOI: 10.36227/techrxiv.24231583.v1

Zhang, C., & Pan, L. (2024). Participatory ethical regulations: Risk challenges of artificial intelligence era and construction of governance logic. *Bulletin of Chinese Academy of Sciences*, *39*(11), 1860–1870. DOI: 10.16418/j.issn.1000-3045.20240417002

Zhang, J., Shao, Z., Zhang, L., & Benitez, J. (2025). Exploring users' post-adoption use of generative AI: An attitudinal ambivalence perspective. *Decision Support Systems*, *197*, 114521. Advance online publication. DOI: 10.1016/j.dss.2025.114521

Zhang, J., & Zhang, Z.-M. (2023). Ethics and governance of trustworthy medical artificial intelligence. *BMC Medical Informatics and Decision Making*, *23*(1), 7. Advance online publication. DOI: 10.1186/s12911-023-02103-9 PMID: 36639799

Zhang, S. (2023). Artificial Intelligence and Applications in Structural and Material Engineering. *Highlights in Science Engineering and Technology*, *75*, 240–245. DOI: 10.54097/9qknfc57

Zu, B., Wang, H., Chen, H., & Li, Y. (2025). Adapting high-level language programming (C language) education in the era of large language models. *Journal of Contemporary Educational Research*, *9*(5), 264–269. DOI: 10.26689/jcer.v9i5.10508

About the Contributors

Debabrata Samanta works as Department Chair and Assistant Professor at the Department of Computing and Information Technologies, Rochester Institute of Technology – Tirana, Europe. He obtained his Ph.D. in Computer Science and Engg. from the National Institute of Technology, Durgapur, India, in SAR Image Processing. He is keenly interested in Interdisciplinary Research and development. He has experience spanning fields of SAR Image Analysis, Video surveillance, a Heuristic algorithm for Image Classification, Deep Learning Framework for Detection and Classification, Blockchain, Statistical Modelling, Wireless Adhoc Networks, and Natural Language Processing. He has completed six Consultancy Projects. Under his guidance, four students have accomplished their Ph.D. degrees. He has received funding of 8,110 USD under the Open Access, Publication fund. He received funding under the International Travel Support Scheme in 2019 for attending the conference in Thailand. He has received a Travel Grant to speak at conferences, seminars, etc. for two years from July 2019. He owns 22 Patents (4 Design Indian Patents and 2 Australian patents Granted, 16 Indian Patents published) and 2 copyrights. He has authored and co-authored over 268 research papers in an international journal (SCI/SCIE/ESCI/Scopus) and conferences including IEEE, Springer, and Elsevier Conference proceedings. He received "Scholastic Award" at the 2nd International Conference on Computer Science and IT Application, CSIT-2011, Delhi, India. He is a co-author of 13 books and the co-editor of 25 books, available for sale on Amazon and Flipkart. He has presented various papers at international conferences and received Best Paper awards. He is the author and co-author of 17 Book Chapters. He also serves as acquisition editor for Springer, Wiley, CRC, Scrivener Publishing LLC, Beverly, USA, and Elsevier. He is an IEEE Senior Member, an Associate Life Member of the Computer Society of India (CSI), and a Life Member of the Indian Society for Technical Education (ISTE). He is a Convener, Keynote speaker, Session chair, Co-chair, Publicity chair, Publication chair, Advisory

Board, and Technical Program Committee member in many prestigious International and National conferences. He has invited speakers at several Institutions.

***

Kashvi Chaturvedi is studying B.Tech with a specialization in Artificial Intelligence and Data Science at Ajeenkya D Y Patil University. She started solidifying her programming skills by completing various certification courses like Data Structures in C, Tableau functions and Operating Systems along with doing few projects using languages like Python, C, C++ and creating Web Page using HTML, CSS and Java Script. She had also attended an Arduino-Based Automation course at Dolphin Labs to enhance her software knowledge. There, she learned how to work with sensors, microcontrollers, and circuit design. She has also written multiple review papers on topics such as Geographic Information Systems, Comparative Analysis of BJT Configurations, Swiss Bank vs. European Central Bank: Data Analysis. She is also researching on and learning many topics such as Small Modular Reactors, Bibliometric Analysis, UNSDGs etc. Because of her interest in latest technologies, she also participated in Global Hyperloop Competition hosted by IIT Madras representing her college as team Vac-Vectoor where she learnt more about various subtopics from the mentors.

Susanta Das is a seasoned educator with a proven record of teaching and mentoring diverse students, working at multiple institutions, and providing service to the various initiatives of organizations. He received his Ph.D. and M.A. degrees from Western Michigan University (WMU), USA, and M.Sc. degree from Banaras Hindu University (BHU), India all in Physics. He continued his research as a Marie-Curie post-doctoral fellow at Stockholm University, Stockholm, Sweden on beam diagnostics for the DESIREE (Double ElectroStatic Ion Ring ExpEriment) in the project DITANET (Diagnostic Techniques for particle Accelerators – a Marie-Curie initial training NETwork), at the Indian Institute of Science Education and Research-Kolkata, India on high-pressure physics as a Project Scientist-B, and at the University of Electro-Communications, Tokyo, Japan on ion-surface interactions as a Post-doctoral fellow. Throughout his career, Dr. Das worked and collaborated with many researchers, Ph.D., master, and visiting students from different countries. He further visited many countries to discuss research and an international conference participant (UK, Italy, Germany, Greece, Belgium, Bulgaria, Romania, Brazil etc.). He worked at several institutions before assuming his current role at Ajeenkya D Y Patil University. He received the Marie-Curie post-doctoral fellowship in Sweden, Science Academies' Summer Research Fellowship in India, Gowen Frostic Doctoral Fellowship, Department Graduate Research and Creative Scholar Award by WMU, and Leo R. Parpart Doctoral Fellowship by Dept. of Physics, WMU, among many others, throughout his academic journey. He co-authored several research articles in WoS/Scopus indexed international journals, conference proceedings, and scholarly book chapters and co-edited several books published by renowned international publishing houses (IGI-Global, Springer Nature, Nova Science Publishers, Wiley, Scrivener-Wiley, Notion Press). At present, Dr. Das continues to delve into cutting-edge fields, with a keen interest in nanotechnology, UN SDGs, and data science. His multifaceted contributions, spanning teaching, research, and administrative leadership, showcase a dedicated professional who is instrumental in advancing the vision and mission of the institutions he serves.

Pooja Dehankar is working in Department of Artificial Intelligence and Data Science, School of Engineering, Ajeenkya DY Patil School of Engineering, Pune. She has completed BE in Computer Engineering from Priyadarshini College of Engineering, Nagpur and ME in Information Technology from Sinhgad College of Engineering, Pune. She has done Post Graduate Diploma in Advance Computing. She is currently pursuing Ph.D. from Symbiosis International Deemed University, Pune. She has 17 years of experience in academics. Her area of interest are Artificial Intelligence, Cyber Security and Data Mining. She has published papers in Scopus Journals. She actively participates in workshops, faculty development programs, short term training programs, conferences and webinars.

Ilham Firmansyah is a third-year undergraduate student in the Department of Informatics Engineering at Universitas Esa Unggul, Indonesia. His academic interests focus on artificial intelligence, data security, and emerging technologies in computer science. He has contributed to research projects exploring quantum-safe cryptography, AI-driven systems, and secure data management. With a growing engagement in scholarly writing, he aims to bridge technical innovation with ethical and strategic perspectives in digital security.

Maksud Madraswale working as an Associate Professor, Department of Management, Presidency University, Bengaluru. For few years he served at Oman and other Arab Countries. To his credit he published five articles in Scopus Indexed journals.

Richa Mehra is working as an Associate Professor of Philosophy and Area chair of Social Sciences and Humanities (SSH) at O.P Jindal Global University, India, she has earned her PhD in Philosophy from Jawaharlal Nehru University, Delhi. While pursuing PhD, she was recipient of Junior Research Fellowship from prestigious Indian Council of Philosophical Research (ICPR). She has completed Masters and bachelor's in philosophy from Miranda House, University of Delhi.

She was awarded with Miranda House award and Delhi University rankers prize for scoring highest marks in bachelor's program. She has also worked at Miranda House, University of Delhi, Amity University, Noida, B.M.L Munjal University and IIIT Kalyani. Recently she has designed a course on Critical Thinking and Analysis for undergraduate business students at O.P Jindal Business School. Dr. Mehra has launched the department of philosophy at Amity University, Noida and hence designed various philosophy course for undergraduate students. She has been awarded with the Excellent Academician Award, in an International Conference organized by University of Sri Jayewardenepura, Sri Lanka. She has presented several research

Bhuvaneswari R. working as an Assistant Professor of English at Dr.Mahalingam College of Engineering and Technology, Pollachi. To her credit she completed 10 NPTEL / SWAYAM and published few articles in Scopus indexed journals.

Velmurugan R. presently working as Professor, Department of Commerce, Karpagam Academy of Higher Education, Coimbatore. He started his career as a Project Fellow under UGC Sponsored Major Research Project at NGM College, Pollachi. He has 19 years of teaching experience has 15 years of research experience. To his credit he produced 25 Ph.D. Scholars and 5 M.Phil. Scholars. At present two scholars submitter his thesis, 6 Ph.D. Scholars are under his guidance. Moreover, to his credit he published 168 articles in various International Journals, of which 116 articles are published in Scopus Indexed Journals and 15 articles in Web of Science and 76 articles in edited volumes. He also participates and presented 27 papers in various International Seminar / Conference and 54 National Seminar / Conference. He acted as an external examiner for various M.Phil. and Ph.D. Viva voce examinations. He acted as a Vice Chancellor nominee for Doctoral Committee Expert at Bharathiar University, Coimbatore and Periyar University, Salem. He acted as a Chairperson at various National Level Conferences. He also acted as an Expert for Syllabus Scrutiny Committee, Question Paper Scrutiny Committee and Expert members for Board of Studies at various reputed Colleges. Considering his meritorious contribution, he received awards like Best Paper Presenter, Best Research Supervisor and Best Faculty Awards from various research foundations and councils. He too acted as a resource person for 27 Guest Lectures, 30 Workshops and 10 faculty development programmes.

Md. Matiur Rahman is a Lecturer in Philosophy at Gurudayal Government College, Kishoreganj, Bangladesh. His research focuses on environmental ethics, justice, and racism, where he aims to develop ethical frameworks for addressing contemporary ecological crises. He is also interested in reflective teaching practices and curriculum reform in higher education. Through my work, He seeks to integrate philosophical inquiry with practical approaches to social and environmental challenges.

Irna Rismayanti is a dedicated researcher affiliated with the Faculty of Computer Science at Esa Unggul University, Jakarta. She possesses demonstrated experience in scientific contributions, including a publication on Service-Oriented Architecture (SOA) in an accredited national journal (Sinta 5). Her current research interest lies in the convergence of IT, Artificial Intelligence (AI), the Internet of Things (IoT), and cutting-edge technology.

Senthilkumar S., currently working as Assistant Professor in Finance and Management, Skyline University, Nigeria. His qualifications are MBA, M.Com, M.Phil, MS, and PhD. He has rich experience in teaching and academic of 18.2 years. He had published 58 papers Publications in National and International Journals and Proceedings. He Authored 4 books in Research Methodology, Corporate Finance, Principles of Accounting and Business Policy & Strategic management. Participated and presented 62 papers in National & International Seminars and Conferences. He acted as resource person and Guest lecture around 25 Programmemes. He guided 225 projects in M.B.A., 36 M.Phil, and 9 PhD. He got Authorized Guide ship for PhD & M.Phil from Indian Universities such as Anna University, Karpagam University, Bharathiar University, Periyar Manimai University and AMIET University and Vinayaka Mission University and Bahir Dar University, Ethiopia. He performed as Foreign examiner for evaluating PhD Thesis around 18 Thesis of Indian universities such as Bharathiar University, Visvesvaraya Technological University, University of Mumbai, MS University and Bharathidasan university.

Binastya Anggara Sekti has been a lecturer at the Faculty of Computer Science, Esa Unggul University, Jakarta, since 2016. He is actively involved in the Artificial Intelligence and Information Security Study Group. He holds a Bachelor's degree in Informatics Engineering from the Bandung Institute of Technology and a Master's degree in Information Systems Management from Trisakti University, Jakarta. Prior to entering academia, he accumulated over 25 years of professional experience as an IT practitioner in various companies across Jakarta. His work focused on developing data centers for internet service providers and delivering IT solutions for the manufacturing and oil & gas sectors. His research interests include artificial intelligence, cybersecurity, and the development of IT infrastructure.

Anisah Sri Utami is an undergraduate student majoring in Information Technology with a strong interest in digital innovation and system development. Throughout her studies, she has actively participated in various academic and project based activities focused on utilizing technology to improve efficiency and information security. Driven by curiosity and a passion for continuous learning, she is dedicated to expanding her expertise in programming, cybersecurity, and artificial intelligence (AI). Anisah believes that technology plays a vital role in creating sustainable solutions to the challenges of the digital era.

Chrisella Natasia Tanujaya is a dedicated Information Systems student at Esa Unggul University, with a strong passion for digital innovation and business process optimization. Throughout her academic journey, Chrisella has authored a book and contributed to a scientific journal, reflecting her enthusiasm for research and continuous learning. She is eager to apply her expertise in leveraging data and technology to design impactful solutions that drive organizational growth and operational excellence.

Agung Mulyo Widodo received a PhD in Computer Science and Information Engineering, Asia University, Taiwan, in 2022, and currently works as a lecturer and researcher at the Faculty of Computer Science, Esa Unggul University, Jakarta, Indonesia. He has worked as a research assistant to his advising professor while a PostDoc Research Fellow at the Artificial Intelligence and Information Security Laboratory, Department of Computer Science and Information Engineering (CSIE), Asia University, Taiwan. Recent, he involves as associate researcher at Intelligent Technology Sustainability Center, National Kaohsiung University of Science and Technology, Taiwan. His previous projects were with Caltex Pacific Indonesia (CPI), Siemens-Telecommunications, Nokia-Siemens-Networks (NSN). Currently, his research focuses on wireless communications technologies including NOMA, OMA, NB-IoT, backscatter systems, cognitive radio, smart antennas, artificial intelligence, and information security.

Index

A

L

M

P

Q

R

S

T

V

www.ingramcontent.com/pod-product-compliance
Lightning Source LLC
LaVergne TN
LVHW060004031026
849161LV00025B/1371